THE BRITISH REVOLUTION

1750–1970

A Social and Economic History

For two and a half centuries Britain has been in the forefront of world social and economic developments. The first nation to evolve an industrial economy, she has since led the way in seeking forms of government and social organisation suited to a modern and responsible state.

In this survey, written to meet the requirements of Examining Boards for C.S.E. and O Level, the story of Britain's pioneering effort is traced as an interaction of facts and ideas. We see problems producing policy, and ideas in their turn shaping events. The approach is broadly topical, with a stress on change and development and the need for continuing evolution.

THE
BRITISH REVOLUTION
1750–1970
A Social and Economic History

By
M. St. J. PARKER
and
D. J. REID

BLANDFORD PRESS
POOLE · DORSET

First published in the U.K. 1972
Reprinted 1979
Copyright © 1972 Blandford Press Ltd.
Link House, West Street,
Poole, Dorset, BH15 1LL

ISBN 07137 0557 4 (*trade edition*)
07137 0558 2 (*school edition*)

*Filmset in Photon Times 11 on 12 pt. by
Richard Clay (The Chaucer Press) Ltd., Bungay, Suffolk
and printed in Great Britain by
Fletcher & Son, Ltd., Norwich, Norfolk*

Contents

Preface

The theme of this survey of British economic and social history since the mid-eighteenth century is the way in which dramatic changes, beginning in the 1700s, combined to produce a new industrial society. This society has had to face completely new problems. Accordingly, to meet the needs of an industrial state, governments have had to shoulder an increasing load of responsibility for the welfare of their people, and have become much more closely involved in their everyday lives. Britain has been quite transformed, both for better and for worse. At the same time, the role of this small country as a pioneer in the evolution of industrial society and the modern state has, we believe, been a significant contribution to the experience of the world as a whole. This, in short, is the British Revolution.

We have tried to outline here the main features of this story, with special emphasis on those parts which have affected most deeply the lives of ordinary men and women. Bearing particularly in mind the needs of those studying for C.S.E. and O Level examinations, we have attempted to give a balanced treatment to the rich and complex detail on which any understanding of the period must be based. But we hope that the evolutionary sweep and flow of this critical period in our history will also appeal to the general reader, interested in discovering how his own way of life has developed.

Inevitably, we owe many debts, both for facts and for ideas, to those who have researched and written in this field. In particular, we would like to acknowledge the inspiration given by the lectures of Professor Peter Mathias, of the University of Cambridge. We are also very grateful to many people who have given help and advice in the preparation of the book: to the publishers, and particularly to Mr John Goulding, who was responsible for seeing it through the press; to Mr R. W. Harris, Master of Studies at The King's School, Canterbury, and historical adviser to the publishers; to Mr Paul Mathias, of Battersea County School, who reviewed the structure of the work and made many valuable suggestions; to Mr J. K. Hodgson, who drew the diagrams; to Messrs P. G. Wenley, R. V. J. Butt and M. J. Hodgson, who gave advice on technical matters; to Miss M. Windham, who prepared the index; and to Mrs F. T. Metherell, who typed a large part of the manuscript. To these and many others we are deeply indebted.

All prices are given in the text in the terms of the period, i.e. £.s.d.

M. St. J. P.

Winchester, July 1971   D. J. R.

Acknowledgements

Acknowledgement is due to the following for their kind permission to reproduce photographs:

Aerofilms Ltd., 32 (*top*); N. J. Bennett, 135; British Aircraft Corporation, 224, 225; Trustees of the British Museum, 45, 93 (*bottom*), 162, 253; B.O.A.C., 221; British Railways Board, 312; British Tourist Authority, 353; Camera Press, 23, 184 (*left*); 196, 204, 211, 212, 244, 288, 301, 321, 329 (*right*), 415; Condé Nast Publications, 347 (*bottom right*); Cooperative Union Ltd., Manchester, 172 (*right*); Courtaulds Ltd., 313 (*both*); Crown Copyright – Central Office of Information, 375; Crown Copyright – Department of the Environment, 32 (*bottom*); Crown Copyright – Ministry of Agriculture, Fisheries and Food, 274 (*bottom right*); Crown Copyright – Ministry of Public Building and Works, 406; Crown Copyright – Science Museum, London, 40, 53 (*top*), 55, 62 (*left*), 90, 203, 222 (*top*), 331 (*bottom left and right*); Cumbernauld Development Corporation, 416, back endpaper; English Life Publications, 92; Farmer and Dark, 373; *Farmer and Stockbreeder*, 274 (*bottom left*), 279 (*right*), 281; *Farmer's Weekly*, 279 (*left*); Folio Society (from *Regency England*, published by the Society for its members in 1964), 50, 54, 359, 360, 361; Ford of Britain, 240, 241, 242 (*both*); *Illustrated London News*, 115, 139, 207, 230 (*bottom*), 260, 261, 351; Imperial Chemical Industries Ltd., 312 (*bottom left and right*); Imperial War Museum, 222 (*bottom*), 289; International Computers Ltd., 312 (*top*); *Lincoln, Rutland and Stamford Mercury*, 328; Lloyd's, 134; London Express News and Feature Services, 322; London Midland Region (B.R.), 234; London Transport Executive, 247; Mansell Collection, 12, 48 (*both*), 53 (*bottom*), 76, 111, 201, 333 (*bottom*), 338, 341 (*left*), 367 (*centre and right*), 376, 389, 395, 400 (*top*), 401; The Marconi Company, 330; Eric De Mare, 49, 63, 88, 93 (*top*), 100; Mary Evans Picture Library, 38, 58 (*bottom*), 78, 144, 156 (*left*), 209; Joseph McKeown (photographs from *London's Industrial Heritage*, by Aubrey Wilson), 71, 153, 159 (*both*), 160, 161 (*both*), 311, 331 (*top*), 335; Museum of British Transport, 232 (*top*); National Coal Board, 320; National Monuments Record, 232 (*bottom*); National Portrait Gallery, 12, 36, 58 (*top*), 74 (*both*), 95, 137 (*all*), 255 (*both*), 256, 367 (*left*), 371 (*both*), 386, 422; National Westminster Bank, 80; Oxford University Press (from *Printed Ephemera*, by John Lewis), 46; Rev. J. W. Parker, 263, 282 (*both*); Paul Elek Productions, 51; Press Association Ltd., 291; *Punch*, 391, 393; Radio Times Hulton Picture Library, 8, 17, 20, 41, 53 (*top left*), 62 (*right*), 83, 119 (*both*), 130, 145, 149 (*both*), 150, 152 (*top*), 154 (*bottom*), 156 (*right*), 172 (*left*), 179, 181, 182, 184 (*right*), 202 (*both*), 205, 208, 215 (*top*), 216, 217, 219, 230 (*top*), 236, 238, 239, 246 (*both*), 302, 304, 305, 306, 316, 317, 333 (*top*), 334 (*both*), 339, 346, 349, 363, 370, 387, 394, 396, 400 (*bottom*), 402, 423, 427, 429; R.I.B.A., 378; Royal Photographic Society of Great Britain, 106; J. Sainsbury Ltd., 409 (*right*); Science Museum, London, 56, 57, 154 (*top*), 200, 266; Sir John Soane's Museum, 384; Sport and General Press Agency, 341 (*right*); Stamford Corporation, 337; Stock Exchange, 81; Tate Gallery, 343; Tesco Stores Ltd., 409 (*right*); *The Times*, 176; T.U.C., 167, 170, 174, 190; University of Reading, Museum of English Rural Life, 39, 265, 274 (*both top*); Vickers Ltd., 223 (*top*), 329; Josiah Wedgwood and Sons Ltd., 96

1 : Population – Explosion and Reverberations

Economic history deals with the way in which people earn their living; social history deals with other details of their day-to-day life. In each case, we have to study people, and so there could be no better place to begin than with an account of the way in which the numbers of people living in Britain have changed during our period, roughly the last two hundred years.

This particular field of knowledge, which is called demography (the charting of peoples or population), is coming to occupy a more and more important place in economic and social history. Demography is a fairly recent development. One reason for this is that the first official census of the population was not taken until 1801, and so we have no reliable figures before then. Such facts as we know have to be found in church registers of births, marriages and deaths, in lawyers' files or wills and other similar sources, which are often incomplete. Such records can never tell us all we wish to know: in the eighteenth century, at least, many people must have lived and died completely unrecorded. None the less, using our limited clues, we can be reasonably certain about the general features of population growth. This chapter will explain how and why the population has increased, and what the results of this have been.

Fortunately, enterprising people from time to time in the eighteenth century took the trouble to make estimates of the size of the population, based on more or less informed guesswork, and these provide a useful cross-check for the deductions of modern historians. The earliest of these estimates of which we have records, and in some ways the most valuable, is that of Gregory King, made in 1696. Although this was well before the start of our period, he wrote at a time when the population was just beginning to rise rapidly after remaining stable for many years. His figures, therefore, are particularly useful.

King's estimate, which modern researchers think was accurate, was that the population of England and Wales in 1696 was about $5\frac{1}{2}$ million. The diagram overleaf shows that by 1750 it was estimated by others to have grown to about $6\frac{1}{2}$ million. This was a steady, but unspectacular, rise. But by the time of the census in 1801, there had been a much greater increase, to 9 million (there were also $1\frac{1}{2}$ million people in Scotland, and 5 million in Ireland). This rise of $2\frac{1}{2}$ million in 50 years may not seem much in terms of mere size when compared with that which took place in the nineteenth

1

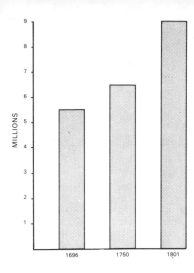

MILLIONS

9
8
7
6
5
4
3
2
1

1696   1750   1801

The population of England
and Wales 1696-1801

century, but in some ways it was more important. This is because it made the breakthrough and established the pattern on which the nineteenth century built. A growth in total population from 20 to 40 million looks more impressive at first glance than a growth from 6 to 9 million; but once the first major increase has been managed, later growth becomes much easier (see diagram opposite).

POPULATION GROWTH IN THE EIGHTEENTH CENTURY

How was this first breakthrough achieved? In order to answer this, we must first see exactly what causes the population to increase. Page 4 shows all the various factors which work together to determine the size of the population. It should be clear that the population will increase if more people are born than die in a given period. For example, if one million die in a particular year and two million are born, then the population increases by one million. The speed of growth will therefore depend on the difference between the numbers of births and deaths (of course, if there should be more deaths than births, then the size of the population will fall). To simplify this, historians usually refer to the birth rate and the death rate; the birth rate is a figure representing the number of babies born in a year for every 1,000 of the population; the death rate is the number of people who die for every 1,000 of the population. If we wish to explain any developments in population growth at any time, we must examine birth rate and death rate first of all. Sometimes we have to take into account a third factor, which is called 'net migration'. This is the difference in number between those who emigrate from the country and those who come into it. If there is a large difference this can have an influence on the size of the population. Normally, however, an understanding of birth rate and death rate tells us all we need to know.

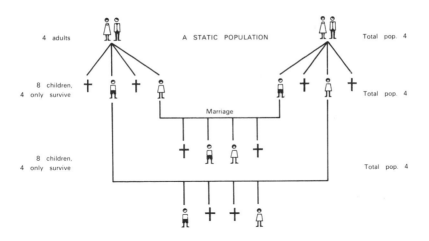

4 adults

A STATIC POPULATION

Total pop. 4

8 children,
4 only survive

Total pop. 4

Marriage

8 children,
4 only survive

Total pop. 4

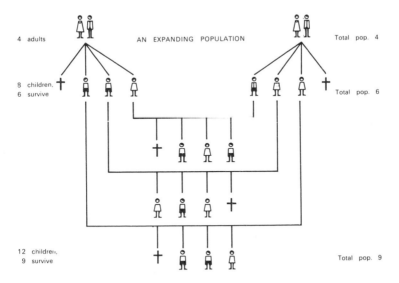

4 adults

AN EXPANDING POPULATION

Total pop. 4

8 children,
6 survive

Total pop. 6

12 children,
9 survive

Total pop. 9

The first stage in the population explosion

BIRTH RATE $\left\{\begin{array}{l}\text{Number of marriages}\\\text{Age of marriage}\\\text{Size of families}\\\text{Illegitimate births}\end{array}\right.$ $\left\{\begin{array}{l}\text{Age structure of pop.}\\\text{Sex structure of pop.}\\\text{Economic conditions}\\\quad\text{(food, jobs, wages)}\\\text{Birth control}\\\text{Welfare services provided}\\\quad\text{by the state}\end{array}\right.$

DEATH RATE $\left\{\begin{array}{l}\text{Deaths of infants}\\\quad\text{and children}\\\text{Deaths of adults}\\\text{Deaths of old people}\end{array}\right.$ $\left\{\begin{array}{l}\text{Wars}\\\text{Epidemics}\\\text{Medicine}\\\text{Diet}\\\text{Hygiene and sanitation}\\\text{Clothing and shelter}\\\text{Economic conditions}\\\text{Safety in factories}\\\text{Services provided by}\\\quad\text{the state}\end{array}\right.$

NET MIGRATION $\left\{\begin{array}{l}\text{Immigration}\\\text{Emigration}\end{array}\right.$ $\left\{\begin{array}{l}\text{Economic conditions}\\\quad\text{at home and abroad}\\\quad\text{(e.g. employment, wages,}\\\quad\text{liberty, gold strikes)}\end{array}\right.$

If a high proportion of the population is of marriageable age, this will help the birth rate.

If there are an equivalent number of men and women, this will help the birth rate.

Birth rate and death rate are in turn a result of several other factors which are shown in the table. It should not be difficult to see how improvements in any of these could lead to a higher birth rate or lower death rate. If there were to be improvements in all of them at the same time, then there would be an enormously fast rate of growth. In fact, this has never happened. But at some times many of the factors have been favourable in this way, and these have been the times when the population has grown fastest. On the other hand, there have been times when the reverse has applied – improvements have been

4   few, and so population growth has been slow.

We can now go on to explain why it was that, after a long period of stability, the eighteenth century saw a faster growth in the population. Obviously, either the birth rate or the death rate, or both, must have been favourable for this to happen. In the early part of the century, there was almost certainly a fall in the death rate. Improvements in medicine, hygiene and food supply enabled people to live longer. In particular more children could survive the first years of life and more mothers could survive to have more children. The terrible plagues which had so often killed large numbers of people in earlier times did not come to Britain after the seventeenth century (although there were several serious epidemics of cholera and typhoid). These developments probably gave the first impetus for population expansion. Similar developments had taken place in earlier centuries, but had always been stopped by some natural checks. In the later eighteenth century, this might have happened again. Indeed the death rate did begin to rise again, especially among children. In some parts of the country, for example, as many as one in every five babies born in 1800 died before the age of one. With the coming of the Industrial Revolution, more and more people went to live in towns, where conditions were very unhealthy for many years. It is a fact that the death rate in towns was much higher than in the countryside.

None the less, the population continued to rise, because by this time the birth rate was beginning to rise at a rate which more than offset the increasing death rate. Men and women began to be married younger and to have more children. Why was this? There are a number of answers, all of which are important. First of all, as we mentioned above, this was a time of change in agriculture, which greatly improved the general standard and availability of food in Britain. It is very important for mothers to be well fed if they are to be strong enough to bear large families, and if their children are to be healthy. If a father knew that good, cheap food could be had, he would not be afraid that a large family would starve.

A second reason was that industry usually provided higher wages than work in the country, so the more people there were who worked in industry, the more could afford to marry young and to have children. The factories provided work for children at a very early age so, in a sense, a large family was an economic advantage since it could bring in a bigger income. This is not to suggest that parents planned their families at this time according to such motives, but matters like this must have been often in the back of their minds. As Arthur Young, a writer of the time, wisely said, 'It is employment that creates population.'

Moreover, the old system of apprenticeship, which required young men to live in with their masters and did not allow them to marry, died down with the new factory system. A fourth reason was that life in the new towns was more likely to lead to marriage than life in the villages, where the choice of partners 5

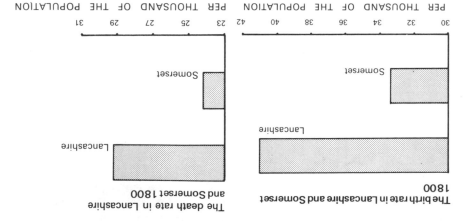

The birth rate in Lancashire and Somerset 1800

The death rate in Lancashire and Somerset 1800

might be very limited. All this helps to explain why the birth rate was usually much higher in the towns than in the countryside.

Many other reasons are sometimes put forward to explain the rise in population at the end of the eighteenth century and there is some truth in most of them. Fewer people were killed in wars than before; the medical care of mothers certainly improved; clothing, housing and other necessities were improved by the new industries. It may even be that the drinking of beer, rather than gin, helped to keep more people alive! But these points were not so important as better diets, and new economic conditions brought about by the Industrial Revolution. This breakthrough in population growth was extremely important. Everyone had to be fed and clothed and provided with basic necessities of life. This gave a great incentive for bigger and better industry and agriculture. Moreover, more people meant more workers to fill the new factories and plants. Above all, the much greater increase in population in the nineteenth century was made possible.

THE GROWTH OF THE POPULATION FROM 1800

Since 1801 an official census has been taken every ten years, so we have accurate figures for population growth since then. (In 1941, because of the war, no census was taken, but a fairly accurate estimate was made.) In addition, we have reliable figures dealing with the birth rate, death rate and migration throughout the period. These make it possible not only to see exactly how the population has grown, but also the chief causes.

The diagrams opposite record some of this evidence. It can be seen at once that the population has risen greatly since 1801. At no time during the last 170 years has the number of people in Britain actually fallen, with the

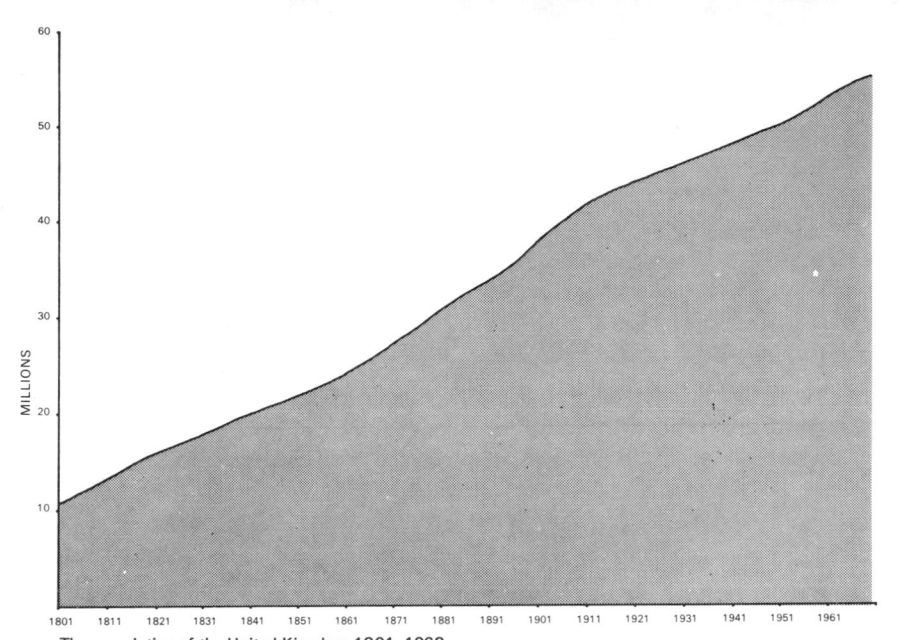

The population of the United Kingdom 1801–1969

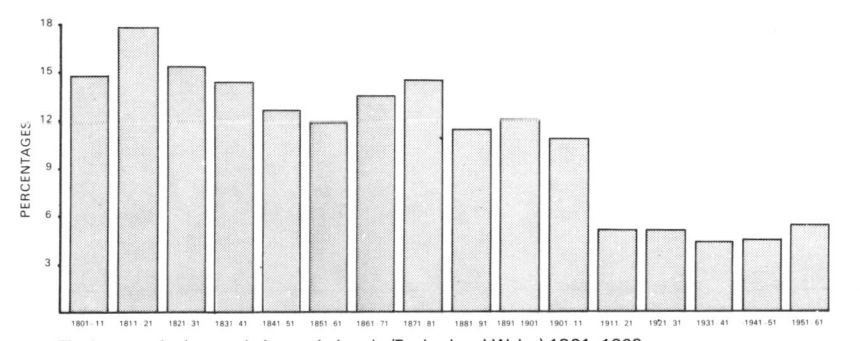

The increase in the population each decade (England and Wales) 1801–1969

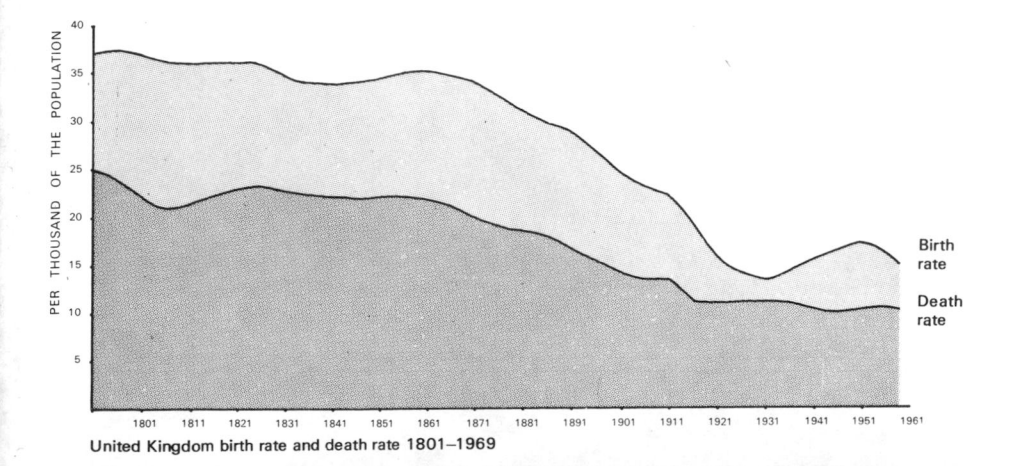

United Kingdom birth rate and death rate 1801–1969

exception of one or two years in the World Wars. Every census has revealed a new increase. But it is also clear that the rate of growth has varied considerably. We can see this if we look at the percentage increase each decade, which is shown in the centre diagram. During the nineteenth century it was always high, but varied from 10.8% to 17.6% per decade. In the twentieth century the rate of growth was as low as 4.5% between 1931 and 1941.

These variations need to be explained. In the previous section we saw how the explanation of changes like this must lie in what was happening to birth rate, death rate and net migration. Let us use these figures to examine the last 170 years, which we can divide into periods. The dates given to these periods are, of course, only rough guides to the time when changes took place in the rate of growth. It should not be thought they began and ended in exactly those years.

1800–35

In this period, the rapid growth in the population, which had begun in the last part of the eighteenth century, continued unabated. The first census results were a shock to many people, who thought that the country was becoming dangerously overcrowded. A clergyman, Thomas Malthus (1766–1834) had just published, in 1798, a book called *Essay on the Principle of Population*. This was a very gloomy forecast of what would happen to society if the population continued to rise rapidly. He felt that food supplies could never keep up with the rising population and so society would be forced down to a general level of poverty, until some disease or war removed large numbers of people. To prevent this, Malthus recommended various measures for keeping the population steady. The 1801 census seemed to confirm his

Thomas Malthus

fears, but luckily they did not really come true, except in Ireland where it did not prove possible to grow enough food to keep many of the people from severe poverty and distress. In some other countries today where the problem is similar, such as India, every effort is made, following the theories of Malthus, to persuade the people to limit the size of their families.

The reasons why the population continued to grow rapidly are that the birth rate remained high, and the death rate, though still high, was on the whole steady and much lower than the birth rate. The factors described in the earlier section on the first population explosion were still operating favourably. In particular, the growth of industry provided greater and greater opportunities for those living in towns. There is no doubt that the population in the towns grew much more quickly than that in the countryside, though it is difficult to be exact about this as the numbers of people pouring into the towns distorted the natural increase among those already living there. Young people living in the towns of Lancashire for example married much earlier than those in the country areas, and this was the kind of difference which pushed up the overall population.

One more feature of this period was the particularly high growth rate in England and Wales, rather than Ireland and Scotland. This was not only because most of the new industry was situated there but also because many thousands of immigrants came in from the other parts of the United Kingdom. There were some very difficult times in Ireland in the nineteenth century, when food supplies ran short and famine resulted. The 1820s saw the first of these black periods, which forced many Irishmen to come to England in the hope of finding new prosperity. They tended to congregate in the northern cities, especially Manchester and Liverpool (and Glasgow in Scotland), and many found employment building the canals or the new railways, as well as in the factories. They were not very popular in England, as they were prepared to work for low wages; they also tended to live in worse conditions than even the poorest Englishman would tolerate. Henry Mayhew, a journalist, described the plight of the Irish in London and the resentment against them, in his work *London Labour and the London Poor* (1861–62). These are two excerpts from his description:

The Irishmen who are in this trade [selling fruit in the streets of London] are also very poor; and I learned that both Irishmen and Irishwomen left the occupation now and then, and took to begging, as a more profitable calling, often going begging this month and fruit-selling the next. This is one of the causes which prompt the London costermongers' dislike of the Irish. 'They'll beg themselves into a meal, and work us out of one', said an English coster to me.

In this second extract, Mayhew describes the standard of living of an Irish widow who sold fruit on the street to maintain herself and her three children: 9

During the spring and summer her weekly average income is about 5s., but the remaining portion of the year her income is not more than 3s. 6d. weekly, so that taking the year through, her average weekly income is about 4s. 3d.; out of this she pays 1s. 6d. a week rent, leaving only 2s. 9d. a week to find necessary comforts for herself and her family. For fuel the children go to the market and gather up the waste walnuts, bring them home and dry them, and these, with a pennyworth of coal and coke, serve to warm their chilled hands and feet. They have no bedstead, but in one corner of a room is a flock bed upon the floor, with an old sheet, blanket, and quilt to cover them at this inclement season. There is neither chair nor table; a stool serves for the chair and two pieces of board upon some baskets do duty for a table, and an old penny tea-canister for a candlestick. She had parted with every article of furniture to get food for her family. She received nothing from the parish but depended upon the sale of her fruit for her living.

Apart from the fact that they lived in such dreadful circumstances, the Irish were mostly Roman Catholics, and it must be remembered that there was still a strong feeling against Catholics in England at this time. Many Scots also came to England at the same time for much the same reasons as the Irish. The crofters of the Highlands of Scotland had never found it easy to make a decent living and now many of them were being turned off their land by the landlords.

1835–55

If the population had continued to grow at the rate of the early nineteenth century it would probably have reached Malthus' forecast of 120 million by the year 2000. (It may do so yet, of course, but it seems very unlikely, unless there is some dramatic change in the present trends.) It did not keep up the early pace, however, and with the exception of 1871–81 there has never been a decade since to match those early years.

For a time, after about the middle of the 1830s, the rate of growth slowed noticeably. As the death rate remained generally steady, the cause lay in a lower birth rate, and also in increased emigration. Both of these changes resulted from an economic depression which lasted from the early 1830s to the late 1840s. This was a time of considerable distress in the industrial areas of Britain, and it took some years to put the economy on a sounder footing. Meanwhile, those who were out of work were not able so easily to marry and to have children, and many decided to leave the country. A novel called *Mary Barton*, written at the time by a Manchester clergyman's wife, Mrs Gaskell, gives a powerful and tragic account of these hard times – often called the 'Hungry Forties'. Children are described dying of famine, and families going to ruin because the father could get no work; finally the hero and heroine solve their problems by emigrating to Canada. In the 1840s came the cruellest blow of all, when famine again struck Ireland. In 1845 the potato harvest, on which the Irish peasants depended, was partially ruined because of a blight or disease which spread throughout the country. In 1846 the crop failed completely and it did not really recover until about 1850. The result was that the population of Ireland was ravaged by poverty, starvation and terrible disease. No fewer than two million people died or emigrated in those five or six years out of a total Irish population of about 8 million. In her book *The Great Hunger*, Mrs Cecil Woodham-Smith quotes many examples of the awful conditions in Ireland during the famine. Here are some typical ones:

> At a farm in Caheragh, County Cork, a woman and her two children were found dead and half-eaten by dogs; in a neighbouring cottage five more corpses, which had been dead several days, were lying: and Father John O'Sullivan, parish priest of Kenmare, found a room 'full of dead people'; a man, still living, was lying in bed with a dead wife and two dead children, while a starving cat was eating another dead infant.

Commander Caffyn, a naval officer concerned in relief operations, described what he saw at Skull, County Cork, a town of 18,000 people:

> Three-quarters of that population were skeletons, with swelling of the limbs and diarrhoea universal. In one cabin four adults and three children were crouched, silent, over a fire, while in another room a man and woman lay in bed, mere skeletons, the woman shrieking for food, the man past speech.

Such conditions, affecting both birth and death rates, were responsible for the slightly less hectic pace of population growth in Britain in this period.

1855–85

In this period the rate of growth recovered to something like its previous level. A glance at the figures shows the causes of this recovery. The birth rate went up again and the death rate at last began to fall. The reasons for these changes were again mainly related to the state of the economy. If the 1830s and 1840s were a time of depression, this was a time of relative boom in the economy. British industry and agriculture flourished in the third quarter of the nineteenth century and unemployment was much lower, apart from occasional difficulties (such as in the cotton industry during the American Civil War, 1861–65, when supplies of raw cotton were interrupted). Wages did not rise much but, on the whole, there was economic security. Moreover, conditions in the towns at last began to improve as the government passed and enforced new laws designed to get rid of the worst problems. Antiseptic surgery and other medical improvements began to have a real effect at this time, so it is clear that most of the economic and social factors were favourable to a faster rate of population growth.

This was particularly true in the later part of the period, from about 1875. From that time, cheap food began to pour in from foreign countries, for reasons described in Chapter 11. The effect was to reduce greatly the cost of **11** living for the poor, who could buy more food of different varieties. The farming community was hurt by the new competition from overseas, but otherwise the cheap food proved a great blessing. As diets improved, so this was bound to make for a lower death rate. The difficulties which British industry began to experience at the same time did not cause enough unemployment to offset this advance.

Lord Lister: his work helped to make surgery much safer

1885–1914

This was a very strange period in the growth of the population. The figures show a dramatic drop in the death rate, caused by a continuation of those improvements mentioned in the previous section. Better food, conditions in towns and medical advances all played their part in this fall, which was so pronounced that one might expect that there would have been a tremendous rise in the population. In fact, this period saw another considerable slowing down. This was for two basic reasons.

First, the birth rate fell even more quickly than the death rate. Several reasons have been suggested for this reversal of the main feature of nineteenth-century demography. One cause was probably that more and more women were beginning to take up their own careers and so refrained from having children until later in their married life. It was about this time that a movement for greater rights for women ('emancipation', as it came to be called) got under way. In 1870 and 1880, two Married Women's Property Acts gave them greater 'emancipation', and the education of girls improved rapidly. The continued expansion and changes in society gave middle-class women, at least, more opportunities to get out of their homes and to follow a career.

Another cause of the fall in the birth rate may have been changes in the laws about children. By the end of the nineteenth century, many Acts had been passed limiting the opportunities of work for children and raising the age at which they might start work. By that time, too, it was compulsory for all children to have full-time schooling up to the age of twelve. These changes meant that children could no longer help to keep themselves by working, as they had done in the past. Each additional child now meant an extra call on the income of the parents, at least up to the age of twelve, with no Family Allowance or any other grant from the state.

It may also be that the drop in the death rate convinced many parents that they did not need to have a large family in order to make sure that some of their children reached maturity safely. Finally, this was the time when some parents began to plan the size of their families more scientifically and reliably, with the use of birth control techniques. However, it took a very long time for these new ideas to gain widespread acceptance in Britain and this factor should not be given too much emphasis before the twentieth century.

We cannot say exactly which of these causes was the most important. They all played their part. But we do know for certain that the average age of marriage and the number of children in each family altered in this period. For example, it has been estimated that the proportion of people in the age-range 20–24 who were married fell by one-third between 1880 and 1900. It has also been suggested that the average size of each family went down from six children to five.

A second basic reason why the population growth slowed down was that the decades at the turn of the century saw massive emigration from all parts of Britain. This subject is dealt with in more detail later, but it should be obvious how the net loss of about two million people from 1881 to 1914 must have affected the growth of the population.

1914–45

The rate of growth of the population in this period was so slow, so different from what had gone before, that many economists and demographers became very alarmed that it might stop altogether. Again, the figures show very clearly where the trouble lay. The death rate over the whole period did not go up much, despite the two World Wars which killed 745,000 and 400,000 Britons respectively. On the contrary, medical advances, such as the development of penicillin by Sir Alexander Fleming, together with continued improvements in living conditions, reduced the death rate even further.

Apart from the war years then, the chief influence on population growth was the birth rate, which continued to fall to an all-time low of 13·9 per 1,000 in 1941. There were two explanations for this. During the war years, with millions of men away fighting, there were bound to be fewer births. And after the First World War the loss of 745,000 young men altered the ratio between men and women for some years and lowered the number of marriages. These were temporary problems, however, and the real weakness lay once again in the economic conditions during the years of peace. The period between the wars was one of severe depression for many people in the older industrial parts of Britain. This fact undoubtedly made it difficult, if not impossible, for many young people to get married and to bring up a large family, for there was still very little help from the state for those in distress or with large families. There is a famous play, written by Walter Greenwood, called *Love on the Dole*, which gives a very good idea of how the harsh conditions made life difficult for people who wished to be married in the impoverished parts of the country.

From 1945

The fears expressed before 1945 about the slow growth of the population have proved unfounded. Since 1945, the rate of growth has accelerated again. It is not yet so rapid as in the nineteenth century, but it is now much faster than between the wars. There have been fluctuations from year to year, of course, as there always have been, but the overall picture is one of steady growth. The death rate has continued to fall, with a host of medical improvements and a rise in the standard of living. It now seems that the death rate is unlikely to fall much further, unless there is a breakthrough in the cure of some remaining killer diseases, like cancer and heart failure. Perhaps the developments in organ transplantation, which began in the later 1960s, will have this effect in time.

The key to the more rapid growth lies once more in the birth rate, which has picked up to a level which is approaching that of the later nineteenth century. The explanation is not hard to find. Since 1945, the people of Britain have enjoyed two things which too many lacked before. One is full employment and a rising standard of living; the second is a welfare state, which has meant that those in distress have been helped by the state. These changes are fully dealt with in Chapter 17. For the moment, it is enough for us to note that the effect upon the birth rate has been impressive.

At the present rate of growth the population of the United Kingdom should reach 70 million by the year 2000. It is far too early to say whether this will, in fact, come about. Demographers have been wrong in the past and they could be wrong again. But it does look as if there will be at least a steady growth, which will raise all sorts of problems.

MIGRATION

Britain has already had long experience of the problems arising from migration, one of the features of population change. So far we have considered migration purely for its importance in determining the overall

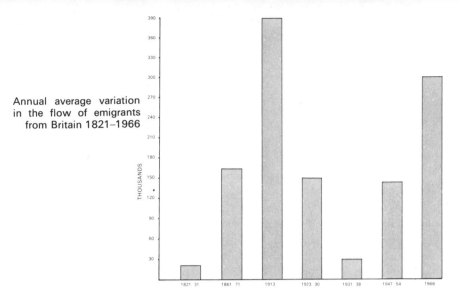

Annual average variation in the flow of emigrants from Britain 1821–1966

population. But the number and type of people leaving Britain or coming to live and work there have had important economic and social effects.

The diagram above shows how many people left Britain for other countries in particular periods in the last 170 years or so. It can be seen that in the early nineteenth century emigration was negligible, yet by the end of the century an average of at least 100,000 left each year. In all, about 25 million people emigrated between 1800 and 1970. This is an enormous total. Why did so many go? A few people still went, as many had done in previous centuries, so that they could live in greater political or religious freedom. The vast majority, however, went because they were not satisfied with the economic and social conditions at home, and felt that they would do better in another country.

Most emigrants from Britain went either to the United States or to one of the countries of the Empire, such as Australia, Canada, Africa or New

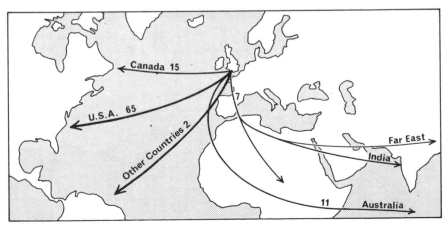

The destination of every hundred emigrants from Britain 1815–1906

15

Zealand. These countries were developing fast in the nineteenth century and offered excellent opportunities to those with the courage and initiative to go out and take their chance. Emigrants with only a little money could expect to do well in business, and those without it could usually find jobs and work their way up. Many countries offered cheap land, or even free land, to those who preferred the rural life. After 1862, for example, settlers in the west of the United States could buy 160-acre farms at 3d. an acre, and in other parts of North America land was usually under 5s. an acre.

Sometimes there was a particular attraction: gold strikes in Australia in 1851, California in 1849 and Alaska in 1896, as well as gold and diamond discoveries in South Africa from the 1880s, lured many thousands to distant parts of the world intent on 'getting rich quick'. In 1852 alone, 86,000 people left United Kingdom ports for Australia, and shipping offices were besieged by would-be prospectors desperate for a quick passage before the gold ran out. Whatever the attraction, conditions were often harsh, but there was always some hope of eventual prosperity.

Emigrants would not have gone, however, if conditions at home had been satisfactory. For many people and for much of the time, conditions *were* satisfactory. But we have already seen how there were several periods of severe depression, with high unemployment and social distress. In such

H E R E   A N D   T H E R E ;

Or, Emigration a Remedy.

This cartoon, dated 1849, makes a stark contrast between life in Britain and in emigrant countries. This is how most emigrants saw the situation

Andrew Carnegie

circumstances it was natural for men and women to think of moving to another country, where the prospects seemed to be better. Often they had to wait years before they had the courage, and the money, to make the move, but the desire to go usually stemmed from a time of depression. This was especially true of emigrants from Scotland and Ireland, who formed a high proportion of the total from Britain. In 1847, for example, 85,000 of the 100,000 emigrants from the United Kingdom were Irish. Even today, in the United States, where many of them went, there are areas dominated by descendants of immigrants from these parts of the United Kingdom.

One famous example is that of Andrew Carnegie (1835–1919). He was born in Dunfermline, Scotland, in a time and area of great poverty. He went to the United States at the age of thirteen and rapidly rose in business. By the time he retired, Carnegie was one of the richest men in the world, owning a large part of the American steel industry, with a personal income of twelve million dollars a year. It is interesting to note that, before he died, Carnegie gave away most of his fortune, building libraries, theatres and other useful projects in both the United States and Britain. He actually died in Scotland, having returned to the country of his youth. For every one example of success like this there were many more of failure, but it was the successful stories which were known about and which acted as magnets to others.

As conditions became better in Britain, with fewer periods of serious unemployment, so the urgent impetus to emigrate fell away; none the less, the figure remained high. In 1968 about 280,000 emigrants left Britain (though this figure contains former immigrants to Britain who decided to return home). In more recent years, new causes of emigration have included discontent at lack of opportunities and facilities for professional men like scientists, doctors and teachers; dissatisfaction at the high level of taxation in Britain (it is lower in most other countries); and perhaps a desire to join relatives already living abroad.

These have been the motives for emigration, but there are other important factors which have made it possible on such a large scale. One is that travel between Britain and distant countries became much easier as the nineteenth century wore on, with the development of fast steamships. In the twentieth century, of course, aeroplanes have made travel even more easy. Ease of travel was an important consideration to an emigrant. In the early nineteenth century, anyone going to Australia was faced with a journey of several months, perhaps as long as a year, depending on the winds. By the end of the century the same journey took about six weeks; the United States and Canada could be reached in under half that time, and wherever the emigrant went, railways speeded his journey inland. As transport improved, fares also came down. These, in fact, were never out of range of the pockets of people who were really determined to emigrate. In the late nineteenth century, for example, the average fare to Australia was about £20, and to North America about £6. Few ordinary emigrants had this amount of money (worth much more in today's values) ready to hand, but most could save it. In any case, the British government paid the fares of many emigrants going to British colonies in the nineteenth century. Later, overseas colonies themselves, anxious for more settlers, paid the whole or part of the fares of suitable emigrants. This practice still applies today in some places—the Australian government offers passages for only £10. Some skilled men in the last century even had their fares paid by Trade Unions, which tried to reduce the number of men in particular trades in Britain in times of depression, in order to give more work to those who stayed at home. Sometimes two or three families might club together to pay the fares for one of them. This family would emigrate and, if they prospered, send back the money for the others to join them.

Emigration societies also played an important part. These were voluntary organisations set up to help people to emigrate. Many would-be emigrants were put off by ignorance of the unknown. In many cases, people suffering hardship and distress were quite unaware of better opportunities elsewhere. Emigration societies offered information and assistance. As early as 1833, a Petworth (Sussex) Emigration Society published a shilling booklet of letters from former Sussex men who had gone to Canada, and the demand for the booklet was so great that a second edition was printed within a year.

As an example of what individuals could do to help, we may quote the work of a remarkable man, Canon Girdlestone, a Devon clergyman. He was concerned with helping farm labourers to move from one part of Britain to another, but the same sort of help was given by many societies and individuals to those going overseas:

Education and a widening of horizons were vital when the labourers, like those in north Devon, had no idea of where better employment was available or how it might be reached, and clung to their squalid cottages and 7s. or 8s. a week rather than face the unknown.

Such ignorance was among the difficulties which Canon Girdlestone had to overcome when he undertook to organise the migration of labourers and their families from his parish of Halberton in 1866. 'Almost everything had to be done for them, their luggage addressed, their railway tickets taken, and full and plain directions given to the simple travellers . . . written on a piece of paper in a large and legible hand. These were shown to the officials on the several lines of railway, who soon getting to hear of Canon Girdlestone's system of migration, rendered him all the assistance in their power. . . . Many of the peasants of north Devon were so ignorant of the whereabouts of the places to which they were about to be sent (in Kent and the northern counties), that they often asked whether they were going "over the water".'

The Canon's efforts – originating in a letter to *The Times* which attracted much attention and many offers of work and money for the labourers – were spurred on by his discovery of the miserable conditions existing in north Devon. . . . The farmers of the district reacted to the Canon's intervention in their affairs by creating opposition in the vestry and absenting themselves from church, but the Canon was not to be so easily deterred. Within six years between 400 and 500 men, many with families, had been moved to high wage areas through this voluntary effort of one individual, and soon the idea spread to the surrounding counties and was taken up by the agricultural labourers' unions in the early 1870's. (J. D. Chambers and G. E. Mingay, *The Agricultural Revolution 1750–1880*.)

In Scotland, the Highlands and Islands Emigration Society, founded in 1851, played a particularly important part in assisting dispossessed crofters to emigrate.

Conditions on the passages to other countries were greatly improved after the early nineteenth century. Emigration was one of the first areas of private enterprise in which the government took a close interest after many revelations, early in the century, that conditions on emigrant ships were terrible. Shipowners packed in as many passengers as possible and gave them as little food as possible, in order to make the maximum profit on each voyage. Many passengers died before they even reached their promised land. From the 1820s a series of Passenger Acts (notably one in 1842) laid down regulations about the accommodation and food which emigrants were to be allowed. The regulations were rigidly enforced by inspectors. However, in exceptional circumstance, for example during the great emigration from Ireland, the inspectors were overwhelmed by sheer weight of numbers. Conditions reached an even worse state. Thus

the *Lord Ashburton*, arrived at Quebec on October 30 (1847), dangerously late in the season, carrying 477 passengers, 174 of whom, Lord Palmerston's tenants, were almost naked: 87 of them had to be clothed by charity before they could, with **19** decency, leave the ship. On the *Lord Ashburton* 107 persons had died on the voyage of fever and dysentery; 60 were ill, and so deplorable was the condition of the crew that five passengers had to work the ship up to Grosse Isle [the quarantine station]. (C. Woodham-Smith, *op. cit.*)

Of the 100,000 emigrants who left Britain for British North America in 1847, it was estimated that 17,000 died on the voyage and that 20,000 died on arrival in Canada, mostly from typhus, a disease which spread easily in the squalid conditions on board ship.

In more normal times tragedies still occurred, as in 1852 when 165 of the 800 passengers on their way to Australia in the *Ticonderoga* died from typhus and scarlet fever, but these cases became more and more rare. Improvements encouraged more emigrants to venture overseas.

Another attraction for emigrants was that there were seldom any formalities to go through. No passports, visas or residence permits were needed, at least until well into the twentieth century. All the emigrant had to do, once he had got on to a ship, was to arrive in the country of his choice. In the case of the United States, millions poured in from all over the world, without any formality whatsoever, and American nationality could be acquired without difficulty after a short time. From the 1920s, the American authorities tightened up considerably. Emigration anywhere is not so easy as it once was, but it is still a smooth process.

EMIGRANTS AT DINNER.

This print is entitled 'Emigrants at Dinner'. Living conditions seem to be relatively comfortable on boa this emigrant ship, but on others life was indescribably squalid

What were the economic and social effects of this massive emigration? As we have seen in a previous section, it directly affected the growth of population in Britain. Not only did it remove large numbers but, as many of the emigrants were young men of marriageable age, it also affected the birth rate. The loss of so many people meant that the demand for goods in Britain was lower than it might have been. Moreover, many of the emigrants were skilled men, whose abilities were lost to the economy. This has become a particularly serious matter in the years since the Second World War, with so many highly trained men leaving for better posts overseas. This 'Brain Drain', as it has been called, has certainly hindered economic growth in Britain.

To set against this, emigration did have some useful effects. People from Britain helped to build up new countries in every part of the world. In the early stages of their development, these countries became valuable markets for British goods, for there was no other country able to supply their needs until at least the end of the nineteenth century. (In the long run, however, some of these countries, such as the United States, became rivals to Britain.) Moreover, emigration did provide a safety valve in times of distress in Britain. It is possible to argue that emigration was vital for preventing revolution in Britain, in the nineteenth century, at least. If so many people had not been able to go abroad to start a new life, to escape from the miseries of their life at home, agitation might have reached a much higher level and possibly exploded into revolution.

Some of the emigrants themselves must have realised how important this was, for a popular song among them in the nineteenth century ran:

> We left our country for our country's good
> And none may doubt our emigration,
> Was of great value to the British nation!

So far, we have only considered one side of migration: emigration. The other side is immigration, the movement of peoples from other parts of the world into Britain. This movement was not very large in the nineteenth century. Political refugees, such as Karl Marx and Lenin, found a home there and a place to live and work in peace and quiet. A few foreign craftsmen came, mainly from Europe, to take advantage of the opportunities offered by the Industrial Revolution, which had not started in their own countries. Occasionally, men of learning and science came to Britain to follow their researches. One of these was William Siemens who came from Germany and developed in England an important steel-making process. Other famous examples included Sir Marc Brunel, the engineer and father of the even more famous engineer, Isambard Kingdom Brunel, and Guglielmo Marconi, the inventor of wireless telegraphy, who also spent many years in Britain.

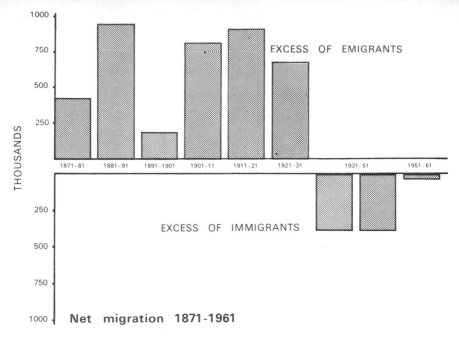

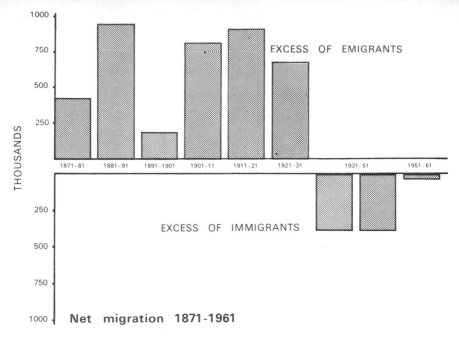

1000

750   EXCESS OF EMIGRANTS

500

250

THOUSANDS

1871–81   1881–91   1891–1901   1901–11   1911–21   1921–31   1931–51   1951–61

250

EXCESS OF IMMIGRANTS

500

750

1000

Net migration 1871-1961

It was not until the twentieth century, however, that immigrants came to Britain in large numbers. It was only in the period after the First World War as the above diagram shows that the number of people entering Britain began to exceed those going out. Immigrants came mainly from two sources. Many continued to come from Europe, and their number was swollen in the 1930s by Jews and other refugees driven out of Nazi-controlled territories. These people were made welcome in Britain and given homes and jobs even though it was a time of depression in large parts of the country. Another growing group of immigrants was from the British Commonwealth. Although a few came to Britain before the Second World War, it was not until about 1950 that large numbers arrived, many of them from Africa, the West Indies and Asia. These Commonwealth citizens looked upon Britain as their 'Mother Country', and had been encouraged by the British government to do so. As British citizens, most of them had the right to come and go as they pleased.

Even though the conditions which they found in Britain were not always as good as they had expected, immigrants were usually much better off than they had been in their own countries. Some became quite prosperous, especially those with a little money who had the initiative to start up businesses. Once a man was established securely in Britain, he usually sent for his relatives to join him, and so the number of immigrants grew. By the early 1960s it was clear that the number had grown so large that serious problems were resulting. Each year, over 150,000 more people were entering Britain to live than were leaving, and in 1962 the government passed an Act controlling immigration.

The population explosion: a dramatic impression of the physical tensions of a growing, urbanised population

Controls became steadily more strict during the 1960s, so that by the end of the decade, emigration and immigration almost exactly balanced.

Immigration has brought advantages to Britain. It has helped to offset the harmful effects of emigration, described above. In the conditions of full employment which Britain enjoyed in the period after the Second World War, immigrants were invaluable additions to the labour force, though their general level of skill was not high. Some immigrants, however, were well-educated and qualified men and women, who helped greatly in key areas of the economy. The best example is that of the National Health Service: many of the doctors and nurses who look after the health of the British people come from overseas.

Unfortunately, immigration has brought serious social problems. The situation has been considerably complicated by an element of bitterness about race and colour. Education and housing are two matters which have produced special difficulties, but these should be overcome with time and patience.

Suggestions for further work and discussion

1. Ask a number of people (your friends, for example) to tell you the size of their own families, and those of their parents and grandparents. Work out how the average size of families has changed over the years. What conclusions can be drawn?

2. Try to find out how the population of your town or village has altered in the last two hundred years. How do you account for these changes?

3. If you visit a churchyard or a cemetery, examine old tombstones and work out the average age of people who died in a given period – the late nineteenth century, for example. Compare the result with the age of people who have died more recently.

4. Compare the results of the 1971 Census with the 1961 figures. What are the most important changes which have taken place?

5. Contrast the history of population growth in Britain with that of any other country. Why have some countries (such as India) such large populations despite their poverty?

6. If no one was allowed to enter Britain or leave it permanently, what do you think the economic and social consequences would be?

Books for further reading:

Henry Mayhew, *London Labour and the London Poor*, 1851–62.
Cecil Woodham-Smith, *The Great Hunger*, Hamish Hamilton, 1962.
John Prebble, *The Highland Clearances*, Secker & Warburg, 1963.

2 : The Agricultural Revolution

Farming is one of the most basic and important human economic activities; it is also one of the most difficult to generalise about safely. It is so greatly influenced by such factors as climate and geology that it can vary a great deal even in quite small countries. There has never been a time when all of Britain was farmed in the same way, and at the beginning of the eighteenth century the differences between one district and another were very great indeed in some cases. In Westmorland, for instance, there were great sheep ranches, where flocks of sheep roamed the bare hillsides, while in Kent fruit and hops were cultivated with other, more 'ordinary' crops in small fields among frequent woodlands, on a system not very far removed from what we now call market gardening.

These regional differences make it very dangerous to attempt a general description of agriculture at the beginning of our period. They also increase the risk of our over-rating the importance of the changes that we see happening in some parts of the country. This should be born in mind as we attempt to describe and analyse the Agricultural Revolution.

One system of farming, however, stands out at the beginning of the period as spreading a fairly uniform pattern of cultivation over a large, fertile and important area of England. This was the 'open-field system', which had been popular in England since the early Middle Ages. It was found especially in the heavy-soil areas of the Midlands; the map on p. 26 gives a clear idea of the extent of its incidence. The working of the open-field system can best be summarised by means of the diagram below it. This of course shows an imaginary example; a good many villages in fact had four great fields, rather than three, and a few had even more; by 1700 most had at least three.

Two main principles governed the working of this system. The first arose from the fact that a farmer who grows the same crop on his land for year after year exhausts the soil, so that yields fall until they are worthless. Since medieval farmers grew little but corn, this was a great problem, which they could solve only by letting the land rest for a year or two, without planting anything on it at all. Fields lying idle for this reason are said to be 'fallow', and open-field villages would cultivate their lands according to a regular timetable based on the 'fallowing' principle.

The distribution of the open-field system: open fields were found chiefly in the shaded area

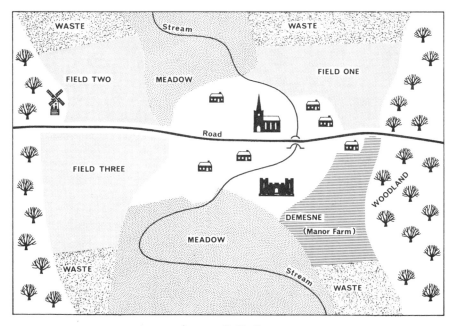

An open-field village

Of course, this routine would not work unless everybody with lands in the great open fields obeyed it; so we have the second of the two principles mentioned above, namely that of 'communal management'. In fact, there was another powerful reason compelling farmers to co-operate, namely the way the fields were sub-divided. It can be seen from the illustration on p. 32 that the great open fields are divided up into strips, which varied in size, but were commonly about a furlong in length by three yards wide. They were privately owned, but their owners usually held them not in blocks, but scattered around. (Some historians believe that this represents an original sharing out of good land and bad in equal proportions to each farmer.) These strips were not fenced or enclosed in any way, merely separated from their neighbours by a narrow unploughed pathway. They could not be worked independently, otherwise there would be chaos; sowing, reaping and above all the 'grazing over' by cattle, who dropped fertilising manure over the land, had to be organised simultaneously. Consequently the management of the fields was a matter for decision by the whole community – usually following ancient customs which had been found to work over the centuries. This was not communism, since the strips and their crops were privately owned; but it meant a much higher degree of co-operation in work than a modern farmer would normally dream of.

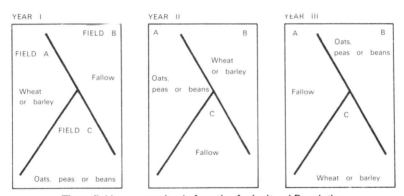

Three-field crop rotation before the Agricultural Revolution

The main objective of a medieval peasant operating this open-field system was to grow enough food to live on for a year. With a fair share of luck he could usually just about manage this. But there was rarely much left over; in other words, the open-field system was not geared to the production of a surplus, and this was still the case at the beginning of the eighteenth century. Thus, for that 80% or more of the English population who lived in the countryside and made their living by farming, work was a matter of supporting oneself rather than supplying a market.

This picture can of course be overdrawn; we must not imagine the farming community as totally primitive in the early eighteenth century. The writings of Danie Defoe (the author of *Robinson Crusoe*), who travelled around the country in the 1720s describing the way people lived, make it clear that many farmers, and indeed whole areas, were specialising in producing goods for which their land was particularly well suited. We hear of vast numbers of cattle, sheep, geese and other livestock being driven from breeding-grounds to grazing-grounds and finally to market, all in widely different localities. There are accounts of great sales of specialised products such as cheeses; and in 1750 nearly a quarter of the year's total wheat crop was actually exported. In other words, what we may call 'commercial agriculture' was already in existence; it was in fact impatience with the unsuitability of the open-field system for a style of farming geared to large-scale production that provoked the great changes that took place in eighteenth-century agriculture.

REASONS FOR CHANGE

If the Agricultural Revolution was founded on a new awareness on the part of farmers of the possibilities offered by a commercial style of farm management, it may seem surprising that it did not happen before the eighteenth century. It is indeed true that, even before the end of the Middle Ages, landlords can be found exploiting their estates for the market, and in the sixteenth century great anger was caused by the activities of a small group of wealthy men who found that it paid them to turn their arable lands (that is, lands cultivated by the plough and used for growing crops) into vast paddocks of grass for feeding sheep. But such early efforts remained comparatively small in scale – all the enclosures of the sixteenth century only reduced the area of open-field in the counties affected by some 2% or 3%. The reason was that a vital factor was missing.

This factor was demand. At no time before the eighteenth century was there a really large population *not* engaged in agriculture and wanting to buy food from those who were. Thus the population explosion described in Chapter 1 really brought about the agricultural changes of this period.

If population growth was the main reason for change, however, there were others which combined with it and were scarcely less important. One of these was the availability of money for investment in agriculture. If a farmer wanted to run his farm on commercial lines, producing for the market, then he had to be prepared to lay out money just like any other expansion-minded businessman. Significantly, it was easier for him to raise money for this purpose in eighteenth-century England than it had ever been before. This was the result chiefly of a great expansion in the banking system, in particular the setting up of 'country banks' (that is, private banks operating in provincial towns), from which enterprising landowners – and tenants – could raise loans.

Another essential factor was the great improvement in transport which took place at about the same time. The new roads and canals described in Chapter 3 enabled the farmers to dispatch their produce (at any rate the imperishable sort) to wherever they thought they could get the best price for it. In this way the opportunity was matched by the ability to make use of it.

THE NEW FARMING

The demand for more food, the availability of capital for improvements and the developments in transport, taken together, opened the way for the eighteenth-century farmer set on commercialising his business. The important question outstanding is, how did he go about it? Part of the answer is, by means of the changes in technique collectively known as the New Farming.

We have grown accustomed in modern times to thinking of progress as largely a matter of improvements in machinery; but the New Farming of this period had practically nothing to do with machinery. The methods of tilling the ground employed by farmers after 1800 were not very different from those which had been used before 1800. Simple and even crude implements such as scythes and flails were still employed for the heavy work of harvesting and threshing, and most other operations remained similarly unchanged. In fact, there were few mechanical inventions to upset the mind of an eighteenth-century farmer, nor was he assisted by any new source of power.

Instead, there were improvements in organisation, particularly of a sort designed to increase the yield of crops and enable the soil to be more heavily and continually exploited. In the Middle Ages, a yield of four to one (four times as much grain gathered as had been sown) was considered a good average. Using the methods of the New Farming, however, eighteenth-century farmers achieved yields of ten to one. This remarkable improvement was brought about largely by the calculated alternation of corn crops with other types of crop, so that the same group of chemicals would not be drawn upon continuously, but would get chances to replenish themselves in the years when crops needing other groups were being grown. Some of the crops used in the new 'rotation' schemes actually restored chemical substances to the land, merely by growing in it. Clover, which 'fixes' atmospheric nitrogen and builds it up in the soil, is a good example of this type of crop. And, of course, there was no longer any question of the land lying wastefully fallow; all the crops in the sequence could be used for something or other. The livestock side of the farmer's operations would benefit particularly, since turnips and other roots, clover and improved grasses, all of which featured in the new rotation schemes, provided fodder for cattle. Larger numbers of stock could be kept and winter feeding presented fewer difficulties. In consequence, there would be more cattle manure available for increasing soil fertility.

Different parts of the country had their own variations of the basic idea, to meet their special needs. On the heavy clay soils of the Midlands 'convertible husbandry' was widely adopted. In this scheme, the land was usually under corn, but the sequence was broken periodically by temporary sowings of grass, called leys. On the lighter soils of East Anglia, a more complex and rigid succession of crops was evolved to cover a four-yearly cycle. This was necessary because the lighter soil was more easily exhausted. This system, which became famous as 'alternate husbandry', or the Norfolk four-course rotation, is explained below.

The Norfolk four-course rotation

YEAR I   YEAR II

Wheat	Turnips
Barley	Clover

Clover	Wheat
Turnips	Barley

YEAR III   YEAR IV

Barley	Clover
Wheat	Turnips

Turnips	Barley
Clover	Wheat

This rotation enabled land to be profitably used every year

The New Farming, of which these systems of rotation were the most important characteristics, did not appear suddenly. On the contrary, it can be seen developing gradually from the middle of the seventeenth century onwards, when clover, turnips and other new crops became popular in eastern England. With it were associated various improvements in efficiency, such as more attention to land drainage and greater care in the breeding of cattle. Some of these improvements are described in greater detail below.

The full effect of the New Farming, however, could not be achieved within the open-field system. Consequently, in the large region dominated by this system, a further fundamental change was necessary. This was brought about by enclosures.

THE ENCLOSURE MOVEMENT

A moment's thought will show that the relatively elaborate patterns of rotation described above could not possibly be put into effect on the strips of an open field, where every step in the farming year had to be taken at the same

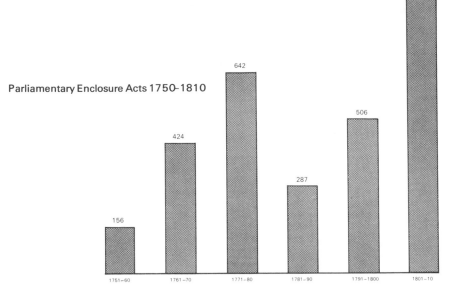

Parliamentary Enclosure Acts 1750–1810

906

642

506

424

287

156

1751–60   1761–70   1771–80   1781–90   1791–1800   1801–10

time as your neighbours, and where animals were let loose periodically to wander over the land at large. Quite early on, therefore, enterprising individuals took to fencing off their strips and if possible building up blocks of strips to achieve greater independence. Once they had achieved the higher profits that the New Farming made possible, their example would be followed and the old pattern of communal agriculture would collapse. Sometimes this would come about spontaneously; but more often there would be a prolonged period of argument, with the more enterprising men making the running. Their aim, briefly, would be to re-divide all the land belonging to the village so that each farmer would own (or rent) a number of enclosures, on average about ten acres each in extent. Within his new fields he could work as he pleased, growing whatever crops he thought best and timing his operations to suit himself, rather than the rest of the village. The field-system which resulted was the one with which we are familiar nowadays – the pattern of enclosures with hedgerows and trees which probably comes into most people's minds when they think of 'the countryside'. (It may be added here that in fifty years' time this image will quite possibly seem as obsolete as do the open fields now.)

The commonest method of bringing about this result and forcing enclosure on objectors was to get a private Act of Parliament passed specially for the purpose. These first became popular in the reign of Charles II and were passed in great numbers during the 150 years following. The acreages involved were enormous. The procedure was for the owners of the major part of the land of a village to petition Parliament to grant them an Act. A committee of the House of Commons would investigate the case, and if there

Above: Open fields, still cultivated on the strip system, round the village of Laxton in Nottinghamshire. *Below:* Fields near Kilby, in Leicestershire; note the strip patterns of the land, showing how it was divided up before enclosure

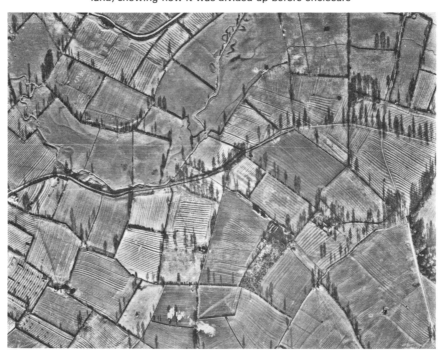

was no effective opposition an Act would be passed appointing commissioners with power to re-allocate the village land in such a way that every owner was given the equivalent of what he had held before – but in the shape of fields, rather than strips.

Of course, the owners of the bulk of the land might not be a numerical majority of all the landowners in the village; but they would be the wealthiest men and it would not be easy for poor and uneducated peasants to oppose them. Generally speaking, the Acts were pushed through with little trouble. There were exceptions, such as the Suffolk village where, on three successive Sundays, the constable charged with the duty of proclaiming the decision of Parliament had his notices torn out of his hands, while he himself was thrown in a ditch and stoned! The procedure was made simpler and smoother by changes in 1801 and 1836, partly to reduce the risk of such difficulties.

Effects of Enclosures

It was generally admitted that the enclosure commissioners did their work reasonably honestly; but there is little doubt that the process of enclosure aided the big landowners and farmers to profit at the expense of lesser men. This was chiefly because the exchange upset the balance of a poor man's economy. When he owned a few strips, together with the right to use the village pasture, woodland and common, he had usually been just able to scrape a living. Under the new, logical, businesslike arrangements the 'marginal benefits' of pasture, woodland and common disappeared, and were not allowed for in the redistribution. The tiny patch of land given as equivalent to the open-field strips would be insufficient to maintain the peasant and his family, and he would be obliged to sell it and earn a living working for wealthier men. One enclosure commissioner admitted that this had often been the result of his work:

> I lament that I have been accessory to injuring two thousand poor people at the rate of twenty families per parish. Numbers, in the practice of feeding on the commons, cannot prove their right; and many, indeed most who have allotments, have not more than an acre, which being insufficient for the man's cow, both cow and land are usually sold to the opulent farmers.

Many villages experienced considerable social change. Where previously there had been a long 'ladder' of ranks and degrees of wealth, people could be divided more and more simply into 'the employers' and 'the labourers'. Even where it had been normal for farmers to employ labourers before, there was often a change – instead of living with their master as part of his family, they would be sent out to dwell apart in a 'tied cottage'.

Enclosure therefore altered more than the pattern of the fields; it changed the shape of rural society, it diminished the number of farms and it increased

33

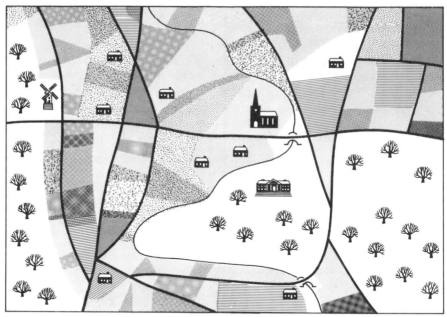
A village after enclosure

their average size. One contemporary estimated that between 1740 and 1788 as many as 50,000 small holdings were absorbed into larger farms over the whole country.

This might perhaps lead one to the conclusion that the Agricultural Revolution was a cruel affair of brutal exploitation, plotted by grasping squires against defenceless peasants. Certainly there were people at the time to whom the changes meant the end of their world. Oliver Goldsmith lamented their plight in *The Deserted Village* (1770):

> Sweet smiling village, loveliest of the lawn,
> Thy sports are fled, and all thy charms withdrawn;
> Amidst thy bowers the tyrant's hand is seen
> And desolation saddens all thy green.

But if we take a long-term view of the whole process we can see that the benefits of the changes outweighed the hardships caused. The new efficient farming enabled the growing population to be fed, and to work for greater prosperity in the new industrial towns, while without the agricultural changes there might have been a serious shortage of food, with incalculable effects. It is not, however, true to say (as many historians do) that the Agricultural Revolution 'caused' a movement of population from country to town. It has often been maintained that the enclosures deprived thousands of people of their livelihoods and drove them into towns, where they became 'fodder' for the new factories. It is, of course, true that many people left the country to live in the towns during this period; but this was nothing new. In fact, the towns of England grew, from the sixteenth century to the nineteenth, chiefly on population drawn from the surrounding countryside. Urban conditions of life were so appallingly unhealthy that many more people died there than were born, every year; in the country, on the other hand, far more people were born, and survived, than died. Agriculture was unable to absorb all the extra rural population, which consequently drifted to the towns. The Agricultural Revolution, indeed, can be seen as positively helpful, in two senses: first, it actually increased the number of jobs on the land (in 1811 697,353 families were engaged in farming, whereas in 1831 the figure was 761,348), and second, it assisted in developing the prosperity of the towns, and thus enabled those who wanted to live in them to find work. What *did* happen was that the proportion of people out of the whole population who were engaged in agriculture began to fall. This fall continued from the end of the eighteenth century onwards, but it was not until the last part of the nineteenth century that the population figures of rural districts began to show a real decline.

PROPAGANDA FOR CHANGE

For those who remained in the country, the general feeling at the time was that life in a village where improvement and enclosure had taken place was really much more prosperous and comfortable than it had been before. Certainly this was the view of William Marshall, a writer who really understood farming and knew perhaps more than anyone else in the eighteenth century about the real state of English agriculture. He wrote a great series of accounts of farming in the Midlands, southern and western England, Norfolk, Yorkshire and other areas, and the arguments he advanced had much influence in government circles.

An even more famous propagandist for the new system was Arthur Young, who lived from 1741 to 1820. In a widely-read series of books and articles he described the different sorts of farming that he came across in his travels at home and abroad. He drew the conclusion that large-scale, capitalist enterprises, organised in enclosures and utilising all the latest techniques, would not only dominate the market for agricultural products, but would also produce a higher standard of living for everyone associated with them.

Young's writings did much to spread the new ideas, but he had a rather undeserved reputation as a failure at practical farming. One man who was able to back up his propaganda with a solid record of achievement was Sir John Sinclair (1754–1835). He owned great estates in Caithness, then a very backward and primitive district of Scotland, which he transformed by great enclosure works and the introduction of New Farming techniques, together with large building and road-making programmes. In fact, he may be said to

Arthur Young in 1794

have introduced the Agricultural Revolution to the Highlands of Scotland. His ideas were taken up by many of his neighbours; in particular, he was largely responsible for a transformation in the management of sheep-rearing and breeding, which played a vital part in the agricultural economy of Scotland. His interests and influence extended very wide; he was a notable figure in the scientific world, particularly in the study of statistics – a word which he is actually credited with having introduced to the English language. He was also a politician of note, and in 1793 became first president of a government body, the Board of Agriculture. This Board was active in encouraging new techniques of farming, and spreading knowledge into all parts of the country: it was the beginning of a long chain of government intervention in agriculture, running right down to the present day.

Among Sinclair's most successful enterprises were the great sheep-shearings which he organised every year on his estates. People were accustomed to come to these from miles around, in the first case for the social merrymakings which were a traditional part of the proceedings. But Sinclair gave them a serious purpose, by turning them into something like a modern county agricultural show, at which there was a great discussion of farming techniques and practical demonstration of the results that could be achieved by the new methods.

Sinclair was followed in this respect by a great Norfolk landowner, Thomas Coke (1752–1842), of Holkham, who also deserves credit as one of the chief propagandists of the Agricultural Revolution. Between 1778 and

1821 he held a great series of meetings known as the Holkham Gatherings, which were immensely popular – it was estimated that 7,000 people attended the last of them – and contemporaries believed that no less than 2,000,000 acres of waste land were brought under cultivation as a more or less direct result of the enthusiasm which they caused.

PRACTICAL PIONEERS

The influence of both Sinclair and Coke owed a lot to the success which they made of their own estates. Coke developed the swede as a valuable crop in a new rotation sequence, and, by studying the fodder requirements of cattle, helped to drive out the old idea that all but the breeding stock must be killed off every autumn because they could not be fed during the winter months.

In most of his innovations, however, Coke was following the lead set a little earlier in the century by another great landowner, Lord Townshend (1674–1738), whose estate was at Rainham, also in Norfolk. The story as usually told is that, after being defeated in political battle by the great Sir Robert Walpole, Townshend retired to the country in disgust, and devoted the rest of his life to developing the turnip: hence his nickname, 'Turnip' Townshend. Quite apart from anything else, this gives the misleading impression that a great nobleman of the eighteenth century would regard life on his estates as a sort of exile from the bright lights of the Court and the capital. In other countries this was in fact true; but in England, for a variety of reasons, the aristocracy felt it no disgrace to live in the country for much of the year. On the contrary, they regarded the efficient running of their lands as their most important and enjoyable activity. (Townshend's successful rival, Walpole, was said always to give priority over all other letters to correspondence from his bailiff.)

The example was set right from the top. George III literally enjoyed the nickname 'Farmer' George, and his Model (or experimental) Farm at Windsor was one of the joys of his life. Lower down the scale, a nobleman might well be seen driving a hard bargain in a cattle market, and a squire would often be quite willing to take his coat off and help with the harvest. When we remember that by far the greatest part of the land of England was owned in the eighteenth century by the aristocracy, it becomes obvious that their willingness to involve themselves in the details of agricultural life was very important in helping to bring about the Agricultural Revolution.

Among these enterprising noblemen, Townshend certainly deserves an honourable place. However, he did *not* import the turnip, as is sometimes suggested, nor clover either. The Norfolk four-course rotation, which he is often said to have invented, was firmly established before he was born. And the idea of spreading marl (a thick, rich soil which occurs in pockets in certain parts of the country) as a stiffener for loose, sandy soil – another notion attributed

Part of George III's Model Farm at Windsor

to Townshend – had been known in Britain since prehistoric times. It was commonly used in the sixteenth century, as this quotation from a Tudor agriculturalist shows:

> Claye marle is of nature fat, tough and clammy. The common people are of opinion that this marle is the fatnesse of the earthe, gathered together at Noah's flood: which is verie like to be true: it is digged or caste out of the pitte, carried to the landes, and their caste either upon the fallow or ley ground unplowed, and this in the summer tyme . . . where it lyeth so on the lande all the somer and winter, the rain making it to melte and run like molten ledde all over the face of the earthe.

In other words, Townshend 'invented' practically nothing. But what he did was to show that it was possible, by skilful use of the new management methods, to make a lot of money from farming. This was really what the Agricultural Revolution was all about, and for this reason he rightly stands among its pioneers.

The same sort of importance should be seen in the work of Robert Bakewell (1725–95), a sheep-farmer of Leicestershire. Bakewell found the type of sheep commonly bred in the early eighteenth century to be unsatisfactory in several respects. So he set himself to improve it by systematic selection for breeding purposes of sheep with desirable characteristics, which he tried to develop from generation to generation. He applied the same technique to cattle and horses; but the strains which he produced are less important than the fact that he popularised the idea of controlled breeding, instead of the old casual system which aimed at nothing more than the production of the

38

greatest possible numbers. This led to much higher profits for the farmer, as can be seen from the table below.

AVERAGE WEIGHTS OF STOCK
AT SMITHFIELD MARKET

	1710	*1795*
	lb.	*lb.*
Oxen	370	800
Calves	50	150
Sheep	38	80

(These figures must be treated with caution, since they disguise certain changes in marketing arrangements.)

A painting of 1809, showing farmers arranging for the hiring-out of rams at Dishley, in Leicestershire. This methodical, commercial approach to sheep-breeding resulted from the work of Robert Bakewell

A man who seems at first sight to be even more scientific in style is Jethro Tull (1674–1740), a farmer of Berkshire. Tull has often been given more credit than he deserves for agricultural inventions – indeed in some accounts he appears almost as the originator of the Agricultural Revolution! In fact he was something of a crank, the unsoundness of whose theories was disguised for a time by the fact that the soil on his farm was rich enough to enable him to grow good crops despite his false ideas. He did, however, make two important linked contributions to good farming practice. He invented a   **39**

A modern artist's impression of Jethro Tull using his seed-drill for the first time

horse-drawn drill for sowing seed in straight lines at a controlled rate; this economised on seed and helped the crop to grow under favourable conditions. Secondly, he laid stress in his book, *Horse-Hoeing Husbandry* (1733), on the need for 'clean' farming – that is, the elimination of weeds. (This of course becomes much easier if it is possible to hoe between the neat drills of young corn.)

Apart from Tull's seed-drill, the Agricultural Revolution owed relatively little to new machinery. An improved plough was produced in 1703, and scythes gradually replaced sickles in the harvest fields. Otherwise the enclosed farms were worked with much the same tools as medieval villagers had used in their open fields. Iron replaced wood to some extent, but a wooden plough (drawn by oxen) was still in use near Brighton in 1850. A threshing machine was indeed invented in 1784, and patents for a number of other agricultural machines were taken out at about the same time. But none of them was a success until the nineteenth century provided a new source of power to replace men and horses. In any case, there was plenty of labour available on the land, and the naturally conservative farmer saw little point in **40** change for change's sake.

Ploughing in 1809: three different types of plough, and teams to match. Many farmers were still little affected by the Agricultural Revolution at this date

SUMMARY

The word 'Revolution' is in some ways a misleading term to use in connection with eighteenth-century agriculture. It suggests a sudden change, an upheaval on a grand scale, and so hardly fits the facts. It is certainly true that the field-patterns round some villages changed strikingly; but in many cases they did not alter at all. Furthermore, enclosures happened piecemeal over more than 150 years. There were practically no inventions of machinery. Such new techniques as there were had often been thought of before. However, there *was* an Agricultural Revolution, in a certain sense. It was a revolution of organisation, and above all it was a revolution of attitude. Its chief feature lay in the fact that farms were converted into profit-making organisations, designed to supply an expanding mass market in the towns. This in turn brought about changes in the shape of village life and village society.

Thus the Agricultural Revolution was intimately linked with the changes that affected other parts of British life in the eighteenth century – it was tied to the Population Explosion and the Industrial Revolution, and forms with them the foundation of modern Britain.

Suggestions for further work and discussion

1. Investigate the field patterns of a chosen local area; try to find out how old they are. Are there any remains of earlier patterns, particularly of medieval strip-systems?

41

2. It is often possible to follow the story of enclosure in a particular locality through the records kept in County Record Offices or other archives. Try to discover what effect the enclosures had on the social life of the area you are studying.

3. Visit an agricultural museum, and examine eighteenth-century implements and other relics of the Agricultural Revolution.

4. Use a book such as G. E. Mingay's *English Landed Society in the Eighteenth Century* (Routledge and Kegan Paul, 1963) to help you find out the income of landowners in the period. How was it made up?

5. Discover how the Norfolk four-course rotation affects the chemistry of the soil.

6. The illustration on page 40 shows Jethro Tull operating his new seed-drill. Describe the reactions of the bystanders. What other agricultural operations can you see going on? How does the drill work?

7. The illustration on page 41 shows three different types of ploughs. Compare the ways in which oxen and horses respectively are secured to the plough. Get a photograph of a modern plough, and see what has changed since 1809.

Books for further reading:

Daniel Defoe, *A Tour thro' the Whole Island of Great Britain*, Cass, 1927, 1968.
The Diary of Parson Woodforde, O.U.P., 1924–31, 1949.
Any of Arthur Young's *Tours*.

3 : The Transport Revolution

Every country has needed an efficient system of transport in order to be able to industrialise. The history of all industrial countries shows how important it has been. In modern economies every effort is made to improve still further existing means of transport and to develop new ones.

It is easy to see why this is so. If an industry can only sell to a few people, its output is bound to remain small. In order to expand, it must be able to sell to a wide market, both at home and abroad. The goods must be able to reach the market quickly and cheaply. With a poor transport system this is impossible. In addition, industry must often be able to obtain supplies of raw materials, like cotton or iron ore, from distant sources. Again, this is impossible or very expensive if the transport system is inadequate. Improvements in transport enable industry to overcome the limitations imposed by distance, and so to produce on a larger scale. This means more efficient and cheaper production, with benefits for the whole of the economy and also for the standard of living and way of life of the people.

If this has been true of all industrial countries, it has been especially important for Britain, the first to industrialise. In the first part of the eighteenth century transport in Britain was quite inadequate, even by the standards and needs of that time. Between 1750 and 1850, however, there took place what has been called a 'Transport Revolution', involving improvements in roads and the development of canals and railways. This transformed the situation beyond all recognition.

TRANSPORT BEFORE 1750

In 1688, when King James II fled to France, it took three months for the news to reach the people of the Orkney Islands. No visitor to Britain in the early eighteenth century, nor any intelligent British traveller, failed to comment on the disgraceful state of communications. It is not much of an exaggeration to say that many of the roads had barely been touched since the Romans left them, 1,300 years before. The main trouble lay in the lack of proper provision for their maintenance. The national government accepted no responsibility and did virtually nothing until military needs forced them to build roads in the Highlands of Scotland after the Jacobite Rebellions of 1715 and 1745. 'General Wade's Military Roads' can still be seen there, little more than tracks today.

By an Act of 1555, each parish in the country was supposed to be responsible for the maintenance of the roads in its particular locality. This arrangement lasted until 1835, but never worked well. In France the *corvée*, or compulsory road labour service, kept up a reasonable standard, but it proved impossible in Britain to get most parishes to make more than token repairs. These were done infrequently and with great reluctance. It was understandable that people living in largely self-sufficient rural communities, with little need to travel far themselves, should be reluctant to go to great expense for the convenience of strangers passing through. Even when roads were repaired, the method was simply to fill up holes with stones, and there was no attempt at building a firm lasting surface.

The result of this was that most roads outside the larger towns, and often within them, became rutted and potholed. They were often unusable in winter, when the rain turned them into a morass of mud. It was not unusual for main highways to be impassable to all wheeled traffic. Local people often earned good money by coming to the rescue with teams of cart-horses to drag the vehicles clear. Roads were often so narrow that even two trains of pack-horses could not pass each other. It was customary for the leading horses to wear bells to give advance warning of their coming, but disputes about who should give way often led to brawls. There were even instances of men drowning in some of the potholes on East Anglian roads! Even where roads were passable, travel was always uncomfortable, and the first springed coach was not invented until 1754.

Arthur Young, who travelled widely in the late eighteenth century, wrote bitterly about this state of affairs. He used words like 'barbarous' and 'execrable' to describe the roads. This is what he had to say about the road between Preston and Wigan in Lancashire: 'I know not in the whole range of language terms sufficiently expressive to describe this infernal road. Let me seriously caution all travellers . . . to avoid it as they would the devil.' Even in London, the roads were sometimes 'an impassable gulf of mud'.

John Metcalf, whose contribution to the improvement of roads is described later, had a bet in 1731 that he could walk from London to Harrogate, in Yorkshire, more quickly than Colonel Liddell, a leading citizen of that town, could get there in his coach. Although blind, Metcalf completed the journey on foot in six days, arriving two days before the Colonel. There is another well-known story which, though it may not be true, gives another idea of the state of the roads. A beggar with one leg was offered a lift by a passing coach. He is said to have replied: 'No, thank'ee. I can't wait. I'm in a hurry!' On the approach to Lincoln, until well into the nineteenth century, there stood a land lighthouse to guide travellers at night, for they would otherwise probably have got lost.

In these circumstances it is not surprising that highwaymen did good
44 business, and that a journey of any distance was usually viewed with the

greatest anxiety and avoided whenever possible. The Revd. T. Broome, of Cheriton, in Kent, when setting out in 1700 for a tour of Britain which eventually took him three years, made preparations which remind one of those made by explorers to Africa in the nineteenth century.

If these were the difficulties facing travellers, the obstacles to the transport of freight were even greater. It was impossible to carry heavy, bulky or fragile goods for any distance, except at great cost. This was a serious limitation on the growth of industry. Attempts to improve matters were rare and sometimes misguided. Such an attempt was that of the government in 1753. It tried then to ban all vehicles with wheels less than nine inches in width from using the roads, to avoid ruts.

A pack-horse convoy. This is a scene from the eighteenth century. Note the bell worn by the leading horse

It was true that heavy goods could be carried by water, and this had been the chief means of freight transport since earliest times. Just one example was the carriage of china clay from South-West England to the Midlands pottery regions via the River Severn. Britain was particularly fortunate geographically in having a large number of navigable rivers which, with coastal routes, were the main arteries of long distance trade. So much cheaper was this form of transport that the Horsehay Iron Co. of Shropshire, for example, found it more profitable in 1775 to send its iron products to Chester, only 30 miles overland, by the roundabout route of the River Severn, Bristol Channel, Irish Sea and River Dee. Most factories were situated by rivers for this reason and also, of course, because water was used to drive the early machines.

There were, however, drawbacks to water transport. Rivers had uneven depths and widths and were subject to flooding. They usually took meandering courses, and particular destinations might not even be served by a river. **45**

By the eighteenth century many rivers were silting up badly and were becoming difficult to navigate. The Dee was one example of this, forcing ships to use the Mersey. This helped the port of Liverpool to grow. Coastal traffic was very much at the mercy of the weather, and privateering was not unknown, especially in war-time.

Thus the traditional means of transport in Britain were unable to support the requirements of large-scale industry. This contributed to a narrowness of social life which made Britain a series of localities rather than one nation. Improvement only came with a complete change, with the turnpikes, canals and railways which made up the 'Transport Revolution'.

THE TURNPIKES

Since the government did not take the lead and the parish neglected their duties, it was left to private enterprise to find a solution to the problem of the road conditions. This solution was the development of the 'Turnpike Trusts'. These were organisations which undertook to maintain certain stretches of road in good order, in return for which they were allowed to charge tolls to passing traffic. This toll system is still used on many European roads, and on some bridges in Britain, though usually under government control. The money for the upkeep of the turnpikes came not only from the tolls, but also from the issue of shares by the trusts.

Turnpikes probably got their name because tollgate keepers usually turned a pike, or pole, to let traffic on to the road. The first one covering any distance was that between Fonthill and Stony Stratford in Buckinghamshire, opened in 1707. Profits were considerable, and so more and more turnpikes were

A Turnpike ticket: this one was issued at Liskeard in Cornwall

LISKEARD TURNPIKE.

Sheviock Gate.

22 day of August 1871

Horses, &c., drawing	No. of Horses	s	d
Carriage - - -			
Chaise - - -			
Phaeton - - -			
Gig - - -			
Waggon - - -	1		6
Cart - - -			
Van - - -			
Dray - - -			

This Ticket frees Crafthole and Cremik Gates.

46

opened. Before 1773 a separate Act of Parliament was needed for each new turnpike and 452 such Acts were passed up until then. After 1773 a General Act enabled a great many more to be built. The earliest turnpikes radiated outwards from London and other large towns and by 1765 virtually all the route from London to Berwick, on the way to Edinburgh (the present A1), had been turnpiked. By 1830 there were about 22,000 miles of turnpike road. Not only did the trusts maintain the roads according to traditional methods but the better ones employed engineers to devise new methods of road construction. The most important of these were John Metcalf, John McAdam and Thomas Telford.

John Metcalf (1717–1810)

'Blind Jack' Metcalf of Knaresborough, in Yorkshire, was a remarkable man. Although he lost his sight at the age of six, he made a successful career. He started as a musician, and played before the Duke of Cumberland after the Battle of Culloden in 1746. Then he became a general dealer and stage-coach operator, before turning his hand to road improvement. His wide travels and business had long since shown him the need for this.

Metcalf's blindness probably helped the development of his other senses, especially his touch. He surveyed routes aided only by a stick to test the nature of ground, and often without assistants. He paid particular attention to the foundation of his roads, using broken stones to provide a well-drained base. His roads followed the easiest gradients and were rather winding, but a great improvement. Metcalf's first road was a new turnpike between Harrogate and Boroughbridge in 1765, which included a fine bridge in the latter town. In the next thirty years he directed the construction of many good roads, mostly in Lancashire and Yorkshire – between Wakefield and Doncaster, Huddersfield and Halifax, Bury and Blackburn.

Perhaps his best feat was the road across the Pennines, between Huddersfield and Manchester. Quite apart from having to cross the hills, this road had to cross a notorious bog. Most people felt that the task was impossible, but Metcalf succeeded after using vast bundles of heather in the foundations. He thus opened up an important new route in the North. 'Blind Jack' died aged 93, after a remarkable contribution to better transport.

John McAdam (1756–1836)

John McAdam, who came from Ayrshire, in Scotland, invented the method of road construction which is still used basically today. His name, in fact, is remembered in the word 'tarmac', or 'tarmacAdam'. He did not invent the use of tar but was responsible for the original surface. His technique was to pack together small, broken stones, often no bigger than pebbles, above the level of   **47**

Thomas Telford   John McAdam

the surrounding land. When rolled tight by passing traffic, this gave a surface which was almost impervious to water, and very long-lasting. When combined with a slope or camber, and drains at each side of the road, this technique solved some of the worse problems of bad roads.

By the time he died, McAdam's technique had been adopted everywhere and he received thanks and a financial grant from a grateful Parliament in 1827. McAdam's roads, as originally conceived, can still be seen in many parts of Europe. They seem primitive today, but to the people of Britain two hundred years ago they made a great difference.

Thomas Telford (1757–1834)

Thomas Telford was one of the most notable civil engineers of the modern age. Another Scot, from Dumfriesshire, he built canals, docks, harbours, bridges and roads throughout Britain and Europe. Most of his works are still in use today. With those of the other great engineers, they remain to provide outstanding monuments of the skill and enterprise of those days.

Among Telford's canals was the Ellesmere Canal, part of the Shropshire Union Canal, linking the Mersey, Dee and Severn. This included the magnificent Chirk Aqueduct, which stands right on the Welsh border near Llangollen. Another was the Caledonian Canal, linking the Atlantic and the North Sea through Loch Ness in Scotland. He also built the Gotha Canal in Sweden. His best known docks and harbours were the St. Katharine Dock in London and most of those on the East Coast of Scotland, from Wick to
Edinburgh.

The Menai Suspension Bridge, one of Telford's greatest works

But it was as a road engineer that Telford really excelled. Working mainly for the Turnpike Trusts, he built nearly 1,000 miles of new road in Scotland, opening up many areas, especially in the Western Highlands and the North, which had been virtually out of reach before, except by sea. The government made a grant for this work, as it did for Telford's biggest project, the rebuilding of the road between Shrewsbury and Holyhead. This road, the old Roman Watling Street and the present A5, was one of the chief routes to and from Ireland; many Irish M.P.s had complained about the dangers and discomforts of the journey.

Between 1815 and 1830 Telford transformed this road, passing as it did through difficult mountain country, into one of the fastest and safest in Britain. The most splendid of all his 1,200 bridges was the Menai Suspension Bridge, which led to Anglesey. This was opened in 1825, replacing a dangerous ferry, and it remains one of the engineering triumphs of Britain.

THE STAGE-COACH ERA

As the roads improved, so the time taken for long journeys was reduced greatly. This can be seen from the example on p. 67. Turnpikes were not always very popular, especially among local people who resented paying the tolls. Tollgates were sometimes destroyed by angry mobs. Despite opposition, a network of mail-coaches and other stage-coaches linked all the major towns   **49** of Britain in 1830. They provided a relatively fast, if not always safe, means of transport; accidents were frequent as rival coach proprietors speeded up their services to attract passengers. Fares were expensive: for example, to go from London to Manchester in 1760 cost £2 5s. inside, half price outside. This did not include expenses on the way. But speeds were remarkable by the standards of the day.

Edmund Burke, statesman and M.P. for Bristol, talked in 1774 of the 'incredible speed' with which his coach had travelled from London to his constituency in 24 hours. An advertisement for the London to Manchester coach in 1754 summed up well the attractions and dangers: 'However incredible it may seem, this coach will actually (barring accidents) arrive in London in four and a half days after leaving Manchester'! By 1830, however, the *Manchester Telegraph* was covering the 186 miles in 18 hours 18 minutes. In that year, too, *The Independent Tally-Ho* reached what seemed to be the ultimate speed, by running from London to Birmingham at an average speed of 12 m.p.h.

By then, stage-coaches were common sights all over the country. Louis Simond, an American traveller in Britain in 1811–12, likened them to 'ships on four wheels', though he did not approve of overloading. 'Stage-coaches continually pass us,' he wrote, 'with their absurd lading of passengers on the top – twelve or fifteen nodding heads.' Typical journey times were London to Salisbury in 12 hours, to Brighton in 6 (with 18 coaches each day) and to Shrewsbury in 16. In 1830 at the height of the stage-coach era, William Chaplin of London, the chief operator, had 3,000 coaches, 150,000 horses and 30,000 employees.

This print, entitled 'The Oxford and Opposition Coaches', is a fine illustration of the stage-coach era

An advertisement for a new
stage-coach service

All this was a great boon to travellers and did much to open up the country. But it was not yet of great value to industry. Despite the improvements, the roads were still seldom capable of bearing heavy loads for any distance. Still only about one-sixth of all roads were turnpiked, and even these were frequently bad. Arthur Young travelled on those between Newport and Chepstow in Monmouthshire. He described them as 'Mere rocky lanes, full of hugeous stones as big as one's horse, and abominable holes'. Moritz, a Prussian visitor, described his journey from Northampton to London in 1782 as a 'perpetual motion or endless jolt from one place to another, in a closed wooden box, over what appeared to be a heap of unhewn stones and trunks scattered by a hurricane'. As late as 1812 Simond could still write sarcastically that 'The English, it is plain, are fond of travelling, and make the pleasure last as long as they can'. The expense, especially with the tolls, of conveying freight by road was still high, and of far greater value to industry were the canals and railways. The latter led to the end of the stage-coach era after the 1830s, although local road transport was given a boost. By and large, however, road conditions relapsed until the arrival of the motor car in the twentieth century.

CANALS

We have seen how rivers were becoming more difficult to navigate by the early eighteenth century. The first attempts to improve matters came well before this, however. These took the form of 'navigations', which were simply improved stretches of river, dredged and widened and sometimes shortened by cuts across big bends. By 1725 there were 1,000 miles of such navigations. But the real answer lay in the digging of canals, artificial waterways, linking rivers, but otherwise completely independent of them.

Canals were not new, for they were already well known in Europe. Captain Perry, an Englishman, had built several for Peter the Great, Czar of Russia, and Louis XIV had had some built in France. They were also quite common in Holland and Sweden, and the Romans had built many in centuries past. In Britain itself, the waterways built to help drain the Fenlands were used for navigation. The major obstacles to further construction in Britain were lack of money and lack of urgency. In Europe, canals were built mostly by the King or government of a country. They found it much easier to raise money than private individuals in Britain. This is why it was not until after 1750 that the needs of a growing economy produced both the incentive and the money for large-scale canals.

The first was the 'Sankey Brook Navigation', from St. Helens to Warrington in Lancashire. It was opened in 1757 and brought together the coal and salt of those regions. This was a proper canal, but owing to the continuing suspicion of canals it was disguised as a navigation. It did not capture public imagination. The Canal Era really began when two men, James Brindley and the Duke of Bridgewater, came together to build the famous Bridgewater Canal.

James Brindley and the Bridgewater Canal

The Bridgewater Canal was hailed as the eighth wonder of the world when it was opened in 1761, and with just cause. James Brindley (1716–72) was a Derbyshire man who became the most celebrated canal engineer, despite his lack of formal education. Indeed, he could read and write only with difficulty. The initial drive and continual inspiration, however, came from the Duke of Bridgewater (1736–1803), and the story shows how much transport improvements were connected with economic need and individual enterprise.

This young man, having failed to marry the woman he loved, decided to give up his social life in London and to devote the rest of his life to improving his estates around Manchester. At Worsley, to the north of Manchester, the Duke had vast coal-mines. The prohibitive cost of road transport to the main market at Manchester, however, and the difficulties of navigating the River Irwell made it impossible to develop these to the full.

He therefore commissioned Brindley to build a canal. The plan finally put into operation, as shown on the map on p. 66, was a bold one. Although the first stage was only seven miles long, the canal involved immense engineering works, the most notable being the Barton Aqueduct over the River Irwell, just west of Manchester. It had several other bridges and tunnels, and ran from

right in the heart of the coal-mines, deep underground. Most people felt that it

The Duke of Bridgewater

James Brindley, with the Barton Aqueduct in the background

was bound to collapse, or that the water would burst through the banks. They ridiculed the canal. But Brindley built it so well, with a water-tight lining of moulded clay, that it remains in use to this day.

It proved an enormous commercial success. The price of coal in Manchester was cut from sevenpence to fourpence per hundredweight, and the Duke made a fortune. Soon Brindley was extending the canal to Runcorn, on the River Mersey. When this was opened in 1767, it provided a new link between Liverpool and Manchester, cutting the cost of the carriage of goods by half.

The success of the Bridgewater Canal had two important results. It did much to help the industrial development of Lancashire, especially

Another view of the Barton Aqueduct on the Bridgewater Canal. The River Irwell is below

Manchester, which doubled its size to about 85,000 between 1770 and 1800. Raw cotton now came up from Liverpool and the finished products returned very cheaply. Secondly, it made a fortune for the Duke of Bridgewater and his company. Although the cost of the whole canal was the then huge sum of £220,000, the annual income was no less than £80,000. These two facts, the industrial and financial rewards, as well as the proof that canals could be built safely, heralded the 'Canal Mania' of the next few years.

The Completion of the Canal Network

In the next few years many canal companies were formed. Brindley himself, Telford, John Rennie and John Smeaton, with some others, built nearly 2,300 miles of canals, with the Midlands as the centre of the network. The main periods of construction were the 1770s and the 1790s. Between 1791 and 1794, for example, 81 Canal Acts were passed and share prices soared during this 'mania'. Some of the 'trunk', or long distance, canals were profitable. The Grand Trunk Canal, linking the Trent and the Mersey, was inspired by Sir Josiah Wedgwood, whose pottery business gained greatly from it. It was opened in 1777 and was 139 miles long altogether. Another successful canal was the Grand Junction Canal, opened in 1805, which linked London and the Midlands. These and some others are still used commercially. Many, however, were not given sufficient forethought, especially those in rural areas, like the Kennet and Avon Canal, linking London with Bristol. These never had enough traffic to make a profit, though they still brought many benefits to the communities through which they passed.

The supremacy of the canals was short-lived as the railways took away much of their business after the 1830s, when the canals went into a decline. Many were taken over by railway companies, perhaps a third of them by 1845. At the height of the canal era, however, the fact that nearly every major city in the country was linked by a relatively cheap form of transport was

A canal scene from the early nineteenth century. Contrast the barges with the sailing boats shown in the earlier prints.

important for social and economic progress. Passengers were carried on most canals – even sleeping accommodation was provided on some barges, such as those between Glasgow and Edinburgh. But the economic importance of the canals was far greater than the convenience of passengers, (see p. 64).

THE DEVELOPMENT OF RAILWAYS

As the Industrial Revolution developed, even the canals found it hard to cope with the volume of freight. Speeds were slow, never more than 3 m.p.h., and locks caused serious delays. The fact that there was no kind of overall control of canals meant that widths varied greatly, and the transfer of goods between barges was costly and timewasting. As time went on, canal companies tended to reduce competition by agreeing on charges. Many provided slow and irregular services with high charges, so that, by the 1820s, there was general dissatisfaction with the canals. Railways provided the answer.

The basic principles of the railway – the use of the rail and of the steam-engine – were well known from an early stage. Railways, or tramways, were quite common in collieries, especially in North-East England. An example was the Killingworth Colliery in Northumberland, where George Stephenson worked. The motive power was usually provided by horses, though fixed steam-engines were sometimes used. There were even some public horse-drawn railways, such as the Surrey Railway from Wandsworth to Croydon, opened in 1805. There were also early experiments in moving steam-engines or locomotives. Richard Trevithick, a Cornishman, ran a steam carriage through the streets of London in 1804, and William Hedley built the *Puffing Billy*, now preserved in the Science Museum in London, in 1813. In 1814 George Stephenson (1781–1848), the most famous of the pioneers, built his first engine, *Blucher*. He soon overcame the problems of adhesion, that is, the

The *Puffing Billy*

Richard Trevithick demonstrating his locomotive *Catch–me–who–can* in Euston Square, London, in 1809. This famous print by Thomas Rowlandson is a mine of information about London life at that time

problem of the wheels gripping the rails. When John Bedlington invented a strong wrought iron rail in 1820, it was only a matter of time before the railways proper emerged.

The Stockton and Darlington Railway, opened in 1825, is usually regarded as the first modern railway. It was certainly important, as it was the first public railway to use steam locomotives. Its main purpose was to carry freight, particularly coal, to avoid the difficult navigation of the River Tees. It still used horses and stationary engines, however. The latter were also used on the Canterbury and Whitstable Railway, opened in 1830. One of the earliest engines on this line, *Invicta*, is displayed in Canterbury by the city walls and a stationary engine can be seen at the university there. Thus it was not for some time after 1825 that the railways really took a hold. That they did so was largely due to George Stephenson, the first man to see the railway not as a novelty but as a revolutionary form of transport which could be established throughout the nation.

The opening of the Stockton and Darlington Railway in 1825

George Stephenson and the Liverpool and Manchester Railway

Stephenson had to overcome much opposition and ridicule, but his chance came when a company was formed to build a railway between Liverpool and Manchester. The charges on the Bridgewater Canal were too high and its capacity too limited. Leading men of both cities felt that a railway might expand trade between the two, as well as providing a handsome profit. Stephenson was given the job of construction and he eventually completed the 69-mile line in 1830. The most difficult part was across Chat Moss, a vast bog. The track was laid across a matting of heather enabling the weight of a train to be spread over a wide area. This involved years of painstaking labour. The Olive Mount Cutting at Edgehill, just outside Liverpool, was another great triumph. As the line neared completion, the directors had to decide what form of motive power was to be used. Locomotives were not yet widely accepted, as many people feared explosions or fires.

In 1829, therefore, a competition was held. A prize of £500 was offered by the directors to the builder of an engine, meeting certain specifications, which most satisfactorily completed a series of trials. The trials, held at Rainhill, near Liverpool, on a level two-mile stretch of line, attracted huge crowds of people. They filled special grandstands erected for the occasion. Most of the 57

George Stephenson

competing engines either failed to start at all or could not complete the course. Only Stephenson's *Rocket* was successful, far beyond anyone's expectations. In the official trial it pulled a load of 13 tons at an average speed of 15 m.p.h., including stops, and reached a top speed of 29 m.p.h. Later, while his rivals struggled, Stephenson drove the *Rocket* back and forth in exhibition runs at speeds well in excess of 30 m.p.h. He was awarded the prize, and the future of locomotives was assured. Nearly 140 years later, in 1968, a ceremony was held at Rainhill to mark the last working run of a steam-engine on the Midland Region of British Rail.

George Stephenson's locomotive works at Newcastle

The opening of the Liverpool and Manchester Railway took place in 1830. It was marred by the death of William Huskisson, who was run over by a train. Despite this bad omen, the opening marked the start of the railway era, just as the Bridgewater Canal had opened the way for canals.

The Spread of the Railways

In the twenty years after the opening of the Liverpool and Manchester, the greater part of the final network was completed, including most of the trunk lines. The first of these was opened in 1838 from London to Birmingham, where the original station can still be seen. The great success of this line encouraged the construction of others; the line from London to Southampton was opened in 1840, and that to Bristol in 1841. In 1840 there were 1,479

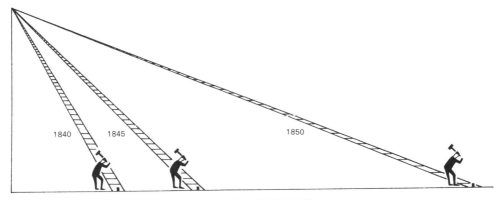

Railway mileage in Britain 1840–50

miles of track, 2,530 in 1845 and 6,559 in 1850. The 1840s, especially 1845–47, saw a 'Railway Mania' on a much greater scale than the 'Canal Mania' of fifty years before. Distances increased, as did speeds, profits and share prices. After 1850 there were many branch lines still to be built and some major projects like the Forth Bridge and the Severn Tunnel, but the pattern was laid out. It took a long time for many to accept the railways, especially farmers and landowners, who disliked the noise, dirt and alleged harm to their livestock. So hostile was one landowner that the engineer had to wait until he was safely in church on a Sunday morning before rushing on to his land to complete his survey in record time! But whatever the opposition, the trains pressed relentlessly on, and had undoubtedly come to stay.

Features of the Early Railways

The most obvious feature of the early railways was the way in which economic necessity was such a driving force. We have already seen this in the Stockton and Darlington and Liverpool and Manchester Railways, and it was true of all the major railways. Many minor lines, however, like the minor canals, could never have paid their way, and were built as purely financial speculations. Freight was the main concern of the pioneers and the passenger appeal which emerged took railwaymen by surprise, for they had considered passenger traffic as of very secondary importance.

This is why passenger trains were only run on the Stockton and Darlington Railway by popular demand. Little attention was paid to passenger comfort for many years, and no composite timetables appeared until Bradshaw's was published in 1839. No one foresaw that one million people would be using the London and Birmingham Railway annually by 1845, or that passenger revenue on most trunk lines would exceed that from freight until the 1850s. This is not to underestimate the importance of freight, of course, but to illustrate the huge, unexpected potential of the railways.

The second feature was the great expense of the railways, perhaps £250 million by 1850. This was not only due to high engineering costs: land prices in Britain were high; bribes had to be paid to landowners, and also to M.P.s to persuade them to pass the necessary Acts of Parliament. The Directors of the London and Birmingham Railway are said to have paid out £750,000 in bribes alone, and it was probably no coincidence that in 1837, 178 M.P.s were also directors of railway companies! A great deal of expensive elaboration, moreover, was used in construction, especially of stations, in order to impress the public. Bristol Temple Meads Station, often mistaken for the Cathedral, is an excellent example of this. Rolling stock and operating equipment were also costly. All this explains why British railways cost in all about £54,000 per route-mile to build, about four times the cost of American railways. Yet, despite the cost, most major companies made big profits throughout the century.

The third feature was the way in which control of the railways quickly passed into the hands of a relatively small number of companies. Mergers and takeovers, not only of other railway companies but also of canals, proceeded rapidly in the 1840s. 200 companies in 1843 were reduced to 22 in 1850, mainly on a regional basis, like the Midland and the London and North Western. George Hudson, of whom a sketch is given later, was the leading figure in this movement.

A final feature was the lack of government intervention or regulation. This was quite in accordance with the beliefs of the age, but it was unfortunate in some ways. There was no overall plan of construction, and as a result there was some unnecessary duplication of lines, like those to South-West England. It even produced two different gauges, the Great Western preferring 7 feet to the standard 4 feet $8\frac{1}{2}$ inches until as late as 1892. There were, moreover, no common standards of safety precautions, though most companies took a pride in their own regulations. These were soon found to be necessary, after several nasty accidents resulting partly from the early practice of regarding railways as turnpikes or canals and allowing anyone to use them after payment. One famous victim of a later crash was the novelist Charles Dickens, who was badly shaken when his train left the line at Staplehurst, Kent, in 1865. Finally, as competition between railway companies declined, it was necessary to have some way of checking unnecessarily high prices and charges.

In 1844 the government of Sir Robert Peel finally passed an Act, for which Gladstone was responsible. This Railway Act laid down some important safety regulations. It also included the famous clause which required all railway companies to run at least one train a day in each direction over all sections of their lines, stopping at all stations and at a fare of not more than one penny per mile. The 'Parliamentary Trains' did much to enable ordinary people to enjoy the benefits of railways. The Act also included the interesting clause, not acted upon, which provided for a possible nationalisation in 1865 of all railways built after 1844.

LEADING PERSONALITIES OF THE RAILWAY ERA

Three men may be taken as representatives of the pioneers of the Railway Era:

Thomas Brassey 1805–70 (Contractor)

Railway contractors have seldom been given the prominence they deserve. They were not usually engineers themselves, but contracted to supply the men and materials and saw that the work specified by the engineer was done. As the scale of operations usually involved thousands of men and hundreds of thousands of pounds, if not millions, this was no mean task.

Thomas Brassey, a Cheshire man, worked with Thomas Telford, before becoming a railway contractor in the 1830s. Much of his work was done abroad after his first major success, the line from Paris to Rouen and Le Havre, finished in 1843. Joseph Locke, the engineer, gained most of the public credit, but Brassey's contribution, with 5,000 British navvies as the core of an international labour force, was immense. The French people were very impressed by his men: 'Mon Dieu, ces Anglais, comme ils travaillent,' was one frequent comment!

By 1850 Brassey had thirty contracts in England, like the London to Portsmouth line, with many more abroad, and he supervised as many as he could himself. In the 1850s his firm built the Grand Trunk Railway in

Canada, and at one time had work under way in all five continents. In the Crimean War, with Sir Morton Peto, another contractor, he built a light railway to take military supplies to the front, charging the government only expenses.

He was even thinking seriously about a Channel Tunnel when he died, leaving £5 million. He was widely mourned, as he was a model employer who looked after his men well. Some of his work can still be seen, especially in France, where the Barentin Viaduct, near Rouen, and the fact that the

Robert Stephenson

Thomas Brassey

trains still keep to the left are just two of the memorials to him. So is the fact that football is now the one really international sport, introduced by Brassey's men playing this British game in their spare time, wherever they went.

Robert Stephenson 1803–59 (Engineer)

The son of George Stephenson, Robert was responsible for the design of many of the major railway lines in Britain and the world. He helped his father to build the *Rocket* and the Liverpool and Manchester Railway. Then he supervised some minor lines on behalf of his father. His first sole responsibility was the London and Birmingham Railway, completed successfully in 1838. This had some major engineering feats, such as the mile-and-a-half-long Kilsby Tunnel near Rugby. His other lines are too numerous to list, but perhaps his most lasting monuments are not the lines themselves, but some of the bridges. In Britain the most impressive are those at Newcastle-on-Tyne and Berwick-on-Tweed and the tubular girder bridge at Conway. His Menai Bridge was also a splendid sight, not far from Telford's road bridge, until it was seriously damaged by fire in 1970 and reconstructed to a new design. It is fitting that when Stephenson died, having received many honours, he was buried in Westminster Abbey alongside Telford. The two Stephensons, with Isambard Kingdom Brunel (1806–59) and Joseph Locke (1805–60), built between them most of the railways of Britain.

The Royal Albert Bridge at Saltash, designed by I. K. Brunel. A goods train, hauled by a steam locomotive, is about to cross the River Tamar.

George Hudson 1800–71 (Financier)

George Hudson, 'The Railway King', was the most influential of all those financiers and businessmen who provided the money for the construction of railways and who made their fortune from them. One of the leading citizens of York, he was associated with most of the railway companies in the North and North-East. In the 1840s he expanded his interests to other areas, and led the way in the mergers described earlier. By 1848 he was chairman of five companies and a director of numerous others. He became an M.P., enormously wealthy and much in demand in London society.

Many of Hudson's business deals, however, were fraudulent and he was very open to bribes. This gradually came out and though he avoided conviction and absolute disgrace, he lost his position and most of his money after 1848. This was an inglorious end for a man who for a brief period was a spectacular example of how the railways could bring rich rewards.

THE RESULTS OF THE TRANSPORT REVOLUTION

The revolution in transport brought profound changes in British social and economic life. The railways were chiefly responsible, but only because of their greater scale and scope. The results of the improvements in roads and canals were basically the same as those of the railways, and they all contributed to the general transformation.

The economic consequences may be divided into five main groups. First, there were important results for industry as a whole. More goods were transported more quickly and more cheaply to wider markets. The canals cut costs by a half, sometimes more. In 1792, for example, land transport from Birmingham to Liverpool cost £5 per ton, water transport £1 10s. per ton. The railway cut costs still further. By 1850 no part of Britain was beyond the reach of most manufacturers. As production increased, so it became more efficient, with new techniques to meet rising demand. There was greater employment for the rising population and so greater prosperity, and an even greater demand for industrial products. It was much cheaper to transport raw materials and coal to the factories which were no longer bound to be located near coalfields. One half of all the freight carried by the railways in the nineteenth century was coal, and in the long run this was an important aid to the beginning of industry in new areas such as the south of England. Better transport meant that workers could travel about the country more easily to find work and this helped to reduce the harmful effects of unemployment. Shops were made more efficient as they no longer had to hold large stocks, but could easily send for new supplies.

Secondly, there were particular benefits for some industries. The heavy industries, notably iron, received a great impetus. A huge quantity of iron was used in the construction of railways. One and a half million tons were used in Britain alone between 1846 and 1850, and much more overseas. More was used in rolling stocks and other equipment; all this had a great effect on the developments in the iron industry in the middle of the nineteenth century. The coal industry also gained from the easier transportation and from the requirements of the engines themselves. Agriculture gained much, for it was now possible to send perishable goods a long distance. Dairy products in particular, especially milk, were sent in special trains to the major cities. Farming even in remote areas became more profitable. The agricultural changes of the nineteenth century owed much to the Transport Revolution.

Even fishing gained; by 1848 the Eastern Counties Railway was bringing 70 tons of fresh fish daily into London, from Lowestoft and Yarmouth; Grimsby, Hull and Aberdeen were other ports which benefited in this way.

Thirdly, there were large gains for Britain's overseas trade. This was speeded up by quicker transport to and from the ports. Since Britain dominated overseas railway construction and the supply of equipment such as rails, carriages, engines and signals, she gained big profits. In the single year 1871, for example, Britain exported over half a million tons of rail to the United States. Her railway investment abroad built up a useful reserve of funds, though in the long run it helped countries such as the United States and Germany to develop into industrial and trading rivals.

Fourthly, the Transport Revolution created new employment opportunities. Roads, canals and railways had to be built, and this offered employment on a scale hitherto unknown. Civil engineering in the modern sense began here, with the appearance of a new class of specialist engineers. John Smeaton founded the Institute of Civil Engineers in 1818, with Telford as President. A class of labourers called 'navvies' also arose, taking their name from those who built the 'navigations'. Permanent employment was offered by the operation of the new means of transport, from tollgate keepers to bargees, engine drivers to repair gangs. New towns sprang up, centred around the canals or railways: such were Stourport, St. Helens, Crewe, Rugby and Swindon. 300,000 men were in some way employed by the railway companies alone in 1848. This meant, with their families, that the railways supported well over one million people. In fact, a whole new form of employment – the transport industry – had arisen.

Fifthly, there were some general effects of the vast sums of money spent on transport development. Expenditure tended to come at times, like the 1840s, when other industries were in difficulties, and so helped to offset general depression. Much was done to improve the financial institutions of the country. The banks and the Stock Exchange had to deal with vast sums of money and were forced to become more efficient and reliable. Finally, it all provided valuable experience of large-scale business organisation, for the railway companies were by far the biggest yet seen.

On the more directly social side, the standard of living was improved in three main ways. First, the cheapening of goods, especially food, and their greater availability had an important effect. Better diets must have aided the falling death rates, especially among infants, and hence led to a higher population. The railways finally removed any fear of widespread famine, though poverty itself was not eliminated.

Second, there were many benefits from the easier spread of newspapers, mail and the electric telegraph, which accompanied the railways. Indeed, the Post Office had been one of the earliest supporters of better transport, and is

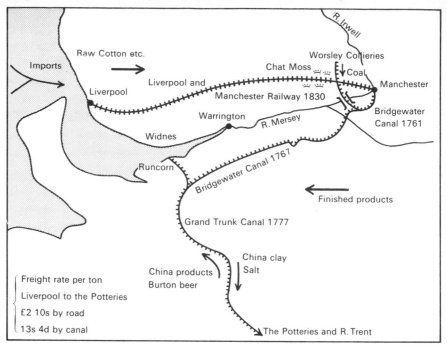

Map of the Lancashire area showing the location and economic importance of early canals and railways

thought to have been responsible for persuading the companies to run trains on Sundays – which many Victorians opposed. The maintenance of law and order was also improved. During Chartist riots in Birmingham in 1839 the harassed local magistrates were able to summon up reinforcements from London by train in a few hours. Even things that we now take for granted, such as a standard time in Britain, only came with the railways. It was impossible to operate railways, for example, while London time was as much as half an hour different from that in some other places.

Third, many ordinary people gained for the first time from being able to travel beyond their own districts. Thomas Cook, the founder of the famous travel firm, was the first agent to organise cheap excursion trips, in 1841, when he laid on one from Leicester to Loughborough for a temperance, or anti-drink, rally. Even before this, the railway companies themselves had organised day trips to places of interest. One day in 1840 a 67-coach train was seen at Leicester with 3,000 passengers on board! This may be taken as a start of the modern 'holiday business'.

In 1851 the railways brought over six million visitors to London for the Great Exhibition. With such bargains as the 3s. 6d. excursion fare from Peterborough, in Northamptonshire, who could resist? People began to visit relatives more often, or to take holidays at seaside resorts like Ramsgate,

66

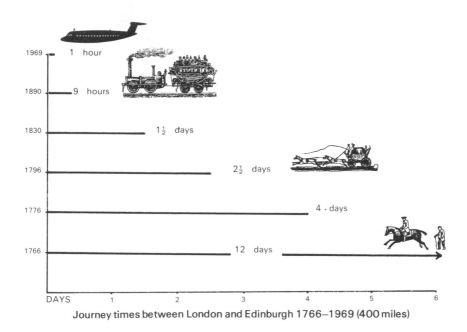

1969	1 hour
1890	9 hours
1830	1½ days
1796	2½ days
1776	4 · days
1766	12 days

DAYS 1 2 3 4 5 6

Journey times between London and Edinburgh 1766–1969 (400 miles)

Bournemouth and New Brighton, which grew up with the railways. Many of the visitors were able to see the sea for the first time in their lives. A very few better-off working people began to go abroad.

All this meant that the revolution in transport helped to break down the limited horizons of the majority of people in the country. Easier travel made Britain much more of a nation. In the twentieth century, the motor car has carried on this process still more effectively, but even before 1850 the Transport Revolution had achieved an impact on social and economic life of profound importance.

Suggestions for further work and discussion

1. Write an account of an imaginary journey between any two cities in Britain in 1750. In what ways would the journey have been different in 1850?

2. Many of the famous works mentioned in this chapter can still be seen. If you live near enough to one, or are on holiday in the area, visit it and find out more about it. It can be a most interesting project to take photographs, make drawings and assemble information about the history and construction of these landmarks in the history of transport.

3. Apart from such famous works, evidence of the Transport Revolution lies all around us. Much is still in everyday use, much is disused and some in museums. Try to discover what there is in your area, and find out as much as you can about its history. Here are some suggestions about what can be found in most parts of Britain:

> Tollgate Houses, milestones, old coach roads (which often run along ridges), coaching inns (sometimes identifiable by their names, such as *The Quicksilver Mail* in Yeovil), timetables, canals, locks, tunnels, barges, aqueducts, old railway branch lines, stations, bridges, engines, signal-boxes and notice-boards.

4. Visit one of the transport museums in Britain, such as those at York and Swindon. (The museum at Clapham, London, is due to be moved to York.) Early engines can be seen at several other places including Darlington Station and Canterbury.

5. Select one (or more) of the engineers mentioned in this chapter, and write a fuller account of his life and achievements. The three volumes of *Lives of the Engineers*, by Samuel Smiles (David & Charles, 1968), contain many interesting details which will help you.

6. Suggestions for essays or discussions:

> What was the importance of railways in the first half of the nineteenth century?
>
> How did ordinary people benefit from improved transport?
>
> How was industrialisation assisted by the Transport Revolution?

7. Many societies are now trying to preserve and operate long-disused canals and railways. Investigate the work of any such society in your locality. Why do you think so many people go to so much trouble to preserve old forms of transport?

Books for further reading:

There are a great many books about the history of transport, and every library will have some. Here are a few which are interesting, and which should be easily obtainable:

> T. Coleman, *The Railway Navvies*, Hutchinson, 1965, Penguin, 1968.
>
> C. Hadfield, *British Canals*, David & Charles, 1969.
>
> C. Hadfield, *The Canal Age*, David & Charles, 1968.
>
> M. Robbins, *The Railway Age*, Penguin, 1970.
>
> L. T. C. Rolt, *George and Robert Stephenson — The Railway Revolution*, Longmans, 1960.
>
> L. T. C. Rolt, *Isambard Kingdom Brunel*, Longmans, 1957.
>
> L. T. C. Rolt, *Telford*, Longmans, 1958.
>
> S. and B. Webb, *The Story of the King's Highway*, Longmans, 1913.

4 : The Industrial Revolution

The advantages of getting someone – or something – else to do your work for you are so obvious that men must always have been on the lookout for ways of improving their position in this respect. The eighteenth and nineteenth centuries are particularly important in the history of the human race because they saw the beginnings of a really big breakthrough in the use of non-human power.

At the beginning of the eighteenth century, industry in Britain was able to draw on three sources of power other than manpower: animals (particularly horses), wind and water. Horses were of such universal importance that they set the standard for every other sort of power, and even today it is not uncommon to find the capacities of engines expressed in terms of horsepower. With a little ingenuity, it was possible to employ horses to drive machinery, such as lifts and pumps, as well as for the more obvious function of drawing or pushing loads.

However, although the horse is a versatile animal, he has his limitations. The use of wind and water power represent attempts to go a stage further.

Water Power and Wind Power

Of the two, water power was more important to British industry. The idea of using the current of a stream to turn a wheel, which itself turned machinery through a system of cogs and gears, was established in Britain early in the Middle Ages. (More than 5,000 such mills are recorded in Domesday Book.) The precise way in which this was managed would vary according to circumstances; there were three main types of water-wheel, each suited to a different sort of river, as shown on p. 70.

The most common use for the water-wheel was, of course, in connection with flour-milling, where its great force might be used to turn the massive stones between which corn could be crushed and ground. There were also other sorts of grinding-mill including snuff-mills such as the one still surviving in part on the River Wandle at Morden, near London. In fact all sorts of machinery could be powered in this way; on the same stretch of the Wandle there were still as many as thirty water-mills in the early part of the present century, working on the manufacture of products as different as tobacco, copper, oil, leather, parchment and paper, besides the snuff-mill and

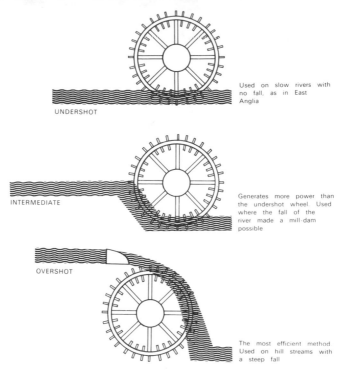

UNDERSHOT

Used on slow rivers with no fall, as in East Anglia

INTERMEDIATE

Generates more power than the undershot wheel. Used where the fall of the river made a mill-dam possible

OVERSHOT

The most efficient method. Used on hill streams with a steep fall

Types of water-wheel

numerous flour-mills. Water power was also used in the iron industry; we find it driving trip-hammers for working iron in Sussex as early as the sixteenth century. Sometimes we find water power employed in rather unusual industries – for example, the flint-mills of Shropshire and the gunpowder-mills at Faversham, in Kent.

The illustration shows a water-wheel which was used for another and very important branch of industry – the manufacture of textiles, in this case the printing of silks and calicoes. Late in the nineteenth century it was owned by a firm which produced a famous type of printed cloth known as Liberty prints.

Water power was probably first applied to the textile industry in the twelfth century, when it was used in fulling (one of the processes in the manufacture of woollen cloth). During the eighteenth century its use was extended by the development of new sorts of machinery to numerous other parts of the textile business. As we shall see shortly, the consequences of these inventions were of the greatest importance.

The third type of power was wind power. This had also been developed during the Middle Ages – there are records of windmills from the late twelfth century. But its usefulness was more restricted and it was employed chiefly for grinding corn in places where water power was lacking. From the seventeenth century, following the example set in Holland, engineers also used windmills to drive pumping engines in the Fens of East Anglia.

The main drawback of wind-powered machinery, which applied to a lesser extent also to water-driven systems, was that it depended on natural forces which could not be relied upon to operate just as and when the miller might want them. The wind might drop, or the stream might fail, just when there was work to be done. For many years men sought to discover a method of producing power which would be entirely controllable; success was finally achieved with the steam-engine.

An undershot wheel

Steam Power

Experiments with what was then called a 'fire-engine' were carried out by various people, such as the Marquess of Worcester, during the seventeenth century. The first machine to work reasonably effectively was a steam-pump developed by Thomas Savery about the year 1698. This operated on the principle explained in the diagram below.

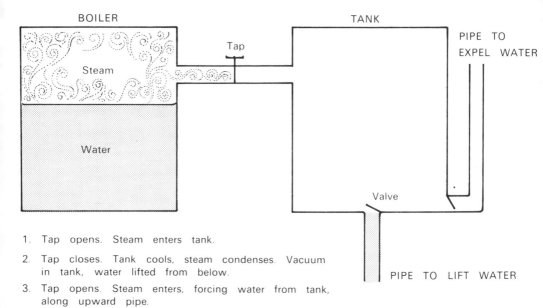

1. Tap opens. Steam enters tank.
2. Tap closes. Tank cools, steam condenses. Vacuum in tank, water lifted from below.
3. Tap opens. Steam enters, forcing water from tank, along upward pipe.

Savery's pumping engine

Savery's machine achieved some success in pumping out mines (for example, tin-mines in Cornwall) and in supplying power to small-scale water-works in and around London. But it was still relatively weak and primitive, and was quite easily superseded by a rather different type of pump, Thomas Newcomen's 'atmospheric engine', which was developed between 1705 and 1720.

The Newcomen engine rapidly came into very general use for all sorts of pumping operations; in 1767, for instance, there were nearly 70 engines in and around Newcastle alone. They were used particularly for pumping out mines, but it also became quite common to use an atmospheric engine to pump water over a water-wheel in order to provide the driving force for a mill. However, the next logical step, namely making the engine itself into the driving-force, had to wait for the discoveries of James Watt.

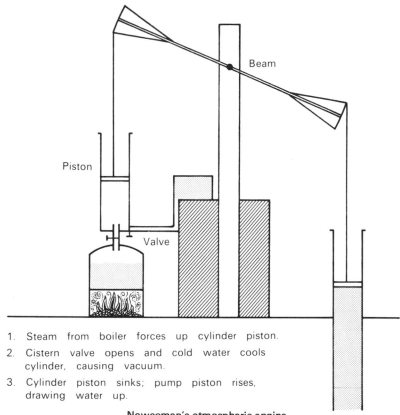

Piston

Beam

Valve

1. Steam from boiler forces up cylinder piston.
2. Cistern valve opens and cold water cools cylinder, causing vacuum.
3. Cylinder piston sinks; pump piston rises, drawing water up.

Newcomen's atmospheric engine

Watt, who lived between 1736 and 1819, came from a well-to-do Scottish family with a background of mathematics and engineering. He demonstrated impressive abilities in these and many other subjects at an early age. In the early 1760s, while he was employed as a maker of scientific instruments for the University of Glasgow, a model of Newcomen's engine came to him for repair, and he turned his mind to the possibilities of improving it. His work on it had two main effects: first, he made the engine much more efficient in itself; secondly, he made it possible to convert what had previously been no more than a pump into a general driving-engine, with (as it eventually turned out) almost unlimited applications.

Although Watt had a brilliant inventive mind, he was not outstanding as a businessman and much of the credit for the rapid success of his steam-engine must go to two other men, ironmasters John Roebuck of Carron and Matthew Boulton of Soho in Birmingham. Roebuck first saw the potential of the invention and entered into partnership with Watt, and then Boulton took Roebuck's place when money ran short. The first working steam-engine of the new sort was set up in 1769, and an improved version followed in 1774.

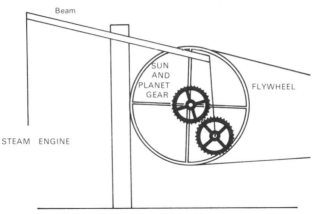

Rotary motion, as developed by James Watt

Despite trouble over patents and pressure from fierce and sometimes un-scrupulous competitors, Boulton and Watt gradually established a position of supremacy in the manufacture of steam-engines, although their enterprise did not show a clear profit until the late 1780s. So in a sense their Soho works can be regarded as the cradle of the Industrial Revolution.

The whole process of development was of course very gradual, and it would be quite meaningless to describe it as if there was one precise moment when the Industrial Revolution 'began', or 'triumphed', or anything of that sort. It is possible, however, to pick on some dates as being especially significant, and one of these would certainly be 1781, when Watt took out a patent for rotary motion. This was the vital process which converted his pumping-engine into a driving-engine, capable of supplying power direct to all sorts of machines. Hardly surprisingly, it was first used to drive bellows, rolling-mills and hammers in the Soho ironworks. A notable ironmaster called John Wilkinson was the first to follow Boulton's example, and after him

Matthew Boulton (*left*) brought organising ability and business flair to his partnership with the brilliant inventor James Watt (*right*)

other ironmasters were quick to order steam-engines for themselves; soon there came a host of others – millers of all sorts, Wedgwood the potter (1782), Whitbread the brewer (1785) and then the various sorts of textile manufacturers. By 1800 11 steam-engines were at work in Birmingham, 20 in Leeds and 32 in Manchester. Soon their numbers could hardly be counted.

THE COAL INDUSTRY IN THE INDUSTRIAL REVOLUTION

Some of the early steam-engines burnt wood; but coal has obvious advantages as a fuel, and the types developed by Watt were coal-fired. Coal is thus essential to the beginnings of industrial development in Britain. It had of course been used long before the eighteenth century; as the forests dwindled it had come more and more to replace wood as a domestic fuel, and even before the Industrial Revolution it was used in some processes of a great many industries. Wool, iron, steel, brick, soap and glass production, tin smelting and sugar refining all used coal at some stage. It is a sign of its importance that the internal trade in coal was second only to the corn trade.

The Newcastle area was so important that it was known in the early eighteenth century as the 'Black Indies', and the coal as 'Black Diamonds'. It was by no means the only area of importance at that time, however; South Wales, Lancashire, Shropshire and Scotland had coalfields which were already beginning to expand, with industries settling around them. There were even exports of coal to some European countries.

Nevertheless, the total output of coal at the beginning of the Industrial Revolution was very small compared with the great potential of the coal seams. Coal-mining was really regarded still as part of the management of a landed estate. So it was mainly a rural occupation in the hands of a few great landowners, like the Duke of Bridgewater. It had serious weaknesses and technical problems which hindered its further development.

Like any industry, coal-mining could only develop on a large scale if there was a big demand for its products. This demand increased very rapidly after 1750 with the general growth of industry; with the invention of steam power which depended on coal; with the closer harnessing of coal to iron production; and, later, with the development of railways and steamships which used vast quantities of coal. All these changes are described more fully in other parts of the book.

To meet this new demand, coal-mining had to become much more efficient. In 1750 most mines were of the open-cast type, in which the coal was extracted from near the surface. As the miners went deeper and deeper, they met serious technical problems. Ventilation methods were primitive, and fresh air was available only from shafts. It circulated through the tunnels by means of trap doors, operated by children. Flooding was frequent, and miners were sometimes drowned. Also, they were occasionally poisoned by carbon dioxide gas ignited by naked lights. Another hazard was the collapse of tunnels, as the custom then was to leave pillars of coal to support the roof and these were not very reliable. Another difficulty was that of raising the coal to the surface. This was normally done manually, and it was not unknown for women to have to carry loads of 170 lb. several hundred yards.

Gradually, most of these difficulties were overcome, and output rose from about $2\frac{1}{2}$ million tons in 1700 and $4\frac{3}{4}$ million tons in 1750 to 10 million tons in 1800 and 30 million in 1830. Really major advances, however, had to wait until the period after 1830.

THE FACTORY SYSTEM

The tremendous developments which we have noticed in the field of power had enormously far-reaching results. In association with the remarkable inventions of machinery which were made at this time, they made possible the development of the factory system and in so doing changed the whole pattern of life and work for vast numbers of people in Britain, and eventually in the whole world.

We have become so accustomed to thinking of industry as an affair of factories, mostly organised on a grand scale, that it is quite difficult to realise that before the Industrial Revolution such organisations just did not exist. Indeed, the word 'factory' had quite a different meaning. Until late in the eighteenth century it signified a place where a trading company maintained an agent (or 'factor') and a warehouse. Thus we hear of the East India Company's 'factories' at Calcutta, Bombay, Madras etc. Our meaning for the word is really derived from a longer form – 'manufactory', a place where goods are made. It was this form which was generally used in the eighteenth century.

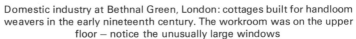

Domestic industry at Bethnal Green, London: cottages built for handloom weavers in the early nineteenth century. The workroom was on the upper floor – notice the unusually large windows

If goods had not been made in factories before the Industrial Revolution, where then had they been made? The answer is that they had been made for the most part in small workshops, or in the homes of individual craftsmen. (There is a picture of a row of houses specially built for such domestic workers on p. 76.) A very wealthy master might gather together a large number of workmen and apprentices in a single workshop: but this would not really be a factory, until certain conditions were met.

The distinguishing marks of a factory are (1) that the work is done by machines, which are *tended* rather than *used* by men, and (2) that production runs continuously and automatically on power other than manpower.

The vital factor here is obviously going to be power. This was recognised at an early date, when, in 1844, a legal definition of a factory was included in an Act of Parliament. It ran as follows:

> The word factory . . . shall be taken to mean all buildings and premises wherein . . . steam or any other mechanical power shall be used to move or work any machinery employed in preparing . . . [in this case, textiles].

This definition effectively rules out early oddities like the giant workshop manufacturing woollen cloth, which the sixteenth-century clothier Jack of Newbury was said to have run, giving employment to 1,040 people; all these people (the figure is certainly an exaggeration) were craftsmen carrying out their tasks by hand, with no power but that provided by their own strength.

The first real factory in England, by the definition given above, was set up by a certain Thomas Lombe, in 1718 or shortly afterwards, on an island in the River Derwent near Derby. It was a big, barrack-like building, 500 feet long and five or six storeys high, housing machines for making silk thread. These machines, which were of a type previously known only in Italy, were powered by a water-wheel. The whole arrangement was a completely new departure for England and excited the amazement of all who saw it. Daniel Defoe wrote:

> This engine contains 22,586 wheels and 97,746 movements, which work 73,726 yards of silk thread every time the wheel goes round, which is three times in one minute, and 318,504,960 yards in twenty-four hours. The water wheel gives the motion to all the rest of the wheels and movements, of which any one may be stopped separately.
>
> (*A Tour Thro' the Whole Island of Great Britain, 1724–7*)

For various reasons the silk industry did not thrive in England, and Lombe's factory looks in retrospect rather like a false start. But the way had been pioneered and when the inventions which Arkwright claimed for his own came to transform the cotton industry, the principle of a water-powered factory was already to a certain extent familiar.

Arkwright's first 'mill' (the word had come to be attached to anything powered by a water-wheel, whether it was a grinding-mill or not) was set up on the Derwent at Cromford in 1771. It can still be seen there today. His machines – heavy, complex and costly – could only be profitably worked in a factory system.

Power was so essential to Arkwright's factory that it is not surprising to find him in correspondence with Watt and Boulton from 1785. He bought a steam-engine from them in 1790. (He had assisted the flow of water over his wheel with a Newcomen engine since 1780.) Thenceforward the steam-engine and the cotton industry progressed together, as the print reproduced below clearly shows.

An early nineteenth-century engraving of power looms in a Lancashire factory; the machines shown were made in Manchester, and cost less than £10 apiece

THE CONDITIONS FOR SUCCESS

We have presented the factory system in terms of power and machinery because this is fundamentally what it is all about. But other factors had to coincide before the system could grow really successfully. First and foremost there had to be a ready supply of capital. This was necessary initially to finance the huge building operations involved in setting up a factory. More capital would be needed to furnish it with machinery and still more to purchase raw materials and pay the workers until enough of the product had been sold to show some sort of profit. England developed a financial system big enough and strong enough to stand this strain for the first time during the eighteenth century; some features of the story are outlined below.

Secondly, the new capitalists could not work all their machines by them-selves. They had to have plenty of labour available – and again this essential condition was met for the first time in England during the eighteenth century. In this case the change was brought about partly by the natural increase of the population, and partly by the effects of another of the great changes of this time of turmoil, the Agricultural Revolution. We have seen how the new developments in farming tended to create a surplus of unwanted people in the villages – people for whom there was no chance of an independent existence, and whom nobody needed as labourers. These people naturally drifted away, looking for work wherever they could get it, and usually ended up in the towns, where they might find employment in the new factories. That is not to say that the factory-owners never had any difficulty in finding workers; on the contrary, we often find them complaining bitterly about the shortage of labour. The balance of population only changed comparatively slowly.

A third essential condition for the factory system was the existence of adequate arrangements for transport. Steam-engines could not run without coal; the machines were useless without raw materials; there was no point in producing vast quantities of goods if they could not be carried to market. The developments in transport, particularly canals, have been fully dealt with in Chapter 3. Here it should be enough to stress once more that the factory-owners were very often right to the fore in promoting new transport schemes, because they could see so clearly that this would serve their own interests. An example is provided by Josiah Wedgwood's promotion of canal schemes in the neighbourhood of his pottery works.

Last of all, the whole paraphernalia of finance, labour, transport and the factories themselves is quite useless if there is no market for the goods which the new system could produce in such unprecedented quantities. This, per-haps above all, is the distinguishing mark of the Industrial Revolution. Pro-ducer and consumer move into a new relationship, based on the assumption of continually expanding demand. There had never been anything quite like it before; more and more people demanding more and more goods, of ever-changing types, and matched by producers able to turn out more and more manufactures, in a way that actually created more wealth, so that standards of living (and thus demand) went up again.

Here we have the marvel of the Industrial Revolution – the change from a stationary to a dynamic economy, the development of a whole set of delicately interlocking factors all exerting pressure on each other towards expansion. Everything affects everything else; to grasp that is to grasp one of the great facts of modern economics.

A splendid example of the way in which different factors worked together to produce the Industrial Revolution is to be found in the contribution of finance. Before the eighteenth century there was nothing that could really have been called a proper financial system – no banks, no Stock Exchange, no safe and regular means of raising credit; there was even a serious shortage of currency. If this situation had remained unchanged, there could hardly have been any Industrial Revolution at all, since it requires a great deal of money to buy steam-engines and power looms, build factories, purchase raw materials and employ workers. Very few men could have afforded to embark on such enterprises out of their own pockets. But the eighteenth century saw enormous changes in the financial picture. Banks were founded, both in the City of London and in the provinces, all of them private at this stage – even the splendidly named Bank of England (founded 1694). There were about 70 London banks in 1800 and about 400 'country' banks, including some names which are famous today, such as Lloyds and Barclays. A big step towards efficiency was taken in 1773, when the London banks established a 'Clearing House' to co-ordinate their dealings; but the system was still relatively primitive and bankruptcies were common. The Stock Exchange was rather less developed, since the law as it stood in the eighteenth century hindered the formation of business companies and narrowly restricted the buying and selling of stocks and shares. The modern Stock Exchange was founded in 1773 and gradually helped more and more industrialists to raise the funds they needed. Finally, the improvements in communications and the founding of banks capable of issuing their own notes did much to produce what economists call greater 'liquidity' in the currency.

A country bank note of the early nineteenth century. The engraving of Telford's Menai Suspension Bridge typifies contemporary pride in such achievements

The Stock Exchange in the nineteenth century

All these improvements and advances meshed together in ways that could not possibly have been foreseen to make it easier for inventors to build their machines, for industrialists to use them and for people of every sort to buy the goods they produced. Historians have argued a great deal over which came first, the financial changes or the industrial changes. The most sensible answer is that they are like the chicken and the egg! Above all, the contribution of individuals must not be forgotten – merchants who made fortunes in overseas trade and invested them in industry (for example, the Liverpool merchants who played a large part in the development of Manchester); landowners who employed the surplus of their agricultural incomes in mining or transport undertakings (for example, the Duke of Bridgewater); and above all, the self-denying energy and vigour of the first capitalists themselves. Perhaps the story of a Yorkshire ironmaster, Samuel Walker, could almost stand as a summary of the way in which the first industrialists made their own finances. He started in 1741, in an old smithy. By 1746 his total capital was £700, and he took in some partners. All the partners drew meagre salaries until 1757, when the capital had reached £7,500 and they allowed themselves the luxury of a small dividend. All the rest was 'ploughed back', until, when Samuel Walker died in 1782, the capital was £128,000. It was this ruthless spirit of determination, very close to that of the seventeenth-century Puritans, that made possible the successful interaction of money and industry in the eighteenth century, and produced the Industrial Revolution.

The finest flower of this interaction was the great textile industry that grew up in the second half of the century, and we will turn to this next to see at work the forces described above.

The manufacture of textiles in this period falls easily into three divisions: the silk industry, the woollen industry and the cotton industry.

Silk

The silk industry was by far the smallest of these, and can be quite quickly dealt with. Silk was essentially a luxury product and, as was the case with most luxury products at this time, its manufacture in Europe was dominated by France. In the sixteenth and seventeenth centuries, however, religious persecution in France had forced numbers of French Protestants, known as Huguenots, to leave their country and settle abroad. Among those who came to England were skilled silk-weavers who established a small but thriving silk industry in a few centres in southern England, notably in Spitalfields, London. Periodic attempts to expand this industry met with little success, chiefly because the Huguenots had not brought with them the secret of spinning silk thread. Consequently this had to be imported at high cost. The experts in the field of silk-throwing, as the spinning was known, were the Italians, and they kept their technique a jealously guarded mystery until in 1716 John Lombe, the brother of the man mentioned above (p. 77), went to Italy as a kind of industrial spy, and at great risk to himself made drawings of the Italian machines. It was these machines which Thomas Lombe installed in the first factory in England in 1718.

Now the English had their own silk-throwing industry. But they still laboured under various disadvantages, the chief of which was a shortage of raw material. They were also seriously hampered by the effective protectionist policies of Continental governments. Some very large factories and workshops were set up in London, Derby, Stockport and other places, and some great fortunes were made. But the silk industry never grew to the point where it could rival the older woollen industry, and it was rapidly surpassed at the end of the century by the new cotton industry. Consequently it is chiefly of curiosity interest, rather than anything more significant in the history of industrialisation.

The great contribution of the silk industry to this history of the British economy was the development of the factory system. It is interesting that, while this new industry nerved itself to take such a step, the far more experienced and wealthy woollen cloth industry seemed for years unable to bring itself to the point and suffered severe troubles in consequence.

Wool

The manufacture of woollen cloth was the great pride and stay of English export business in the sixteenth and seventeenth centuries. Many types of cloth were produced, of which the most famous and popular was broadcloth. The main cloth-producing areas are shown on the map on p. 94.

The industry was organised on what is known as the domestic, or outwork, system. That is to say, the various processes were carried out by craftsmen working in their own homes, using tools and machinery which in many cases would be their own. It might be that only the raw material, from wool to finished cloth, was owned by the 'clothier' (i.e. the merchant-capitalist who supervised the whole operation, and under whose name the cloth would finally be sold). The clothier would arrange for the material to be moved from one craftsman to another, and would pay the men at piece-rates.

This system sounds rather sprawling and inefficient; but we have already tried to explain how there was little point in trying to centralise industry until the development of power-driven machinery made factories worthwhile and indeed essential. Certainly it proved possible to make great fortunes from the industry, even organised as it was. So much was this the case, in fact, that the clothiers became set in their ways.

Spinsters at work

During the eighteenth century the demand for cloth grew very greatly in England, and also overseas, partly at least because of the increase in the population. This should have prompted the clothiers to examine their methods of production, to see if they were the best that could be devised. In fact, the domestic system was not well suited to the business of supplying an expanding mass market. It tended to be rigid, and slow to respond to fluctuations in demand; and, of course, the numerous small craftsmen, only loosely organised by the master-clothier, found it difficult to adjust their limited skills to the production of the new sorts of cloth demanded by an increasingly fashion-conscious public.

Despite all the good reasons for trying to alter the domestic system, however, the majority of clothiers actually resisted change. They had got things cosily organised to their own satisfaction and, up till then, to their profit as well; they did not want to have to start again from scratch. They did not wake from their complacency until their position had been fatally weakened by upstart rivals – the 'cotton lords', as many people called them at the time. The great East Anglian industry centred on Norwich disappeared almost without trace, and even the proud clothiers of the West Country were reduced to tiny shadows of their former selves.

Not all the manufacturers of woollen cloth were so stupid. The men of Yorkshire, stimulated by the competition and following the example of their rivals, the cotton lords of Lancashire, met the challenge of modernisation with

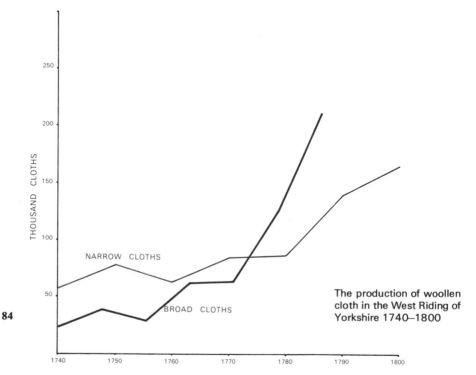

NARROW CLOTHS

BROAD CLOTHS

THOUSAND CLOTHS

The production of woollen cloth in the West Riding of Yorkshire 1740–1800 success and actually improved their position to the point where practically all the woollen manufacture of England came to be concentrated in the West Riding, especially in the cities of Leeds, Huddersfield, Bradford and Halifax.

The chief reason for this success, apart from any possibility of superior personal qualities on the part of the Yorkshiremen, is curiously complicated. Labour in Yorkshire was at first cheaper (i.e. wages were lower) than in the East or South-West, which made it possible for an enterprising businessman to make a fortune by conventional 'domestic' methods; with prosperity, the price of labour rose and forced the employers to turn to mechanisation – just in time!

The new machines were adopted in Yorkshire, though not as quickly as in the Lancashire cotton industry. The first machines to be taken up were, significantly, those like the spinning jenny and the flying-shuttle (see pp. 90, 92) which could be fitted into the domestic system. Only gradually, during the first quarter of the nineteenth century, did the powered combing-machine and the power loom force the development of a factory system, against the bitter opposition of the numerous small masters.

The following tables show the development of the woollen industry in the period:

WOOLLEN GOODS IN RELATION TO TOTAL EXPORTS,
1700–1830

	Woollens and worsteds	
	Value, £'000	*Percentage of total exports*
1700–09	3,095	70
1710–19	3,222	67
1720–29	3,116	64
1730–39	3,581	63
1740–49	3,453	53
1750–59	4,239	48
1760–69	4,448	44
1770–79	3,991	43
1780–89	3,518	35
1790–99	5,234	30
1800–09	5,982	24
1810–19	5,617	16
1820–29	5,553	12

Notice the fluctuating rise in the value of woollen exports and the steady fall in the share of total exports.

The figures represent annual averages per decade.

	Broad cloths	Narrow cloths
	(To the nearest thousand)	
1730	32	—
1740	43	61
1750	61	74
1760	49	75
1770	93	90
1780	98	98
1790	187	155
1800	286	169

The next diagram illustrates the main stages in the manufacture of woollen cloth; it also applies, broadly, to cotton cloth.

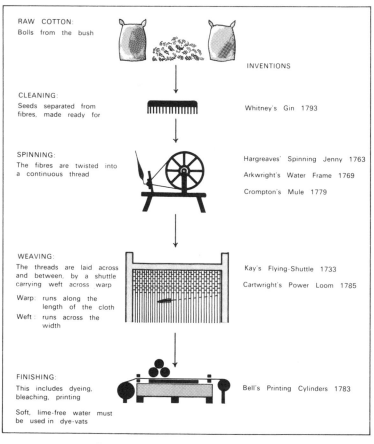

RAW COTTON:
Bolls from the bush

INVENTIONS

CLEANING:
Seeds separated from fibres, made ready for

Whitney's Gin 1793

SPINNING:
The fibres are twisted into a continuous thread

Hargreaves' Spinning Jenny 1763

Arkwright's Water Frame 1769

Crompton's Mule 1779

WEAVING:
The threads are laid across and between, by a shuttle carrying weft across warp

Warp: runs along the length of the cloth

Weft: runs across the width

Kay's Flying-Shuttle 1733

Cartwright's Power Loom 1785

FINISHING:
This includes dyeing, bleaching, printing

Soft, lime-free water must be used in dye-vats

Bell's Printing Cylinders 1783

Stages in the manufacture of cotton textiles

Cotton

The last section to be considered is also the biggest and the most important part of the textile industry at the time of the Industrial Revolution. The cotton industry grew during this period from practically nothing into the greatest industry in the country. Contemporaries were staggered – some were appalled – by this mushroom growth and the fortunes which were made out of it. The figures indeed speak for themselves, especially when we remember that the cotton industry grew like Jack's beanstalk in a society which had been economically quiet for a long time.

THE GROWTH OF THE COTTON INDUSTRY

	Raw cotton, retained imports '000 lb.	*Total cotton exports*	
		Value, £'000	*Percentage of total exports*
1700–09	1,000 (app.)	13	0
1710–19		8	0
1720–29		16	0
1730–39		15	0
1740–49		11	0
1750–59	2,820	88	1
1760–69	3,531	227	2
1770–79	4,797	248	3
1780–89	14,824	756	7
1790–99	28,645	2,631	15
1800–09	59,554	9,995	39
1810–19	96,339	18,712	53
1820–29	173,000	28,800	62

Note: all figures represent annual averages per decade.

Textile goods as percentages of total exports 1700–1800

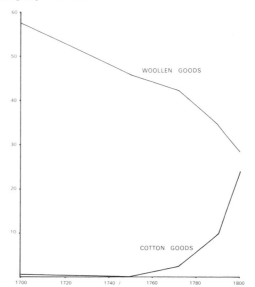

A cotton warehouse in Manchester, built astride a canal; its size hints at the vast scale of the industry by this time (1836)

The clue to this almost incredible expansion was of course the adoption of the factory system, with its powered machinery. We have already seen that the development of machinery was a necessary part of the process which led to the factory system; but in the case of the cotton industry the story of mechanical invention is quite extraordinarily brilliant. Machines of ever-increasing sophistication and complexity followed each other in a succession which almost seems to excuse the examination candidate who answered the question, 'What was the Industrial Revolution?', by describing it as 'a wave of gadgets that swept over England in the eighteenth century'!

Nor is the interest confined to the machines. Their inventors are at least as fascinating – a strange collection of geniuses and frauds, dazzling successes and abject failures, attractive personalities competing with some men of quite outstanding nastiness. The whole story of the rise of the cotton industry is larger than life – if we saw it in the cinema without knowing anything about it beforehand, we would quite probably be tempted to dismiss it as unhistorical exaggeration. But it really happened.

To make sense of this vast picture it will be necessary to pick out a small selection of the most important men and their machines, setting them against the background of a brief outline of the industry's history.

1 Origins. Cotton cloth was first manufactured in this country at the very end of the sixteenth century; but few people took much notice of it before the beginning of the eighteenth century. During the reign of Queen Anne, merchant ships (particularly those belonging to the East India Company) began to bring back large quantities of cotton cloth from the Far East, especially India. This cloth, which was light to wear, easy to wash and attractive to look at with its bright colours and gay patterns, quickly became very popular. It was generally agreed to have many advantages over the thick, heavy woollen cloth which had been in general use up to that time and which had been England's biggest industry for so long. We have already seen how the manufacturers of woollen cloth failed to meet the challenge of cotton in the home market. The great success story of the eighteenth century, however, is the way in which the obscure, small-scale cotton industry expanded and developed to meet the new demand, so that they were able first to imitate, then to compete with and finally to defeat the cottons imported from abroad.

The raw material came in the earliest days from the East, particularly through Smyrna (a port in Turkey). But during our period more and more was imported from the Americas and the West Indies. The chief port for this import trade was Liverpool   in the first instance for no special reason other than the fact that it was well placed for the Atlantic trade, but soon because it provided an easy entry to Lancashire, a district which was quickly found to have a number of natural advantages in the manufacture of cotton cloth.

The chief of these advantages was the climate. Lancashire's high rainfall may not be a tourist attraction, but, in association with the even temperature, it ensured the permanently damp atmosphere which was necessary in the early cotton-mills to keep the fibres in easily manageable condition. In addition, the water tumbling in streams down the steep hillsides provided a convenient source of power. And finally, the geology of the region gave the water a chemical quality which turned out to be especially valuable for treating the cloth at various stages of its finishing.

To these physical advantages we can add two fortunate coincidences. First, it so happened that the growth of population and the state of trade in Lancashire produced a plentiful supply of cheap labour, just at the moment when the early cotton manufacturers needed all the workmen they could get. And secondly, the fact that up till this time there were not very many big towns in the county meant that the medieval gild system, with all its restrictive practices and petty regulations, could easily be evaded by employers who would have found it an intolerable drag on their efforts to start factory production.

89

2 Processes. Like wool, cotton had to go through a number of stages before it was finally turned out as finished cloth. These stages were similar to those for the woollen industry; they are shown in the diagram on p. 86.

3 Kay's Flying-Shuttle. At first all these stages were done by hand, with little benefit from machinery. The first important step towards mechanisation was taken by John Kay (1704–64), a weaver and mechanic in the woollen industry. In 1733 he brought out a simple but important improvement to the traditional weaving-loom, namely the flying-shuttle.

Poor Kay must have bitterly regretted the day he announced his invention. He was first persecuted by weavers who feared that the new high-speed machine would make them redundant, and then defrauded by manufacturers who were enthusiastic in favour of the machine but refused to pay him royalties. In 1753 Kay's house was sacked; he himself was beaten up on several occasions – once he had to escape hidden in a sack of wool. Finally, he fled the country.

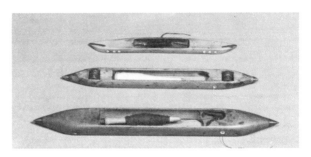

Shuttles of the type invented by Kay

The flying-shuttle was 'intended', so to speak, for the woollen industry; but we have seen how slow the clothiers were to adapt to new techniques. In fact, the machine was taken up on a big scale by the cotton manufacturers of Lancashire, who found that it enabled them to increase their output of woven cloth at a dramatic rate. There was the further advantage that thread made out of cotton fibres proved easier for machines to handle than thread spun from wool.

4 Spinning Machines. The expansion made possible by the flying-shuttle in itself, however, created problems, because the supply of spun cotton thread could no longer keep pace with the demands of the weavers. The next step, therefore, was the mechanisation of the spinning process. There were numerous attempts at this around the middle of the century, particularly by two partners, John Wyatt and Lewis Paul, who patented a spinning machine in 1738. Their invention had many faults and neither Wyatt nor Paul seems to have been much of a businessman – they frequently experienced desperate poverty and occasionally came very close to starvation. When they finally went bankrupt in 1742 their machines were bought by a speculator named Cave, who set them up at Northampton in a building with a water-wheel to provide power. So, though not otherwise specially notable, Cave has the distinction of having established the first cotton-spinning factory in the proper sense of the word. More important than this unsuccessful venture, however, was the fact that the idea was almost certainly taken over by the great Richard Arkwright.

5 Richard Arkwright. Arkwright, who lived from 1732 to 1792, was the most strikingly successful of the eighteenth-century cotton pioneers. He began life in humble circumstances and was for a long time a rather unsuccessful barber; but before he died he had gained a knighthood and could boast capital assets of half a million pounds (at a time when money was worth many times what it is now). His fortune was founded on a chain of mills, using first water and, later, steam power to drive cotton-spinning machinery which was given the name of the 'water-frame'. Arkwright claimed to have invented this machine and actually took out patents for it, and for a number of other machines as well. But in a series of great legal battles various competitors and inventors successfully cast doubt on this claim, and in the end his patents were taken away. There is little question that Arkwright made clever use of other men's work without acknowledging his debts to them. However, his defeat in the courts did not stop him from making a fortune, as we have seen, and the reason for this was that he turned out to be a businessman of the very highest order. He was one of the first to make a real success of the factory system in the textile industry, and he came to be regarded as typical of the

Richard Arkwright, 'self-made man' and pioneer of modern business methods

91

new sort of man produced by the Industrial Revolution. He was always on the lookout for a new way of making money, and he never let an opportunity slip. He showed great shrewdness in driving bargains and was a fierce and unscrupulous competitor. He took the broadest possible view of industry and was ready to engage in all sorts of projects if he thought they would help him to produce and market his cotton – he would have approved of what we now call 'diversification'. He drove his men hard, but he drove himself as well; he travelled a great deal, visiting his various mills and enterprises, and always moved at top speed in a fast private carriage, writing and conducting business as he went, to the amazement of all who saw him. This in fact is his real claim to fame – that he was the first man to appreciate the real potential of the factory system, and that, by his efficient high-speed methods, he set a new standard for management and money-making.

6 Hargreaves' Spinning Jenny. Arkwright's water-frame was patented in 1769; in 1770 another spinning machine was patented, by a rather obscure man called James Hargreaves. This machine, called the 'spinning jenny', was not a factory machine, but was more suitable for domestic use. To that extent it was in the older tradition of the textile industry. But in fact the two types of spinning machine produced slightly different types of thread, which happened to be convenient, in that the water-frame thread was suitable for use as warp, while the spinning-jenny thread was better used as weft (see diagram, p. 86). The two types of spinning went on side by side, entirely superseding the traditional spinning wheel in the last part of the eighteenth century.

Hargreaves' Spinning Jenny, a domestic machine

Crompton's Mule, factory machines

7 Crompton's Mule. Gradually, however, they were superseded in their turn by a machine known as the 'mule', because it combined the qualities of both to produce a thread that was both fine and strong. The mule was developed by Samuel Crompton in the 1770s, but was not adapted for powered factory use until after 1790. After that date the spinning jenny declined rapidly.

8 Cartwright's Power Loom. This left only the weaving process in the hands of the domestic, as opposed to the factory workers; and for a short time they experienced great prosperity, with more work than they could easily handle, at prices of their own asking. This state of affairs was ended, and the triumph of the factory system completed, by the somewhat improbable figure of the Revd. Edmund Cartwright, poet and former Fellow of Magdalen College, Oxford (1743–1823). He was a complete amateur and no businessman, but out of intellectual interest he invented and patented a power loom in 1785, and subsequently improved it to a very fine pitch. His first efforts at commercial exploitation were completely disastrous; but the tide of events was running in his favour, and by the early 1800s the power loom was sweeping the country.

Power looms, as invented by Cartwright. They are driven by the belts running from overhead transmission shafts

The handloom weavers did not disappear altogether; on the contrary, they hung on until 1850 or even later, finding it harder and harder to get work and more and more difficult to break out of their dead-end occupation. But apart from this depressed group, the cotton industry flourished mightily in its factories, and English cotton goods went all over the world in enormous quantities.

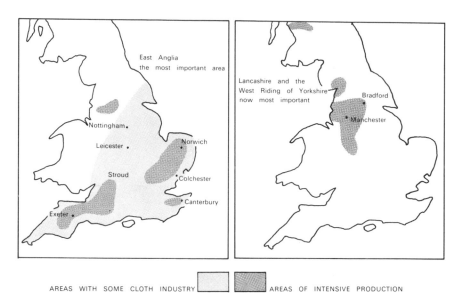

AREAS WITH SOME CLOTH INDUSTRY ☐ ▨ AREAS OF INTENSIVE PRODUCTION

Textile manufacturing, before (*left*) and after (*right*) the Industrial Revolution

JOSIAH WEDGWOOD AND THE POTTERY INDUSTRY

Before leaving the Industrial Revolution itself, we must look briefly at another area of expansion and innovation, the pottery industry. This is of special interest as providing a smaller-scale counterpart against which to measure the gigantic achievements of the cotton industry. It is also of importance in its own right, since it involves one of the most outstanding figures of the Industrial Revolution, a great man in several senses of the word – Josiah Wedgwood. Finally, the pottery industry can be shown to combine in classic manner several of the principal factors for economic change – capital, transport, technology, management, marketing. The one exception – power – is in itself significant.

Before the eighteenth century the production in Britain of what today we often call china was very limited. Little pottery of any good quality was made, and ordinary crockery was crude and rough. Techniques of production were primitive and unreliable, and the difficulty of transporting such fragile goods was another problem which hindered development. Good china products had to be imported from such places as Limoges in France and Dresden in Germany. By 1800, however, there was an industry employing thousands, and English ware was famous throughout Europe and America. This change was mainly the work of Josiah Wedgwood.

Wedgwood was born in 1730, at Burslem, in Staffordshire, the son of a potter who died when he was young. He began work at the age of ten and was almost entirely self-educated. Throughout his life he read widely and corresponded with many scholars and scientists, becoming a learned and cultured man. As an apprentice, Wedgwood soon showed great skill, and became expert in all branches of the trade. He began business on his own in 1759 with only a very little capital. Yet within ten years he had become a rich man, official potter to the royal family and flooded with orders from all over Europe. He achieved this success and fame for several reasons.

First of all, Wedgwood was able to improve, out of all recognition, the quality of pottery. He was not a trained scientist or technologist, yet he conducted a great many experiments in all stages of the making of pottery. He improved practically everything from the selection and blending of clays to the throwing, firing and finishing of the product. As a result he was able to turn out stronger, cheaper and more uniform articles for the mass market such as plates, cups, saucers and teapots, with a glaze or finish which had previously been seen only on the best and most expensive European pottery. Wedgwood's 'creamware', which he later called 'Queen's Ware', was his basic product, but he made a number of other types of pottery as a result of his experiments with different clays. His most famous, for the luxury market, was called 'jasper'. This ware was usually in lilac or blue, with white designs, and original pieces are now very valuable. For these technical feats, Wedgwood was elected a Fellow of the Royal Society in 1783.

Josiah Wedgwood, a portrait cameo
made at the Etruria works

Wedgwood was not only a skilled craftsman and scientist, but an artist of great ability. It is true that most of his designs were copied from other artists like John Flaxman, or from classical works of art, but he reproduced them on his pottery with genius. He applied his gifts to all his decorative ware, whether for mass consumption, or for specially ordered works costing hundreds of pounds. Wedgwood was especially interested in Roman and Greek designs and some of his copies in pottery, like those of the 'Barberini Vase', are acknowledged as among the finest English works of art in the eighteenth century. In 1774 he made two dinner services for Catherine the Great, Empress of Russia, totalling 950 pieces. These were of ordinary creamware, and the basic cost was £52. Each piece was decorated with a different view of an English country scene, and this added over £2,000 to the cost. These magnificent services can still be seen in the Hermitage Museum in Leningrad.

Wedgwood was also a very good businessman and employer. Realising the importance of advertising, he kept a showroom in London and had agents in many European countries. He printed his catalogues in French, Dutch and German. He was always on the lookout for new fields to conquer and towards the end of his life began to manufacture earthenware water pipes. Wedgwood realised the importance of good transport for his fragile goods and took a part in the building of turnpikes in Staffordshire. His main achievement in transport was the building of the Grand Trunk or Trent–Mersey Canal. This was opened in 1777 and proved extremely valuable to his business, as he made sure that it passed right through his works at Etruria. The Etruria works, near Stoke-on-Trent, were named after the old Roman territory, now called Tuscany, and were opened in 1769. These works produced the bulk of his output.

Small beginnings: eighteenth-century potters at work

Conditions of work at Etruria were good, as Wedgwood was always concerned for the welfare of his employees. He built houses, schools and churches for them and gave generously to other projects in the area. In return, he always insisted upon the highest standards of workmanship. He usually did the finer pieces himself and ruthlessly smashed any of his own or others' work which did not measure up to his standards.

When Wedgwood died in 1795, he left behind him a flourishing industry. Others followed his example, and he was not the only eminent potter of the time. There was Josiah Spode (1754–1827), for example, and Worcester Ware was also famous. But Wedgwood was the first and most influential. The region known today as the Potteries owes its existence mainly to him. When Wedgwood began his career there were only ten houses in Stoke. When he died it was a prosperous town of several thousand people. In the nineteenth century the area was, as it still is, the centre of an industry which sent its products all over the world. Even in 1763 Wedgwood sent 550,000 pieces abroad. Some years later, a traveller was able to write:

'In travelling from Paris to St. Petersburg, from Amsterdam to the farthest point of Sweden, from Dunkirk to the southern extremity of France, one is served at every inn from English earthenware. The same fine article adorns the tables of Spain, Portugal, and Italy; it provides the cargoes of ships to the East Indies, the West Indies, and the American continent.'

Suggestions for further work and discussion

1. Relics of the Industrial Revolution are still fairly common, though they have often suffered alteration. Look for: eighteenth-century factory and warehouse buildings, water-wheels, steam-engines and other machinery.

2. Make working drawings of the following machines:
    Kay's fly shuttle
    Arkwright's water-frame
    Hargreaves' spinning jenny
    Crompton's mule
    Cartwright's power-loom.

3. Find out more about the career of *one* notable industrialist of the eighteenth century, e.g. Wedgwood, Boulton, Arkwright or Strutt. What made them so successful?

4. Subject for an essay or discussion: which was most important to the Industrial Revolution, new machinery, new power or the factory system?

6. The illustration on page 83 shows spinsters at work. (The woman   97

on the right is working a clock-reel, for winding yarn.) Compare this scene, with the illustration of mule-spinning on p. 93. Where would you prefer to work? Why? Which is the more realistic picture, in your opinion? How are the mules powered? What can you see that might be dangerous in the factory scene?

Book for further reading:

> Paul Mantoux, *The Industrial Revolution in the Eighteenth Century*, Cape, 1961.

1751

1851

Main industrial areas

5 : The Birth of Industrial Society

We have now described some of the new types of industry which grew up during the Industrial Revolution, and we have seen that the one thing which all these new industries had in common was the factory system. The simplest way of dealing with the effects of the Industrial Revolution is to begin at the same point and to look at the factory system as it worked on the lives of masses of ordinary people.

INDUSTRY AND THE MOVEMENT OF POPULATION

One of the chief features of the factory system is that it requires a large group of workmen to operate all in the same building. In the period we are studying there was no transport that these workmen could use to get themselves to work. Almost inevitably, this meant that their houses clustered closely round the factory gates. In this, the factory system is different from the domestic system which it replaced. The craftsmen of the domestic system might live widely scattered around the countryside, especially if, as was often the case, they spent a part of their working time on another job such as farming.

We can see, therefore, how the growth of new, concentrated settlements of population was bound to be an early result of the adoption of the factory system. As soon as Richard Arkwright and the other pioneers of the period set up their new mills, they created what economists call a focus of employment.

In some cases this focus of employment would be situated in an already existing town. The works of Boulton and Watt, in Birmingham, would be an example of this. Birmingham was already a centre of manufacturing, though of course on a tiny scale by comparison with what it later became. There are obvious advantages in siting a factory in an existing town, not least of which would be the fact that there would be a supply of labour already in existence and (presumably) quite easy to tap. In these cases the factories would still alter the life of the town enormously; but at least a completely fresh start would not be necessary.

More often than not, however, we find the new factories being set up outside the towns, sometimes quite a long way away from any existing settlement. This may at first seem rather stupid, but there were good reasons prompting Richard Arkwright, for example, to pick on the village of Cromford in Derbyshire for the site of his first mill.

The chief of these reasons concerned the power, without which the factory was useless. Arkwright's machines were driven at first, as we have seen, by water power; so he had to find a site for his mill by the side of a strong, fast-flowing stream of water. Cromford was on the Derwent, at a point where the river comes down from the hills and runs swiftly through a gorge. It had the further, unusual advantage that a little way upstream there was a spring of warm water, which flowed into the river and kept it from freezing over in winter. This meant that Arkwright was less likely to have his milling operations stopped from lack of power.

Generally speaking, it is true that a small stream running down a hill can generate more power than a much bigger river meandering quietly along on

Arkwright's Cromford Mill, recently restored; notice the hillside rising steeply behind the building

the flat. So, many of the early water-powered factories were situated either in the hills or else at the base of the slopes. We find them particularly around the Pennine range, the highest in England. Dotted along the steep, narrow valleys, some of the old mill buildings are still standing. And, if they have not been swallowed up by more recent expansion, we can often see the cluster of cottages, of the same date as the mill itself, grouped around its walls.

The search for a satisfactory source of power, however, was not the only factor which caused the creation of new settlements at this time. In the case of the textile industry, we have seen earlier how the irksome restrictions of the old gilds drove many of the new manufacturers to abandon the well-established towns, even when they might otherwise have been suitable sites for their factories. In the iron industry the need to be as near as possible to the heavy raw materials, which were so hard to transport, brought about a similar result.

By the beginning of the nineteenth century, therefore, industry had created a large number of new settlements in certain parts of the country. When this process takes place at the expense of existing centres and areas (as it did in this case), it is known to economists as 'relocation of industry'.

Many of these new settlements, however, remained small, sometimes growing no larger than little hamlets. One good reason for this can be seen straightaway – there is not going to be room or opportunity for more than one water-mill to operate beside a stream at any given spot. The mills tended therefore to be strung out along the valleys, rather than concentrated into what we should call 'new towns'.

A further change came about when the inventions of James Watt made it possible to use steam-engines to drive machinery, instead of water power. Water supplies would still be necessary, but practically any water would do, and it might even be pumped from some distance through a pipe. As Watt's engines became more widely used mill-owners began to consider a further relocation of their activities. There was after all a lot to be said for coming down out of the hills. In a town nearer to the coast, they would be able to get hold of labour more easily. They would also enjoy the advantages of being closer to market, and perhaps, in the case of the textile industry, closer to the seaports through which they were supplied with raw materials. Finally, they would very probably reap the benefits of much improved transport facilities.

So, in the end, the new towns of industrial England came to be built, not among the high hills, but more often in the lower country. In a sense, however, this is only a matter of detail; the really big relocation of industry was not so much a matter of hills or plains, but of North and South, as can be seen from the maps on p. 98.

The decline of industry in the South and its growth in the North was a process started by the development of water-powered factories and clinched by the introduction of the steam-engine. In the first case, the most suitable streams for providing water power were found in the North; then the great northern coalfields offered the opportunity of almost unlimited fuel for the steam-engines.

THE NEW TOWNS OF THE INDUSTRIAL REVOLUTION

The new industrial towns and cities of the North were unlike anything that had been seen in England before. They must have come as a great shock to people visiting them for the first time — especially, perhaps, to those agricultural labourers uprooted by the changes on the land, wandering in search of a job, far from the quiet villages in which they had grown up. Even today, after many changes, these towns make a striking impact, especially on people from the South of England.

There had of course been big towns before — London had for a long time been one of the greatest cities in Europe, and Norwich, York, Bristol were all accounted major centres. But these old towns, with their churches and cathedrals, their markets and fairs, their rows of shops and craftsmen's booths, their theatres and palaces and lawcourts, their gay and varied social life, were nothing like these new towns.

The pictures on p. 104–5 and p. 106 give some idea of what conditions were like. The early immigrants to the industrial towns would have had to live in whatever accommodation they could find — cheap lodgings, cellars, old houses in which people were allowed to sleep, sometimes twenty to a room, for a penny a night.

When more houses became available the change was often not much of an improvement. Many terraced cottages were put up by factory owners to house their workers; still more were the work of builders anxious to cash in on the boom by buying plots of land and covering them with cheap housing which would then be offered for sale. (This type of business is called 'speculative building'.) The results were much the same in either case — rows of little four-roomed slums, end-to-end and often back-to-back as well.

A variation on this 'alley' system was the 'courtyard' layout. This was popular in London and a number of big towns, and the following description from Nottingham, dated 1845, could have been equalled in many of the new towns:

The courts are almost always approached through a low-arched tunnel of some 30 or 36 inches wide, about 8 feet high, and from 20 to 30 feet long. . . . They are noisome, narrow, unprovided with adequate means for the removal of refuse, ill-ventilated, and wretched in the extreme, with a gutter, or surface-drain, running down the centre; they have no back yards, and the privies are common to the whole court: altogether they present scenes of deplorable character, and of surpassing filth and discomfort . . . In all these confined quarters, too, the refuse is allowed to accumulate until, by its mass and its advanced putrefaction, it shall have acquired value as manure; and thus it is sold and carted away by the 'muck majors', as the collectors of manure are called in Nottingham.

(From a report to Parliament made in 1845)

The houses in these slums were flimsily built of the cheapest brick and slate; often the walls were only one brick thick. There might be no proper foundations; floors were usually made at ground level of bricks laid on the bare earth, and for the upper storey of timber so thin and weak that it was common for people to fall through into the room below. Piped water supplies were totally inadequate, as the following extract shows, and of course water closets were unknown in such slums.

[In certain districts of Liverpool] there is a great deal of broken ground, in which there are pits; the water accumulates in those pits, and of course at the fall of the year there is a good deal of water in them, in which there have been thrown dead dogs and cats, and a great many offensive articles. This water is nevertheless used for culinary purposes. I could not believe this at first. I thought it was used only for washing, but I found that it was used by the poorer inhabitants for culinary purposes.

Was that owing to the want of a supply of water? – There is a good supply of water for the poor, if they had the means of preserving it. The water is turned on a certain number of hours during the day, four hours, perhaps; the poor go to the tap for it; it is constantly running; and each poor person fetches as much as they have pans to receive; but they are not well supplied with these articles, and in consequence they are frequently out of water. It is not sufficient for washing, or anything of that kind.

(From a report to Parliament made in 1840)

Nowadays we take care to avoid such problems by insisting on the observation of numerous rules and regulations governing the number of houses that can be built on a given area, the quality of the building and the supply of 'services' (water, sanitation, etc.). Such rules did not exist in the eighteenth and early nineteenth centuries. This was partly because when the population had been much smaller and much more scattered there had been no great need for them.

Another reason why the building of towns was so badly regulated at first was the speed with which the development took place. It surprised even the people who profited from it, so that they had no time to stop and think about what they were doing, even if they had cared. Demand for houses was tremendous and the builders could sell everything they could knock together, no matter how badly it might be constructed. The shortage can be judged from the fact that every census in the first half of the nineteenth century showed that one house in every five was inhabited by two families or more. Remember that families then were generally a good deal bigger than they are now!

A third reason for the failure to regulate the quality of the houses in the towns was the sheer ignorance of even the most educated people about elementary facts of hygiene. Cases are recorded of families living in a single room directly on top of a boarded-over cess-pit. In the early days of town growth, filth thrown into the streets was bought by farmers for manure; before long there was so much that the townsmen had to pay the farmers to take it away. (Sometimes the farmers got more than they bargained for; when two ditches were emptied in Windsor in 1842, the manure was so strong that it killed the grass in the meadows where it was spread.) In the end, even this system broke down, as we can see from the fact that in 1833, when an outbreak of cholera led to a purifying campaign in Leeds, no fewer than 75 cartloads of filth were removed from a single small cul-de-sac, called Boot and Shoe Yard. (It is perhaps worth adding that this yard was regarded by the landlords as one of the most profitable properties in the city.) In some courtyards in London it was recorded that the drinking water from the single

One of the new industrial towns: part of a panoramic view of Leeds in the mid-nineteenth centu

pump that served the whole yard was a dark brown from the human excrement that had seeped into the well below. The worst case of the accumulation of filth in the streets was perhaps that recorded in Greenock in 1842.

In one part of Market Street is a dunghill — yet it is too large to be called a dunghill. I do not misstate its size when I say it contains a hundred cubic yards of impure filth, collected from all parts of the town. It is never removed; it is the stock-in-trade of a person who deals in dung; he retails it by cartfuls. To please his customers, he always keeps a nucleus, as the older the filth is the higher the price. The proprietor has an extensive privy attached to the concern. This collection is fronting the public street; it is enclosed in front by a wall; the height of the wall is almost twelve feet, and the dung overtops it; the malarious moisture oozes through the wall, and runs over the pavement.

The effluvia all round about this place in summer is horrible. There is a land of houses adjoining, four stories in height, and in the summer each house swarms with myriads of flies; every article of food and drink must be covered, otherwise, if left exposed for a minute, the flies immediately attack it, and it is rendered unfit for use, from the strong taste of the dunghill left by the flies.

(From a report to Parliament made in 1842)

Nor was this state of affairs confined to poor people: even in the wealthiest houses, the drains were amazingly primitive, so that grand social occasions were occasionally spoiled by revolting smells. Indeed, Prince Albert himself

A remarkable early photograph, taken in Newcastle during the 1880s. The houses date from well before the Industrial Revolution, and their state of decay, more squalid than picturesque, illustrates the fate of most such buildings in the teeming towns of nineteenth-century England

is thought to have died of typhoid fever contracted as a result of the insanitary drainage arrangements at Windsor Castle. Sewage was discharged direct into the rivers, and it was notorious that the Houses of Parliament in London became virtually unusable in the height of a hot summer, because of the vile stench which came off the polluted Thames. M.P.s sometimes complained of the difficulties of debating in the House of Commons, when it was filled with a noxious blue haze that made it almost impossible to see the Opposition on the other side!

To show the level to which housing conditions could sometimes sink, here is a description of a really extreme case, recorded in London in 1849:

On entering the precincts of the pest island the air had literally the smell of a graveyard, and a feeling of nausea and heaviness came over anyone unaccustomed to imbibe the moist atmosphere. Not only the nose, but the stomach told how heavily the air was loaded with sulphuretted hydrogen; and as soon as you crossed one of the crazy and rotten bridges over the reeking ditch, you knew, as surely as if you had chemically tested it, by the black colour of what was once white lead paint upon the door posts and window sills, that the air was thickly charged with this deadly gas. The heavy bubbles which now and then rose up in the water showed you whence at least a portion of the mephitic compound issued, while the open doorless privies that hung over the waterside, and the dark streaks of filth down the walls, where the drains from each house discharged themselves into the ditch, were proofs indisputable as to how the pollution of the ditch occurred.

The water was covered with scum almost like a cobweb, and prismatic with grease. In it floated large masses of rotting weed, and against the posts of the bridges were swollen carcases of dead animals, ready to burst with the gases of putrefaction. Along its shores were heaps of indescribable filth, the phosphoretted smell from which told you of the rotting fish there, while the oyster-shells were like pieces of slate from their coating of filth and mud. In some parts the fluid was as red as blood from the colouring matter that poured into it from the reeking leather dressers' close by.

(Henry Mayhew: letter to *The Chronicle*, 24 September 1849)

It astounds us, when we read of such cases nowadays, that they could ever have been tolerated. It is not that people actually preferred living in such terrible conditions − that they did not goes without saying. But those who experienced them at first hand were too poor to do anything about them. More fortunate people tended to be either indifferent or resigned to the problem. It was generally felt that such squalor was unavoidable, a necessary if regrettable part of the business of economic growth. A northern proverb grew up to the effect that 'Where there's muck, there's money'. Indeed, it was observed in 1843 that 'There are . . . numbers of persons in Sheffield who think the smoke healthy'.

The small number of people who tried to do something positive to put matters right were met with the fierce opposition of those who believed that it was wrong for the state, or any outside authority, to intervene in the private affairs of citizens. The defenders of freedom maintained that 'The Englishman's home is his castle', and that if his home was really only a foul little hut, then it was up to him to improve it if he could. This *laissez-faire* attitude had hardly changed before the middle of the nineteenth century.

As conditions in the towns grew worse, the urban death rate climbed. The figures in the table give an idea of the risks of town life at this period.

LIFE EXPECTANCY IN 1842

| | Average age of death (*years*) | |
Classification	In Manchester	In Rutland
Professional persons, gentry and their families	38	52
Tradesmen, farmers and their families	20	41
Mechanics, labourers and their families	17	38

(From a report made to Parliament in 1842) **107**

HOW TO AVOID THE CHOLERA:

BEING

PLAIN DIRECTIONS FOR POOR PEOPLE.

By DR. CHALLICE, of Bermondsey,

AUTHOR OF "MEDICAL ADVICE TO MOTHERS ON THE MANAGEMENT OF CHILDREN."

☞ *Whatever may be the cause of Cholera, thus much is certain, that hitherto, almost without exception, this pestilence has been the portion of the poor, and we know that those who are in want of food and clothing most readily fall the victims of this disease. Let therefore the working man, the head of a family, reflect, that by idleness or drunkenness he not only exposes himself, but in all probability his wife and his children, to the attacks of Cholera, by depriving them of the comforts and the necessaries of life.*

1. Good health, good spirits, and industry, are the best preservatives. If you are ill, send for a doctor.

2. Keep the whole of the body clean; do not spare soap and water; rub the skin well dry after washing. Cholera is fond of *filth*. Parents, apply this rule to your children.

3. Live plainly, and avoid all excesses. Go early to bed; the hard-working man requires rest, not excitement, after his day's work. Drunkenness and late hours are great friends of the Cholera.

4. Sleep as few in the same room, or in the same bed, as possible; make every shift, rather than be crowded at night.

5. Early in the morning, remove all dirty or offensive matters, open your windows and doors, turn down the bed-clothes, to let the fresh air pass over them.

6. Do not take your meals in the bed-room; if you cannot help yourselves in this respect, there is still greater necessity for cleanliness and fresh air.

7. Washing or drying clothes in the bed-room is always bad, and, in times of sickness, very dangerous.

8. EAT ONLY OF GOOD FOOD. Half a pound of good meat is better than one pound of bad. One good loaf is better than two bad ones. Cyder and sour or hard beer are injurious. Let not your children stuff themselves with apples, plums, pears, or sweet stuff. Rice, tapioca, barley, and oatmeal, are cheap, nourishing, and wholesome.

9. Cleanse out, and thoroughly scour, your water-butts or cisterns; boil the water before you drink it or give it to your children. Impure water is the cause of many diseases.

10. If there be offensive smells in your house, from sewers or cesspools, complain to your landlord; if he take no steps for removing the nuisance, complain to the parish authorities; if they don't assist you, apply to the magistrates. The *law* now protects from *poison* as well as starvation.

11. If you get wet, change your clothes as soon as you can; warm and dry clothing, however homely or coarse, will do much to keep off Cholera. Flannel should be worn next the skin round the body, and the feet be kept dry and warm with worsted stockings.

12. Go out, and take your children, into the fresh air as often as you can; pure air and wholesome exercise may keep off Cholera, as well as Fever.

13. Take no *strong physic*, as Epsom salts, senna, &c. If opening medicine is wanted, a small tea-spoonful of powdered rhubarb, with a little ginger and carbonate of soda, or a small wine-glassful of the compound tincture of rhubarb, or the compound *rhubarb* pill, (which may be bought for 4d. or 6d. per dozen,) may either be taken with advantage. For children, nothing is better than rhubarb with magnesia, in *small doses*, repeated every four hours till the proper effect is produced.

14. If you have bowel complaint, leave off work. Rest and lying in bed are most necessary; many a working man has lost his life by neglect of this rule. Get this mixture, for preparing which a druggist ought not to charge a poor man more than sixpence:—

1 drachm	of	Aromatic confection.
1	„	Prepared chalk.
1	„	Sal Volatile.
½	„	Laudanum.
2	„	Tincture of ginger
2	„	Tincture of kino.
3 ounces	of	Cinnamon water.

A table-spoonful to be taken every two hours till the relaxation is stopped. A child under ten years, half the dose; and from three to five years old, a fourth part only. For infants it is not suitable. Broths and hot tea are injurious, and increase the relaxation of the bowels. Arrowroot, or rice boiled in milk, or gruel, with some grated ginger or cinnamon powder, should be taken, and these not *hot*, but nearly cold.

15. Should the Cholera, however, attack you, or any in your house, don't be alarmed—it is not catching—the disease is now better understood than heretofore; mild cases are easily cured, and the worst cases are not always fatal.

16. Neighbours and friends have a bad custom of crowding a sick room. Where there is *Cholera*, it makes the disease more dangerous; therefore, don't do it.

17. As a measure of precaution, every family should, if possible, have a pound of the best mustard, one quart of vinegar, half a pint of brandy, (which must be close corked and sealed,) and two pounds of salt, in the house; also, the fire laid ready for lighting at a moment's notice, with a large kettle full of water on the hob. Then, in case of sudden attack before a doctor can be fetched, apply a vinegar-and-mustard poultice over the whole belly, as long as it can be borne, or at least for twenty minutes, and let the arms, feet, and legs be constantly rubbed with flannels dipped in hot vinegar. Constant friction in this manner may save many a life. The body of the sufferer becomes in the same state as one nearly dead from drowning or suffocation, and every one knows how often life is restored in such cases by persevering exertion for *hours*. Two of these pills should be taken at *once*, with a table-spoonful of brandy, and one pill with a table-spoonful of brandy-and-water, cold, every half hour. But don't delay getting a doctor.

Cayenne Pepper	12 grains.
Camphor	12 „
Calomel	12 „

Aromatic confection sufficient to make into twelve pills.

Brandy is certainly most valuable in Cholera to those who have not been in the habit of spirit-drinking: those who have constantly taken it, derive little or no good from it.

Lastly. It cannot be too often repeated, that bad bread or bad vegetables, unsound meat or stale fish, tend most powerfully to derange the stomach and bowels, and to bring on Cholera. Let the *dealers* in these staple commodities of life reflect on their very serious responsibility at the present moment, and on the public indignation which will most justly fall upon them should *human life* be sacrificed by the sale of unwholesome food—a too common practice, and a wicked imposition upon the poorer classes.

LONDON: HENRY RENSHAW, MEDICAL PUBLISHER, 356, STRAND.

Savill & Edwards, Printers, 4, Chandos-street, Covent-garden.

The normally high death rate was sent rocketing from time to time by outbreaks of disease, particularly typhoid and cholera, which ravaged the country on a number of occasions. There were severe outbreaks of cholera, for example, affecting most of the big cities, in 1831–33, 1847–48 and 1865–66. Such outbreaks naturally led to an outcry for improvements but, since it was not generally understood what caused the diseases, effective action was slow in coming. It is significant that the broadsheet, 'How to Avoid the Cholera', reproduced on p. 108, begins, rather pathetically, 'Whatever may be the cause of Cholera . . .'. The first Act of Parliament to deal with the problem was the Public Health Act of 1848, following the second great epidemic. It set up a Board of Health with powers to advise and assist towns which wanted to improve their sanitary arrangements. The Board did a great deal of good work in the years that followed, but was hampered by much opposition and by the fact that it had been given little power of compulsion. Some measure of its problems can be gathered from the fact that it had difficulty in persuading people to accept such elementary ideas as the undesirability of keeping pigs in a kitchen.

The worst problems were undoubtedly those connected with private housing. But there were others as well. The factories poured the smoke from their tall chimneys in great clouds into the atmosphere, blackening the buildings, the clothes, the faces and the lungs of the citizens. Industrial waste was dumped wherever it was out of the way – often in a river or canal. Trees and green spaces were devoured by speculative builders and the jumble of ugly, unplanned streets sprawled ever wider into the countryside.

But the sheer filth and ugliness of the new towns were not the only things about them which made life so miserable. After all, as we have already pointed out, there had been big towns before, and they too had had drainage problems. What was really new was the fact that these towns, unlike their older predecessors, grew so fast that their inhabitants could not easily feel that they belonged to a real community. Later on, as we shall see, the great industrial towns developed a strong life of their own. But up till the middle of the nineteenth century many of them were just vast collections of swarming human beings, all fighting and struggling with each other in the cruel battle for survival, with no sense of unity or common interest. The towns in fact were a kind of man-made jungle.

This is very clearly brought out in the history of local government in this period. Many of the industrial towns grew from tiny beginnings, so that there was no existing system of local government to administer them. With almost incredible laziness, the central government in London allowed this state of affairs to drift on, so that Manchester, for example, was still run as a village in 1831 when the census recorded a population of 142,000. Nothing was done to alter this until 1838.

Such unregulated growth did not produce any of the organisations and institutions which make life in large communities pleasant and civilised. There were no theatres, libraries or museums, and few churches, schools, meeting halls or places of amusement other than the most sordid drinking dens. The life of the new towns, in fact, was concentrated entirely on the business of bare survival for the poor, and profit for the rich.

The great Prime Minister, Benjamin Disraeli, who was also a writer of successful novels, left a powerful description of such a town, which he called Wodgate, in his novel *Sybil*:

> Wodgate had the appearance of a vast squalid suburb. As you advanced, leaving behind you long lines of little dingy tenements, with infants lying about the road, you expected every moment to emerge into some streets, and encounter buildings bearing some correspondence, in their size and comfort, to the considerable population swarming and busied around you. Nothing of the kind. There were no public buildings of any sort; no churches, chapels, town-hall, institute, theatre; and the principal streets in the heart of the town in which were situate the coarse and grimy shops, though formed by houses of a greater elevation than the preceding, were equally narrow, and if possible more dirty. At every fourth or fifth house, alleys seldom above a yard wide, and streaming with filth, opened out of the street. These were crowded with dwellings of various size, while from the principal court often branched out a number of smaller alleys, or rather narrow passages, than which nothing can be conceived more close and squalid and obscure. Here, during the days of business, the sound of the hammer and the file never ceased, amid gutters of abomination, and piles of foulness, and stagnant pools of filth; reservoirs of leprosy and plague, whose exhalations were sufficient to taint the atmosphere of the whole kingdom, and fill the country with fever and pestilence.

WORKING CONDITIONS IN THE FACTORIES

Such were the conditions in which people lived. They may be said to have been the products largely of accident. The conditions under which the new industrial labourers worked, on the other hand, were affected by much more positive factors, especially the desire of the employers to save as much money as possible to avoid reducing their profits. As a result, the factories and mines of the Industrial Revolution present scenes in some ways even more horrifying than the slums just described.

Seen from the outside, the first factories were not all like the 'dark Satanic mills' of William Blake's poem 'Jerusalem'. The architecture of many of them has come to be admired in recent years, and some, such as Robert Owen's mills at New Lanark in Scotland, are now carefully preserved. But whatever the outside appearance of the early factories, their interiors were almost invariably bad as places to work in. The ceilings were low, to save space; the machines, treacherously unguarded and ranked closely side by side, thundered and rattled deafeningly. They were mostly driven by belts, which ran

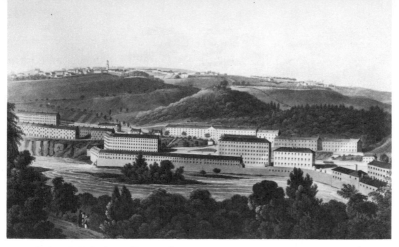

Industrial idealism: Robert Owen's model settlement at New Lanark

from the central engine, and were rarely boxed in. The air was often foul and full of dust and dirt, without any attempt at regular ventilation. In cotton factories a damp atmosphere was deliberately created in order to make the cotton fibres easier to work. Lighting arrangements were usually hopelessly inadequate, even when candles were replaced by gas early in the nineteenth century. Even lavatories were in short supply.

> In the manufactory, with 200 machines, there are only two privies, which were designed for the separate use of the men and women, but the fact is that they are promiscuously used by both sexes. Both these privies are in sight of three of the shops where men work.
>
> (From a report made to Parliament in 1843)

Working under conditions such as these, the employees were often driven hard by profit-conscious foremen and managers. Working-days of fourteen hours were not uncommon in textile mills of the 1780s. It is not surprising that tired workers frequently made fatal slips among the whirling machinery. Determined to keep the weary men up to the mark, supervisors all too often resorted to brutal methods; in fact, one of the more shocking cases recorded in the Parliamentary Papers for 1831–32 concerned a young woman:

> At the time I was in the mill, there was a young woman who had been kept seven months in the gaol at Dundee for deserting this mill; and she was brought back, after having been in the gaol for seven months, to make up for lost time and the expenses incurred. One day I was alarmed by her cries. She was lying on the floor, and the master had her by the hair of her head, and was kicking her in the face till the blood was running down.

111

Although violence as shocking as this may have been rather exceptional, unscrupulous exploitation of every sort was certainly very common. Imagine the reaction of a modern Trade Union to the following story:

> It often happens that when the weaver goes to work in the morning, he finds the clock fifteen minutes forwarder than when he left in the evening. The hands on the factory clock do not always move from *internal wheels*, but very frequently from a little external aid; this always takes place after the hands have left the place in the evening. . . . The reader will best understand why this is done, when we inform him that *thirty* or *forty* people may be frequently seen at the lodge door locked out, in the morning, while the person with the *fine-book* has been through the rooms of the mill, taking down the numbers of the looms of those that were absent. On one occasion, we counted *ninety-five* persons that were thus locked out at half-past five o'clock in the morning. . . . These ninety-five persons were fined three-pence each.
>
> (From a book written by a Manchester working-man, published in 1844)

If we were able to go back and visit one of these early factories now, one of the things that would possibly strike us most forcefully would be the effect which the conditions of work had on the people at the machines. This is how their appearance was described in 1833:

> . . . an uglier set of men and women, of boys and girls, taking them in the mass, it would be impossible to congregate in a smaller compass. Their complexion is sallow and pallid – with a peculiar flatness of feature. . . . Their stature low – the average height of four hundred men, measured at different times, and at different places, being five feet six inches. Their limbs slender, and playing badly and ungracefully. A very general bowing of the legs. Great numbers of girls and women walking lamely or awkwardly, with raised chests and spinal flexures. Nearly all have flat feet, accompanied with a down-tread, differing very widely from the elasticity of action in the foot and ancle, attendant upon perfect formation. Hair thin and straight – many of the men having but little beard, and that in patches of a few hairs, much resembling its growth among the red men of America.

In the middle of so much misery, it is hardly surprising to find that women and children suffered worst. They were employed in large numbers by the early factory owners, especially in the textile industries. This was partly because demand, and the inventions designed to make it possible for supply to meet the demand, both expanded so fast that there was a general shortage of labour in the first phases of the Industrial Revolution. Women and children could fill the places in the mills, because the new machines were relatively simple to operate, and did not require skilled workmen with years of training. Equally important was the fact that the power to move the machinery was now supplied from a non-human source – a water-wheel or a steam-engine. From the point of view of the employers, there were considerable advantages in having a labour force composed chiefly of women and children. They were generally considered to be more easily disciplined and managed than men; and (a still more powerful argument) they were much cheaper, since their rates of pay were well below those for men. In the 1780s, for example, a man might earn between 10s. and 15s. a week, while a woman could not hope to get more than 5s., and a child might be paid as little as 1s. a week, working perhaps twelve hours a day for it.

The factory workers themselves rarely complained about the employment of women and children. The people who moved from the countryside into the towns at the end of the eighteenth century did so in most cases with the hope that they would be able to make more money by working in industry. They were not likely to object, therefore, if the chance arose for every member of the family to earn a wage, instead of the father only. Besides, there was nothing absolutely new about the idea. The wives of labourers were accustomed to doing jobs such as spinning wool and making clothes for their families; it must have seemed to them at first as if they were now being paid for doing their ordinary housework! Children, too, had always been treated as assistants to their parents in whatever work was being done. This, in fact, was their preparation and training for adult life. Once again, therefore, it seemed quite right and reasonable that they should join their parents in the factories – all the more so if they could actually bring home a few pennies in payment for their efforts.

Very quickly the new pattern of universal employment became established. We have already seen, in Chapter 1, how the working classes came to regard their children very often as economic assets. It became quite common to find that fathers were the worst taskmasters of their own families, frequently beating them severely if they gave any cause for annoyance, as for example by dozing off at the machine after a fourteen-hour day with no proper mealtimes.

It may seem almost unbelievable that small children of seven should have had to work for fourteen hours in a day, six days a week, and often on Sundays as well, throughout the year. But here is the evidence of a supervisor in a Lancashire factory, given to a Parliamentary inquiry in 1816:

> What were the hours of work? – From 5 o'clock in the morning till 8 at night all the year through. What time was allowed for meals? – Half an hour for breakfast and half an hour for dinner. . . . Did they, beyond working those 15 hours, make up for any loss of time? – Yes, always. They continued working till 9 o'clock, sometimes later.

The children who were the subject of this particular piece of evidence were actually 'workhouse children'. That is to say, they were orphans or the children of very poor people, who had become the responsibility of the parish authorities. These authorities were required by law to look after such children and to fit them for after life by apprenticing them to a trade. In theory, again, this was a reasonable and even a generous system. But in practice the parish authorities were interested only in getting rid of their responsibility, and they found that they could do this by virtually 'selling' the unfortunate children to factory owners, who undertook to feed, house, clothe and 'train' them for a given period of time – often until they were 21. This meant, in practice, that the factory owners got a ready supply of cheap labour; and it was rare for anybody to come round and check whether the terms of the apprenticeship agreement were being carefully observed. The children were, in fact, treated simply as slaves, as the following quotation from a speech made by an M.P. in 1815 shows clearly:

> These apprentice children were often sent one, two, or three hundred miles from their place of birth, separated for life from all relations, and deprived of the aid which even in their destitute situation they might derive from friends. . . . It had been known that a gang, if he might use the term, of these children had been put up for sale with a bankrupt's effects, and were advertised publicly, *as a piece of the property*. A most atrocious instance had come before the court of King's Bench two years ago, in which a number of these boys, apprenticed by a parish in London to one manufacturer, had been transferred to another, and had been found by some benevolent persons in a state of absolute famine. Another case, more horrible, had come to his knowledge while on a committee upstairs; that, not many years ago, an agreement had been made between a London parish and a Lancashire manufacturer, by which it was stipulated that with every *twenty sound* children, one *idiot* should be taken!

One of the fullest and most horrific accounts of the sufferings of a factory apprentice was given by a boy who survived and whose story was written down and published in 1828 and 1832 as part of a campaign to change the law about children in factories. His name was Robert Blincoe. He told how his foreman used to invent ingenious tortures by way of punishments, such as filing down the apprentices' teeth, making them work naked in winter, loading them with weights and hanging them up over moving machinery which would catch and mangle them if they did not keep their knees lifted. When Robert's scalp became infected as a result of the many times he had been hit about the head, the cure used was to pour hot pitch over it, allow the pitch to cool into a solid cap, and then rip it off, so that all the hair was dragged off with it. The apprentices were virtually allowed to starve; in the factory yard the employer used to keep pigs, and when these were fed the children used to fight and struggle with the animals to get at the swill in the troughs. It is not surprising that attempted suicides were common.

When we read accounts such as this, it is impossible to avoid the conclusion that the Industrial Revolution brought out the worst in some of the men

whom it enabled to rise to riches and power. It is important to remember,

Industry idealised: a nineteenth-century artist imagines the scene as one of the first government inspectors visits a factory to check on child employment. (The first Factory Act providing for such inspection was passed in 1833.)

however, that up to a point at least the evil lay in the system, as well as in the men who worked it. The factories represented a new type of organisation and it took some time (much too long, admittedly) for people to realise that this new form of industry required a different approach from the old system.

It had been reasonable for the children of domestic weavers to assist their parents at the loom; it was another matter for them to be employed as independent wage-earners under the supervision of employers who were not in the least concerned for their welfare. But the problem went deeper than that. There were, after all, some employers who, for religious or humanitarian reasons, did a great deal to look after their employees. We read of one man who gave his apprentices wheaten bread and milk porridge, meat almost every day and fruit from his own orchard. Others are praised for the standard of the clothing, the housing, the education which they provided. Yet even in these factories the children suffered what we should nowadays consider terrible hardships. The reason for this was that these early factories, which were the results of the inventions of machinery, were themselves very like gigantic machines. There was one central source of power and all the machines were driven from it simultaneously. If something went wrong and made a single machine stop, the work of the whole factory might easily be disrupted. The children were employed, in textile factories at least, chiefly on simple maintenance work — oiling and cleaning the parts while they were in motion, re-tying broken threads, supplying raw materials. They were considered specially suitable for this work because they were small and nimble and could get in among the whirling wheels where no men could reach. But the results were all too often frightful.

If these complex, machine-like factories were to run at all, they had to run regularly. Everybody had to begin work at the same time, carry on at the same speed and stop together. This was anything but popular with most of the workers. People who had been accustomed, under the domestic system, to being their own masters and working as and when they pleased did not take kindly to rules and regulations and compulsion. It might be true that they could earn more money this way. But many seem to have thought it was not worth it. One of the most pathetic groups in the history of the working classes in the nineteenth century was composed of skilled craftsmen, such as hand-loom weavers, who stuck to a dying trade long after it had ceased to provide them with an adequate living, partly at least because they placed such a high value on their independence. These were the men who at first tried to bring down the factory owners by smashing their machines (the Luddites), and who were later most active in political agitations such as Chartism.

The factory owners complained not merely of an independent spirit among the workers, but of downright laziness and refusal to co-operate. It is true that the domestic workers had acquired a wide reputation for slack and irregular work habits, before the factory system made them redundant. But it must have been very difficult for a man of spirit to keep his temper when faced with a set of rules such as the following, in force at a Manchester factory in the 1840s:

> 1st. The door of the lodge will be closed ten minutes after the engine starts every morning, and no weaver will afterwards be admitted till breakfast-time. Any weaver who may be absent during that time shall forfeit three-pence per loom.
> 2nd. Weavers absent at any other time when the engine is working, will be charged three-pence per hour each loom for such absence; and weavers leaving the room without the consent of the overlooker, shall forfeit three-pence.
> 9th. All shuttles, brushes, oil-cans, wheels, windows, etc., if broken, shall be paid for by the weaver.
> 11th. If any hand in the mill is seen *talking* to another, *whistling*, or *singing*, he will be fined sixpence.

12th. For every rod broken, one penny will be stopped.

16th. For every wheel that breaks, from one shilling to two and sixpence, according to size. Any weaver seen from his work during mill-hours, will be fined sixpence.

Such rules show the employers in a thoroughly bad light – mean, harsh, oppressive. They would doubtless have answered that they were dealing with a working class of extraordinary laziness, stupidity and viciousness, and they would have been quite largely right. One of the most striking – and horrifying – things about the Industrial Revolution is the way in which it 'dehumanised' people. Achievements and sufferings alike were on a gigantic scale, and the individual was lost in the huge, smoky frenzy of it all.

THE MINES

If anything could surpass the horror of the factories at this time, it was the condition of workers in the mines, especially the coal-mines. What is more, these conditions were allowed to last rather longer than was the case with the factories, perhaps because investigators somehow found the prospect of going down into these 'hell-holes' to see for themselves what they were like just too unattractive to be borne!

A notable difference from the state of affairs that prevailed in the factories was the backwardness of technical improvement in the mines. In the factories much of the hardship was caused by the very nature of the new machines. But in the mines, it was the absence of machinery that rendered the work so hard and dangerous. The whole process, cutting the coal, hauling it to the base of the main shaft and then lifting it up the shaft to the top, where it would be sorted and taken away, was done in practically every case by human labour – men, women and children working with nothing more than picks and shovels, trolleys and baskets, ropes and pulleys. Almost the only significant piece of machinery employed until the middle of the nineteenth century was the steam-pump, for emptying the diggings of water.

The shafts and tunnels and galleries were of the most primitive type. The danger of explosions caused by gas was regarded by most people as an unavoidable hazard. Ventilation was crude; the method which gradually became universal in the early nineteenth century was to instal a system of doors, which were opened and shut as the baskets and trolleys of coals went past, thus creating a minimum of draught.

In these tiny, dark, airless warrens, sometimes several hundred feet underground, the miners tunnelled like a race apart, almost unknown to ordinary folk above ground. The occupation was virtually hereditary. Children went down the mine sometimes as early as four years old, and were almost invariably at work by the time they were seven or eight. The mining villages were generally isolated and self-contained, so that there was little hope of other employment. Besides, generations of work in these degrading conditions had produced a race that was scarcely human, so some observers thought, and was so stunted and degraded that they could hardly be considered for other jobs even if they had had the chance to look for them. One traveller who had the courage to descend into a mine near Whitehaven, in Cumberland, in 1813, wrote a peculiarly atmospheric and impressive account of the experience, which he published the following year. Here is his description of the miners:

> All the people whom we met were distinguished by an extraordinary wretchedness; immoderate labour and a noxious atmosphere had marked their countenance with the signs of disease and decay; they were mostly half-naked, blackened all over with dirt, and altogether so miserably disfigured and abused, that they looked like a race fallen from the common rank of men, and doomed, as in a kind of purgatory, to wear away their lives in these dismal shades.

The smallest children, as we have seen, were set to man the ventilation doors. They would usually work at this task, known as 'trapping', for twelve hours at a time, sitting all alone in the dark among the rats, having no contact with humans apart from the occasional older child or woman pushing a loaded trolley along the tunnel. At the age of eight or nine, the child would graduate to 'hurrying' – moving the coal from the working face to the pit shaft. The labour involved in this is described in a Parliamentary Report of 1842:

> She has first to descend a nine-ladder pit to the first rest, even to which a shaft is sunk, to draw up the baskets or tubs of coals filled by the bearers; she then takes her creel (a basket formed to the back, not unlike a cockle-shell flattened towards the neck, so as to allow lumps of coal to rest on the back of the neck and shoulders), and pursues her journey to the wall-face. . . . She then lays down her basket, into which the coal is rolled, and it is frequently more than one man can do to lift the burden on her back. The tugs or straps are placed over the forehead, and the body bent in a semi-circular form, in order to stiffen the arch.
>
> Large lumps of coal are then placed on the neck, and she then commences her journey with her burden to the pit bottom, first hanging her lamp to the cloth crossing her head. In this girl's case she has first to travel about 14 fathoms (84 feet) from the wall-face to the first ladder, which is 18 feet high; leaving the first ladder she proceeds along the main road, probably 3 feet 6 inches to 4 feet 6 inches high, to the second ladder, 18 feet high, so on to the third and fourth ladders, till she reaches the pit-bottom, where she casts her load, varying from 1 cwt. to $1\frac{1}{2}$ cwt., into the tub.
>
> This one journey is designated a rake; the height ascended, and the distance along the roads added together, exceed the height of St. Paul's Cathedral; and it not unfrequently happens that the tugs break, and the load falls upon those females

who are following. However incredible it may be, yet I have taken the evidence of fathers who have ruptured themselves from straining to lift coal on their children's backs.

Boys would eventually take their places hewing coals at the face; but girls stayed at the work of hauling coal very often for the whole of their lives, until their health broke down. The pictures on this page, which were published in the Report of 1842 mentioned above, give an idea of this work. Women usually worked naked to the waist, because of the heat and filth in the tiny tunnels. The men often worked entirely naked. It is hardly surprising that, as the Report of 1842 said with pompous horror, 'where opportunity thus prevails sexual vices are of common occurrence'. Once again, we are impressed by the sheer inhumanity of the total picture; the mines were places where men, women and children were turned into filthy animals.

Prints published as part of the agitation against child labour in coal-mines; the upper one appeared in the Shaftesbury Report, which led to the Coal Mines Act of 1842

119

The coal-mines and the cotton-mills would not have developed as they did if there had not been an overwhelming pressure working to produce such a result. This pressure, as we have already seen, was the demand – for coal, cloth and goods of every description. Never before had there been such demand, and never before had there been such opportunities of riches for those who could satisfy it.

But, of course, not everybody was so fortunate as to be a member of the group which profited from the Industrial Revolution. On the contrary, the number of people who won riches and success in this way was, relatively speaking, tiny, when compared with the vast masses of workers who spent their short and wretched lives slaving for the barest minimum of wages. To some contemporaries, the most significant aspect of the Industrial Revolution was the effect which it had on traditional social patterns and relationships.

There had been very rich men before, of course, and a great many very poor ones. Nor did the traditional forms of wealth disappear with the coming of industry. Indeed, it was probably not until the middle of the nineteenth century that the fortunes made from business could be compared with those of the great landed aristocrats such as the Dukes of Devonshire, Bedford and Newcastle. But what *was* undoubtedly new was the appearance of men who were the direct employers of several hundreds, or even two or three thousands of workers, all concentrated together in one spot and working under direct control. The landed estates, by contrast, were delicately balanced affairs, in which very large numbers of people were involved *at different levels*; they did not contain such an overwhelmingly large proportion of landless labourers – most of the land was held by tenant farmers, and the Duke of Devonshire himself, for example, employed relatively few labourers.

The new employers are referred to by economists as 'capitalists'. This is because their position was based on the fact they owned the capital without which industry cannot operate. Capital means wealth not needed for immediate expenditure – often, therefore, money apart from income. This money can be turned into factory buildings, the machinery in them, raw materials and a paid labour force.

It is true that in broad terms there must always have been capitalists, in the sense of people with surplus money to spare for investment. The majority of capitalists before the Industrial Revolution, however, were landowners, or financiers, or merchants. People, in other words, not involved with industry. The majority of those who produced goods were little more than craftsmen, operating on a small scale and at a very simple level. Most of them did not employ labourers – just an apprentice or two. There were exceptions; as early as the sixteenth century we find ironmasters in Sussex and master clothiers in the Cotswolds who can perfectly well be described as capitalists. But the Industrial Revolution brought new forms of capitalism forward, particularly in association with the factory system, and did so on a scale that justifies our talking about the industrial capitalists of the late eighteenth century and early nineteenth century as a new class.

It is interesting to look into the origins of this new class. The first and most obvious candidates might seem to be the inventors of the new machinery; they, surely, should have been in a position to set up factories and make big profits. The evidence, however, does not bear this out. Very few actual inventors became capitalists or made great fortunes. Indeed, many of them, such as Kay and Crompton, might have done better financially if they had not meddled with machinery at all. There were a few exceptions; James Watt was lucky enough to find for a partner a businessman who was honest as well as hard-headed. The Darbys of Coalbrookdale were wise enough to keep the news of their invention quiet until they had made a lot of money from it. The biggest apparent exception to the rule, Arkwright, was most probably not an inventor at all in the strict sense of the word. The reason for the failure of the inventors to become capitalists may be partly connected with the inventor's temperament, if there is such a thing. But more probably in each case it came down to a matter of hard cash. The money must have come from somewhere; it is not enough to have bright ideas.

For much the same reason, relatively few of the capitalists seem to have risen through the industries themselves, though a few did so. Most, on the contrary, began as 'outsiders' who could bring a little spare money and a good deal of sharpness to the exploitation of a new idea. Interestingly, relatively few came from the ranks of the established large capitalist classes, the landowners and merchants. Very often, though, they would be men whose daily work brought them into contact with new ideas and opportunities and whose income was perhaps slightly irregular, so that they were not unwilling to take a gamble on a likely-sounding chance. Arkwright, one of the most successful of them all, falls into this category.

Another important group began as yeomen or small farmers who also worked at domestic industry in the evenings. In such cases as these, income from the farming side may have been turned into capital for the industrial side. The families of Robert Peel, Joshua Fielden and Jedediah Strutt, three of the greatest names in the history of textiles in Britain, can be traced back to this sort of origin.

It is therefore difficult to make general statements about the social origins of the industrial capitalists. But it would certainly be true to say that, as a group, they are marked by outstanding energy and dynamism, and also by powerful organising ability. Their task fell into at least three sections. They had first to get together and pay for premises and equipment; then they had to organise the manufacture of the product, which would mean dealing both with mechanical problems and with the difficulties of handling a labour force; finally, they had to sell their goods at the best price possible.

Some of the men who achieved success in all these three fields undoubtedly deserve great admiration. We have spent a lot of time in this chapter describing the horrors of the Industrial Revolution; but it must not be forgotten that there were also factories run by men of high principles and real civilisation, men who cared for their workers and set themselves the highest standards in everything they did. Matthew Boulton ('Princely' Boulton), Josiah Wedgwood and Robert Owen stand out as special examples of this type; but they were certainly not alone.

As time went on, businessmen of all types tended to imitate the manners of the landed gentry who still dominated the English social scene. They bought estates with big houses in the country, sent their sons to public school and university and ventured into London society or the hunting field of Leicestershire. Possibly as they did so they lost some of their original drive and determination.

Up to 1850, though, they seemed to be in no serious danger of losing their way. On the contrary, the period is marked by the clear emergence of the business interest as a pressure group on the national level. As early as 1785, the determined opposition of a group of merchants and manufacturers caused William Pitt the Younger, then Prime Minister, to abandon an important scheme for the improvement of economic relations with Ireland. After the Napoleonic Wars the business group was active in pressing for Free Trade; and they scored a brilliant success, in their own estimation at least, when their organisation, the Manchester-based Anti-Corn Law League, played a big part in the repeal of the Corn Laws in 1846.

Their chief interest as a group, however, probably lay in the suppression of working-class attempts to improve wages, hours and conditions. Businessmen in Parliament were responsible for many of the eighteenth-century attacks on working men's societies. In 1782 they inspired drastic legislation against workers who broke looms or damaged employers' property. And they are known to have drawn up 'black books', in which were recorded the names of 'troublesome' workers; copies of these black books would be available to employers, and workmen who were active in campaigning for their rights might find it impossible to get work, no matter where they went.

Once again it is only fair to add that not all businessmen acted in this way. It was a businessman, Sir Robert Peel the Elder, who passed the first of all Factory Acts; and many industrialists were prominent in nineteenth-century campaigns to improve worker's conditions.

In all clashes between capitalists and workers the dice were heavily loaded
on the side of the capitalists. The workers obviously had no capital. Their

only 'asset' was their physical strength and possibly their trained skill. In the new conditions of industry they found themselves at a terrible disadvantage. On the whole they made peaceful, though slow progress; but the issue was frequently in doubt, and at times it seemed that the gulf between the capitalists and the workers would never stop widening. Some writers in the nineteenth century, of whom the most famous was Karl Marx (1818–83), thought there could be no way out save revolution. But fortunately they have been proved wrong.

The changes came about very gradually; but the final effect was to alter the whole pattern of British society. The possession of land ceased to be the sole guide to a man's status, and capitalists took their place among the rulers, as magistrates, Members of Parliament and so forth, to be followed in due course by the workers.

Suggestions for further work and discussion

1. Study of street-plans can often show up the stages of a town's expansion, and buildings can usually be dated by their appearance; try to find out how your town grew in the Industrial Revolution, and relate your findings to the economic life of the area.

2. Find out what building regulations apply when new houses are being constructed today. How long have they been in force? Who sees that they are observed?

3. Find out how water is supplied to your town, and how sewage is disposed of. Some Victorian waterworks and pumping stations are magnificent examples of municipal engineering, and well worth a visit if it can be arranged.

4. It is possible to discover statistics for cholera and typhoid deaths in the nineteenth century. Draw a graph to show the incidence of mortality. How were matters improved by public health measures? Use your local resources (church registers, etc.) to find out if the epidemics hit your own town.

5. Why were the early factories and industrial towns such terrible places, on the whole? Why were they only put right so slowly?

6. The illustration on page 115 shows a government factory inspector. How realistic do you think this picture is? Was the artist on any particular 'side'? What sort of questions would the inspector be asking?

7. The two illustrations on page 119 show children working in the coal-mines. How old are the children? How high are the tunnels? How much light would there be? What is the purpose of the door in the lower illustration. How heavy would the coal be in the trucks?

Books for further reading:

Mrs Gaskell, *Mary Barton*, 1848.
Charles Dickens, *Hard Times*, 1854.
Royston Pike, *Human Documents of the Industrial Revolution in Britain*, Allen and Unwin, 1966.

6 : Overseas Trade

The Growth of Trade

Overseas trade had always been important for Britain. The rich could only get from abroad some of the luxury goods they wanted – tobacco, silks, wines, spices. The table below shows the wide variety of goods imported through one port in a single year. In exchange, British merchants sent home-produced goods, mostly woollens and grain before 1700, to profitable markets in other countries. This had been the basis of Britain's external trade for centuries. It was a valuable part of economic life, but with the coming of the Industrial Revolution it became vital. Some historians even go so far as to state that without a substantial overseas trade, the changes in industry might not havè come about so soon.

SHIPS ARRIVING AT BRISTOL JUNE 1699 TO JUNE 1700

Origin of ships	Number of ships	Cargo
Virginia	29	Tobacco
Antigua/Nevis/St. Kitts	28	Sugar, Cotton, Logwood, Dyes
Jamaica	18	Sugar, Cotton, Ginger, Molasses
Newfoundland/New England	9	Oil, Fish, Rice, Skins, Furs, Timber

(Adapted from C. McKinnes: *Bristol: Gateway to Empire*)

This was because Britain had few natural resources or raw materials of her own, apart from coal and wool. Raw cotton and good iron ore, for example, could only be obtained from overseas. Moreover, industry could only grow on a really large scale if it could sell to the markets of the world and not just to those at home. Thus a prosperous overseas trade was essential if Britain was to become a great industrial country.

It was an advantage, therefore, that Britain already possessed a considerable overseas trade at the beginning of the eighteenth century. In the Middle Ages the chief areas of trade were western and northern Europe, but from the time of Queen Elizabeth I, adventurous merchants began to branch out to more remote regions.

Much of the trade was in the hands of great trading companies. These were called 'Chartered Companies', and they were given the sole right to trade in certain areas. The best known was the East India Company, founded in 1600. It traded in India and the Far East. In its fine ships, 'the East Indiamen', it brought to London luxuries such as tea, spices, perfumes, jewels, silks, porcelain and cotton goods. The last were so popular that British manufacturers began to make them, and imports of finished cotton were eventually banned. A fascinating illustration of the East India trade is provided by the life of Edward Barlow, a mariner in the late seventeenth century. He ran away to sea as a boy and rose to be chief mate on a number of vessels, mainly engaged in trade with Asia for the East India Company. Barlow wrote down his experiences in his journals, and these may still be seen in the National Maritime Museum at Greenwich. These journals give us valuable evidence of conditions at sea in those days, and of the nature of trade. We may take as one example Barlow's last voyage, as chief mate of the *Fleet Frigate*, 270 tons, under charter to the Company.

The *Fleet Frigate* left Deal on 8 March 1702, bound for Canton in China. The outward cargo included glassware, cloth, guns and sword blades, but consisted mainly of coins to pay for the return cargo, as the Chinese imported few goods in those days. After a non-stop passage of nearly four months, the ship arrived at the Dutch port of Batavia in Java (now Djakarta in Indonesia) on 13 July, to take on provisions and fresh water. As the captain was incompetent, Barlow was in fact responsible for the navigation and sailing of the ship, and he took the *Fleet Frigate* through the dangerous channels north of Batavia. On 25 August the Portuguese port of Macao was sighted and, after several days' haggling with local officials, the ship was cleared to proceed to Whampoa, about ten miles from Canton, where the main trade was carried on at that time. It was six months since the ship had left England.

No trade could be done without bribing local officials, and a present of about £666 had to be made to the chief officer of the port. After these preliminaries, negotiations began, but it was not until the following February that the return cargo was fully loaded and the ship could sail for home. The cargo list was as follows:

205 chests of Chinese and Japanese porcelain, 507 chests of copper, 122 chests of quicksilver, 416 tubs and baskets of sugar candy, 155 bags of nux vomica, 42 bags of galingall, 28 bags of gourege [drugs and spices], 28 chests of rhubarb, 14 small scrivetories, 13 chests of laquered ware, 23 chests of Chinese lacquer, 481 balls or bundles of raw silk, 2 chests of fans, 2 tubs of oil for lacquering, 1 chest of turtle shell, 4 chests of vermilion, 83 chests of tea, 60 large jars of green ginger, 4,822 pieces of Chinese wrought silks, 70 chests of screens and a large quantity of miscellaneous Chinese and Japanese earthenware.

One wonders how all this was loaded on to such a small ship! It was a typical cargo from China, and when it was brought back to England it would have made a large profit for the East India Company. The *Fleet Frigate* reached England in November 1703, the whole voyage therefore lasting twenty months.

The Company governed and defended many of the regions in which it traded. It fought many wars against native leaders and rival traders, such as the French, Dutch and Portuguese. Vast fortunes were made by some of the Company's employees. When these 'Nabobs', as they were called, returned to Britain with their riches, they were often a force in politics and society. Such a man was 'Diamond' Pitt, the father of the statesman, William Pitt the Elder; another was Robert Clive, who conquered large parts of India in the Seven Years' War (1756–63). The political power of the East India Company did not finally end until after the Indian Mutiny of 1857.

There were other important Chartered Companies. The Hudson's Bay Company, for example, traded mainly in furs from the desolate regions of Northern Canada. The Merchant Venturers traded with the Netherlands and Germany, while the Levant Company opened up direct contact with Turkey and the Near East. The Baltic Company began the trade with Russia and the Baltic region. The magnificent gift of silver sent by Queen Elizabeth I to Ivan the Terrible, ruler of Russia, to improve relations and to encourage trade can still be seen in Moscow.

THE SLAVE TRADE

One rather different company was the Royal African Company, which took part in the notorious 'triangular' slave trade. The diagram below shows the nature of this trade. On the first leg, ships left London, Bristol and some other ports for West Africa. They carried cargoes of glass, beads, trinkets, coloured cloth and other goods likely to appeal to native chiefs. One ship in the early eighteenth century, probably typical, left Bristol with a cargo of

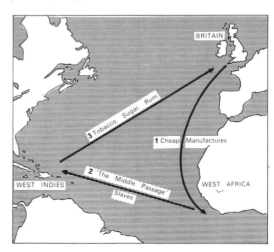

The Triangular Slave
Trade

clothes, guns and iron, valued at £1,226. In West African territories such as the Gold Coast or Ivory Coast these articles were exchanged for Negroes. Arab traders who brought the Negroes down to the coast from the interior sometimes acted as agents. More often, deals were done directly with the coastal chiefs.

Then began the infamous 'middle passage', across the Atlantic to the West Indies. The Negroes were often transported in terrible conditions, packed together below decks for months on end. Usually there was not enough food or water. Even though it was in the interests of the ships' captains to keep the slaves alive, many died. There were even examples of Africans leaping into the sea in mid-passage to escape the torments of the voyage. Vast numbers of Negroes were carried. In 1771 alone, 192 British ships sailed from West African ports with 47,146 Negroes on board. It has been estimated that 2,000,000 slaves were transported between 1680 and 1786, to British possessions alone. When the ships arrived in the West Indies or mainland American colonies, the surviving 'cargoes' were sold as slaves to the tobacco and sugar planters. It was felt by then that only Africans, used to the tropical conditions, could do the necessary work on the plantations.

By the early eighteenth century, male slaves were fetching about £15 each in the West Indies and higher prices were not unusual on the American mainland. In South Carolina, in 1755, as much as £40 a head was paid for good-quality male slaves. These prices in themselves gave excellent profits, but the proceeds were normally reinvested in cotton, sugar, tobacco and rum, the produce of the colonies – and when these goods were resold in Britain after the third and final leg of the voyage, enormous profits could be realised.

A pamphlet of 1749 stated that 'our West Indian and African trades are the most nationally beneficial of any we carry on . . . the Negro trade . . . may be justly esteemed an inexhaustible fund of the wealth and naval power of this country'. Huge fortunes were certainly amassed by those engaged in it. It was the basis of the prosperity of several ports. In Bristol many fine houses and churches of the period still stand to remind the visitor of the days when the city was one of the richest in England. Some place-names remind us that Negroes were even brought to England. They were sold technically as ser-

vants rather than slaves, as slavery was illegal in England itself. At this time it was very fashionable for rich families to have black boys as page-boys. In Bristol they were sold at a market on 'Blackboy Hill', buyers approaching along 'Whiteladies Road'. Liverpool, too, gained enormously from the trade. The father of Mr. Gladstone, several times Prime Minister in the nineteenth century, made some of his fortune from the slave trade in which he was engaged from Liverpool. Eventually the trade was stopped in 1807, after many people had become convinced that it was wrong.

Not all trading companies were successful. Some were disastrous failures or fraudulent, like the South Sea Company, which caused a financial collapse in 1720. This resulted in much harm. Nor was all trade in the hands of companies. An increasing number of independent merchants traded with areas outside their control, such as North America. Some bold 'interlopers' even began to cut into the areas reserved for the companies. Between them all, the merchants made England one of the chief trading nations of Europe by 1700. Only Holland and France were major rivals.

GOVERNMENT REGULATION OF TRADE

The government took a close interest in commercial matters, for three main reasons. In the first place it was felt that a prosperous trade meant a more wealthy country. If more was exported from Britain than was imported, there was a favourable balance of trade, as it is called. This meant an increase in the wealth of the country. From this, secondly, came the view that the richer a nation was, the more power it enjoyed in the world. As Sir Josiah Child, a businessman of the seventeenth century, once said: 'Profit and Power do jointly go together.'

Finally, trade was regarded as of particular importance to Britain as a means of training seamen. As an island, Britain depended on naval power for her security. An expanding trade meant a bigger merchant fleet for both coastal and overseas voyages. Thus a ready supply of trained sailors was always available in war-time. Then the 'press-gang' went to work to get unwilling recruits for men-of-war.

This is why, in the seventeenth century, the government developed a system for the regulation of trade, called the 'mercantilist system'. It had

Calcutta in 1756. This was an important centre of the East India Company's trade

several features. First, it placed a great emphasis on a favourable balance of trade. Everything possible was done to ensure that exports exceeded imports. Measures taken ranged from giving bounties, or grants of money, to exporters to banning the export of machinery or skilled workmen, which might enable other countries to start up rival industries. Likewise, imports were discouraged by high tariffs, or customs duties, which made the price of imported goods high. The overall result was a favourable balance of trade in goods right through the eighteenth century. Tariffs did not apply to imports of raw materials, such as cotton, which were used in home manufactures. Nor were they imposed on goods like sugar and tobacco, which were brought to Britain and then re-exported to other countries.

Re-exports came mostly from British colonies, and a second feature of mercantilism was the emphasis on the development of colonies. They were considered as essential parts of a flourishing system of trade, supplying the raw materials which could not be produced in Europe. Many people believed that the amount of trade available in the world was more or less a fixed quantity. The more of it that Britain could control, the less would be available for rival nations.

This feeling lay behind much of Britain's foreign policy in the seventeenth and eighteenth centuries and helps to explain why there were so many wars over colonial disputes. Britain fought several wars against the Dutch in the seventeenth century, and against the French and Spanish in the eighteenth, mainly arising from colonial questions.

Work at a London
warehouse in full swing

As a result of these wars, Britain gained a considerable Empire in Asia, Africa, the West Indies and North America. The mercantilist view was that the colonies should be controlled solely in the economic interests of Britain, the 'Mother Country', as she came to be called. No other country should be allowed to take advantage of them. So, under the Navigation Act of 1660, trade with the colonies could only be carried on in colonial or British ships. Most goods could only be exported to the colonies from Britain. Most important, many colonial goods could only be sold in Britain. This applied to articles 'enumerated' in the Act, like tobacco, sugar, naval stores (timber) and rice. As Britain imported from the colonies far greater quantities of these goods than she could possibly use at home, and as there were few other sources of supply, a proportion of them was re-exported to Europe. This was a most valuable trade. When other products such as Newfoundland cod and Indian tea were taken into account, re-exports usually amounted to one-third of Britain's total exports. Two-thirds of the tobacco and one-third of the sugar coming to Britain in 1700 was sent on to Europe.

The mercantilist system reached its peak in the eighteenth century, under Prime Ministers like Sir Robert Walpole (1721–42). Later, it came under attack, and a demand for freer trade grew up, as we see later in this chapter. But it served Britain profitably until then, as well as providing the colonies with secure markets for their goods.

The 'Commercial Revolution'

Overseas trade was therefore important and profitable for Britain, but it was not until the mid-eighteenth century that it became big enough to cause industrial change. Indeed, between about 1690 and 1740, trade experienced certain difficulties which caused it to grow only slowly. From about 1740, however, there was such a transformation of British trade that it has been called a 'commercial revolution'. The extent of this change can be seen from the accompanying diagrams.

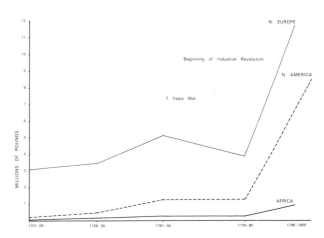

The growth of exports to three markets 1700–1800

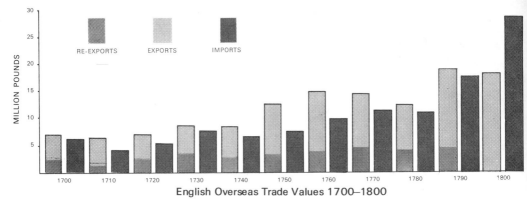

English Overseas Trade Values 1700–1800

The cause was a great expansion of demand for British goods. This demand came from the colonies, rather than from Europe. The colonies at last became important purchasers of British goods. This was for two main reasons. First, wars added greatly to the size of the Empire, especially after the Seven Years' War. By the Treaty of Paris (1763) Britain gained new territories in India, the West Indies and Canada. Second, and more important, the older territories had now reached quite an advanced state of development.

Unlike the colonies of some other countries, like Holland, the British colonies were quite thickly settled and their population grew rapidly. This was certainly the case in America. The population of the American colonies in the 1770s was about three million, or half that of England and Wales. Moreover, the average wealth was probably higher by this time, and new development was going on all the time. The Americans had few industries of their own. British laws discouraged them, and most Americans preferred to work the plentiful land. Most of the manufactured goods they needed, then,

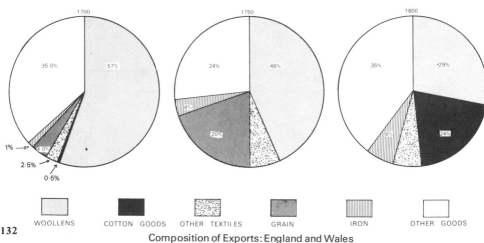

Composition of Exports: England and Wales

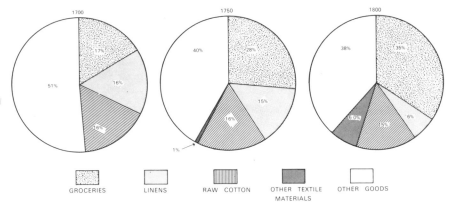

Composition of Imports: England and Wales

GROCERIES LINENS RAW COTTON OTHER TEXTILE MATERIALS OTHER GOODS

had to come from Britain, even the commonest everyday articles. Nearly all the needs of all sections of this expanding American society had to be met by British industry. Here was a fine market for British trade.

So hammers, nails, pots, pans, guns, axes, buttons, silks, woollens, even beaver hats and, later, cottons were sent in greater and greater quantities to satisfy the never-ending demand across the Atlantic. The colonists eventually gained their independence in 1783, but even after this a favourable treaty ensured that Britain retained the lion's share of the American trade.

What was true of the American colonies was also true, to a lesser extent, of other parts of the Empire. In 1700 the American colonies, together with the East and West Indies, supplied 33% of British imports, but took only 13% of British exports. By 1773 these figures were 60% and 46%. These colonies were buying more British goods than European countries were.

This was the chief change in the pattern of British trade, but there were others of importance. The composition of exports changed considerably. Woollens no longer dominated to the extent that they had done in the past. By 1800 cotton exports, very small before 1750, had almost caught up wool. Cotton had many advantages over wool, in cost and comfort, especially for hot climates. When technical changes came in the industry in Britain, there was a ready market overseas.

The export of iron products also increased significantly, though they remained relatively expensive until the nineteenth century. It is also noticeable how Britain gradually ceased to export grain. As the home population rose, not only was there little surplus to export, but it became necessary to import more and more foodstuffs of all kinds. Another change in imports was the increase in raw cotton, needed for the growing cotton industry of Lancashire.

133

The results of the revolution in commerce were extremely important. The most obvious was the expansion of British shipping and ports. By the mid-eighteenth century there were about 6,000 merchant ships, totalling some half-million tons. The average size of ships doubled to about 100 tons during the century, and the table below shows how the volume of shipping leaving the ports grew. Upwards of 100,000 men were given employment at sea, in what was probably the biggest single industry after agriculture. Employment was also given to shipbuilders, and shipbuilding was soon one of the staple, or basic, industries of Britain.

TONNAGE OF COMMERCIAL SHIPPING LEAVING
ENGLISH PORTS 1700–1801

	Tons
1700	317,000
1764	658,000
1801	1,924,000

In time, many British sailing ships were used to carry the trade of other countries as well. This 'carrying trade' earned valuable revenue, or 'invisible income' as it is called. So the basis was laid of yet another activity in which Britain was to be supreme in the nineteenth century.

The port which grew most of all in the eighteenth century was Liverpool. In the previous century it was little more than a fishing village. The slave trade was the cause of its early growth, so that Daniel Defoe was calling it 'one of the wonders of Britain' in 1720. Then the cotton trade with America brought a new expansion in the later part of the century. It received the raw

Lloyd's Subscription Room in 1800. Most shipping insurance business was done here, and Lloyd's developed into the most important insurance market in the world

St Katharine Docks, built by Thomas Telford. These were the first artificial docks constructed in London

cotton for manufacturers in Lancashire to process and sent back the finished products. In 1700 its population was only 5,000, yet by 1801 this had risen to 77,000. It boasted many fine houses, churches and public buildings. It was so famous that Arthur Young, on one of his tours, went out of his way in order not to miss it.

Some ports, like Bristol and Chester, suffered relative decline. This was mainly because silting up of their approaches made it less easy for larger ships to reach them. Others, such as London, still the chief port, and Glasgow, went from strength to strength as trade increased.

The most important consequence, however, was the contribution of overseas trade to the Industrial Revolution. The causes of the Industrial Revolution form a subject for much argument, but there is no doubt that without an increase in demand for goods there would have been no incentive for change.

The home population was growing in the mid-eighteenth century, but slowly. The people were generally poor. Therefore, home demand was sluggish. But, as we have seen, overseas demand for British products was becoming more dynamic, especially in the colonies. This was, perhaps, the real spark behind the Industrial Revolution, the real incentive for change. It has been estimated that industries producing for export increased their output by 80% between 1750 and 1770, compared with only 7% by the industries producing for British customers.

To meet the growing overseas demand, which provided such profits for manufacturers and merchants, there had to be change. The traditional system of manufacture in the home was too inefficient and too small in scale to cope. This was especially true as the home labour force was rising too slowly, more slowly than the urgent orders flowing in from overseas. There was, therefore, every incentive to produce labour-saving machines and to bring work into the larger and more efficient factories. This came more quickly in cotton than in wool production for reasons given in Chapter 4.

Equally important, the profits of trade over the years meant that capital was available for investment in the more expensive industrial projects. The merchants formed a new and rich middle class. As merchant clothiers, some had already taken an interest in the domestic manufacture of the goods which they sold, notably woollens. They were not slow to make money available now, where and when it was most needed. It was no coincidence that the main industrial growth areas of Britain at this time lay within reach of the major ports. Not only did it make economic sense to be near the ports, but it was there that the merchants were most willing to invest. Thus Liverpool merchants helped to build up Lancashire industry. The Clyde Valley and South Wales industries owed much to Glasgow and Bristol merchants. They knew that in the long run such investment would expand their own business enormously.

This was how British overseas trade helped industrialisation to begin. Once it was under way it was no less important. The markets, ships and experience were all there to profit from, and to keep up, the industrial supremacy which Britain soon built up. In the early nineteenth century two-thirds of all cotton produced in Britain, and much of the iron, was exported. The vast increase in trade to all areas was a real reflection of industrialisation, and also of the demand created by the Napoleonic Wars, which only Britain could meet.

Exports helped to pay for the imports of raw materials, foodstuffs and luxuries. All this eventually enabled the standard of living of everyone to rise. The more goods bought from overseas, the more foreigners were able to buy from Britain, so a system evolved where everybody gained. The fact that British trade was mainly in goods originating either in Britain itself or in her colonies abroad provided security for the future. The importance of Britain's overseas trade was recognised and admired everywhere. Voltaire, a French observer, once wrote of British commerce: 'This is the foundation of the greatness of the state.' When, in the early nineteenth century, there seemed to be a stagnation in trade, this caused general alarm and despondency. It also gave force to the growing demand for tree trade, since this was thought to be a new recipe for trading prosperity.

FREE TRADE

The mercantilist system, described earlier in this chapter, served Britain well for a long time. By the late eighteenth century, however, a growing number of people began to feel that such close regulation of trade had outlived its usefulness. They felt that, far from helping trade to expand, mercantilism was actually restricting it. So a movement, called the free trade movement, grew up in opposition to mercantilism. As the name implied, it favoured a policy under which trade would be carried on completely freely, without government interference or regulation. Goods would be able to come into and go out of Britain without hindrance. There would be no Navigation Acts, monopoly companies, import controls and export bounties. Only a few small import duties, to provide some revenue for the government, would be allowed.

A system which had lasted for several hundred years could not be destroyed overnight. Parliament and political leaders, responsible for the laws,

Adam Smith

William Pitt the Younger

had to be convinced that mercantilism really was harmful and that free trade really would be a better system. In order to convince them and the many opponents of free trade its supporters put forward a great many arguments in its favour.

Adam Smith (1723–90), a Scottish economist, outlined many of these arguments in a famous book, *The Wealth of Nations*, which was published in 1776. In it Smith argued that free trade was essential for Britain to sell goods in the widest possible markets, and to admit imports which would raise the general standard of living. His ideas were taken further by later writers and they had a very great influence. The Younger Pitt, Prime Minister at the end of the eighteenth century, made some changes, but progress was none the less slow until after the Napoleonic Wars, when British trade became sluggish and industry got into some difficulties.

These problems persuaded statesmen such as William Huskisson, Sir Robert Peel and W. E. Gladstone to work for free trade. The most important measures were passed in Peel's Ministry of 1841–46, ending with the repeal

Sir Robert Peel

W. E. Gladstone

of the Corn Laws, which had hindered trade in grain since 1815. This was a triumph for the principle of free trade and, although the last important tariff barriers were not removed until about 1860, Britain was really a free-trade nation some time before.

The Results of Free Trade

What were the results? After about 1850, world and British trade increased rapidly. British industry expanded to the peak of its supremacy. So did shipping, insurance and other services. The quarter-century after 1850 was really the high water mark for British industry and even for agriculture. The 'Hungry Forties' gave way to a period in which ordinary people enjoyed a higher standard of living.

The Great Exhibition of 1851 had, as one object, the demonstration of how free trade had contributed to British success. This may have been premature, but free trade certainly did have very great effects. It is impossible to say exactly to what extent it caused the expansion, but we must not imagine that it was entirely responsible. Change was due, not just to free trade, but also to the money which Britain was investing abroad. This was spent on railways,

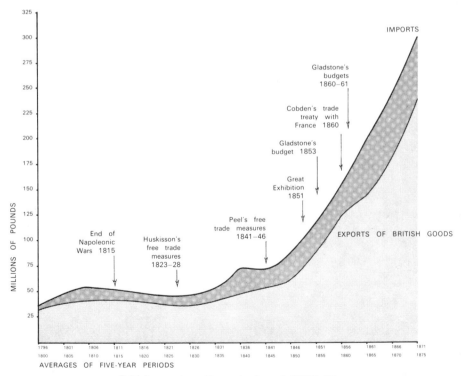

British exports and imports of goods 1800–75

The Crystal Palace, seen after it was moved from Hyde Park to Sydenham in South London. Notice the huge areas of glass used to overcome the problem of lighting a building of this size. The Crystal Palace was destroyed by fire in 1936.

machinery and similar industrial equipment, enabling foreign countries to increase and cheapen their production. Moreover, the spread of railways at home had much to do with the growth of industry after the 1840s. These factors must not be separated.

To sum up: the results of free trade, together with other causes, were first, that world trade was able to grow after a stagnant period, and British trade with it. Second, this assisted the growth of British industry and, with the imports of cheap food later in the nineteenth century, a much improved standard of living for the people was achieved. But finally, in the long run, by providing an open market for the products of other countries, free trade did much to help those countries to build up their industries to the point where British industry and agriculture were seriously challenged. When this happened in the late nineteenth century, a more depressed period set in.

The last point explains why, not long after the triumph of free trade, men like Joseph Chamberlain were clamouring for the return of protection. 'Fair Trade' not 'Free Trade' became the cry, and though it was ignored for a long time, it eventually brought about the return of protection in the 1930s.

Suggestions for further work and discussion

1. If you live near or visit a port which was flourishing in the eighteenth century, such as Bristol, Liverpool or London, discover as much as you can about its history. You can probably visit (with permission) original docks and warehouses. Local museums will certainly have documents and paintings of former days. If you can find records of cargo-lists, examine them carefully and see how cargoes changed over the years.

2. Give an account of a voyage in an 'East Indiaman', using Edward Barlow's experiences as a guide.

3. Examine more fully the life and achievements of Robert Clive or 'Diamond' Pitt.

4. Find out more about the slave trade. Why were men so indifferent to the fate of Negroes? What effect did the slave trade have on the history of the United States? Of Africa? How was it finally stamped out?

5. Trade rivalry was an important cause of war in the seventeenth and eighteenth centuries. What were the trading disputes which helped to start the Seven Years' War (1756–63)? What colonies did Britain gain at the end of that war? List the British colonies in 1815.

6. Subject for an essay or discussion:
   What was the importance of overseas trade for the Industrial Revolution?

7. Visit the National Maritime Museum at Greenwich. *H.M.S. Victory* and the Victory Museum at Portsmouth are also most interesting to look round.

Books for further reading:

A. G. Course, *A Seventeenth-Century Mariner*, Muller, 1965.
C. McKinnes, *Bristol: Gateway to Empire*, David & Charles, 1968.

7 : The Old Staples

The only industry described in detail in Chapter 4 (The Industrial Revolution) was the cotton industry. The special treatment given to cotton is not accidental, since it was this industry that pioneered new methods of production and forms of organisation. The result was that the most startling achievements, in terms of output, exports and profits, are also to be found in the cotton industry. It would not be going too far to say that the Industrial Revolution began as a Cotton Revolution.

Chapter 4 also made clear, however, that these great changes were not brought about without the help of coal and iron. These two industries were intimately bound up with the early stages of the Industrial Revolution, though they were not in the forefront of the advance. In this chapter we shall be describing how they took over from cotton in the middle of the nineteenth century and became for a while the leading sections of the British economy.

Part of this story is necessarily dealt with in other chapters, those covering overseas trade during this period, and transport developments. Here we will be concerned almost entirely with developments inside the industries themselves.

By the second quarter of the nineteenth century the prospects of the cotton industry were beginning to cause serious alarm to numbers of well-informed people. As output increased, retail prices inevitably fell; but the costs of manufacture showed no signs of falling, and so margins of profit were reduced. At the same time, the market showed a disturbing sluggishness; home demand remained more or less constant, since the economic difficulties kept standards of living from rising; and even foreign countries failed to buy as much as the British manufacturers wanted, and indeed needed, to sell. The signs of difficulty were clear in the 1830s and 1840s, which from the point of view of the social historian were two of the most disturbed and dangerous decades of British history since the Civil War. They were clear also to the economist, since Britain began to experience balance of trade difficulties from 1826 onwards — not as serious as the troubles that caused so much worry in the 1960s, but still bad enough.

The most alarming aspect of the situation was the fact that, if cotton went into decline, the whole of the economy might collapse. The extent of Britain's dependence on cotton can be measured from the fact that in the years 1815–40 roughly one half of *all* British exports consisted of cotton goods. Consequently when Lancashire sneezed in the mid-1830s, all Britain seemed on the point of catching a cold.

Disaster was averted by coal, iron and steel, and the products derived from them. Before we trace the progress of these industries it is necessary to explain how they fit into the pattern of economic development on the big scale.

The early phases of the Industrial Revolution had indeed been revolutionary; and yet they had gone only so far. The pattern of production had in certain respects been changed very sharply; but the economy as a whole was not yet an industrial economy. This is a difficult point to grasp. It may perhaps be most easily understood if we point out that in the 1830s by far the biggest categories of occupation were agriculture, domestic service and building, in that order. These are the activities of an undeveloped nation. And although cotton came fourth in the list, it was really little more than an expanded version of one of the old 'service crafts', like shoemaking or hat-making.

A truly *industrial* economy, on the other hand, is one in which industrial occupations are the most important; and these industries must include some which are concerned with the production of capital, as opposed to consumer goods (say, machines as opposed to shirts). Thus it will be an economy of which the various industrial parts sustain each other, creating and satisfying demands among themselves; agriculture, and not manufacturing, will be the 'service' section of the economy.

This short section of economic theory must be understood before we can grasp the full significance of the developments that took place in Britain in the period between the 1830s and the 1870s. In effect, new pressures both of need and opportunity created (though not quite from scratch) vast new industries, particularly those concerned with coal, iron, steel and their products. These – loosely referred to as the 'capital goods industries' – transformed the basic structure of the economy. Thus it was around the middle of the nineteenth century that Britain became decisively an industrial nation.

Significantly, this was the period of free trade, when Britain relaxed restrictions both on the export and import of goods. It was possible to do this because the economy had become in a real sense an industrial affair; this put it at a bargaining advantage with other countries, who could not possibly turn their raw materials into industrial goods. The success of the free-trade policy was clearly seen in the unprecedented rate at which exports expanded. Between 1845 and 1855 the total went up by 7·3% every year. A large proportion of this increase was made up of the new capital goods, as the following table shows:

	Total value of exports (£m. annually)	Capital goods exports (Percentage of total)
1840–42	55·4	11
1857–59	100·1	22
1882–84	230·3	27

The most important role of the heavy industries, however, lay not in the export field but at home. A large part of the huge increases in output revealed by the table below was swallowed up by the domestic market.

	Coal output and exports (million tons)		Iron output and exports (thousand tons) (inc. steel)	
1800	11·0	0·2	100	33·3
1830	23·0	0·2	740	180
1850	49·4	3·3	2,200 (est.)	1,225
1870	121·3	12·31	6,378	2,965

(Note: figures weighted to minimise short-term variations)

The cue for this tremendous expansion, and the direct cause of a good deal of it, was the growth of railways. This has already been described so it is only necessary to point out here that the railway system consumed vast quantities of coal and iron, in numerous ways. The great numbers of workers required for these undertakings were able to inject their increased spending power into the consumer goods industries, and so there began a rising cycle of expansion. Nor must we neglect the purely financial side; the great manias for railway investment in 1835–37 and (much more important) 1845–47 may have been largely artificial in themselves, and unprofitable to many of the investors; but they performed a very important function in spreading over the industrial field the fertilising capital which had been built up during the previous period of cotton prosperity, but had found no outlets and had consequently accumulated in useless heaps.

Against this background we must now trace the progress of the principal industries often known as the 'old staples'.

THE COAL INDUSTRY 1830–70

Down to the early nineteenth century, coal-miners faced considerable physical hazards in the most primitive conditions. The only significant improvement of the eighteenth century had been the development of efficient pumping machinery to stop flooding. Wooden pit-props were introduced in about 1810, and as a result tunnels became rather safer and less coal was wasted by being left to prop up the roof. However, the risk of underground 143

The dangers of mining in the nineteenth century: following an explosion, a crowd had gathered at the Oaks Colliery, near Barnsley, when the mine blew up (1866).

explosion and fire, an ever-present possibility because of the gases to be found in natural deposits in coal seams, was not reduced until 1815, when Sir Humphry Davy (1778–1829) invented the miners' safety lamp. In this device the candle, or other naked light, was protected by a mesh of metal gauze, which allowed the light to pass through, but reduced its temperature by absorbing the heat. This saved countless lives, and was not generally super-seded by electric lighting until the twentieth century.

If mining became rather safer, though, technical limitations stopped mine-owners from exploiting their resources to the full until at least the 1830s. The best coal was often to be found in very deep seams, but these of course were very hard to work. The spread of pit-props helped, and a steam boring-machine first used in 1830 made easier the task of sinking immensely deep vertical shafts from the surface. About the same year, the introduction of pithead winding-engines made it possible to lift coal without sending miners climbing endless series of vertical ladders, carrying baskets on their backs. A logical extension of the lifting business followed in 1835, when a metal cage was introduced on the Durham coalfield, for moving the miners up and down the shaft; but movement in the 1,000-foot pits that were becoming common must have remained perilous until the wire cable was invented in 1839 to replace the weaker hempen rope.

As a result of all these improvements deep mines became common by 1850 in the coalfields of the Midlands and the North-East. Those pits were ambi-tious affairs, on a big scale, and the great coal-owners were very wealthy men. The Earl of Durham and Lord Londonderry, for instance, each had more than half a million pounds sunk in mines of this type. The investment proved

A whimsey, or pithead winding-engine of a type used in the Staffordshire collieries

well worthwhile, however, since the Northumberland and Durham mines yielded as much as a third of total British production at this time. Elsewhere, the deep pits were still a rarity, though rising demand was bringing about a rapid expansion of the industry in South Wales, especially in the Rhondda.

Some problems still hampered the miners. The deeper they dug, the more difficulty they had with ventilation. Variants on the furnace method of raising a draught had obvious disadvantages, and it was not until the 1850s that steam airpumps and fans became common. Even then, further improvements were necessary in the 1860s. Another major difficulty was connected with the movement of the coal from the working face to the bottom of the shaft. A certain Richard Reynolds had introduced tramways into his Shropshire pit as early as 1767, but the cramped tunnels of the mines at that time made tramways of little general use. Wider, higher tunnels assisted the development on a limited scale of mechanical haulage in the 1820s, but it proved difficult to develop a system which could cope with long distances, corners and changes of level. Down to about 1840, women and children were extensively employed in the business of haulage, but then Lord Shaftesbury inspired an investigation, the report of which caused a sensation by its horrifying revelations. This finally prompted the government to pass a Mines Act in 1842, which banned the employment in mines of all females and all boys under 10. In the next 30 years there were several Acts controlling conditions in the **145** mines. One effect of this first one was that mine-owners had to develop a better transport system for underground working. Extensive railways were laid down and ponies were used to haul truckloads of coal. Kept, and eventually bred, underground in stable-caverns, the ponies eventually developed into something like a special breed of their own. Some were still employed until the 1960s.

The work of the miner himself remained almost unaltered, however, throughout the period. A piston-driven pick was invented in 1861, and rotary cutters were tried in the 1870s, but even if these were practical they were very little used, since the employers enjoyed the luxury of a large pool of cheap labour and the miners were not anxious to be made redundant by machinery. In 1851 the industry employed 219,000 men and the number continued to rise, to 438,000 in 1870. On the other hand, output per man also rose from an average 276 tons per man in 1860 to 310 in 1869.

Many of these improvements represent response to the demands of industry (nor must we forget the rising domestic demand for house-coal). We have seen how important the railways were as a source of this demand; they were equally important as the transport which enabled the coal-owners to move their product all over the country, to markets wherever it would sell. To this day the siting of coalyards beside the railway stations, often still with nineteenth-century buildings around them, is a continuous reminder of the intimate link between railways and coal. The spread of the rail network led to the establishment of a matching pattern of coal exchanges all over the country, where merchants bought from owners, with the intention of passing the coal on to retailers.

Both the housewife and the industrialist felt such tremendous benefits from the coming of cheap coal that it must have been easy to forget the struggle that mining still was, throughout this period, for the men directly engaged. Not only were physical conditions hard and accidents appallingly common, even after all the improvements listed above, but the organisation of labour was managed in a reactionary fashion. In the North, until 1866, miners were still often bound to the mine-owner by a 'yearly bond', a relic of the days when miners had been little better than slaves. In the Midlands a system of subcontracting by men called 'butties' led to many abuses, which only died away slowly, and could still be found in some pits at the end of the century. It was a sign of the depressed condition of miners as a class that payment 'in kind' – the 'truck' system – although officially outlawed in 1831, still lingered on in South Wales in the 1870s.

This suffering was tolerated, or rather ignored, because the rush to produce coal could never keep pace properly with the expansion of demand; now it is time to look at the iron and steel industries which, above all others, devoured

the coal in such prodigious quantities.

The Making of Iron and Steel

It is important first of all to understand some of the process by which iron and steel are made. The diagrams below illustrate the main stages, which are:

1 The Smelting of Iron Ore. Iron ore is taken from the ground and burned, or 'smelted', together with limestone, to remove the worst of the chemical impurities which it contains. The resulting metal is called 'pig iron'. If it is poured into a mould, or 'cast', it becomes 'cast iron'. This is hard and rigid and will not bend, but can easily be shattered by a sudden blow.

2 The Processing of Pig Iron. If pig iron is then burned further, to remove more of the impurities, a more flexible type of iron is produced, called 'wrought' or 'malleable' iron. This is then 'finished' by beating it into the shape and size required.

3 The Production of Steel. Steel is made by treating, or 'refining', the pig iron still further and adding certain elements to it, such as carbon and manganese, to make it especially tough.

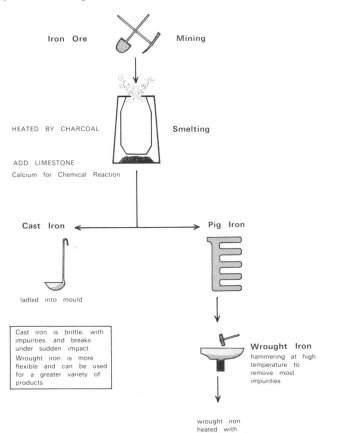

Iron Ore   Mining

HEATED BY CHARCOAL   Smelting

ADD LIMESTONE
Calcium for Chemical Reaction

Cast Iron   Pig Iron

ladled into mould

Cast iron is brittle, with impurities, and breaks under sudden impact.
Wrought iron is more flexible and can be used for a greater variety of products.

Wrought Iron
hammering at high temperature to remove most impurities

wrought iron heated with carbon to make it harder

Iron and Steel Production 1700

147

Iron at the End of the Seventeenth Century

The iron industry was of ancient origin in Britain, and by 1720 its annual output was about 17,000 tons. The main iron smelting centres were the Weald in South-East England and the Forest of Dean. These are not industrial areas today, but at that time their forests provided the charcoal which was then essential for iron smelting. The working of wrought iron took place in various centres, of which the most important was Birmingham. In towns of the west Midlands like Walsall, Wolverhampton and Dudley, small iron products – such as locks, nails, horseshoes, harness, axes and household fittings – were made.

Though well established, the industry was in difficulty by the early eighteenth century. The chief reason for this was that it depended for its fuel on charcoal, which could only be obtained in wooded regions. The manufacturers had not yet found how to use coal in such a way that the sulphur and other impurities which it contained would not harm the metal. The supply of charcoal was diminishing as the forests were exhausted and it was in any case expensive to transport the iron ore to the few remaining charcoal areas. Nor was charcoal even a particularly efficient or cheap fuel.

For these reasons, the iron produced in Britain in the early eighteenth century was generally poor in quality, limited in quantity and expensive. In fact, by far the best iron came from countries like Sweden and Russia, which exported a good deal to Britain.

Most of these problems were overcome by 1850.

PIG IRON PRODUCTION
1720–1850

	Tons
1720	17,000
1788	68,000
1806	260,000
1830	700,000
1850	2,225,000

Abraham Darby and the Use of Coke. Darby (1677–1717), a Quaker, was an ironmaster from Bristol, who moved to Shropshire in 1707. His new works at Coalbrookdale, by the River Severn, were well situated. In the vicinity were iron ore, coal, limestone and wood, and the River Severn was one of the main trade routes of that time. At Coalbrookdale, Darby was almost certainly the first man to find a way to use coal in iron smelting. He did this by first turning the coal into coke. The coal was heated, without letting it catch fire, and this drove out the sulphur, leaving coke to be used for smelting.

This technique first showed its potential about 1709, but it was many years before it was extensively used even at Coalbrookdale, because of early difficulties. But it was gradually adopted elsewhere, and greatly improved the quality and quantity of pig iron.

148

A romantic view of the Industrial Revolution: Darby's Coalbrookdale works, in Shropshire

The Coalbrookdale works became celebrated throughout Britain and it was at the initiative of Darby's grandson, also called Abraham, that the world's first iron bridge was built. It spanned the Severn a short way from Coalbrookdale, and was opened in 1779. It can still be seen today, at the town of Ironbridge, which grew up around it. The iron for the bridge, however, was actually cast by another great ironmaster, John Wilkinson.

John Wilkinson. John Wilkinson (1728–1808) was a neighbour of the Darby family, with an ironworks at Broseley, a few miles away. He, too, developed the use of coke, probably independently, and became so enthusiastic about the possibilities of iron that he was known as 'Iron-mad' Wilkinson.

Ironbridge, on the Severn near Coalbrookdale

His chief skill was in the manufacture and boring of cannons. His firm supplied a great many of those used in the Napoleonic Wars. He could bore the barrels to 0·05 in., which was remarkably accurate for those days. He was also the first man to launch an iron boat, which he did on the Severn, in 1787; he even insisted, before he died, that he should be buried in an iron coffin!

Trade tokens issued by John Wilkinson, 'Iron Master', in the 1780s

Matthew Boulton. Matthew Boulton (1728–1809) was the Birmingham ironmaster who did most to aid and encourage James Watt in the development of the steam-engine. In 1762 he opened his works at Soho, which quickly became renowned for the good quality of its products. Apart from producing steam-engines, Boulton specialised in coin-minting. In 1790 he produced a machine which revolutionised this process, and he took orders for coins from the Royal Mint and from many foreign countries. Boulton was a fine employer, who looked after his men well, and he was a model of the new type of entrepreneur produced by the Industrial Revolution. He once laid on a banquet for 700 employees, as part of the celebrations for his son's twenty-first birthday. A visitor once described him as 'an iron captain in the midst of his troops'.

John Roebuck. John Roebuck (1718–94) started his career as a doctor, but was very interested in industrial chemistry and eventually turned to iron **150** production. He set up his Carron ironworks at Falkirk, in Scotland, in 1760.

This may be fairly taken as the foundation of the Scottish iron industry, which is still so important today. Roebuck used coke and, like Wilkinson, was also a specialist in cannon. His own 'carronades' became famous in naval warfare. He was a friend of Boulton, and was the first to give money to James Watt for his experiments. He was eventually ruined by an unwise business venture, but his ironworks continued in other hands and grew steadily.

All these men were important for expanding and improving the production of pig iron, but that of wrought iron lagged behind until the end of the century, when a new process was devised.

Henry Cort and the Puddling and Rolling Process. Henry Cort (1740–1800) was at first a naval agent, responsible for obtaining supplies for Royal Navy ships and dockyards. He found that British wrought iron was so bad that the government would allow only expensive Russian iron to be used in the metal parts of a ship. Cort was convinced that there was a better way to make wrought iron than the traditional method of heating it and beating it with hammers. He set up an ironworks near Fareham in Hampshire, and in 1784 perfected his 'puddling and rolling' process. The basis of puddling was to stir molten pig iron in a 'blast furnace', together with iron oxide. The oxide combined with carbon impurities to form a gas which could easily escape. Cort was then able to pass the metal, as it cooled, through rollers, which could produce any length or shape. Like Roebuck, Cort was later ruined financially, but his processes, improved by Samuel Homfray of South Wales in later years, transformed wrought-iron production.

After all these improvements, the iron industry at the beginning of the

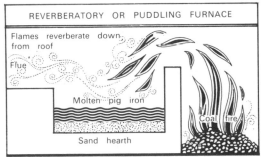

REVERBERATORY OR PUDDLING FURNACE

Flames reverberate down from roof

Flue

Molten pig iron

Coal fire

Sand hearth

Stirred by the puddler

Henry Cort's Inventions

As it cools, iron is passed in balls, or "loops", to grooved rollers, which shape it into, e.g., rails.

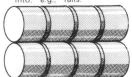

Henry Cort. The original portrait inscription describes him as 'the Tubal Cain of our century and of our Country'

nineteenth century was in a position to undertake a considerable expansion of output. As yet its size was relatively insignificant – in 1802 total iron production was only a little over 100,000 tons for the whole country. By 1850 pig-iron output had reached $2\frac{1}{4}$ million tons, and by 1880 it was $7\frac{3}{4}$ million. Clearly the Industrial Revolution only really happened in the nineteenth century, so far as iron was concerned.

The reason for this tremendous growth was, as we have come to expect by now, a change in the pattern of demand. New uses were found for iron in the first half of the nineteenth century; it was employed in the construction of buildings, ships, railways and machines; and, a little later on, it was converted in enormous quantities into steel, which was itself used to replace all the earlier iron structures – so that iron might in a sense be used twice over for the same job.

Clumsy, often inefficient, strength characterised the beginnings of the nineteenth-century age of iron; this derelict steam hauling-engine was used at Coalbrookdale

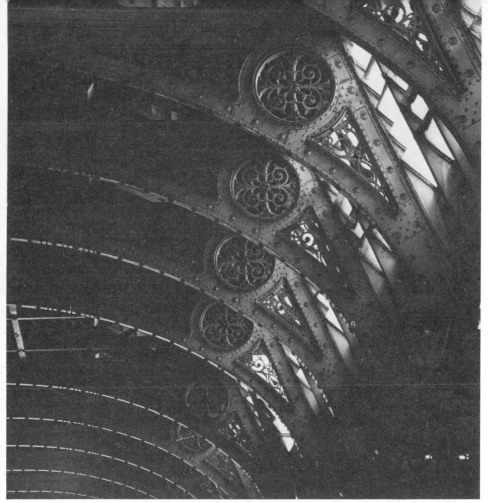

Industry sometimes aspired to produce art: the ornate cast-iron girders of Smithfield Market in London

After the inventions already described, there were relatively few major innovations in the techniques of iron making (as opposed to steel – see later). In 1829 James Neilson, a Scottish gas manufacturer, perfected a process begun by Roebuck, which enabled coal rather than coke to be used in the puddling process. By passing a blast of hot air through the furnace he achieved considerable economies of time and fuel and revolutionised the Scottish iron industry. Previously minute, this grew so that by 1850 it was responsible for a quarter of the total British output. (The other major areas were South Wales, Staffordshire and Shropshire.) Apart from this, the major improvements were connected with the introduction of machinery to various stages of the iron-making process. A good example would be the marvellously

153

The power
of Vulcan:
Nasmyth's steam
hammer caught
the imagination
of contemporaries

versatile steam-hammer invented by James Nasmyth in 1842 – 'capable', it
has been said, 'of cracking the top of an egg in a wineglass at one blow, and of
shaking the parish at the next'.

The scale of some of the iron firms was stupendous, by the standards of the
time. In the 1840s, for instance, Sir John Guest of Dowlais, near Merthyr
Tydfil in South Wales, employed 6,000 men producing 20,000 tons of pig
iron a year. He had £1,000,000 of capital sunk in the business, of which part
was dramatically seen in his 18 blast furnaces roaring together. He supplied
12 British and 16 foreign railway companies with iron rails.

Yet the supremacy of iron was rapidly overhauled after the middle of the
century by the new material – steel. It is to this that we will turn next.

Bessemer converters
working by night

The Development of Steel

It has been explained that steel is really a form of super-treated iron. It is a much more versatile material than iron – it can be made rigid, or flexible, or sharp, or hard – and modern steel has of course been developed in many subtle forms, of which stainless steel is one of the most commonly used around the house. Unfortunately, it is not easy to make.

In the 1740s a Doncaster clockmaker named Benjamin Huntsman (1704–76) perfected a method known as the crucible process. He obtained small quantities of cast, or crucible steel, by smelting bar-iron at a very high temperature in sealed clay crucibles in the middle of a furnace. The crucibles also contained small quantities of charcoal and ground glass. This steel was good for watch springs and knives, but it was difficult to get in large quantities.

Sealed Clay Crucible
Containing "blister" steel and charcoal (carbon)

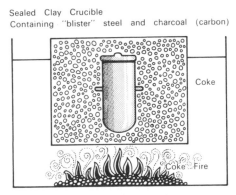

Benjamin Huntsman's Crucible Steel-making
Process

The process hardly changed until 1856, when a professional metallurgist named Henry Bessemer (1813–98) published a paper astoundingly entitled *On the Manufacture of Iron Without Fuel.* This title was in fact something of a publicity gimmick, since Bessemer was not proposing to dispense with fuel altogether, merely with a second heating. He ran the molten pig iron straight from the blast furnace into a tipping vessel (the 'Bessemer converter'), through which compressed gas could be forced to produce unprecedentedly high temperatures. In fact, this discovery was related to Neilson's hot blast of the previous decade. The malleable iron and steel thus produced had certain disadvantages, but these were more than outweighed by the enormous savings in time – steel could now be made in half an hour, instead of taking seven or eight days – and the prospect of mass-production of a material which had previously been almost a precious metal.

A dramatic moment in the steel-making process, witnessed by the Prince of Wales in Sheffield, 1875

Sir Henry Bessemer

British manufacturers, however, reacted conservatively – the arteries of the Industrial Revolution were already beginning to harden. To convince them, Bessemer started up his own firm in Sheffield and made 100% profit every two months for 14 years! He was followed in 1859 by the famous firm of John Brown; the army started using his steel in 1863, and railways began experimenting with steel rails in 1864.

While this was still happening, another discovery further simplified the business of manufacturing steel. William Siemens, an engineer of German origin, but settled in Britain, developed a new type of furnace, which became known as the 'open hearth' furnace, since (like the Bessemer process) it dispensed with crucibles. He too employed the principle of using gases rather than fuel to achieve a heat, but he also devised a way of using up to 80% of iron and steel scrap, instead of iron ore, in the furnace, thus saving on materials. The precise quality of the product could also be more carefully controlled. The only disadvantage was that this process took 6–8 hours.

The last major technical innovation of this series was the work of a Welshman, Sydney Gilchrist Thomas. He was a clerk in a police court, but his amateur interest in chemistry led him to attend evening classes in that subject, and on one occasion he heard a lecturer remark casually that there was a fortune waiting for anyone who could make steel out of phosphoric ore. Thomas set himself to work on this problem and in 1879, aided by the backing of the great Bolckow Vaughan works at Middlesbrough, he invented his 'basic' process – often known simply as the Gilchrist Thomas process. 'Basic' is itself the name of a material rich in metallic oxides; Thomas lined his furnace with bricks of this material, which effectively dephosphorised the molten metal, and made possible the use of a much wider range of ores. He made the promised fortune. By 1889 14% of the steel output of the United Kingdom was made by his process, and by 1939 the figure was 77%.

Iron and Steel Producing Areas 1750 and 1850

By the 1870s, therefore, steel was poised on the brink of a vast expansion, much as iron had been 70 years earlier. Production was still relatively small – about 480,000 tons. But the potential demand, and the capacity to meet it, were both there.

SHIPBUILDING

One of the chief consumers of iron (and then of steel, as it became available) was the shipbuilding industry. The story of the development of new types of ship – iron ships and steam ships instead of wooden sailing ships – is told in Chapter 9. We need not go over that ground here; but shipbuilding as an industry is distinct from 'shipping' as a subject, and in fact it is generally counted among the 'old staples'.

The importance of shipbuilding to a maritime trading nation must be obvious; but the considerable success achieved by British shipyards by 1870 might have surprised somebody surveying the situation 40 years earlier, and for some time to come after that. Contrary to popular legend, British ships have not always been the best in the world. For long periods other nations – the Dutch, the Spaniards, the French and, in the nineteenth century particularly, the Americans – have led the way in marine architecture and aspects of ship design and propulsion. For most of the first half of the nineteenth century   **157** a mixture of laziness and conservatism seems to have kept British ship-builders lagging well behind, so that more and more British trade was actually getting carried in American ships.

The sudden development of the iron and engineering industries, however, forced change on the shipyards around the mid-century and a period of rapid expansion followed. The numbers of men employed doubled between 1850 and 1880, and output rose rapidly. This was accompanied by a shift in the centre of the industry, from the South-East, where it had been focused on the Thames, to the North, the Mersey, the Tyne, the Wear and, above all, the Clyde. The northern rivers had obvious advantages of size and depth; but above all they were better able to draw on the materials of shipbuilding – iron and steel, as these were increasingly coming to be. London struggled on for a surprisingly long time; as late as the 1860s Prussian warships were still being launched on the Thames. But a severe slump in 1866 virtually killed off the remains of this once proud shipbuilding centre.

The shipbuilding industry is, to some extent at least, a rare example of supply operating on demand, rather than the other way round. We may perhaps take it as an illustration of the fact that Britain had now become a fully industrialised nation, capable of generating its own industrial activity from within.

ENGINEERING

The youngest of the old staples was engineering, the product entirely of the Industrial Revolution (unlike all the others, which had existed previously and were expanded rather than created).

The first engines – steam-engines or machines of any sort – were built as unique creations. There could be no question of ordering a Model X – you would have one made specially for you and specially for the job. When it was complete, it would be moved to the place where it was intended to work by a skilled representative of the makers, who would instal it and stay with it until he was sure that it was working properly and that its new operators knew how to handle it. If anything went wrong thereafter, the makers would have to be called in again and a new part made specially to replace the part that had broken. It is difficult to realise quite what this must have meant until we learn that every single nut and bolt was custom-made; not one would fit any other, not even if they were side by side securing the same plate.

From about 1790 onwards a number of great engineers worked to rational-ise this situation. Not only did they improve machines as such, and refine the methods by which they were constructed; they invented machines intended specifically for making other machine-parts or tools. Such devices are called machine tools. The most important inventions were those of Joseph Bramah (1748–1814), Henry Maudslay (1771–1831) and Joseph Whitworth (1803–

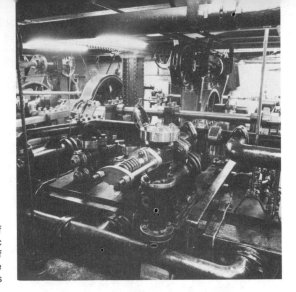

One of the masterpieces of nineteenth-century hydraulic engineering: the machinery of Tower Bridge, dating from the 1890s

1887). In the years between 1790 and 1800 Bramah invented the wheel-cutting machine, the hydraulic press and a number of lock-making tools. Together with Maudslay, he invented the screw-cutting lathe and the slide-rest. This last was a simple device for holding a tool firm against whatever it was working on; it was one of those obvious, practical things that makes an

A hydraulic devil, or quay crane, installed at St Katharine Docks in 1860

159

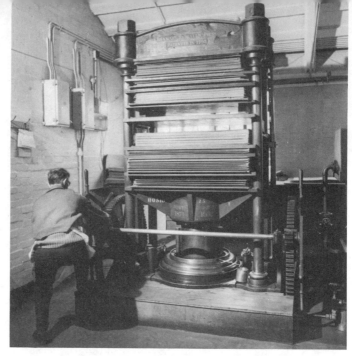

Hydraulic press by Joseph Bramah, dating from about 1800; a fine early example of such machinery, it gave 1 ton pressure in response to a manual force of a few pounds

almost immeasurable difference to a craftsman's work – think of trying to draw a geometrical circle without a compass! The screw-cutting lathe made it possible to cut screws quickly and accurately; but it was still not until 1841 that Whitworth suggested that screw threads should be standardised, and not until 1861 that his suggestion was put into general effect. In the early 1800s Maudslay invented a mortising machine (which suggested to another engineer, Roberts, the idea of slotting metal pieces together). His other chief work was connected with measurement; he designed a measuring machine which was accurate to one ten-thousandth of an inch. This was of the greatest importance in the development of precision engineering and standardisation. Maudslay's work was carried on by his pupil, Whitworth, who produced a machine that could measure one two-millionth of an inch. Such accuracy is hardly believable, and can only be surpassed by modern electronic methods.

The facts about the two measuring machines must demonstrate more clearly than any amount of explanation the superb quality of these early nineteenth-century engineers' work. Many of their machines are still to be seen today, in perfect order, and often doing the work for which they were

originally designed.

Apart from the sheer ingenuity of these inventions, they had the greatest significance for British industry. They made possible mechanisation on a vast scale, and, in interaction with transport developments and the metallurgical discoveries, they gave effective meaning to the expression 'an industrial economy'.

Engineering the steam-engine: a plate-edge planer, dating from 1888; it was used for chamfering boiler-plates

Mechanisation of hand processes: a cold-rolling machine, of about 1890, designed for straightening steel plates warped in storage

THE TEXTILE INDUSTRIES

Before leaving this account of the staple industries in the period to 1870, it is necessary to look briefly at the history of the textile industries. It was made clear at the beginning of the chapter that these played, relatively speaking, a reduced role in the nineteenth-century economy. None the less, they continued to expand, and the woollen industry made tremendous strides to make up for its earlier eighteenth-century slowness in adopting the changes of the Industrial Revolution.

In cotton, the high tide of prosperity was first checked by depression in 1833 and, though that soon passed away, trouble returned on a more serious scale in the period 1837–42. The basic problem was that the cotton industry had expanded as much as an otherwise under-developed economy could bear; 161

but the situation was considerably complicated by a general trade crisis and European depression. In 1841–42 the consumption of raw cotton actually fell slightly. But collapse was averted by the growth of other sectors of the economy, as described above, and the cotton manufacturers, always buoyant, pressed ahead with technical developments and rebuilding programmes. 'Self-acting' and 'double-decker' mules increased output per man to double the previous rate in the spinning-mills, while in weaving the general adoption of the power loom raised output per man two and a half times. (This had one bad side-effect, however, in that it led to unemployment and misery for the handloom weavers. The numbers of these unhappy people were slowly reduced by economic hardship, from the half-million of the 1820s to some 40,000 in the late 1840s. Their despair made them willing recruits for radical and revolutionary movements, and they provided much of the force for the Chartist agitation that disturbed Britain between 1839 and 1848.)

Mechanisation even spread into the one part of the industry which had been almost unaffected by the eighteenth-century changes – it was during the 1840s that the first sewing-machines began to transform the making up of cotton cloth into finished garments. Much of the work was still done by women working in their homes or in small workshops, but the crippling dependence on the hand-worked needle was reduced, with great gains in human happiness, as well as output. One important result of the increasing reliance on efficient machines was a rise in the proportion of women workers – a feature of the textile and clothing industries in general during this period. By 1870 nearly twice as many women were employed as men.

One highly significant feature of the cotton industry during the mid-Victorian boom was its growing reliance on export markets. By 1860 only 20% of output was consumed at home, and the 1872 figure was even lower – 12%. This clearly indicates Britain's mid-century reliance on her position as the workshop of the world (a phrase proudly used at the time). Such a reliance had its dangers, however, as was clearly seen in the years 1861–65, when the American Civil War cut off Lancashire's supplies of raw cotton and caused a crisis in the industry. The danger was overcome by a switch to Indian sources, but the risks of such dependence had been clearly shown and the future had to some extent been revealed.

The development of cotton was broadly matched in its phases by that of the woollen textile industries, though here the picture is rather more complicated. Strictly speaking, there are two sorts of woollen fabrics, namely woollens proper and worsted. The original difference between the two lay in the choice of the type of wool used – in the case of woollens, short-fibred and curly, and for worsteds long-fibred, straight and silky. This difference led to variations in the methods of manufacture, and during the nineteenth century worsted came to be made, sometimes at least, out of a mixture of cotton and wool. The fabrics that resulted were naturally quite opposite in type – woollen fabrics tending to heaviness and possibly to roughness, worsteds to lightness and smoothness. The old centre of the woollen industry was the West Country, while worsteds were concentrated in East Anglia.

Wool as a material is less easy to treat with machines than cotton, and this, combined with conservatism, made the woollen manufacturers slow to take up the inventions of the Industrial Revolution. Consequently their products suffered in competition with the cheap cotton goods. In the West Riding of Yorkshire, however, enterprising businessmen still using the old methods set up a competitive worsted industry at the end of the eighteenth century which rapidly brought decline and ruin to the old worsted centre, Norwich. Then, aided by a great increase in the supply of raw material after Australian wool began to come on the market in the early 1830s, they expanded their operations and took over the orthodox woollen manufacture from the West Country centres, such as Frome. By the middle of the nineteenth century 95% of all worsted manufacturing was carried on in the area around Bradford, and 40–50% of the woollen manufacture.

Mechanisation came to both branches in the 1830s, when power looms

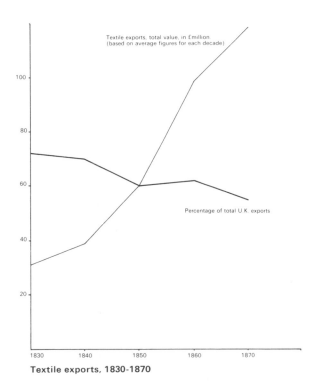

Textile exports, total value, in £million (based on average figures for each decade)

Percentage of total U.K. exports

Textile exports, 1830-1870

spread rapidly; handloom weaving still survived in the 1850s and '60s, how-ever, partly because it was able to cater for the fashionable market in the light worsteds. By 1850 there were about 10,000 power looms (taking woollens and worsteds together), but perhaps as many as 120,000 handloom weavers.

As in the cotton industry, there was a crisis of excess capacity in 1840–42, but once this had been overcome progress was rapid. The 'combing' operation was successfully mechanised in the late 1840s, after defeating the ingenuity of inventors for nearly three quarters of a century. The man who produced the combing machine, Samuel Cunliffe-Lister, became a great figure in Bradford. He like to boast that there was not a man in England who had worked as hard as he had, which may have been an exceptional claim but accurately expressed the common attitude of the West Riding clothiers, and more gener-ally of the industrialists of this period of aggressive mid-Victorian boom.

Thus, although the relative importance of textiles declined between 1840 and 1870, the industries continued to expand. This apparently contradictory pattern, and indeed the position of the staple industries in general during this period, can best be summarised in the graph below. Nothing could illustrate more clearly or succinctly the meaning of the phrase used to describe Britain in this heyday of the old staples – the workshop of the world.

Suggestions for further work and discussion

1. What is self-sustained economic growth? How did it come to Britain?

2. Technical exploration: find out how hydraulic machinery works; how do you set about measuring one two-millionth of an inch without elec-tronic apparatus? How do Bessemer furnaces work?

3. Search for relics of industrial activity in the mid-nineteenth century. How do they differ from those of the eighteenth century? In particular, look at the arrangements for supplying coal to your own town.

4. Further details of British staple industries in this period can be found in Peter Mathias, *The First Industrial Nation*, S. G. Checkland (Methuen, 1969), *The Rise of Industrial Society in England* (Longmans, 1964) and E. J. Hobsbawm, *Industry and Empire* (Weidenfeld & Nicolson, 1968). Use the material you find there to make graphs to illustrate the meaning of the term, The Workshop of the World.

5. The illustration on page 145 shows a pithead engine. How does the haulage system work? Where does the water for the boiler come from?

Book for further reading:

Aubrey Wilson, *London's Industrial Heritage*, David & Charles, 1967.

8 : Labour and Society

Before the Industrial Revolution, Britain's small population was scattered throughout the land. There were few large towns, few industrial enterprises with large numbers of employees. Most men lived and worked in small groups, isolated from each other by bad communications. News travelled slowly and many country people never ventured beyond their own parishes. There was no feeling of solidarity or common interest between men in different parts of the country – little idea of joining together in any way to press for improvements in their condition. Few could see any connection between their own position and that of working people elsewhere. In short, there was no real concept of a 'working class' as such.

The Industrial Revolution changed all this. The population grew rapidly and with industrialisation came a growing number of working men wholly dependent on industrial employment. They began to live crowded together in large numbers in the expanding towns, and to work in larger and larger groups in the factories. Problems were discussed, ideas exchanged, and these began to spread as communications improved. Gradually, a feeling of comradeship developed and the idea of a working class emerged – the idea, that is, of a separate section of society, with common interests and an identity of its own. These interests were quite distinct from those of the upper and middle classes, whom working people were increasingly reluctant to bow down to, or to rely upon. Many began to feel that they could now achieve, by joining together, a great improvement in their social and economic conditions. Indeed, as other sections of society seemed determined to resist change and progress, it seemed as if they had to unite, to create a movement and organisation of their own, in order to gain their objectives.

This movement is usually called the 'labour movement'. It had many different sides. Trade Unionism is the best known. But Friendly Societies, Chartism, workers' educational movements, Co-operative societies, socialism, the Labour Party – all these are important aspects of this wider 'labour movement'. The working class had to be educated and organised in many different ways. In the end, political power itself had to be fought for and won, before the final acceptance of a new social order. These other aspects, however, have all been closely associated with Trade Unionism, and it is to the history of this movement that we turn now. Trade Unionism has been largely responsible for the triumph of the labour movement, and with it the dramatic change in the social and economic status of the majority of people in Britain.

COMBINATIONS

Even before the Industrial Revolution there were some large groups of men working together, and so there were instances of workers combining. But these were usually on special occasions, often at times of high bread prices. In 1727, for example, a mob of Cornish tin-miners descended on Falmouth to prevent by force the export of corn. In 1739 and 1740, when there was particular hardship in North-East England, a widespread uprising took place, led by Newcastle keelmen. These men, who worked on the coal barges, were well organised at times; for example, they struck successfully for higher wages in 1763.

It was not until the middle of the eighteenth century, however, with the changing industrial situation, that permanent Combinations were formed. These Combinations, or Trade Clubs as they were sometimes called, were the forerunners of modern Trade Unions. By 1800 they had appeared in many trades. Sheffield ironworkers combined in 1787, as did Glasgow wool workers; in 1792 cotton workers in Bury and Bolton formed a Combination and this gave way in 1799 to a Society of Cotton Weavers, covering a wider area of Lancashire. Kent paper workers combined in 1795, and there were many other examples.

Combinations usually catered for skilled tradesmen or craftsmen, since such men were in a better position to bargain with employers or hold successful strikes. Employers found then, as they still do, that it was far more difficult to replace skilled than unskilled employees. The aim of Combinations was to keep up wages and improve conditions of work, by bargaining, by strike action, if necessary, and by controlling the number of new workers in their industry. It would be a mistake, however, to regard Combinations as Trade Unions in the modern sense. As the details above show, they were local rather than national in scope, often only on a factory or workshop basis, and their organisation was often poor.

FRIENDLY SOCIETIES

The majority of workers could not join Combinations, but they could and did help themselves in another way. This was done by forming or joining a Friendly Society. This was in some ways an ancestor of the modern Insurance Company, or of the National Insurance System (see Chapter 17). Workers paid weekly subscriptions, usually only a few pence, and in return they received money from the society if they were sick or out of work. The society might also pay for the funeral of any member who died, an important benefit to many poor people. They dreaded that they might have to be buried 'on the

An early 'union card'

parish', i.e. at the expense of the parish authority, in the plainest fashion possible. A proper burial was important to men and women of the time because they felt that whatever the misery they suffered on earth, things were bound to get better after death. They and their relations were determined that there should be a decent start to this new life.

'The Incorporation of Carters in Leith' (Edinburgh) was founded as early as 1555 and there were other Friendly Societies in Scotland before the first English one in the early eighteenth century. They were admirable examples of 'self help', a doctrine that was widely followed in those days, and in the nineteenth century as well. The upper and middle classes were pleased to see working men making efforts to help themselves to overcome their difficulties. Friendly Societies were given official encouragement, which helped them to flourish. In 1793 a Friendly Societies Act gave their funds legal protection, and by 1815 there were over 7,000 societies with no fewer than one million members. Most societies were purely local, but some, like the 'Order of Oddfellows', founded in Manchester in 1810, came to have branches throughout England and even in the Empire.

Difficulties of Combinations

While Friendly Societies grew rapidly, Combinations soon met with difficulties, arising mainly from the opposition to them from employers and the authorities. Employers naturally resented any organisation which might force them to pay higher wages. The government was hostile for another reason: Combinations were thought to be dangerous because they might encourage political agitation. Such feeling reached new heights after 1793 when the wars against France began. Most people in authority were terrified lest something like the French Revolution should break out in Britain. They feared that Combinations could be the basis for such an upheaval. New members of   **167**

Combinations often went through elaborate initiation ceremonies, including an oath of loyalty and secrecy.

Benjamin Disraeli, in his novel *Sybil* (1845), gives a description of such a ceremony. The language used was, perhaps, rather more extreme than that of earlier years, but the form of ritual was the same:

> Mick found himself in a lofty and spacious room lighted with many tapers. Its walls were hung with black cloth; at a table covered with the same material, were seated seven persons with surplices and masked, the president on a loftier seat; above which, on a pedestal, was a skeleton complete. On each side of the skeleton was a man robed and masked, holding a drawn sword; and on each side of Mick was a man in the same garb holding a battle-axe. On the table was the sacred volume open, and at a distance, ranged in order on each side of the room, was a row of persons in white robes and white masks, and holding torches.
>
> 'Michael Radley', said the president, 'Do you voluntarily swear, in the presence of Almighty God, and before these witnesses, that you will execute with zeal and alacrity as far as in you lies, every task and injunction that the majority of your brethren, testified by the mandate of this grand committee, shall impose on you, in furtherance of our common welfare, of which they are the sole judges; such as the chastisement of Nobs, the assassination of oppressive and tyrannical masters, or the demolition of all mills, works and shops that shall be deemed by us incorrigible? Do you swear this in the presence of Almighty God, and before these witnesses?'
>
> 'I do swear it', replied a tremulous voice.
>
> 'Then rise and kiss that book'.
>
> Mick slowly rose from his kneeling position, advanced with a trembling step, and bending, embraced with reverence, the open volume. Immediately every one unmasked; Devilsdust (his friend) came forward, and taking Mick by the hand, led him to the president, who received him pronouncing some mystic rhymes. He was covered with a robe and presented with a torch, and then ranged in order with his companions. Thus terminated the initiation of Dandy Mick into a TRADES UNION.

Such rituals were really designed to awe a new member and give him the feeling of solidarity with his fellows, but they convinced the authorities that Combinations were dangerous and revolutionary. This was an understandable attitude at a time of great national crisis.

It was for these reasons that the government took action against Combinations. In the eighteenth century there were many Acts banning them in particular trades, as many as forty by 1800. In itself this was a sign of how the movement was spreading, but the Acts were not very effective. In 1799 and 1800, however, general Anti-Combination Acts were passed by the government of the Younger Pitt.

These Acts were sweeping, and made it illegal for employers or employees
to plan or take any joint action in connection with wages or conditions of

work. They hit the workers hardest, of course, since no action was ever taken against employers. There were several prosecutions of employees and the Acts certainly delayed the development of Combinations. Despite this, however, they were not as effective as the government hoped and Combinations were able to survive.

For one thing, it was possible for a Combination to disguise itself as a Friendly Society, and so to continue to operate. The Cotton Spinners Association did this, for example, and it was even able to organise a strike in Manchester in 1810, and pay out £1,500 a week in strike money. Conditions were certainly difficult for Combinations, but not impossible.

The Repeal of the Anti-combination Acts 1824–25

In 1824 and 1825 the government took action at last to repeal the Anti-Combination Acts. In the years after 1815 it had continued to act harshly against any demonstrations. As time went on, however, the danger of revolution seemed to get less and less, and pressure for change brought results.

Francis Place (1771–1854) was behind much of this pressure. He was a London tailor who had suffered years of poverty before becoming successful in his trade. He was active in various London radical movements before beginning his campaign for the repeal of the Anti-Combination Acts in 1814. Place worked in association with Joseph Hume, a Radical M.P., and in 1824 the government at last agreed to set up a parliamentary committee to investigate the question. Place and others put evidence very skilfully to this committee, and it recommended repeal. This happened in 1824, and from then on Combinations were legal, even though the law was tightened up slightly again in 1825.

This was a great step forward, but unfortunately there were still legal difficulties. The law was not clear about the right of Combinations to organise strikes, and this right had to be fought for in the years to come. Moreover, there were other laws which could be used if necessary, as in the case of the Tolpuddle Martyrs.

THE TOLPUDDLE MARTYRS

1834 was a year of distress in many areas, especially in the countryside. At Tolpuddle, in Dorset, six farm labourers, led by George Loveless, joined together to try to find some way of getting conditions improved. They were sober and respected Methodists, certainly not revolutionaries. But the local authorities were afraid of an uprising in the district and farm workers, who had scarcely tried to organise themselves before this time, had been easily dominated by their employers. The men of Tolpuddle were reported as dangerous and it was decided to make an example of them. They could no longer be prosecuted for forming a Combination, but it was known that they had **169**

CAUTION.

WHEREAS it has been represented to us from several quarters, that mischievous and designing Persons have been for some time past, endeavouring to induce, and have induced, many Labourers in various Parishes in this County, to attend Meetings, and to enter into Illegal Societies or Unions, to which they bind themselves by unlawful oaths, administered secretly by Persons concealed, who artfully deceive the ignorant and unwary,—WE, the undersigned Justices think it our duty to give this PUBLIC NOTICE and CAUTION, that all Persons may know the danger they incur by entering into such Societies.

ANY PERSON who shall become a Member of such a Society, or take any Oath, or assent to any Test or Declaration not authorised by Law—

Any Person who shall administer, or be present at, or consenting to the administering or taking any Unlawful Oath, or who shall cause such Oath to be administered, although not actually present at the time—

Any Person who shall not reveal or discover any Illegal Oath which may have been administered, or any Illegal Act done or to be done—

Any Person who shall induce, or endeavour to persuade any other Person to become a Member of such Societies,

WILL BECOME

Guilty of Felony,

AND BE LIABLE TO BE

Transported for Seven Years.

ANY PERSON who shall be compelled to take such an Oath, unless he shall declare the same within four days, together with the whole of what he shall know touching the same, will be liable to the same Penalty.

Any Person who shall directly or indirectly maintain correspondence or intercourse with such Society, will be deemed Guilty of an Unlawful Combination and Confederacy, and on Conviction before one Justice, on the Oath of one Witness, be liable to a Penalty of TWENTY POUNDS, or to be committed to the Common Gaol or House of Correction, for THREE CALENDAR MONTHS; or if proceeded against by Indictment, may be CONVICTED OF FELONY, and be TRANSPORTED FOR SEVEN YEARS.

Any Person who shall knowingly permit any Meeting of any such Society to be held in any House, Building, or other Place, shall for the first offence be liable to the Penalty of FIVE POUNDS; and for every other offence committed after Conviction, be deemed Guilty of such Unlawful Combination and Confederacy, and on Conviction before one Justice, on the Oath of one Witness, be liable to a Penalty of TWENTY POUNDS, or to be committed to the Common Gaol or House of Correction, FOR THREE CALENDAR MONTHS; or if proceeded against by Indictment may be

CONVICTED OF FELONY,

And Transported for SEVEN YEARS.

COUNTY OF DORSET.
Dorchester Division
February 22d. 1831.

C. B. WOLLASTON,
JAMES FRAMPTON,
WILLIAM ENGLAND,
THOS. DADE,
JNO. MORTON COLSON.

HENRY FRAMPTON,
RICHD. TUCKER STEWARD,
WILLIAM R. CHURCHILL,
AUGUSTUS FOSTER,

G. CLARK, PRINTER, CORNHILL, DORCHESTER

A public notice issued by Dorchester magistrates in 1831. These were the offences for which the Tolpuddle Martyrs were sentenced to transportation

taken oaths and gone through initiation ceremonies. They were tried, therefore, on charges under the Unlawful Oaths Act of 1797. Despite a national outcry, the six men were transported to Australia as convicts. They were eventually pardoned and brought back to England, but not before five years had elapsed. The case of the 'Tolpuddle Martyrs' became famous in Trade Union history and showed the difficulties that still had to be overcome. The publicity surrounding the affair, however, won sympathy for the victims and their aims, and in future the government was more cautious.

There were other problems to be overcome besides legal ones. Economic conditions were not favourable to Combinations. The first half of the nineteenth century saw long periods of unemployment, during which strikes could not usually succeed, as employers could get other workers. (It has always been the case that Trade Unions are strongest in times of full employment, when employers may be forced to give way in a dispute, having no other workers available.)

Finally, poor communications in the country made it difficult for Combinations to develop on a national scale. Workers in different parts of the country were still unable or unwilling to act together. The labour movement had begun, but it could not really prosper until the idea of a massed working class, throughout the whole country, developed. This time had not yet come.

There were, none the less, some attempts to form national Trade Unions in the years immediately after 1825. The most famous of these was the Grand National Consolidated Trades Union, founded in 1834. Its aim was to cater for all working men in the country, of all trades and skills. It had a brief success, claiming 500,000 members in a few months. Not many of these paid their subscriptions, however, and within a year the Union collapsed in financial difficulty, having spent a good deal of what money it did have in fighting for the Tolpuddle Martyrs.

Robert Owen (1771–1858) was the inspiration behind the G.N.C.T.U. He came originally from Newtown, in Montgomeryshire, where his grave may be seen today. By the age of nineteen he was managing a cotton mill in Manchester with five hundred employees. He eventually became a wealthy mill-owner, with extensive works at New Lanark in Scotland. Owen's main importance, however, was not so much as a manufacturer, but in the ideas which he tried to put into practice. He believed that the characters of men and women could only be improved if the society in which they lived were made as ideal as possible. This is why he spent a good deal of his life trying to establish, at New Lanark and in the United States, model communities in which people could live and work happily; decent housing and all other facilities, like schools, churches and places of entertainment, were provided by the community. Owen was not entirely successful in this, but his ideas were very far-sighted and are widely accepted today. He proved that employers could be human and still make a profit – in fact, humanity paid!

Owen also felt that working men should help themselves as far as possible, and this is how he became connected with Trade Unionism. In addition, his ideas were the basis of the Co-operative movement, in which working men formed societies to run their own shops. This enabled them to buy goods at lower prices, as the Co-operative Societies were not concerned to make large profits, as private shopkeepers were, and if profits were made, they were given back to members in the form of a dividend, according to the amount they had spent. There were several such societies in the early nineteenth century; one was the London Co-operative Trading Society, founded in 1829. None of these gained lasting success, however, and historians agree that the modern Co-operative movement began with a shop in Toad Lane, Rochdale, in 1844. The Rochdale Pioneers, as they came to be called, were good organisers, and their success enabled the movement to spread rapidly.

In 1863 the Co-operative Wholesale Society was established in Manchester, to produce and sell goods to individual societies. A similar organisation was set up in Scotland in 1868, and in the following year the Co-operative Union was founded to provide a central advisory body for the $\qquad$ 171

Left: Robert Owen. *Above:* The original co-operative store of the 'Rochdale Pioneers', opened in Toad Lane Rochdale, in 1844

movement. By the late nineteenth century it had really caught on. It attracted many working people as a way of purchasing cheap goods, without having to pay the profits of middle-class shopkeepers. The dividend was a convenient means of saving, as it was paid out in bulk every so often, usually just before Christmas. Above all, it was a movement which represented a real effort by working people to help themselves to raise their standard of living, in a truly socialist way.

By the twentieth century co-operation had spread to every aspect of retailing and services. Banking, travel, insurance, housing, education, health and funeral services were among the many fields developed by co-operation, which was also popular in other countries. The International Co-operative Alliance was founded in 1895 and helped to spread the movement throughout the world. In Britain it was even strong enough by 1917 to enter politics seriously, with the formation of the Co-operative Party. As many as twenty M.P.s, sponsored by the Co-operative movement, and pledged to look after its interests in Parliament, have been returned on occasion. In recent years, however, Co-operative Party members have been virtually indistinguishable from those of the main Labour Party, with which they always worked closely.

The high points of the Co-operative movement came before the First World War, and between the wars. After about 1942, however, a gradual decline set in. As society became more prosperous, the need for co-operation became less urgent and the dividend less attractive. Early socialist zeal began to wear off and serious problems set in. In the 1960s the Co-operative Union

172

and individual societies started a policy of bringing the movement up to date, improving its image and fighting back against competing forms of retailing. In 1970 there were still 600 societies, with 13 million members and 30,000 shops doing over £1,000 million worth of business each year. Co-operative societies accounted for about 8% of all retail trade, and a much higher proportion of trade in some goods such as bread and milk. These figures show how much the movement had spread, and reflect the importance of co-operation in the history of the labour movement as a whole.

In his last years, Owen devoted himself to the cause of education. He went much further in all his campaigns than even the most benevolent of his fellow employers, and seems now to have been far ahead of his time. Owen was a greatly loved ally of working men and did much to help them in these difficult years.

Better Prospects

By the 1840s Combinations were not much further forward than they had been in 1825. There were about 100,000 members in a variety of small and local organisations, but these bore little resemblance as yet to modern Trade Unions. Yet by 1850 the prospects were brighter. Trade and industry were growing again. The railways were bringing much better communications between various parts of the country. The failure of Chartism was turning many men back to Trade Unionism. The fear of the government and employers that Unionism might lead to revolution was slowly fading. All this meant that a new attempt to spread Trade Unionism might succeed.

The next hundred and twenty years or so saw a remarkable expansion, with enormous benefits for everyone. No one living then could have foreseen that in time some ten million people would belong to Trade Unions: both men and women, skilled and unskilled, professional and wage-earning. None could have foreseen that Trade Unionism would become one of the most powerful forces in the country, with a strong influence over the policy of the government. As if to emphasise this great change, at a dinner held in 1968 to mark the hundredth anniversary of the Trades Union Congress, not only were the Queen and members of the government present: perhaps most important of all, there were also some of the leading employers. This event symbolised the triumph of the labour movement as a whole, bringing changes which have done so much to improve the well-being and standard of living of the people. This is why it is so important to continue to follow in detail the long and often bitter struggle which produced such success.

THE AMALGAMATED SOCIETY OF ENGINEERS AND THE 'NEW MODEL UNIONS'

The Amalgamated Society of Engineers (A.S.E.) was founded in 1851. It was created by bringing together various small trade societies in the engineer-   173 ing industry. Its most prominent members were William Allan of Crewe, who became Secretary, and William Newton of London.

The A.S.E. is normally regarded as the first modern Trade Union. This is mainly because its organisation was very much like that of modern Unions. It was the first successful national Union, with headquarters in London, and branches in the main industrial towns. It had full-time paid officials, like Allan. Control was in the hands of an Executive Council, which was elected by the branches. Most of the funds were kept in London and no strike money could be paid out without the agreement of the Council. This meant in practice that any strike had to be approved by the Council. Membership was restricted to skilled craftsmen or artisans, who were often quite well off and so able to pay the relatively high membership fees. This enabled the A.S.E. to build up big funds, amounting to £73,000 in its first ten years alone.

In its first year the A.S.E. attracted 12,000 members. Despite an unsuccessful strike in 1852, it continued to grow and had 33,000 members by 1867. Others followed this example. The A.S.E. became the model for Unions in other skilled trades, especially those concerned with building and manufacturing. The Amalgamated Society of Carpenters and Joiners was one of these newcomers, which are known to historians as 'the New Model Unions'. Like the A.S.E., they catered only for skilled men, the aristocracy of the working class. They did not, therefore, affect directly the vast majority of working people. There was still only a total of 290,000 members in 1871. None the less, by their aims, example and accomplishments, the New Model Unions had a profound influence on the later growth of Unionism for all working men.

The success of the New Model Unions was due in part to the formation of Trades Councils in various cities. These organisations brought together the leaders of the various Unions and enabled them to work out some common policy and action. There were important ones in the provinces – in Glasgow, Sheffield and Manchester, for example. By far the most influential, however, was the London Trades Council. This was formed in 1860 and contained the

Robert Applegarth

Secretaries of the main Unions – men like William Allan, Robert Applegarth (Carpenters and Joiners) and George Odger (Ladies' Shoemakers). These men and their colleagues were later called the 'Junta'. This word means a small group of men with power and influence. This was apt, as the Junta formed a kind of 'cabinet' of the Trade Union world.

The chief aim of the New Model Unions, of course, was to look after the welfare of their members. They continued to pay out friendly benefits – sickness pay and so on. But they also wanted to improve pay and conditions of work. If possible, they wanted to control the entry of apprentices to their trades and to keep up standards of work. None of this could be done unless the Unions survived, and the survival of the New Model Unions was perhaps their greatest achievement. After the collapse of the first strike by the A.S.E., in 1851, it was realised that extreme action would only lead to hostility and repression, as it always had done. It might even lead to extinction; for the 1852 strike cost £43,000, a sum that could not be afforded too often. Therefore the New Model leaders acted cautiously. They tried to win over employers by peaceful bargaining, to get themselves accepted as moderate and respectable. The pictures of Union leaders of this time give an idea of this almost middle-class image – of well-dressed portly men, with gold watches and chains. Strikes were avoided whenever possible, even after a successful one in the London building trade in 1860–61. Gradually the movement became accepted, and the Unions could become more forceful.

Instead of striking and attacking employers, the Junta concentrated its efforts on trying to persuade the government to grant two things. The first was more factory and social reform. The second, much more important to them, was legal security for the Unions. Propaganda was put out and efforts made to influence elections in the 1860s. No real progress was made until the 1870s, however. When it came, it was due not only to the efforts of the Junta but also to those of a new organisation, the Trades Union Congress.

THE FOUNDATION OF THE TRADES UNION CONGRESS

The Trades Union Congress (T.U.C.) first met in Manchester in 1868. It was not the idea of the London Junta, but of Samuel Nicholson, President of the Manchester and Salford Trades Council. Many trade unionists outside London were rather dissatisfied with the progress which the Junta was making and disliked some of its tactics. Nicholson thought that a national Congress, or meeting, would give all unionists a chance to air their views. This would give an impetus to the movement. Thirty-four delegates, representing 118,000 Union members, assembled at the first Congress. It was so successful that it became an annual event, as Nicholson hoped. At first the Junta stayed aloof, suspicious of what seemed like a new rival to its authority. After two or three years, however, it saw the value of the T.U.C. and joined in.   175

At first the T.U.C. was simply an annual meeting. In 1871 it appointed a Parliamentary Committee to keep an eye on matters relating to Unions during the remainder of the year. Its chief task was to bring pressure on Parliament for reforms. The Parliamentary Committee was replaced by the modern General Council in 1921. This had thirty-five members, all leaders of major Unions, and by 1970 it also had a permanent staff, headed by a General Secretary (in 1970 this was Mr Victor Feather). The T.U.C. has never had any compulsory powers over its member Unions. During the first hundred years of its existence, however, it built up a great reputation and prestige through tact and persuasion. It provided a more or less united leadership and policy for the Trade Union movement. It solved many disputes between Unions, helped to make them more efficient and had influence over governments. In 1969, for example, it was able to persuade the government to

A scene from the T.U.C. conference at Brighton in 1967. Among the leaders shown are George Woodcock and Vic Feather

drop its proposed legislation about Trade Unions, in return for a promise by the T.U.C. that it would do all it could to stop harmful, unofficial strikes. In its early years it was a very loose organisation, but its very existence gave new force to the struggle in which the Junta was already engaged.

THE FIGHT FOR LEGAL SECURITY

When the Junta and the T.U.C. talked of legal security, they meant three things. First of all, they wanted Unions to be given a proper standing in law. Although Unions had been permitted since 1824, their legal position was not at all clear, especially with regard to their funds. Secondly, they wanted the law to be made clear about the right to strike and to picket. (This means to enforce a strike by persuading men not to work. Picketing would normally be peaceful, with strikers on duty at factory gates with placards asking men not to work, or it might sometimes be violent, with strikers assaulting those who wished to work.) Thirdly, they wanted the Master and Servant Laws repealed. These laws gave an employer the right to have an employee sent to prison if he broke his contract of work.

Trade Unions could not possibly achieve very much without a clear right to strike, to picket and to build up funds, free from the danger of imprisonment. Their unsatisfactory status in law was underlined by two incidents in the 1860s. The first was the outbreak of violence in Sheffield in 1866, known as the 'Sheffield outrages'. Some extreme Union leaders stole the tools and damaged the machines of some of the men who refused to join in a strike in the cutlery trade. They even blew up the home of one man by dropping gunpowder down his chimney! These events did much harm to the reputation of the Unions.

The second incident was a decision in the legal case of *Hornby* v. *Close* in 1867. This is sometimes known as 'The Bradford Boilermakers' Decision'. The Boilermakers' Society sued the Treasurer of its Bradford (Yorkshire) branch for £24, which he was accused of stealing from the funds. The judges decided that the Union could not sue in the courts, as it had no legal standing. Individuals could sue. So could companies. A Trade Union was neither, and so it could not. This was serious, as it meant that Union funds could not be fully protected.

So great was the anxiety over these matters that the government appointed a Royal Commission in 1867 to enquire into the whole legal position of Unions. It had a Union representative, Frederic Harrison, as one of its members. The Junta, led by Robert Applegarth, bombarded it with skilful evidence. In the end it issued two reports. The first recommended only small changes in the law. The second (Minority) Report wanted wholesale changes in favour of the Unions. Unfortunately, this disagreement held up action for some years. In 1867 the second Reform Act gave the vote to many working men in towns. This fact began to make statesmen more interested in doing something for the Unions. This was especially true after the T.U.C. Parliamentary Committee was founded in 1871. A majority of the 290,000 members of Unions affiliated to the T.U.C. had the vote, and so it became politically important to meet their demands. At last, between 1871 and 1875, in the ministries of Gladstone and Disraeli, Acts were passed which seemed to give the Unions what they wanted. A standing in law, safeguards for their funds, the right to strike and to picket peacefully – the Unions gained all these. Time was to show that there were still some legal problems, but all seemed clear in 1875. It was a great triumph for the New Model Unions which had shown the way. They had survived. They had grown. Their organisation was excellent. Above all, they had persuaded the government to grant them legal security, without which Unionism could not grow much further. During this period, as well, there had even been some experiments in arbitration. This means the settling of disputes by a neutral person, and A. J. Mundella, a Nottingham manufacturer, led the way in this. Now the main work of the pioneering New Model Unions was done. The way was clear for the benefits to be extended to the working class as a whole. All this, and especially the change in the attitude of politicians, was most important in the progress of the labour movement. Now it could be widened to embrace all types of labour.

THE SPREAD OF 'NEW UNIONISM'

In the last few years of the nineteenth century a different type of Trade Union began to appear, catering for all workers. These Unions became known as 'New Unions' to distinguish them from the New Model Unions. The latter did not disappear. Some opened their ranks and became very much like the New Unions. This happened, for example, in the case of the A.S.E., which eventually became part of the huge Amalgamated Engineering Union (now the A.E.F.) founded in 1921. Others, however, continued to admit only skilled craftsmen. There are still many of these craft Unions, most of them small, like those in the printing trades.

But these faded into the background as the New Unions spread. Unionism had so far scarcely touched the great mass of unskilled workers. Their position, though certainly better than in the 1840s, was still one of poverty – when sixpence an hour was considered a good wage in the docks, and fifteen shillings a week on the farms. There was every reason for more working men to combine together. After the 1870s a great many more did so. There were three main features of the New Unions. The first was their size and scope. They were quite unlike the New Model Unions. Instead of being small and exclusive, they were prepared to admit anyone in the trade who wanted to join. They were the fore-runners of the huge modern general or industrial

Joseph Arch

Unions, like the Transport and General Workers' Union (T.G.W.U.), or the National Union of Mineworkers (N.U.M.). Membership fees were low, so that even the poorest worker could afford to join. The aim was to attract as many members as possible. The more members there were, the more representative and powerful the Unions could be. This policy did mean, however, that the New Unions could not spend much on friendly benefits, nor even on strikes.

There was something of a false start in the 1870s. Joseph Arch, a Warwickshire farm labourer, founded the National Agricultural Labourers' Union in 1872. This had 100,000 members by 1873. It collapsed, however, soon afterwards, when agricultural depression set in. This was a good example of how Unions declined in times of unemployment. Farm labourers had particular difficulty in forming a Union, because they normally worked in small groups in remote areas. Alternative employment was not often available, and most farm workers depended very much on the good will of their employers. There was a surplus of labour on the land, in any case, and so only when agriculture was expanding rapidly did the workers have much hope of continuing successfully. The Amalgamated Society of Railway Servants (A.S.R.S.) also started in 1872, but did not prosper until much later. The real spread of New Unions did not come until the late 1880s. Dockers, miners, gasworkers, seamen, railwaymen and building labourers – these were just some of the many unskilled and semi-skilled men who now became organised into Unions for the first time. In 1871 there had been only 290,000 Union

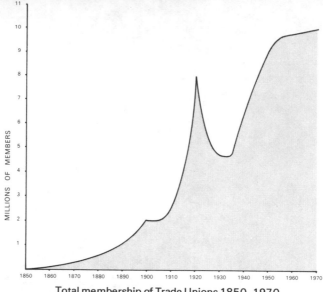

Total membership of Trade Unions 1850–1970

members. In 1901 there were two million – still only a small proportion of the working population, but a vast increase none the less.

The second main feature of the New Unions was the strong influence on them of socialism. Socialist beliefs, partly based on the teachings of Karl Marx, the German thinker, were becoming more widespread in the late nineteenth century. Men who believed in the control of industry and the government by the workers themselves formed societies to spread their views. Two which had a strong effect in Britain in the 1880s and 1890s were the Social Democratic Federation, whose chief spokesman was H. M. Hyndman, and the Knights of Labour, which came from the U.S.A. Most of the New Union leaders were strongly influenced. Men like John Burns (A.S.E.), Ben Tillett (Dockers), Will Thorne (Gasworkers) and Keir Hardie (Miners) were convinced socialists. These leaders were quite unlike those of the Junta. They were mostly rough working men, with little formal education, but inspired with a burning zeal to help their fellow workers and put society to rights. They usually had the vital gifts of passionate oratory and a genius for administration.

This leads on to the third main feature of New Unionism. This was its militancy, or aggressiveness. The cautious and moderate approach of the Junta did not suit these men. They did not believe in co-operation with employers or with the government. To them, Trade Unionism was part of a fight. It was a class struggle, in which employers and authorities had to be defeated, perhaps even destroyed. As Tom Mann said bitterly in 1886, 'The true Unionist policy of aggression seems entirely lost sight of; in fact, the average Unionist of today is a man with a fossilised intellect, either hopelessly

John Burns addressing London dockers during the bitter strike of 1889

apathetic, or supporting a policy that plays directly into the hands of the capitalist exploiter.'

This was fighting talk. The result was a series of sensational strikes which were given wide publicity. Several hundred match-girls showed the way with a successful strike in 1888. 1889 was the great year, however; first of all, the London gasworkers struck for an eight-hour day, and won. This success inspired Ben Tillett and the London dockers to launch a strike which lasted several weeks before the employers gave in to most of the demands. The main demands were for a basic wage of sixpence an hour (famous as 'the Dockers' Tanner'), and for a minimum of four hours' work each day. Two important features of 'The Great Dockers' Strike' were the huge, orderly demonstrations and processions which Ben Tillett and his colleagues organised, and the way in which Australian Trade Unionists sent £30,000 to help keep the strike going, when it was near collapse. This was a sign of the growing international bond of friendship between working men of various countries.

The success of these strikes led on to the main development of New Unions in the 1890s. There were several results.

First, as we have seen, Trade Unionism spread among a much wider section of the working population. Secondly, the aggressiveness of the Unions revived fear of their power and of the possible revolutionary results of their activity. Employers themselves began to get together, as in the Shipping Federation of 1890. This was one of the forerunners of the modern employers' organisation – the Confederation of British Industries. The courts began to look more closely at Unions. Thirdly, a pattern of forcefulness began that was to lead to violence, and eventually to the General Strike of 1926. Fourthly, the rise of the New Unions helped to bring about the formation of a new political party. This was the Labour Party, and its origins will always be associated with the name of Keir Hardie.

The labour movement had dabbled in politics for a long time, though without much success. Sometimes, however, working men had been returned to the House of Commons. In the 1870s, for example, Alexander MacDonald, the Scottish miners' leader, was an M.P. Henry Broadhurst, an Oxford stonemason, even became a junior minister in the government of Gladstone in 1886. But these men were elected and sat as radical Liberals. They were unable to act independently of the Liberal Party and were therefore much less of a force than they might have been.

By the end of the nineteenth century many labour leaders felt that the time had come for a completely new political party, a working-class party which would represent the interests of labour in Parliament. The time was ripe, as after 1884/5 a majority of working men had the vote and were becoming more aware of the potential power which this gave them. In the 1890s Trade Union leaders became alarmed at the growing hostility of the courts, which is described in the next section. The Liberal Party was not a working-class party, and in any case it was reluctant to admit more than a handful of working men to the ranks of its M.P.s. This was the background for the birth of the Labour Party, which was in time to undermine and then replace the Liberal Party as one of the two great parties in British political life.

Keir Hardie (1856–1915) was the first Independent Labour M.P. He had grown up in poverty in Glasgow, before organising the Ayrshire Miners' Union in 1886. He soon rose to fame as a labour leader and was elected M.P.

Keir Hardie

for West Ham (London) in 1892. Hardie caused a sensation in the House of Commons, with his working man's clothes and cloth cap, which contrasted strongly with the morning suits and top hats worn by most M.P.s at that time.

The Independent Labour Party was formally organised in the following year, 1893, and for several years this was the main socialist political body. But it failed to make much progress, and in 1900 it joined with other organisations to form the Labour Representation Committee. This was not really a party, but an alliance of the Independent Labour Party, socialist societies such as the Social Democratic Federation and the Fabian Society, and various Trade Unions, mostly the New Unions of unskilled workers. The objective of the L.R.C. was to return as many M.P.s as possible to Parliament. It was faced at once with a general election in 1900, and so unprepared was it that it could only raise £33 to sponsor candidates! This was a foretaste of the kind of financial difficulty which has dogged the Labour Party since its foundations. None the less, although only two M.P.s were returned in 1900 (including Hardie), a start had been made.

The turning point for the L.R.C. came with the Taff Vale case of 1901 (see p. 186). This great legal case seemed to threaten the very existence of Trade Unions, and they rushed to support the L.R.C. as the best means of putting pressure on Parliament to reform the law. As a result, the L.R.C. was able to field 50 candidates in the 1906 election, and 29 were elected. This caused a sensation at the time, and marks the real beginning of the modern Labour Party. This was not just because it was the first time that the labour movement was represented in any strength in the House of Commons, but also because the first act of the new M.P.s was to rename the party, giving it its modern title of the 'Labour Party'.

Keir Hardie was the first leader of the Labour Party, though he was only known as its 'chairman'. This was because the early Labour M.P.s did not like the idea of a permanent leader, which they thought was undemocratic. In addition, Hardie was an irritable man and a poor parliamentarian, and this helped to get agreement that the chairmanship of the party should be passed on every two years. After 1908, therefore, Hardie gave way, first to Arthur Henderson, and then to George Barnes. J. Ramsay MacDonald, who, like Hardie, had been a miner, took over the chairmanship in 1911. He continued to be the dominant figure for many years, though not always technically leader. MacDonald had been associated with the labour movement from his youth, and had been Secretary of the L.R.C. In 1924 he was to become the first Labour Prime Minister.

The Labour Party, in fact, was in a rather weaker position in 1906 than it seemed, in the flush of its victories at the polls. For one thing, it remained badly short of cash. For another, it was still very dependent on the Liberal Party. This was not intentional, but the result of an electoral agreement in

Ramsay MacDonald   Arthur Henderson

1906, whereby the two parties had arranged not to oppose each other in certain constituencies. This gave the Labour Party a feeling of dependence, which was reinforced by the fact that it was obliged to vote for the new Liberal government's measures in the Commons, since it could hardly oppose the forward-looking Bills which were then being introduced. The Labour Party was supposed to be very much a Trade Union party — indeed, individuals were not allowed to join the party at that time and could only do so through a Trade Union or socialist society. Yet in Parliament, the party often seemed no more than a wing of the Liberal Party which, of course, included many employers and 'bosses'. This unfortunate situation caused bitter dissension among labour leaders, and the more extreme socialists, like Hardie, grew disillusioned with it. Hardie was very suspicious of the younger men who were coming to the top of the labour movement, believing that they were not true working men, and certainly not true socialists. He wrote in 1909:

> I suppose we are in for another year of Henderson's chairmanship, which means that reaction and timidity will be in the ascendancy with disastrous effects to our side of the movement in the country.... There are times when I confess to feeling sore at seeing the fruits of our years of toil being garnered [gathered] by men who were never of us, and who even now would trick us out . . .

It is hardly surprising, in view of these facts, that the years after 1906 were difficult ones for the Labour Party. A major blow fell in 1909 when the Osborne Judgement (see p. 186) had the effect of cutting off funds from Trade Unions. As M.P.s received no official salaries at this time, the judgement seemed likely to ruin the Labour Party before it had really got into its stride, for few of the working-class M.P.s had the means to support themselves for long without income. A tremendous strain was imposed on the remaining funds of the party by the two general elections of 1910, and the finances were practically exhausted.

Fortunately, however, the Liberal government needed the support of the Labour Party after 1910, in order to get some important legislation through Parliament. This legislation included reform of the powers of the House of Lords and a National Insurance Act (both 1911). In return for this support (which the Labour Party was glad enough to give, as it could not face another general election) the government met two of the demands of the Labour leaders – M.P.s were given salaries in 1911, and the Osborne Judgement was reversed in 1913.

The Labour Party was now saved from financial extinction, but it was still in a delicate condition when war broke out in 1914. The First World War led to a deep division in Labour's ranks. The bulk of the party supported the war and were caught up in the enthusiasm for it. Others felt that it was the duty of working men to try to put a stop to the war; indeed, socialists in many countries had been discussing for years how best this might be done. Hardie was convinced that international solidarity by the working class could and ought to have prevented the outbreak of war, and when he died in 1915 he was a disappointed and disillusioned man. He had never thought he would see Labour leaders in a Cabinet helping to wage war.

Yet this is exactly what happened. From 1915 Arthur Henderson and other leaders were included in the coalition governments of Asquith and Lloyd George. Although this move was not entirely successful, it was a great step forward for the labour movement. Its leaders were now regarded as sufficiently responsible to share in government at a time of national crisis. The great contribution of working men and women everywhere to the war effort did not go unnoticed either, and the whole labour movement emerged from the war with greater respect and prestige. In 1918 the Labour ministers withdrew from the government and began to make important changes. Individuals were allowed to join the party for the first time, and by 1920 there were over four million members, though this figure dropped away with the coming of economic depression in the 1920s. The Labour Party was becoming a major force in opposition. As the Liberal Party declined, partly because of feuds among its leaders, the Labour Party took over the role of the principal opposition party. At the general election of 1924 sweeping gains were made. Although not the largest party, Labour held the balance in the House of Commons. When the Conservative government of Stanley Baldwin resigned, Ramsay MacDonald was invited by King George V to form the first Labour government. Many people opposed this at the time, fearing that the Labour leaders were incompetent to govern, and that revolution was about to begin in Britain. But the King decided that Labour must be given its chance. **185**

In the event, the government, without a majority in the Commons, was not a success, and it was to be many years before a Labour government, with real and effective power, came into office. Later developments are part of another story (see Chapter 17), and we can turn again to the Trade Union movement itself, having seen how in such a short time the whole political scene had been changed by the Labour Party, and how, with it, the prospects for social progress had become much greater.

LEGAL DIFFICULTIES: THE TAFF VALE AND OSBORNE JUDGEMENTS

After the 1870s the Unions felt absolutely safe from any kind of legal action in connection with their activities. Their behaviour in the 1890s, however, began to turn opinion against them. It was not long before the Unions were given a rude shock. Out of several legal cases affecting the Unions at this time, the two most important were the Taff Vale and Osborne Judgements.

The Taff Vale Judgement of 1901 was a quite unexpected blow. It came after a strike in 1900 on the Taff Vale Railway in South Wales. The Amalgamated Society of Railway Servants (A.S.R.S.) prevented the company from obtaining non-Union labour to break the strike. The company then sued the Union for damages. Eventually, in the House of Lords, the highest court in the land, it was ruled that the A.S.R.S. had to pay £23,000 damages to the company. This amazed all Trade Unions. No Union could now safely call a strike without the danger of having to pay huge damages. This was an intolerable situation. It did much to speed up the foundation of the modern Labour Party in 1906. The many Labour M.P.s of various sorts elected in that year were enough to persuade the Liberal government to act. By the Trades Disputes Act of 1906, it was made clear that Unions could not be sued for damages as a result of a strike, unless they committed some criminal act, such as smashing up machinery. This safeguarded Union funds, but another shock soon came.

The Osborne Judgement, made final in 1909, arose from the fact that most Unions paid part of the membership fees to the new Labour Party. As has been seen, in those days M.P.s were not paid official salaries, and so money was necessary to enable working men without private means to sit in Parliament. Osborne was Secretary of the Walthamstow (London) branch of the A.S.R.S. He was a supporter of the Liberal Party, and objected to his money going to the Labour Party. He eventually got the House of Lords to rule that it was illegal for a Trade Union to pay money to a political party. This was another blow, as it meant that the Labour Party, which was of great assistance to the Union movement, might now collapse. The labour movement seemed seriously threatened. Pressure again brought help from the government, and M.P.s were given small salaries in 1911 (£400 p.a. compared with £3,250 in 1970). Then, in 1913, the Trade Union Act made it legal for Trade

Unions to contribute to the funds of a political party. Any member not wishing to pay was allowed to opt, or contract, out. Most, of course, never bothered to do so.

VIOLENCE AND THE GENERAL STRIKE

The Unions survived these legal difficulties. Though they were given a severe fright, they emerged safely and total membership grew to four millions by 1914. Some of the reforms they had been demanding for years were granted by the Liberal government just before the First World War. The most notable of these was the establishment of Labour Exchanges in 1909. These helped the unemployed by putting them in touch with employers who had vacant jobs. Other reforms included the setting up of Conciliation Boards to bring Unions and employers together if a strike seemed likely. Old age pensions and national medical insurance also came before the First World War. These did not help Trade Unions directly, but did improve the security of many working people.

The Chancellor of the Exchequer in Asquith's government between 1908 and 1916 was David Lloyd George. He was a friend to the labour movement. Though not a socialist, he believed in social reform and was especially favourable to the Trade Unions. Lloyd George actually intervened on occasions to settle strikes, persuading employers to make concessions. This recognition showed how far the Unions and the labour movement had already come in sixty years. It was at this time, too, that the movement launched its own national newspaper – the *Daily Herald*, started in 1911.

The years before the First World War were very troubled, however. Prices were rising steadily and socialism was getting stronger. Extreme socialists, known as 'Syndicalists', were now preaching the use of outright violence.

Ben Tillett speaking at a typical strike meeting in London in 1911

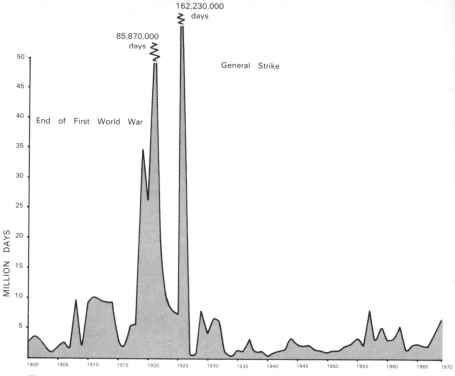

162,230,000 days

85,870,000 days

General Strike

End of First World War

Total number of working days lost each year through industrial disputes 1900–1970

They felt that only a general strike, a strike of all trade unionists, could lead to the social and political changes they felt to be necessary. Working men's discontents were stirred up. There was a considerable response, which helps to explain why there were so many grave, and often violent, strikes between 1910 and 1913 (see graph above). The major industries experienced the first national strikes. Some were successful, like the dockers' strike of 1911. Others were disastrous for the Unions, like the miners' strike of 1910 and the transport strike in 1912. In the former, troops had to be sent to Tonypandy in South Wales to stop riots, and one striker was killed. These events showed how dangerous big strikes could be, for the economy and for public safety. It is only fair to say, however, that at no time did violence reach the level of that in some other countries, especially in the United States.

Then came the First World War. Many trade unionists opposed the war on principle, but very few refused to fight when called upon. On the home front, Trade Unions gained credit for co-operation with the war effort. Membership rose greatly as new workers, many of them women, flooded into the factories. All efforts were devoted to the victory which was expected to produce a fine new world. Partly in return, at the end of the war, the government established some Joint Industrial Councils to bring employers and employees together.

These Councils were known as Whitley Councils, after the chairman of the Committee which recommended them to the government. They did not spread very far beyond the Civil Service and Post Office. An Industrial Court, for voluntary arbitration, was also set up in 1919.

The Britain of 1919 was very different from that of 1914, despite the efforts of some people to pretend that it was not. Many social changes had taken place. Practically the whole population had shared in the massive tasks of war, and the gulf between the classes had narrowed. The social divisions of the pre-war world were not swept away entirely, of course, but they were definitely weakened.

Unfortunately, however, the economic position of the working people failed to improve. On the contrary, after a short period of relative prosperity in 1920–21, Britain entered a depth of depression which was to last for many years, and which was far worse than anything experienced in Edwardian days. It was against this background of deteriorating economic conditions that the labour movement grew restless, disillusioned and bitter. What did it matter that working men and women had gained respect and gratitude for their role in the war, if they were unemployed and near to starvation? To most people the promised fine new world seemed as far off as ever, if not further.

In 1926 the General Strike, which had been feared for so long, at last took place. When it came, many people thought that it was a political event – an attempt at revolution, such as had taken place in Russia in 1917. This was wrong, except perhaps for a very small minority of strikers. The General Strike was certainly the last fling of those who thought that the Unions had to use extreme methods. But it was really an economic event. This economic hardship, and the reasons for it, are described in detail in Chapter 12. It is sufficient here just to state a few facts. Unemployment was always above the one million mark right through the 1920s. In some towns, such as Barrow, in Lancashire, 50% of the working population was out of work, for year after year. Even for those with work, wages were often cut. The worst hit were the miners. Many lost their jobs altogether, as the mines got into difficulties. Others suffered big wage cuts, as much as 50% in South Wales. Other industries – iron, steel, shipbuilding and cotton – suffered less severely, but still very badly.

It is not surprising, therefore, that many trade unionists became desperate. Demand became more insistent for the use of the ultimate weapon, the General Strike, to force the government into doing something to help the workers. Other developments made a General Strike more likely. In the first place, Trade Union organisation had improved considerably in previous years. In 1915 a 'Triple Alliance' was formed between the Miners, Railwaymen and Transport Workers. Each group agreed to support the others if a strike was called. In 1921 the T.U.C. General Council was formed, giving better leadership. After the war many Unions combined into much bigger and stronger ones. Examples of this were the Amalgamated Engineering Union (A.E.U.) (1921) and the Transport & General Workers' Union (T.G.W.U.) (1922), the start of a process of amalgamation which is still going on.

Secondly, the government never really understood the position or aims of the Unions. Part of the trouble was that there were several different governments between 1918 and 1926. Even the first Labour government, headed by Ramsay MacDonald, lasted only for a few months in 1924.

Thirdly, various misunderstandings and disagreements blew up to produce a bitter atmosphere in which compromise was impossible.

In the build-up to the General Strike, the first event of importance came as early as 1921. The Miners asked their Triple Alliance partners to come out on strike. Owing to a disagreement their plans collapsed almost at once on a day known as 'Black Friday' because it was regarded as a tragedy. This broke up the Triple Alliance. The main importance of these events was to give warning to the government. It began to make preparations in case of a General Strike, which gave it the whip hand when the strike came.

By 1925 profits in the mines had fallen so low that the owners were forced to withdraw a wage increase that they had only just granted. This infuriated the miners, who asked the T.U.C. to organise a strike. The General Council made some plans, but at the last moment the government acted. The Prime Minister, Stanley Baldwin, set up a commission under Sir Herbert Samuel to enquire into the miners' grievances. The strike was postponed, on a day which came to be known as 'Red Friday', as the government's action was looked on as a triumph for socialism.

It was a short-lived triumph, however. Early in 1926 the Samuel Report was published, and it was a bitter disappointment to the miners. Although it was basically favourable to them, the Report said that the miners must accept

A. J. Cook

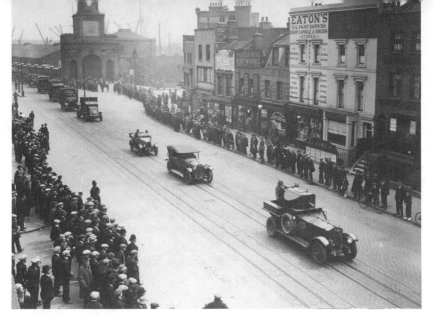

Armoured vehicles escorting a food convoy along the East India Dock Road, London, during the General Strike of 1926

some wage cuts for a time. This was quite unacceptable to the miners' leaders, A. J. Cook and H. Smith. 'Not a penny off the pay, not a second on the day' was their fighting slogan. Plans for a General Strike were revived and brought up to date.

The T.U.C. did not really want a strike but felt that it had to back up the miners. First there were long discussions, between the T.U.C. and the government, which did not want it either. They nearly came to a last-minute agreement, but this fell through, due to yet another misunderstanding. On 4 May 1926 the General Strike began.

Though known as the General Strike, it was never really general. Nor was it supposed to be. The leaders themselves, of whom Ernest Bevin emerged as the main figure, preferred to call it a national strike. They did not want everyone out on strike. Their aim was to call out those in the key industries, mostly manufacturing and transport. It was, in fact, what we would call today a sympathetic strike, in support of the miners. Looked at in those terms, it seemed at first to be a great success. Two and a half million men, virtually all those called out, downed tools. Nearly all remained firm to the end. It was a remarkable demonstration of working-class solidarity.

The strike was managed by a Strike Organisation Committee, which kept contact with local Committees of Action in the main cities, by telephone and by messengers on motor-cycles. Communications and the major industries came virtually to a halt. There was little violence except in some cities like

Newcastle and Glasgow, and this was not serious. In Plymouth, things were so quiet that strikers and police played football against each other! As the *News Daily* said at the time, 'Truly, we are a funny nation.' Police and troops were not used to suppress violence so much as to move essential foodstuffs and other supplies.

This is where Baldwin and his government held the upper hand. Its careful preparations enabled it to keep the country going as far as was possible. Volunteers came to its aid. Members of the aristocracy helped load lorries. Undergraduates from universities drove trains and buses. Only a very few middle-class socialists, like Hugh Gaitskell, later leader of the Labour Party, helped the strikers. The public did not really suffer a great deal of personal inconvenience. The government held firm. It controlled the BBC and put out more propaganda through an official newspaper, the *British Gazette*, edited by the Chancellor of the Exchequer, Winston Churchill. Its theme was that the General Strike was an attempted revolution. Lord Balfour put it plainly in the issue of 10 May:

> It is what I have called it – an attempted revolution ... from such a fate may the courage and resolution of our countrymen save the civilisation of which they are the trustees.

The strike leaders answered as best they could in their own paper, the *British Worker*. But their position, never strong, was weakening all the time. They had never really been prepared to take their policy to the bitter end, and now some lost their nerve. Bevin and his colleagues saw that to go on would do much more harm than good. On 12 May, only nine days after the start, the strike was called off. There were no concessions by the government. Only the miners, bitterly disillusioned at what they thought was betrayal, kept up the hopeless struggle for several more months.

The failure of the General Strike was a great humiliation for the Trade Union movement. It failed because the government was better prepared and stood firm; because probably a majority of the population opposed it; above all, because the English political tradition discouraged this form of direct action.

The strike had several important results. First, it marked the end of the violence and extremism which had been a major feature of Trade Unionism for so long. Secondly, it ruined much of the good work that moderate trade unionists had done in building up the movement. Unions lost a good deal of prestige, and much of their money. The next few years, which would have been difficult anyway in a time of depression, had to be devoted to the task of rebuilding and restoring a good image. Thirdly, the government reacted in a practical way. In 1927 it passed laws banning general strikes and making it more difficult for Unions to contribute to political party funds. These laws

Ernest Bevin

were repealed in 1946. Fourthly, the General Strike, by holding up production and trade, did great damage to the British economy at a time when this could least be afforded. All in all, the labour movement had suffered a great setback, from which it was to take years to recover.

TRADE UNIONISM AFTER THE GENERAL STRIKE

Recovery

The chief task facing Union leaders in the years after 1926 was to revive the power and prestige of the movement. That this was done quickly was largely due to the work and influence of two men; one was Walter Citrine (later Lord Citrine) who came from the Electrical Trades Union (E.T.U.) and who was General Secretary of the T.U.C. from 1926 to 1946. Ernest Bevin (1881–1951) was the other. His career was a remarkable illustration of how a Trade Union leader could become a social and political force in the twentieth century.

Ernest Bevin was born in Somerset. As a youth, he worked in a variety of humble unskilled jobs in Bristol. He educated himself and became leader of the Dockers' Union at the age of thirty. In 1920 he became famous when he put the grievances of his men brilliantly before a Committee of Enquiry. He even brought into the room the exact quantity of food that dockers could buy with their meagre wages. For this, he became known as the 'Dockers' K.C.' In 1922 Bevin brought together over thirty Unions to form the Transport and General Workers' Union, then the largest in the world. As a member of the T.U.C. General Council, he emerged as the dominant personality and took charge of the General Strike. After his work in the 1930s to raise the fortunes of Unions, he was asked in 1940 by Winston Churchill, his old enemy, to join the war-time coalition cabinet. As Minister of Labour and National Service he did excellent work. In Attlee's government after 1945 he was a popular and effective Foreign Secretary. In this remarkable career he had gone from the back streets of Bristol to the Foreign Office.

Citrine and Bevin worked together in the 1930s. They were able to revive the authority of the T.U.C. over the Unions and the Labour Party. At a time when economic conditions were desperate they worked successfully to keep Unions going as far as was possible and to prevent any rash actions which might ruin them. The lessening of strike action can be seen in the graph on p. 188. Unionism slowly regained its strength. In 1935 Citrine was offered a knighthood, which he accepted, a sign of the new social status of the leaders. By 1939 the T.U.C. was again being consulted by the government. Joint plans were drawn up in case of war. When this came, the appointment of Bevin as Minister of Labour ensured that there would be close co-operation for the duration.

The other features of recent Trade Union history came in very different conditions after the Second World War. Full employment and general prosperity as usual meant that Unions were now in a much stronger position, with several results.

New Fields

Unionism began to spread rapidly among people who had so far not been much influenced by it – women and 'white-collar' workers. There had been Unions for women in the late nineteenth century. Other women, of course, joined mixed Unions, especially in the First World War. It was only after the Second World War, however, with more women working permanently, that Trade Unionism really caught on among them. In 1970 there were well over two million women trade unionists. The main issue in which they were interested was that of equal pay – the same pay for both men and women doing the same work.

'White-collar' workers are professional, office or other non-manual workers. Their number increased considerably in proportion with the coming of automation and the expansion of the professions. The first non-manual Union seems to have been the National Union of Elementary Teachers, founded in 1860. Again, however, real progress was only made after the Second World War. Among Unions which were either founded, or which grew rapidly, after 1945 were the National and Local Government Officers' Association (NALGO), National Union of Teachers (N.U.T.), the Union of Shop, Distributive and Allied Workers (U.S.D.A.W.), the British Airline Pilots' Association (BALPA), Equity (the Actors' Union), the Professional Footballers' Association (P.F.A.) and the National Union of Bank Employees (N.U.B.E.). The leading figure in this movement among 'white-collar' unionists was Clive Jenkins, General Secretary of the Association of Scientific, Technical and Managerial Staffs (A.S.T.M.S.). Against considerable obstacles he worked hard to recruit and organise professional men and women, with much success. Overall, however, the number of Trade Union members remained steady — about 40% of the working population, with other Unions losing members as some industries, like mining, declined.

Fresh Legal Difficulties

As Unions grew stronger again, new legal difficulties arose. The courts became more concerned to check abuses of power, and several important cases occurred. In 1961 the High Court found that some communist officials of the E.T.U. had rigged elections in order to win power and to keep it. The Union was expelled from the T.U.C., new elections were held and the communist officials removed before things returned to normal. This case showed up clearly one of the difficulties of modern Unions — the apathy of members. Because so few ever bothered to vote in elections for officials, the communists had no difficulty in gaining control. In many Trade Union elections, fewer than 10% of members bothered to vote, and even fewer troubled to attend branch meetings.

There were also numerous cases involving disputes between Unions and members. The most famous was the case of *Rookes* v. *Barnard* in 1963, which gave the Unions almost as big a fright as the Taff Vale case had sixty years before. Douglas Rookes, a draftsman employed at London Airport, had a quarrel with his Union, the Draftsmens' and Allied Technicians' Association (DATA). When the Union forced his employers, B.O.A.C., to sack him, by threatening to call a strike, Rookes went to court. The case dragged on for several years before he was finally awarded £7,000 damages against the Union leaders. This judgement seemed to put Union funds in danger once again. Moreover, the case raised doubts about the use of the 'closed shop'. This is the practice of Unions insisting that only Union members should work in a particular factory or industry. The 'closed shop' has been operated in a variety of places and jobs, like the printing trades and the music profession. It has caused much criticism as it seems to deprive individuals of the right to join a Union or not as they wish, and even of their right to work, if the 'closed shop' is operated effectively. On the other hand, if a Union succeeds in getting better pay and conditions of work, this usually benefits all workers, whether or not they are Union members, and it is a fair argument that all those who gain from the work of a Union should belong to it. The loopholes in the law, exposed by *Rookes* v. *Barnard*, were filled in by a new Trades Disputes Act favourable to the Unions, which was passed in 1965.

Union Power and Strikes

The Unions made every possible use of their power after 1945. This was understandable. They had behaved cautiously for many years. They were led by men who had suffered much in the depression. Now they were strong enough to press for big wage increases and other improvements. A large number of strikes resulted. In 1946 Citrine claimed that the unionists had 'passed from the era of propaganda to one of responsibility'. Events in the next twenty years made most people disagree with him.

Many disputes were not between Unions and employers at all, but between Unions themselves. Some concerned the question of which Union workmen should join. A dispute of this sort went on in the docks from 1954 to 1959. Others, called 'demarcation disputes', were about which Union should do certain types of work. There were many other strikes about wages and conditions of work, most of which resulted in large gains for the Unions. The more serious of them, like the seamen's strike of 1966 and the dockers' strikes of 1967 and 1970, did considerable damage to the national economy.

Some put the blame on shop stewards. These men and women are not officials of a Union, but are elected by Union members in a factory or other place of work, to look after their interests at a local level. They emerged first of all in the First World War and have got more powerful ever since, as there are not enough full-time Union officials to be in complete touch with all the members, or to know exactly what the problems are in all factories. There is no doubt that the vast majority of the shop stewards are extremely valuable, doing important work on a purely voluntary basis. In the boom conditions of the 1950s and 1960s, however, a few abused their power and defied their Unions by calling unofficial strikes, i.e. strikes which did not have the official support of the Union. The London Docks strike of 1967, the Liverpool bus strike of 1968 and the Pilkington's glass strike at St. Helens in 1970 are examples of this harmful type of strike. It seems as if an ever-deepening gulf is developing between the leadership of Trade Unions and the rank and file members. In the Pilkington's strike, for example, Union leaders lost all control over the situation. Often, the shop stewards have acted in what they

Jack Dash

thought was the best interest of their followers, but sometimes communists, like Mr Jack Dash in the London docks, have been accused of stirring up trouble for political reasons.

Proposals for Change

These unofficial strikes have lost much prestige for the Unions, as they did harm to the economy at a time when Britain could least afford it. The general economic difficulties which faced Britain after the early 1960s meant that irresponsible strikes could only weaken the chance of recovery. Many unionists did not accept that responsible behaviour would lead in the long run to a much better standard of living all round, when Britain had recovered from her difficulties. So long as exports were undermined by strikes, there was little hope of such a recovery.

The T.U.C. did what it could to stop the Unions from going too far along this dangerous path and to exercise a greater control over them. George Woodcock, General Secretary from 1960 to 1969, did much good work and persuaded the Unions to agree to some co-operation over such matters as the Prices and Incomes Policy. Despite this, general dissatisfaction with the Unions led to a Royal Commission, the Donovan Commission, which enquired for three years into all aspects of Trade Unionism. Its published Report in 1968 disappointed those who hoped for sweeping changes. It showed up many weaknesses and problems, but had few suggestions for putting them right. In 1969 the government did put forward limited plans for Trade Union reform, but these were dropped after a long struggle with the T.U.C. In 1971 the Conservative government passed an Industrial Relations Act, designed to achieve a complete overhaul of the whole system.

Conclusion

This rather unhappy period of Trade Union history, however, ought not to make us forget the real success story of the wider labour movement. Using all the means described in this chapter, working men and women have brought about tremendous social change. They have made sure that the benefits and rewards of a prosperous Britain have been shared among the majority of those who have worked so hard to make it so. This has been achieved without the violence and destruction which has taken place in some other countries – a great tribute to the determination and good sense of all those who have worked for this goal for so long.

Suggestions for further work and discussion

1. Find out more about the career and achievements of:
   (a) Robert Owen, (b) Keir Hardie, (c) Ramsay MacDonald, (d) Ernest Bevin.

2. What are your reactions to the passage from *Sybil*, quoted in this chapter? Why do you think that it was necessary for trade unionists to hold such ceremonies?

3. Subjects for an essay or discussion:

How has the Labour Movement helped to improve the standard of living of working people in Britain?

What were the causes of the General Strike? Why did it fail?

How has the Labour Party grown from its humble beginnings into one of the two major parties of government?

4. Select any recent or current industrial dispute and examine its causes and results. How has the dispute affected the well-being of (*a*) the Union members, (*b*) the national economy?

5. Make a survey among men whom you know. Ask them whether they are Trade Union members. If not, why not? If they are, what benefits do they feel they gain from membership? Do they vote in Union elections? How do they feel about shop stewards?

6. The Industrial Relations Act was due to come into operation in 1971. What difference has it made to relations between Unions and management?

7. The co-operative movement has been in difficulties for some years. Why is this? How has the movement attempted to fight back? With what success?

8. Give an account of the life of Karl Marx. Why is he regarded as so important by socialists? His grave may be visited in Highgate Cemetery, London.

Books for further reading:

H. Pelling, *A History of British Trade Unionism*, Macmillan, 1963, Penguin, 1970.
L. Buch (ed.), *A History of the T.U.C., 1868–1968*, Hamlyn, 1968. (This book was published to mark the centenary of the T.U.C. in 1968, and contains many interesting photographs and documents.)

9 : Transport – Ships and Planes

As we saw in Chapter 3, improvements such as turnpikes, canals and, above all, railways had enormous and far-reaching effects on the economy and way of life of the people in the nineteenth century. But the effects of improved transport did not end there. In the last hundred years there have been many technological breakthroughs, radically altering existing forms of transport and creating new ones. Diesel and electric trains, steamships, aeroplanes, motor vehicles, hydrofoils, hovercraft – all these have carried on the improvement of the working of the economy and raised the standard of living of people in Britain and throughout the world.

In a sense, these new forms of transport have evolved naturally from the older ones. Just as steamships and giant tankers have followed naturally from the sailing vessels, once technology made this possible, so the motor car has succeeded the stage coach. Electric engines now haul vast loads at speeds undreamed of by the early rail pioneers. Perhaps only aeroplanes represent a completely new form of transport.

This theme of evolution can be carried further. As the early forms of transport helped to expand the economy and change society, so the need for better and more efficient transport inspired inventors. New, improved methods emerged. It has been a never-ending process of change, and must continue to be so in the future. Transport cannot stagnate. Whatever the means in operation at any given time, they have only a limited capability, and are soon overloaded and swamped by economic and social pressures, unless further change takes place. This is why the story of transport has been so exciting, and so important.

SHIPPING

In order to give a complete picture of developments in shipping we must go back to the early nineteenth century.

Sailing Ships

Around 1800 Britain had an important merchant fleet, dominated by the East India Company as we saw in the chapter on Trade. The ships of the East India Company, however, were not exceptionally large in comparison with those of some other countries. The largest was only 1,200 tons, a size which the Company had found most suitable for its needs. Because the Company

An East Indiaman, the *Earl Balcarres*, under full sail

(together with the Royal Navy) was by far the most important purchaser of ships in Britain, technological change in shipbuilding tended to come only when it fitted in with Company requirements. This meant that important developments in naval design and engineering were made in other countries, particularly the United States.

In 1833, however, the monopolies of the East India Company were abolished, and as trade became more free, a demand grew for bigger and better ships. The British shipbuilding industry responded very quickly and before long had reasserted itself as one of the best in the world. Nearly all important inventions or improvements in shipbuilding in the nineteenth century and well into the twentieth were pioneered either in Britain or the United States. So far as sailing ships were concerned, the most important and dramatic change was the building of the 'clipper' ships, in the 1850s and 1860s.

The clipper was a great improvement on the old East Indiaman. It represented a new design, its main feature being much greater length, allowing improved performance through the water. Better rigging, with wire rope in use from the 1850s, made the ship easier to handle with fewer men. These magnificent ships, truly the 'monarchs of the seas' in those days, were built in both Britain and the United States. Perhaps the finest builder was Donald McKay (1810–80) of Boston, Massachusetts. Many of the ships which he built were sold to British owners. One, the *Lightning*, during its maiden voyage from Boston to Liverpool in 1854, set up what is believed to be still the record for a day's run by a sailing ship – 436 miles. This was exceptional, but when one remembers that a run of 150 miles was considered good in an East Indiaman, the improvement achieved by the clippers is obvious, even in those early days.

The *Cutty Sark*. Compare her design with that of the East Indiaman

Probably most people in Britain know something about clipper ships, thanks to the preservation of the *Cutty Sark*. This fine ship, regarded at the time as the most superb sailing ship ever built, was designed by the then unknown naval architect, Hercules Linton, and launched at Dumbarton, on the Clyde in 1869. Although she was not a large ship, only 963 gross tons, the *Cutty Sark* was faster than any other ship of her time, steamships included (given good winds, of course). She could sail regularly at 17–18 knots, and could also sail closer to the wind than most other sailing ships. These factors gave her a great advantage in the trade in which she was engaged – the tea trade with China. At that time, clippers were used mainly on the Far East runs, where they still had the advantage over steamships. The usual voyage was outward to Australia with cargo, such as iron for the railway construction there, or with emigrant passengers. Until the 1870s there was little bulk cargo to bring back from Australia, and so the clippers went on to China to pick up cargoes of tea to carry home to Britain.

One day, in 1872, the *Cutty Sark* left Shanghai on the same day as her great rival, *Thermopylae*. Quite apart from the prestige involved, the first ship home with its tea would sweep the market and fetch the highest prices for its cargo. So a race began, and the public in Britain followed it with the greatest interest and enthusiasm. Each ship had its supporters, and bets were struck on the outcome of the race. At first, the *Cutty Sark* took the lead, but when next sighted, 28 days out from Shanghai, the ships were neck and neck, with *Thermopylae* only a mile and a half ahead. When better winds blew, however, *Cutty Sark* raced away and soon built up a seemingly unassailable lead of over four hundred miles. Then disaster struck: she lost her rudder, and while she was making repairs, *Thermopylae* went by, to win by a week. It is

The clippers *Ariel* and *Taiping* racing home with tea from China in 1866

interesting to note that the passage of 115 days was about half the length of time taken by Edward Barlow, in the *Fleet Frigate* in 1703 (see pp. 126–7).

Later, the *Cutty Sark* was employed in the Australian wool trade, in which she made several fast passages. In 1887–88, for example, she set up a record of seventy-one days from Sydney to London. The ship passed from owner to owner over the years, until she was finally bought by the Cutty Sark Preservation Society. In 1954 she was put into a special dry dock at Greenwich, fully restored to her former glory, and there she may be seen, the only surviving example in good repair of a tea clipper.

The *Cutty Sark* was a 'composite' ship, that is, of a mixed construction, wood and iron. Sailing ships had no difficulty in adapting to iron and, later, steel hulls. For a long time they could also stand up to competition from steamships, as these had difficulty with fuel on long runs and sailing ships were very economical to run, and this is why they survived for so long. British sailing ships were engaged in overseas trade until as late as 1929, and there are still a very few used in coastal trade. Today, however, apart from these and preserved ships, only training ships like the *Sir Winston Churchill* can remind us of the great days of sail.

Melbourne in 1855, after the discovery of gold, which was a great boost to Australian trade

Once changes in the iron industry had made it possible, it was only a matter of time before wooden ships were replaced by iron, and then steel. Once men like 'Iron Mad' Wilkinson (see Chapter 7) had proved that iron-hulled ships could actually float, it was not long before most mariners accepted that iron was a better material for ship construction. As if to give proof, when the *Great Britain* went aground in Ireland in 1846, and could not be removed for nearly a year, she needed only limited repairs, and served for years afterwards. A wooden ship, aground for that length of time, would probably have been totally destroyed.

It was more difficult, however, to adapt steam power for practical use in ships. There were many experiments, in Britain and in the United States, as the enormous value of success could easily be seen. Which steamboat first ran successfully is a matter of dispute, but in 1802 the *Charlotte Dundas* certainly ran reliably on the Forth–Clyde Canal in Scotland. From 1807 steamboats were making regular passages up the Hudson River in the United States, and in 1819 the *Savannah* crossed the Atlantic, using steam power for part of the voyage. The first ship to cross the Atlantic using steam power all the way was the *Sirius* in 1838. To begin with, steam was seen as an auxiliary form of power, to be used when winds were unfavourable. Later, sails were carried for emergency or supporting power, and it was not until quite late in the nineteenth century that steam power became reliable and efficient enough to be used alone.

A model of the *Charlotte Dundas*, one of the earliest steam-boats

203

The *Great Britain* being raised on a pontoon in the Falkland Islands, before being towed to Bristol in 1970

Only a few hours after the *Sirius*, in 1838, the *Great Western* reached New York, having crossed under steam power. She was the first of three great steamships built by Isambard Kingdom Brunel. This famous engineer was mentioned earlier as the architect of some of Britain's most important railways and bridges. He worked mainly for the Great Western Railway Company, and had the idea of a continuous route from London to New York, via Plymouth, using steam power all the way. It was a grand vision, and although his later ships were fated with bad luck, the *Great Western* was extremely successful and Brunel must be remembered as one of the most important ship designers of the nineteenth century.

Brunel's second ship, the *Great Britain*, was launched at Bristol in 1843. It was the largest iron ship built up to that time, and the first ocean-going ship to be constructed entirely of iron. More important, it was the first to use screw propulsion, instead of paddles. This was not Brunel's invention, but he was the first to have sufficient faith in it to use it in a large ship. Mechanically, the *Great Britain* was a highly successful ship, but she proved uneconomical in service. She also suffered unfortunate accidents, such as the grounding in Ireland in 1846, mentioned earlier. Like the *Cutty Sark*, she had a chequered career later on, before being abandoned finally in the Falkland Islands in 1886. This was not the end of her, however, for in 1970 she was repaired sufficiently to enable her to be towed to Bristol, where it was hoped to restore her in the yard where she was built, and to preserve her, not far from one of Brunel's other masterpieces, the Clifton Suspension Bridge.

Brunel's last great ship, the *Great Eastern*, was a disaster. This was a gigantic vessel of 18,914 tons displacement, and easily the largest ship ever built up to that time. In fact, the *Great Eastern* was six times the size of any existing ship, and it was to be many years before a larger one was constructed. Naturally, she attracted enormous attention, and created much controversy. She was built on the Thames, at the Isle of Dogs, Millwall, where she became a familiar sight, attracting thousands of visitors, and gradually dominating the skyline. Mariners sailing to and from London passed within a few hundred yards of what was intended to be the greatest ship in the world, in all senses of the word.

But the ship was dogged by ill fortune, though construction work went smoothly enough considering the enormous problems involved. Because of her size, the *Great Eastern* was given a double hull for additional strength. This was a new method, and it is still the practice in shipbuilding today. The ship required three million rivets, and it took two hundred rivet gangs nearly three years to fit them. Considering the number of men involved, and the dangers, it was a reflection of Brunel's safety precautions that only a handful of men were killed. One worker fell to his death between the two hulls, and an unproved legend has it that he was never found, until in 1889, when the ship was broken up, his skeleton was discovered by terrified dockers. One visitor to the ship was particularly unlucky. He was 'prying about' and was 'bending over the head of a pile, when the monkey [hammer] came down, flattening his head'.

Isambard Kingdom Brunel standing in front of one of the cables which helped to launch the *Great Eastern* in 1857

Such accidents were unfortunate, but not unexpected. The real trouble arose from a constant lack of funds and continual interference with the work by the directors of the company which had ordered the ship. This rose to a climax at the launching, which was a tragic affair. Brunel had worked night and day for several years on this project, and the strain involved in the last few months ruined his health. Because the ship was seven hundred feet long, and the Thames is narrow at Millwall, it had been decided to construct the ship, and launch her, sideways on to the river. This was an entirely untried method, with a ship of unprecedented size. The launch presented problems which taxed the abilities of even such an experienced engineer as Brunel. He needed luck and general co-operation, if all was to go well. James Dugan, in his book *The Great Iron Ship*, has given the following graphic account of what happened, based on descriptions written at the time:

> The ship lay on two timber cradles, which rested on 120 iron rollers, placed across 160 railway rails, supported on a two foot layer of concrete, in which were embedded two thousand timber piles driven thirty feet through mud to the gravel base of the Thames. She lay 330 feet from the high-tide mark, on an incline of one in twelve feet. As the last plates were riveted in September, 1857, there arose a speculation and a clamour for the launching date. Brunel reminded the directors that he would have to have adequate power to get her into the water. The *Great Eastern* was the heaviest object that man had attempted to move.
>
> To overcome her twelve thousand inert tons, Brunel would need sufficient hydraulic rams to push her, steam tugs on the river to pull her, gigantic steam winches on shore to let her down the ways and huge windlasses to check the mass when it slid too fast, operations which would require miles of massive chain cable. The directors borrowed chains from the Admiralty and gathered tugs and winches, but gave Brunel only two small hydraulic rams. Despite misgivings, Brunel announced the launching for November 3, 1857, when the ship could be floated on a rising tide.

Brunel expected the launch to take place with only a few privileged spectators, for he needed absolute silence if the complicated task was to be carried out safely. But without his knowledge the directors issued thousands of tickets, and over ten thousand people from all walks of life were present on the great day:

> A clerk stood at each launching cradle with a blackboard to record her movements for Brunel; no voice could be heard above the crowd. The engineer waved his white flag to release the bow and stern fastenings, and to slack off chain on the two drums that were to check the slide. The mighty ship gave a shuddering rumble, and stood and groaned for ten minutes, a convulsion so majestic that people were knocked dumb. The very mud beneath them quaked.
>
> 'She moves!' they yelled. 'She moves!' The stern slid three inches. Brunel

This view of the launching of the *Great Eastern* shows the enormous size of the ship and the complicated arrangements for launching her

waved his red flag for the hydraulic rams to push. There was a scraping squeal, the earth shook, and the *Great Eastern* started to slide. Among the thousands who simply stood and sighed was the gang on the sixty-ton stern checking drum. The ship took up the slack of their chain and sent the windlass spinning in reverse. The huge handlebars caught a dozen workers and threw them above the heads of the crowd. Spectators and workers ran in panic, except for Brunel and the foreman of the forward drum crew, Ned Hepworth, a Yorkshire yeoman shipwright, who applied his brake. The ship stopped with a horrible complaint of iron. The crews of the river barges lost their heads and leaped into the river.

Five men were carried off, of whom two died. Brunel couldn't find the frightened barge crews. He ordered the lighters to be cut out of the river organisation and went on with steam tugs alone. The crowd was readily cleared from the launching gear as Brunel organized another attempt. A heavy rain began to fall. He signalled the tugs to take up bow and stern tackle, and started the steam winches and hydraulic rams. The ship would not move. The *Great Eastern* groaned and grumbled, inert and motionless. The bow winch stripped its gears. Chains snapped and flailed links as thick as a man's arm at screaming, running people. Brunel signalled the end of the day's efforts.

It took three more months to launch the ship. Vast amounts of equipment were brought in, and much of it was wrecked. Eventually, on 31 January 1858, the *Great Eastern* was afloat. It is interesting to note that, though the ship herself never recovered from these early misfortunes, the designer of the launching rams – Sir Richard Tangye – made his fortune and laid the basis of **207** prosperity for his company. As the company was to say later, 'We launched the *Great Eastern* and the *Great Eastern* launched us!'

Brunel died soon after these events, and he was perhaps fortunate not to see the later fate of the ship. She could have been profitable only on the Far Eastern runs for which she was designed. But the *Great Eastern* was never put into service in the Far East. She proved most unprofitable on the route to New York, and became a huge 'white elephant'. For a time she was used as a cable-laying ship, and actually laid the first Atlantic cable in 1866, before being sold eventually for scrap. It was a sad end for such a magnificent conception.

Men aboard the *Great Eastern* prepare to recover a broken cable during the laying of the Atlantic telegraph in 1865–66

The trouble with many of the early steamships was that they were so expensive to run. Fuel costs were very high, and so it was profitable to use them only on relatively short runs. This is why sailing ships remained in business for so long, especially on the Far Eastern voyages. Not only was it too expensive to use steam for all that great distance, but it was physically impossible to carry sufficient coal. It was estimated that in the mid-nineteenth century a ship could only carry enough coal for a voyage to Australia if it used all its cargo space! Sailing ships boasted of their 'free coal' (wind), and kept this advantage until several changes combined to bring about their extinction.

One was the opening of the Suez Canal in 1869, which cut the route to Australia by several thousand miles. Coaling stations were gradually set up along the route to enable ships to carry less coal. Merchants became more and more attracted by the regularity of steamship services. Above all, **208** technical improvements finally overcame remaining disadvantages.

The opening of the Suez Canal in 1869. The canal was an enormous help
to trade in the East, and after 1875, Britain owned nearly half the shares

TECHNICAL IMPROVEMENTS IN PROPULSION AND NAVIGATION

After screw propulsion, the next vital invention was the compound expansion engine, developed in Britain by John Elder in 1854. This employed a
second cylinder where steam was used at lower pressure after it had done its
work in the first. Later, a triple expansion engine was produced, and finally a
quadruple expansion engine. These engines achieved a remarkable saving in
fuel costs. As steam was used four times, much less coal was needed. By the
end of the century 1 lb. of coal per horse-power per hour was required,
compared with about 5 lbs. in 1850.

In 1894 Sir Charles Parsons (1854–1931) invented a more efficient
engine, the turbine. This engine works on roughly the same principle as a
windmill. Just as wind moves the sails to drive the machinery of a windmill,
so the turbine uses steam operating on a series of blades to create a rotary
action. In the case of a ship, this action drives the screw propellers, and
Parsons found it to be an excellent means of propulsion. In order to attract
attention, he took his trial ship, the *Turbinia*, to the Naval Review at Spithead
in 1897, and suddenly appeared among the fleet travelling at the astounding
speed of 34 knots. One can imagine the consternation of the naval authorities,
who were reluctant to accept any technical change. The dignity of the
occasion was quite ruined by the small vessel darting in and out of the huge
ships drawn up so impressively in review order! The *Turbinia* easily outpaced
the despairing guardships which tried to head her off, and she more than
proved her point. It was some years before various snags were ironed out, but
the turbine, using gases rather than steam, and modified in more recent years,
was to become widely used. After the First World War, diesel engines came
into use, and a great many vessels are now powered in this way. In the late
1950s the first nuclear powered ships appeared, and it seems likely that more

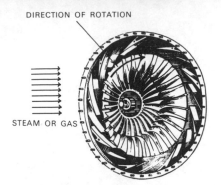

DIRECTION OF ROTATION

STEAM OR GAS

The pressure of steam or gas on the turbine-fans rotates the engine, which is connected by a shaft to a propeller

How a ship's turbine works

and more will be built, if the capital costs (of construction) are reduced. Navigation became much more reliable once a means had been discovered in the eighteenth century of determining longitude at sea. But it was still not wholly reliable until the twentieth century, in which important new techniques have been invented. Probably the most useful of these are the gyrocompass, first produced in 1908, which enables a ship to steer an absolutely accurate course; radar, which enables obstructions to be seen at night or in poor visibility; and the Decca navigating device, by means of which a ship (or aircraft) can determine its position to within a hundred metres. These last two inventions were developed in Britain during the Second World War. They have not replaced old navigating methods, but added greatly to their reliability. Unfortunately, the growth in the volume of shipping, and in the size and speed of ships, has meant that even these devices have not prevented a rising number of collisions and other mishaps at sea.

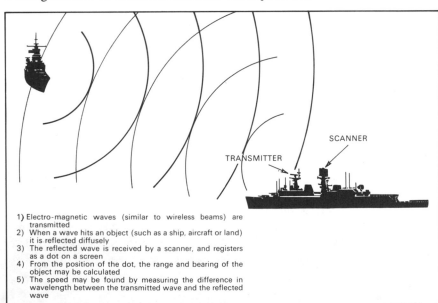

SCANNER

TRANSMITTER

1) Electro-magnetic waves (similar to wireless beams) are transmitted
2) When a wave hits an object (such as a ship, aircraft or land) it is reflected diffusely
3) The reflected wave is received by a scanner, and registers as a dot on a screen
4) From the position of the dot, the range and bearing of the object may be calculated
5) The speed may be found by measuring the difference in wavelength between the transmitted wave and the reflected wave

210

How radar works

Larger Ships

All the new forms of propulsion and navigation, described above, have been fitted into larger and larger ships. For many years the largest ships, like the *Great Britain*, were passenger ships. Before aeroplanes provided an alternative, ships were, of course, the only means of travelling overseas. As early as 1840 Samuel Cunard founded his famous transatlantic shipping line, providing regular services to a fixed timetable. The quicker passages and more comfortable conditions attracted a growing number of passengers, and other companies followed. In time, very large ships indeed were built for the passenger service. Not all were British, by any means – French, American and German shipping lines ordered huge ships. None the less, three British liners won a commanding position in the transatlantic service. These were the *Mauretania* (31,000 tons), launched in 1906; the *Queen Mary* (81,235 tons) in 1934, and the *Queen Elizabeth* (83,673 tons) in 1938. Today, however, such ships seem to be outdated, as air transport offers so many advantages. Those which remain, and new ones built, like the *Queen Elizabeth II*, are engaged more and more in cruises, rather than regular runs. The *Queen Mary* and *Queen Elizabeth* were both sold to new American owners, for use as floating conference and exhibition centres in the United States. In 1970 the *Queen Elizabeth* was resold, to be used in Hong Kong as a floating University.

While the days of the large passenger ships now seem numbered, this is certainly not true of cargo vessels. Inevitably the passenger liners have attracted most publicity over the years, and were very profitable until quite recently. Economically, however, cargo ships have always been of greater importance for Britain. We have seen how much Britain depended on trade,

The *Queen Elizabeth II* going down the Clyde after her launching in 1969. She is the most recent of many famous passenger ships built on the Clyde

on imports of food and raw materials, and exports of manufactured goods, in the nineteenth century. This has been equally true since, with imports of finished products having a greater role. The health of Britain's economy has always depended to a large extent on a thriving overseas trade, and this in turn has relied on a strong and reliable shipping service.

In the nineteenth century Britain's merchant marine was so strong that it carried not only the British trade but also goods for other countries. A large profit was made in this way, and London became the centre of the world's shipping business for a time. Although this position has changed, some parts of it, like shipping insurance, remain strong.

In both the First and Second World Wars merchant ships played a vital role in keeping Britain and her allies supplied with essential goods. A great many ships and lives were lost. In the First World War alone, nearly eight million tons of British shipping were lost, mainly sunk by the Germans during their blockade of trade to and from Britain and the colonies. This loss was quickly made up after the war, but unfortunately world trade suffered a setback and British shipowners were in difficulty until the later 1930s. A number of ships had to be scrapped, as there was just not enough freight to go round.

Since the Second World War this problem has disappeared, and British-owned vessels again play an important role in world trade. Although aircraft carry a growing quantity of freight, it seems impossible for them ever to carry sufficient cargo cheaply enough to replace ships. New types of cargo ship have appeared. Giant tankers, some now over 200,000 tons displacement, carry oil, gases and chemicals from one specially prepared port to another.

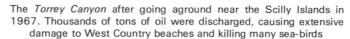

The *Torrey Canyon* after going aground near the Scilly Islands in 1967. Thousands of tons of oil were discharged, causing extensive damage to West Country beaches and killing many sea-birds

The dangers of these vast ships were seen in 1967 when the *Torrey Canyon* went aground on rocks near the Scilly Islands, disgorging thousands of tons of oil, and seriously damaging beaches for hundreds of miles along the coast. In 1970 a similar disaster was only narrowly averted when the *Pacific Glory*, laden with 70,000 tons of oil, was involved in a collision off the Isle of Wight. Oil pollution seems likely to be one of the greatest maritime problems of the future.

Container ships, in which cargo is packed in regular containers for easy handling, are coming into use. Other new ideas include sea-going barges, towing containers behind them, for simple transhipment at river ports. Computers are transforming problems of handling cargo, and the time seems to be approaching when the crews of large vessels will be reduced to the role of supervisors of sophisticated electronic equipment.

Of course, such ships are still the exception rather than the rule. Small tramp steamers still ply from port to port, picking up cargo where they can, and the traditional methods will be used for many years to come. But in shipping the future is clear – the importance of men is being reduced and the machine is taking over, a process which we can now see repeated in other forms of transport.

HYDROFOILS AND HOVERCRAFT

After the Second World War two new forms of water transport were developed, each with considerable potential for the future.

The hydrofoil is a ship with underwater wings which lift the vessel clear of

British Rail's hovercraft *Princess Margaret*. This is an example of the many hovercraft now in service between Britain and the Continent

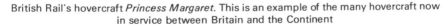

213

the water at the bows when travelling at speed. This cuts down friction and permits very fast speeds, in excess of fifty knots. Hydrofoils were developed in Germany and Italy, and have come into widespread use, mainly as passenger ferries. Few have come into service in Britain, however, possibly because a hydrofoil is limited to a certain size for technical reasons, and because it can only operate in reasonably good water conditions. It is best suited to lakes and rivers, and, unlike some Scandinavian countries, for example, Britain has few of these large enough to justify a hydrofoil service. The use of the hydrofoil for cargo seems unlikely.

The hovercraft was a British invention, though like some other British inventions of the post-war period it took a long time to gain recognition and support, with the result that other countries have been able to take advantage of it. The hovercraft is technically an aeroplane, since it travels on a cushion of air a few feet above the land or water. The inventor was Sir Christopher Cockerell, whose prototype SRN 1 crossed the English Channel in 1959. After a long struggle, the government eventually appreciated the potential of the machine, and gave financial support. The hovercraft soon attracted great interest. Its principal advantage lies in the fact that it is amphibious. It can travel over both land and water, and is thus ideal for use in difficult marshy country, as well as ordinary terrain and water. Hovercraft are now coming into service all over the world – mainly for passenger or military purposes. They have proved especially well suited for use as car ferries – across the English Channel and to various islands. The size of a hovercraft does not seem limited by technical factors, as is the case with a hydrofoil, and as larger ones are developed there should be no reason why hovercraft should not be used more and more for carrying freight.

AIRCRAFT

Man's conquest of the air has produced a spectacular advance in transport. Even though it was only in 1903 that an aircraft first flew under its own power, development since then has been so rapid that today aircraft capable of carrying hundreds of passengers at twice the speed of sound are being successfully tested. The scale of speed exceeds even the wildest dreams of the early pioneers of flight. Even space flight has become a reality, though not yet for passengers. In this dramatic development, British science and technology have played a full part.

Early Flight: Balloons and Airships

It has always been man's ambition to fly like the birds. From earliest time there were experiments, nearly all of the 'flapping-wing' variety. Most people know the legend of Icarus, who flew too close to the sun. There were many others who perished, though not for the same reason! This form of experi-

A balloon ascent at Vauxhall Gardens, London, 1849. Such ascents were very popular attractions

ment could never succeed, as man is simply not equipped with muscles sufficiently strong to operate wings big enough to lift his weight. By the eighteenth century, therefore, attention turned to balloons filled with hot air and then hydrogen, to make them lighter than air. At a surprisingly early date, 1783, such balloons flew successfully in France, and they came into wide use in the nineteenth century. In Britain they were used mainly for recreation, until it was discovered that they had a military use – for reconnaissance, sighting for artillery, even for bombing raids. In the World Wars, of course, fixed balloons were valuable as anti-aircraft barrages.

The airship R 100 under construction. The figures in the foreground give an idea of the size of the structure, which looks rather like a modern spaceship

215

The balloon as such could hardly be called a form of transport, however, until it was provided with a motive power of its own to make it more reliable and manoeuvrable. In 1903 the first practical airship was launched. Much of the early work was done in Germany by Count Zeppelin, who gave his name to the airships which did some damage to London during the First World War. The success of these machines encouraged other countries to build them. In Britain airships were built with government aid, and for a time were extremely successful. In 1919 the R34 made the first crossing of the Atlantic, from Scotland to New York. This flight heralded a boom period for airships, and many passenger flights were made, the airships being fitted with comfortable accommodation. However, there was always a fear that disaster might strike, with the inflammable gases on board. This unfortunately happened in 1931. The R101, on its maiden flight to India, crashed at Beauvais in France. There was a great loss of life, including several important government and aviation officials. Although an enquiry showed that the accident was due to a fault in design, this disaster caused the government to abandon all manufacture of airships, and public confidence waned. The airship was dead in Britain. This did not matter too much, as the future of aviation clearly lay in another direction. Airships had advantages, but they were slow and unwieldy. Heavier than air machines were eventually fast and manoeuvrable, and made airships obsolete.

Early Days of Powered Flight

Although the first successful trials of heavier than air machines flying under their own power were made in the United States, Britain may claim to have played a vital part in pioneering work. Sir George Cayley (1773–1857) was the first to understand fully the principles of powered flight, and his researches were invaluable. As early as 1866 the Aeronautical Society (now the Royal Aeronautical Society) was founded, and it conducted many important experiments.

The Wright Brothers making the first powered flight at Kitty Hawk in the United States, in 1903

Louis Blériot and his aeroplane, after becoming the first man to fly the Channel in 1909

The American brothers Wilbur and Orville Wright, however, succeeded first in actually flying a machine. On 17 December 1903 their craft flew for periods of between twelve and fifty-nine seconds, at Kitty Hawk, North Carolina. Later, Wilbur Wright came to Europe, and his exhibitions of improved aircraft captured the imagination of the public. But it was in France, rather than Britain, that most work was done, until in July 1909 Louis Blériot made his famous flight from Calais to Dover.

Blériot's tiny plane was made of ash and poplar wood, and weighed only 45 lb.! This is how he described his flight, in an interview published in the *Daily Mail*, which had offered a prize of one thousand pounds to the first man to fly the Channel.

At 4.30 a.m. we could see all round. Daylight had come. A light breeze from the S.W. was blowing. The air was clear. Everything was prepared. I was dressed as I am at this moment, a 'khaki' jacket lined with wool for warmth over my tweed clothes and beneath my engineer's suit of blue cotton overalls. My close-fitting cap was fastened over my head and ears. I had neither eaten nor drunk anything since I rose. My thoughts were only upon this flight, and my determination to accomplish it this morning. 4.35: 'tout est prêt'. Le Blanc gives the signal and in an instant I am in the air, my engine making 1,200 revolutions – almost its highest speed – in order that I may quickly get over the telegraph wires along the edge of the cliff. As soon as I am over the cliff, I reduce my speed. There is now no need to force my engine.

I begin my flight, steady and sure, towards England.... The motion of the waves beneath me is not pleasant, but I drive on. Ten minutes have gone. There is nothing to be seen.... I am alone. I can see nothing at all – 'rien du tout'. For ten minutes I am lost. It is a strange position to be alone, unguided, without compass, in the air over the middle of the Channel. I touch nothing. My hands and feet rest

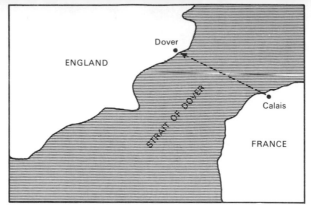

Blériot's historic flight

lightly on the levers. I let the aeroplane take its own course. I care not whither it goes. For ten minutes I continue neither rising nor falling, nor turning. And then, twenty minutes after I have left the French coast, I see the green cliffs of Dover, the Castle and away to the west the spot where I had intended to land.

Now it is time to attend to the steering. I press the lever with my foot and turn easily towards the west, reversing the direction in which I am travelling. Now I am in difficulties, for the wind here by the cliffs is much stronger and my speed is reduced as I fight against it. Yet my beautiful aeroplane responds. Although I am confident that I can continue for an hour and a half, that I might indeed return to Calais, I cannot resist the opportunity to make a landing upon this green spot. Once more I turn my aeroplane, and, describing a half circle, I enter the opening in the cliff, and find myself again over dry land. Avoiding the red buildings on my right, I attempt a landing; but the wind catches me, and whirls me round two or three times. At once I stop my motor, and instantly my machine falls straight upon the land from a height of 20 metres [65 feet]. In two or three seconds I am safe upon your shore. The flight could easily be done again.

A memorial stands on the cliffs at Dover near the spot where Blériot landed at the end of his historic achievement, which seemed to show that Britain could no longer rely on the sea power which had stood her in good stead for so long.

Blériot's flight stimulated interest in Britain, where the first powered flight had been made in 1908. J. T. C. Moore-Brabazon (later Lord Brabazon) gained the first pilot's licence in 1909. In 1910 a race from London to Manchester, for which a prize of ten thousand pounds was offered, not only created great excitement, but showed that aircraft were capable of long and reliable flights. In this race Claude Graham-White made the first night-flight, relying on the headlights of cars to guide him, and to assist his landing. By the First World War aircraft were still rare in the skies of Britain, but they had definitely come to stay.

The war itself proved decisive in the development of aircraft. As with so **218** many things, the urgent needs of war produced rapid change towards better machines. At first regarded as useful only for helping the ground forces by observation, aircraft quickly came into their own as offensive weapons. In 1914 the average speed of aircraft was 70–80 m.p.h. and their maximum height was seven thousand feet. In 1918 the figures were 140–150 m.p.h. and thirty thousand feet. The R.A.F. had over twenty-two thousand planes, some of them capable by the end of the war of bombing Berlin.

THE GROWTH OF COMMERCIAL AVIATION

So far, flying had not been put to much commercial use, apart from some airmail services. Flying was still too expensive, as well as dangerous and uncomfortable, to attract passengers and cargo. The war changed this, however, and as soon as it was over many aviators tried to adapt their war-time experience to commercial flying. Public interest and confidence increased as many dramatic flights opened up new routes. In 1919 John Alcock and Arthur Whitten-Brown made the first crossing of the Atlantic in their Vickers Vimy warplane. They flew from St. John's, Newfoundland, to Ireland, a distance of 1,890 miles, in sixteen hours, at an average speed of 118 m.p.h. In the same year the first flight to Australia was made by Captain Ross Smith and Lieutenant Keith Smith.

In 1927 came perhaps the most famous flight of all – that of Charles Lindbergh. A prize of twenty-five thousand pounds had been offered for the first man to fly alone from New York to Paris, and Lindbergh, an American airmail pilot, was determined to win it. Having flown first from California to New York, setting up a record in the process, he set off for Paris at 7.52 a.m. on 20 May 1927. Few knew of his departure, but as soon as the news spread there was enormous interest on both sides of the Atlantic. For hour after hour Lindbergh battled on in his tiny, 220-h.p. Ryan monoplane, named *The Spirit*

Charles Lindbergh and his *Spirit of St Louis*, after completing his historic flight from New York to Paris in 1927

219

of St. Louis, fighting against bad weather conditions and fatigue. On more than one occasion ice on the wings threatened to bring disaster. At times the plane was no more than a few feet above the Atlantic waves. Cramped in his tiny cockpit, and unable to let his concentration drop for a moment, Lindbergh flew on all that day and night. There was no news of his progress for the anxious millions. Then at last he sighted Ireland beneath him, and his problems of navigation were over. But after so many hours without rest, Lindbergh was finding it very difficult to concentrate. Huge crowds gathered at Le Bourget Airport in Paris. Darkness fell and still there was no sign of him. But at about 10 p.m. (local time) on 21 May, Lindbergh saw the lights of the city ahead of him, and the crowd saw him approach. At 10.24 p.m. he landed safely to a rapturous reception.

This epic flight had lasted over thirty-three hours. It was a tremendous tribute to Lindbergh's physical endurance and flying skill, as well as to the reliability of his aircraft. The pilot became a hero throughout the world. He toured widely and made other trail-blazing flights, spreading the gospel of aviation wherever he went and inspiring others.

There were heroic fliers in Britain too. A woman, Amy Johnson, flew from England to Australia alone in 1930. Francis Chichester, better known today perhaps for his sailing exploits, was also a pioneer of flying in Australia and New Zealand in the 1930s.

All these flights and many others helped to popularise flying. By 1924 there were several companies operating in Britain, and a regular service between London and Paris had been opened as early as 1919. It was expensive, however, and not altogether reliable. Fares were between 15 and 20 guineas (perhaps £50 in terms of today's prices). It soon became clear that airlines had to have government support in the early years if they were to survive economically, so in Britain, as in most other countries, such support was given. In 1924 the government organised Imperial Airways Ltd. This was an amalgamation of several small companies, and it received subsidies so that it could offer lower fares. Passenger traffic gradually built up, so that by 1929 over forty-eight thousand passengers were travelling to and from Britain by air, compared with six thousand in 1920. In the 1930s services were opened up to nearly all parts of the Empire, and to many foreign countries. Two of the most important routes were to India and Australia. Air mail services to Australia were begun in 1932, and passengers were carried a year later. This was the longest route of all – 12,700 miles from London to Brisbane; journeys started from Croydon Airport (which was not replaced by London's Heathrow until 1946). On many routes passengers travelled in huge flying-boats where they found a standard of service and comfort rivalling that provided in ships. The Empire flying-boat offered de luxe cabins and a smoking cabin, as well as excellent food and other amenities. Though the

An Imperial Airways Empire
flying boat

journey took twelve and a half days, in easy stages, this compared most favourably with the six weeks or so needed by sea. The single fare to Australia was £195, but passengers reckoned this as good value, and the service did very well.

Though it was not until 1938 that transatlantic services began, Imperial Airways continued to expand. In 1939 the company operated seventy-seven aircraft and had a staff of three thousand five hundred. It merged in 1939 with a newcomer, British Airways, to form the British Overseas Airways Corporation (B.O.A.C.) and this company was nationalised. Internal and European services were reorganised in a separate company in 1945. This was British European Airways, and since that time, independent companies have been concerned mainly with charter business. Two of the most important independent companies, Caledonian and British United, merged in 1970 to form a stronger 'second force' airline. It is hoped that this will prosper under private enterprise, without damaging the nationalised companies, which are now profitable, after some difficult years.

The growth of air passenger services is illustrated in the table below. As fares came down and speeds and comfort improved, more and more passengers took to the air. By 1970 Britain was linked to all parts of the world by air, with a wide internal network as well.

PASSENGER-MILES FLOWN BY UNITED KINGDOM AIRWAYS 1945 AND 1969

	Millions of passenger-miles
1945	302
1969	10,089

THE AIRCRAFT INDUSTRY

The British aircraft industry grew naturally with the acceptance of flying and the need for more and more military and commercial planes. It has always been among the leaders in world aviation; it has contributed a great deal to Britain's technological reputation, helped to pioneer new ideas in the air, boosted the balance of payments with overseas sales and aided victory in war.

Aircraft production in Britain really began, in fact, with the First World War. With the financial support of the government, famous firms such as de

221

A Bristol Fighter. This was one of the most famous aeroplanes in the early history of the Royal Air Force

Havilland, Sopwith, Bristol, Short, Handley-Page and Vickers built aircraft with historic names: Snipe, Camel and F.B.2 (the 'Gunbus').

After the war the military demand fell, and it was some years before production was able to expand rapidly again. As commercial air services grew, however, so did construction, and it became one of the important 'new' industries which helped to relieve the unemployment caused by the decline of others in the 1930s. Famous planes produced in Britain during the inter-war period included the Vickers Valentia, Hawker Demon and Asprey, Handley-Page Heracles class, de Havilland Rapide and Moth, Armstrong-Whitworth Argosy and Short Empire flying-boat. In the later 1930s the government began a policy of rearmament as war seemed possible, and the aircraft industry had to expand enormously. The whole art of warfare had been changed by the new concept of air power. Events in Spain in the Civil War there (1936–39), and in the first months of the war in Europe (1939–40), showed the devastating effects which aircraft could have in war. Very quickly, Britain had to construct sufficient planes to ward off an attempted invasion by Hitler. A Ministry of Aircraft Production was set up under Lord Beaverbrook. Britain was saved as much by the efforts of those who worked so hard to build the planes as by the brave men who flew them. The Spitfire, Hurricane, Lancaster, Wellington and Mosquito were among the many new types of aircraft produced which have since become household names. It is a

A formation of Spitfires. The safety of Britain depended very much on these fighters and their pilots in the summer of 1940

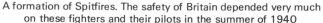

Wellington bombers under construction. Aircraft construction was one of the most vital parts of war production

remarkable fact that the aircraft industry became the largest single industry in Britain during the war. 22,750 Spitfires alone were produced. At one time over two million men and women were employed. Inevitably there was a cut-back once the war was over, but the post-war industry found a new field of work in the production of jet aircraft.

Most of the pioneer work on the jet engine was done in Britain, by Sir Frank Whittle. His first successful engine was made in 1937. Though the first jet aircraft – the Heinkel 178 – flew in Germany in 1939, Whittle's Gloster E 28/39, which first flew in 1941, and his later Gloster Meteor, proved more successful. They came too late to be used much in the war itself, but they were the forerunners of the modern jet aircraft which are in service in all parts of the world.

The principle of the jet engine is very simple. Everyone knows that when a rifle is fired there is a recoil. The movement of the bullet in one direction reacts on the gun and pushes it in the other. With a large gun the movement of the shell may drive it several yards on its gun carriage. A jet engine works on the same principle, except that it uses very hot gases, ejected in a steady flow. These give the effect of a constant recoil, and thrust the aircraft forward. A

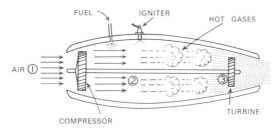

How a jet engine works

1. The forward movement of the aircraft draws air into the engine
2. The compressor forces the air through. It mixes with fuel and is burned to create hot gases
3. The gases drive the turbine, which forces them from the engine, giving forward momentum to the aircraft. The turbine also drives the compressor.
N.B. In a "turbo-prop" the turbine is also linked to propellers, which suck in air

gas turbine engine is used to heat incoming air, mixed with fuel, and force the resultant gases out again. The diagram on p. 223 shows how a pure jet (which should properly be called a 'turbo-jet') works.

A modification of the pure jet is the 'turbo-prop.' In a turbo-prop some of the gases are ejected, but much of the energy is used to drive propellers, which draw air into the engines. Turbo-props are more efficient than pure jets at low altitudes and on short journeys; and so are widely used.

Several outstanding jet and turbo-prop aircraft have been produced in Britain during the years since 1945. The most successful have been the Viscount, Britannia, Comet, One-Eleven and VC-10. Many hundreds of these have been sold all over the world, helping to keep the aircraft industry competitive and profitable in times of growing overseas competition and bringing in thousands of millions of pounds' worth of foreign earnings. Competition has become a serious problem, however, as the industries of other countries have grown, especially that of the United States, and also France. Government policy has made British airlines buy British planes whenever possible, but the home market is not big enough to support the

A BAC One-Eleven nearing completion

industry by itself. Planes have to be sold abroad, and this is difficult when other governments naturally try to protect their own industries, or give subsidies to lower prices and increase their own sales.

Thus the British government was forced to act again in 1960. The aircraft industry was not nationalised, but reorganised, to make it as efficient as possible. From that time only two large companies, both depending substantially on government aid, have made fixed-wing aircraft – the British Aircraft Corporation and Hawker-Siddeley Aviation, both descendants of early pioneering companies which gradually merged into larger and larger concerns. As well as these, there are some smaller companies making light aircraft, and Westland Aircraft Ltd, which manufactures helicopters (and hovercraft). In addition, two aircraft engine companies – Rolls-Royce and Bristol Siddeley – produce what are commonly agreed to be the finest engines in the world. Even aircraft designed and built in the United States often use British engines.

Concorde 002 landing at Fairford, Gloucestershire, after its maiden flight in 1969

Despite these changes of organisation, however, the industry is now in an uncertain position. Only a limited demand for military planes remains, and the new field of rocketry is hardly developed in Britain (see below). Thus civil aircraft simply have to be sold abroad in large numbers if the industry is to survive. Much depends on the success of the Concorde project. While the Americans were concentrating on building enormous conventional jets (Jumbo-Jets) in the late 1960s, British and French companies, supported by their governments, decided on a joint effort to produce a supersonic plane, 225 capable of travelling at a speed of 1,400 m.p.h. At enormous cost, this plane has been built, about five years ahead of American and Soviet rivals. After successful tests beginning in 1970, it is hoped that the Concorde will come into service within three or four years. Many people, however, have doubts about the usefulness of such a plane, and wonder whether it will be profitable. Concern about the noise of the aircraft has lessened after the early trials, and with the probability that it will not be allowed to travel at supersonic speed over land. The great cost (£1,000 million by the end of 1970), much of it borne by the taxpayers, is also under attack. But it is hard to see how the industry can carry on if Concorde is not allowed to come into service and perhaps sweep the world market.

SPACE FLIGHT

Although space travel could hardly be called a form of transport, it seems likely that the journeys of so many science-fiction stories over the years will one day become reality. Even by 1970 many men and one woman had travelled in space – the first was Yuri Gagarin of the Soviet Union in 1957 – while three parties of Americans, the first led by Neil Armstrong in July 1969, had actually set foot on the moon. These travels have not affected directly the lives of ordinary people, apart from the human interest of millions all round the world, but some by-products of them have done so. The work involved in sending men into space, and their experiences, have produced what is called 'spin-off', that is, new techniques which can be used in quite different fields, such as industry, communications and medicine. As a result of the many satellites placed in orbit around the earth, for example, tele-communications have been much improved throughout the world. Some of the equipment in the rockets and satellites sent up has been made in Britain, and all-British satellites have been launched by American rockets. But apart from this, Britain has played little part in the space race. At one time it was hoped that Britain might become more involved, and this was one reason for the reorganisation of the aircraft industry in 1960. But since then economic difficulties have made it impossible to continue with a number of projects. It was only in 1970 that an attempt was made to launch an all-British satellite with a British rocket, the Black Arrow. This launch, in Australia, was a failure, and another attempt was planned for 1971.

Many critics of space flight are glad that Britain has played such a small role in space travel, but there is little doubt that a larger involvement would have provided much needed work for the aircraft industry.

In one allied field, however, important advances have been made in the post-war period – in navigation and air safety devices. With larger and faster aircraft, old methods of navigation and equipment on the ground are no 226 longer good enough to prevent disasters. British technology has made many contributions to better equipment, including the Decca navigating device and the 'Black Box' flight recorder, an instrument which keeps a complete record of the flight of an aircraft. It can often determine the cause of a crash, and so help to prevent a repetition. Both these devices, and others, have gained acceptance throughout the world.

THE IMPORTANCE OF AIR TRANSPORT

Obviously the most imporant result of air transport has been to speed up travel. Even before the advent of Concorde, no part of Britain was more than about two hours' flying time from London; New York was only five or six hours away, Cape Town twelve and Sydney twenty-four. This great increase in the speed of travel has brought all parts of the world within easy reach of Britain. The world, so to speak, has 'shrunk'. The Atlantic has become no more than a 'river', to use a slogan from airline advertisements.

Internally, Britain has gained less than some other countries. In the Soviet Union, for example, aeroplanes have cut down the journey from Moscow to Vladivostok from ten days (by train) to ten hours. Britain, as a small country, cannot boast such dramatic improvements. Yet for the outlying parts of Britain, air transport has been vital in keeping communities going. The Western Islands of Scotland, for example, benefit from their mail, newspaper, hospital and passenger air services. These are provided by aircraft maintained, at considerable cost, by government subsidy, in order to help the islanders. So far as other parts of Britain are concerned a wide network of services has helped businessmen and others pressed for time, but the difficulties of travelling between airports and city centres, as well as higher fares, have made most people prefer the railways. These have been able to compete favourably since the construction of better lines, and provision of better services, in the 1960s (see Chapter 10). Only a fraction of internal freight is carried by air, because of the high cost, which railways and road haulage can undercut.

Internationally, however, air transport has had a greater effect. Trade and tourism in particular have gained enormously from the ability of people to reach all parts of the world quickly and comfortably. But the full potential is far from being reached, as fares are still too high to attract travellers in a hurry. Airlines are bound by agreement not to cut fares, and so many planes fly half empty, especially on highly competitive routes, such as those across the north Atlantic. Although the number of passengers flying to and from Britain is rising steadily, only lower fares seem likely to turn this into a flood.

International air freight is a fast growing business, and vital for British firms competing in markets where punctuality and regularity of delivery are essential. But air freight is expensive, and not really able to cope with very large consignments. For these reasons carriage by sea continues to account for the vast bulk of overseas freight transport.

227

Suggestions for further work and discussion

1. If possible, visit the *Cutty Sark* at Greenwich and the *Great Britain* at Bristol. Make a fuller study of the romantic history of these ships.

2. Show how the design of ships has changed during the period covered by this chapter. Why have these changes taken place?

3. Navigation difficulties and oil pollution have become the two greatest problems created by modern super-tankers. Suggest ways in which they can be overcome.

4. Investigate in more detail the working of:
(a) the turbine engine, (b) the jet engine, (c) radar, (d) the Decca navigating device.

5. Some heroic early flights are mentioned in this chapter. Try to find out more about these pioneering efforts, and about some of the many others which took place. Why did men take such enormous risks?

6. There have been many well-known aircraft designers, including A. Santos-Dumont, A. V. Roe, T. Sopwith and Dr Barnes Wallis. Select one of these, or any other aircraft designer, and examine his work.

7. Subjects for an essay or discussion:
Why did the airship fail?
What are the arguments for and against *Concorde*?
Why has Britain played such a small part in space exploration?
Why do many passenger aircraft fly half-full, and yet still charge fares which ordinary travellers cannot afford?

Books for further reading:

P. Brickhill, *The Dambusters*, Evans, 1963, Pan, 1969.
Sir Francis Chichester, *The Lonely Sea and the Sky*, Hodder, 1964, Pan, 1967.
Joseph Conrad, *The Nigger of the Narcissus*, Heinemann, 1949.
R. H. Dana, *Two Years Before the Mast*, Blackie & Sons, 1964, N.E.C., 1965
A. de Saint-Exupéry, *Night Flight*, Heinemann, 1942 (in French).
J. Dugan, *The Great Iron Ship*, Hamish Hamilton, 1953.
J. Gilbert, *The Great Planes*, Hamlyn, 1970.
B. Lubbock and S. Mason, *The Romance of the Clipper Ship*, Macmillan, 1958.
N. Shute, *No Highway*, Heinemann, 1951, Pan, 1968.

10 : Transport – Rail and Road

Although the basic network of British railways was laid down by about 1850, the system continued to expand for many years. A great many branch lines were built, and some important improvements were made to older ones. An example was the line through Westbury on the Great Western Railway, which provided a much faster route from London to the South-West than via Bristol. It was not until 1930 that the peak route mileage (20,405) was reached. The new construction included some of the most famous engineering works of the Victorian Age – for example, the Severn Tunnel (opened in 1885), the Forth Bridge (1890) and the Tay Bridge (1887). In fact, the last-named was the second bridge to be built across the River Tay to Dundee, a route which considerably shortened the journey to the north of Scotland. The first bridge was opened in 1878, and was over two miles long. It was an impressive structure, and Queen Victoria herself travelled across it, as if to give confidence to the public. But the bridge had not been fully tested in high winds, and in a great gale on 28 December 1879 the centre part collapsed. A train crossing the bridge pitched headlong into the river below, with the loss of seventy-eight lives. There were no survivors. It was a terrible tragedy, and led to much tighter regulations in the future. The unfortunate designer, Sir Thomas Bouche, who had earlier been knighted for his work, died the following year, a broken man. It says much for engineers of the time that a new bridge was built so quickly – one that has stood safely to this day.

Speeds increased until several main-line trains averaged 60 m.p.h. by the end of the century. Of course, the weight of the load was much less then than it is today, as a rule, but this was still an impressive achievement. Services improved in other respects, too. The first proper sleeping cars were introduced on the West Coast route to Scotland in 1873, and the G.W.R. pioneered regular restaurant car services from 1893. These were the most competitive days of the railways, for there was often a choice between two or more routes, and each company strove to outdo its rivals in speed and service.

One of the most competitive routes was that between London and Scotland, and this gave rise in 1895 to the famous 'races'. They were not officially encouraged, or even acknowledged, of course, because of the danger involved. But night after night, each pair of companies did its utmost to get its train to Aberdeen quicker than their rivals. The London and North Western Railway, **229**

The Forth Bridge in the days of steam

with the Caledonian Railway, operated the West Coast route from Euston via Crewe and Carlisle; the Great Northern and North British Railways commanded the East Coast route from King's Cross, through York, Newcastle and Edinburgh. Each night large crowds cheered the rivals off, and turned out at stations along the way. Train crews and station staff did everything they could to speed their trains along. Inside, excited passengers enjoyed the thrill of the race at unprecedented speeds for hour after hour. In the end, both routes were covered in the remarkable time of 518 minutes, but the West Coast route of 541 miles was rather the longer of the two. As an accident soon put a stop to further racing the contest was never fully resolved!

The Tay Bridge disaster: this dramatic picture from *The Illustrated London News* shows the vain search for survivors

An early nineteenth-century train

Such events added excitement in the heyday of the railways, but in the following years difficulties began to grow. Before the First World War road transport offered no serious competition, but during the war the railways suffered a good deal from wear and tear. The demands which the war made upon the system were very great. A vast amount of freight and passenger traffic had to be carried, and there was no time to put in hand anything but essential maintenance and repairs. The private railway companies were controlled by the government during the war and were run efficiently, but at considerable cost. It was during the war, in 1915, that Britain's worst train disaster occurred. This was at Quintinshill, in Scotland, where a troop train crashed and was consumed by fire, with the loss of two hundred and twenty-six lives.

In 1921 the railways were returned to private ownership, but they were completely reorganised. The 125 companies which had existed before the war were grouped into four—the L.M.S., L.N.E.R., S.R. and G.W.R. This was probably a sensible decision as only large companies like these had any chance of raising the money needed for essential improvements. Not only had the damage of the war to be put right, but the railways had to meet serious competition from road transport for the first time.

The companies made a big effort to meet the problems which faced them. One success was the electrification of most London suburban routes. This project was begun as early as 1898, and was largely complete by 1939, bringing a tremendous improvement in conditions for London commuters. Glamorous services were introduced to try to maintain the appeal of rail travel: the *Silver Jubilee* Express ran from London to Newcastle in four hours in 1935, and in 1937 the *Coronation Scot* set up new records on the London to Glasgow service. In the following year the *Mallard* set up a world speed record for a steam engine of 126 m.p.h. (This record still stands, and the engine is preserved at Clapham.)

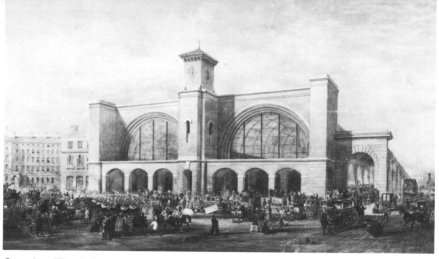

Crowds milling in front of King's Cross Station in 1853, the year after it was opened. The original building remains largely intact

These were some of the highlights of the inter-war period, but otherwise it was a gloomy time, as the railways lost more and more ground to road transport. At first it was freight services which suffered most – between 1920 and 1938 rail freight dropped by 17%. But as the number of motor cars rose, so passengers turned to them or to buses, especially for shorter journeys. The number of passengers carried by rail in 1938 was only 60% of the 1920 total. Although the Second World War diverted traffic back to the railways again, it also imposed new strains, and all the companies found themselves in serious financial difficulty.

St Pancras Station and Hotel. The buildings remain today as monuments to Victorian railway architecture

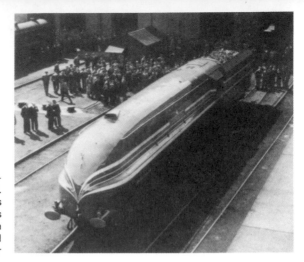

Interested onlookers inspecting the *Coronation* in 1937. Streamlined engines of this class hauled famous expresses like the Coronation Scot before the Second World War

This was the situation which faced the Labour government after 1945, and it decided to nationalise all rail services. Nationalisation became effective in 1948, and though there was much sadness at the passing of famous companies, especially the G.W.R., it was clearly the only thing to do, in view of financial weakness and the vast amount of money which was needed to modernise the railways and make them more attractive and competitive.

British Railways have made a valiant effort to avert complete collapse. A 'Modernisation Plan' was launched in 1954, and this has led, among other things, to the replacement of steam engines by electric and diesel engines. Many were sad to see the last of steam power, but other forms of traction are cleaner and more efficient to run. The main line between Euston and the North has been completely rebuilt, with overhead electric traction, bringing Birmingham to within one hour and three-quarters of London, and Manchester to within three. Eventually the whole of the main line to Glasgow will be electrified, and in the more distant future it is planned to introduce 'Advanced Passenger Trains', based on quite new concepts, which will allow remarkable speeds and timings. These measures have been essential in order to compete not only with road transport but also with internal air services. In addition, British Railways have attempted, with some success, to win back freight traffic: 'freightliner' services offer fast trains running to fixed schedules, and with good connecting road delivery services, using containers. It is possible, if a Channel Tunnel is built, that a great new area of expansion will be opened up.

None of this has been particularly controversial, so far as the general public is concerned, but British Railways' other main policy in its fight for survival has caused much dispute. This is the withdrawal of services on many unprofitable lines. Dr Richard Beeching, who was in charge of British Railways at the time, recommended in 1963 that five thousand miles of

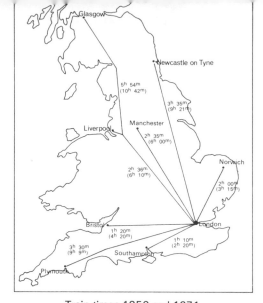

Train times 1850 and 1971

(N.B. 1850 times are in brackets. In some cases the route was different.)

unprofitable line should be closed, and that the main effort should be concentrated on main-line and commuter services. Not all of Dr Beeching's proposals have been put into effect, as some areas would suffer badly if services were withdrawn. But many have been implemented, and route mileage had been cut to under 13,000 by 1970. It is likely that more cuts will be made in the future. However, the changes which have been made since nationalisation have put the railways on a new and much more secure footing, and they continue to play a vital part in the economy of the country.

An express train travelling at over 100 m.p.h. on the high-speed electrified line between London and the North-West. At this point, near Watford Gap, the line runs alongside Britain's first motorway, the M1

We may note, in passing, that Britain's canals were also nationalised in 1948. They are administered by the British Waterways Board. Although only a few still carry commercial traffic, mainly in the north, there has been a growing interest in using canals for pleasure cruising. A number, like the Llangollen Canal, have been re-opened to provide such facilities. However, there has been a certain amount of public disagreement over waterways policy, and demands for-more vigorous maintenance have come from commercial as well as 'amenity' interests.

MOTOR TRANSPORT

Early Road Vehicles

With the success of the railways, long-distance stage-coach services dwindled and road transport was neglected until the arrival of the motor car. Many people think that the 'horseless carriage' was an invention of the late nineteenth century, but this is not so. Steam carriages were developed much earlier. Richard Trevithick built one as early as 1804, and he demonstrated it in the streets of the City of London. By 1827 there were steam coach services between London and Bath. But such vehicles were difficult to run, as they needed frequent intakes of water, just like railway engines. They were also very heavy, and the roads were hopelessly inadequate for them. Moreover, they were regarded by the authorities as dangerous, and efforts were made to discourage them. At last, an Act of 1865 laid down that each steam vehicle had to be preceded by a man on foot carrying a red flag, at a maximum speed of 4 m.p.h.! Not surprisingly, therefore, steam carriages remained few and far between on the roads (though traction engines were used quite widely in agriculture).

In fact, the first new road vehicle which caught on widely was the bicycle. This was invented in France, and various versions reached Britain in the 1870s. These included the 'penny-farthing', so named because of the appearance of its wheels. It needed skill to master a 'penny-farthing', and one can see from examples which survive in museums why it had only a brief period of fashion. In the 1880s, however, a new 'safety-bicycle' of modern design came on to the market. One of its chief attractions was the pneumatic tyre, invented by John Dunlop in 1888. With its separate inner tube, it gave a much more comfortable ride, and it was, of course, also an important contribution to the development of the motor car. The 'safety-bicycle' was the basis of a very wide sale of bicycles for many years to come. For many people the bicycle offered the first means of personal transport, cheap to run and very flexible in its operation. Until surprisingly recent times, even adults worked and saved to   **235**

Problems of early bicycling!

buy a bicycle in the way they do today for a car. In many respects the bicycle had an effect, in miniature, much like that of the car later on. The manufacture of bicycles became a major industry, centred in Birmingham, and a substantial export market was built up.

In 1859 a Frenchman, Étienne Lenoir, produced a new gas engine. This was the prototype of the internal combustion engine, which was to revolutionise road transport, just as the jet engine came to transform flying. The working of the engine is shown in the diagram below. When it was fully developed, it proved to be so effective a means of propulsion that it has come to dominate land transport all over the world. Nikolaus Otto first invented a four-stroke compression engine in Germany in 1886, but both he and Lenoir used coal gas as fuel. This was inefficient, and it was another German – Gottlieb Daimler – who first discovered how to use petrol, which was refined from crude oil. Daimler made this discovery in 1883, and four years later this first petrol-driven four-wheeled car was successfully tested. This moment could fairly be called the start of the modern motor age.

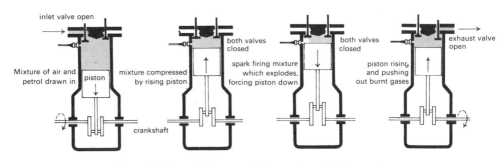

The principles of a four-stroke internal combustion engine

The Development of Motoring in Britain

Apart from the pneumatic tyre, mentioned above, all major technical developments in motor engineering took place outside Britain in the early years. This was rather curious, considering the important role which British inventors and engineers had played in the past. It was partly due to backwardness in technical education and research (see Chapter 15) and partly to the deterrents against mechanical road vehicles which the authorities had imposed. 1896 saw a change, however. In that year F. W. Lanchester built the first British four-wheeled car, and the English Daimler Company set up a factory at Coventry. Most important of all, Parliament was at last persuaded to repeal the notorious 'Red Flag Act'. Henceforth the speed limit was set at 14 m.p.h., but this proved to be so farcical that it was raised to 20 m.p.h. in 1903. Even so, it was largely ignored, and was soon changed. The repeal of

The 1907 Rolls-Royce 'Silver Ghost'

the Act was hailed as a measure of 'emancipation' or freedom, and an 'emancipation run' was held from London to Brighton in celebration. This became a tradition, and every year vintage car enthusiasts cover the same course as a tribute to those motor pioneers.

Cars were very expensive at that time, of course, and so only rich people could afford to buy them. One vehicle which was very fashionable among the wealthy was the Rolls-Royce 'Silver Ghost'. This was built by Henry Royce and Charles Rolls in 1906, and set a standard of luxury and quality for which the firm has remained famous ever since. But this was far beyond the means of ordinary people, who could never hope to own any kind of car, let alone a Rolls-Royce. It was the American, Henry Ford, who made the breakthrough in manufacturing which brought motoring within the reach of many more   **237** people. Using techniques of mass production on one standard model aimed at the mass market, he produced his famous 'Model T Ford', affectionately known as the 'Tin Lizzie'. Ford was able to keep his selling price low as a result of his efficient means of production, and was thus able to reach a wide market all over the world. The more he sold, the more he could drop the price. By 1915, six years after the first model was sold, the price had dropped to £115. No fewer than fifteen millions were sold in eighteen years. Britain was a good market for Ford cars, and gradually engineers and businessmen came to realise that what Ford could do in the United States they could do in Britain.

Two men in particular launched mass production of cars in Britain. They were William Morris (1877–1963) and Herbert Austin (1866–1941). Both men started in a humble way. Morris was the son of a farmer, and began work in a cycle repair shop in Oxford; Austin was an apprentice engineer in Birmingham. Morris built his first car, the Morris 'Oxford', in 1913, and later produced the Morris 'Minor'. These cars, together with the Austin 'Seven', did for the British motor industry and for British motoring what Ford had done in the United States. They both built up large manufacturing empires, which were the basis of today's British Leyland Company. (Both men, incidentally, were given peerages – Morris took the title of Lord Nuffield – and both gave away much of their fortunes for good causes. Lord Nuffield is thought to have given away £25 million during his lifetime.)

The Austin 'Seven' cost £165 in 1922, and though this was still too much for most working-class people, there were still plenty of middle-class buyers for the new British cars. Luxurious models like the Armstrong-Siddeley

238

Lord Nuffield arriving at Guy's Hospital, London, in 1934, to lay the foundation stone of a new building

An Austin Seven, one of the first cheap British family cars

continued to be built, of course, but the system of taxation in Britain favoured smaller or 'baby' cars. This was because the tax increased with the size of the car. In the early days cars were not popular with everyone. They were smelly, noisy and often dangerous. They were resented, especially by those who still worked with horses, or who had charge of animals. Many furious scenes took place between irate farmers and motorists whose cars had terrified livestock. But none of this could stop the spread of private cars, any more than similar opposition could stop the railways in the nineteenth century. By 1939 there were 2,000,000 private cars in Britain, compared with 132,000 in 1914 and 20,000 in 1903.

By this time the internal combustion engine had been adapted to other kinds of vehicle. Buses, lorries, motor-cycles – all these were developed, and became widely used. Many were powered by diesel engines, which were cheaper to run, though noisier, than petrol engines. They were named after Rudolph Diesel, who invented the engine in 1892. Heavier motor vehicles showed their worth during both World Wars, transporting men and materials with much greater ease and speed than the old horse-drawn vehicles. Tanks (invented in 1915) and armoured vehicles provided entirely new weapons of war.

MOTOR VEHICLES IN BRITAIN 1945–69
(in thousands)

	Goods vehicles	Private cars
1945	488	1,521
1959	1,378	4,972
1969	1,640	11,238

In recent years the number of motor vehicles in Britain has risen enormously, as the table shows. This is chiefly a result of the growth in the standard of living since 1945, which has meant that all but the poorest families can now afford to buy a car. Indeed, many families now have two cars, perhaps a family saloon and a smaller one for the wife to take the children to school, do **239** the shopping and visit friends. The car is no longer considered a luxury, as it once was. It is now thought by many to be an essential part of living, almost as important as a house. The 'car-culture' flourishes despite a very considerable increase in price in recent times, a result of generally rising costs of production. Only fairly modest new cars can now be bought for less than a thousand pounds. Partly because of this, the smaller car has become popular again, and some models have been as successful as their counterparts of the inter-war period. The Morris and Austin 'Minis', introduced in 1959, have been especially popular, with economy of size and low running costs, yet with a high standard of performance. In general, technical improvements have increased performance and comfort. Two examples among many are hydrolastic suspension and disc brakes. The Wankel rotary engine, developed on the Continent, may prove to be another startling advance.

So motoring in Britain has reached a mature stage, and we must assess the results of this for the economy and society. But before we do so, let us look briefly at how the roads have kept pace with the traffic upon them.

Modern mass production: part of the Capri assembly line at the Ford Halewood plant, near Liverpool

The finished product: a Ford Capri

Roads

Motoring in the early days was always uncomfortable and often dangerous. The roads had been neglected since the days of stage-coaches. They were unsurfaced, and so drivers faced mud in the winter and dust in the summer. The first cars gave little protection anyway against the weather, and certainly not against these conditions. Therefore motorists set out as if on an expedition, wearing elaborate protective clothing. The well-dressed motorist of the Edwardian Age sported overalls, a cape, goggles and gloves! The roads were so rough that it was most unusual to complete a journey without at least one puncture. Moreover, the roads were quite unsuitable for high speeds, and there were many accidents.

The first move to improve this state of affairs was to surface the road with tar. The benefits which this brought can easily be judged by anyone who drives on some unsurfaced roads in other countries, even today. The work took a long time, and was costly. Some of the money was obtained from the motorists; from 1903 onwards the motorist has been subjected to ever-rising taxation, and the only compensation is that some of it has gone into road improvements. In 1919 the Ministry of Transport was set up to supervise all matters relating to transport, and one of the things which it undertook was a road building programme. The British preference for small cars may have made the need for big roads seem less urgent than it really was. In any case, there was just not enough money available in the inter-war period to do very much, and so Britain fell far behind some other countries. In Germany and Italy, for example, many hundreds of kilometres of new roads were constructed to accommodate the swelling volume of traffic, but not enough was done in Britain. (The German *Autobahn* was the model for the eventual British motorway.) By 1939 this was becoming a serious matter, as the volume of traffic was beginning to swamp the roads, especially with more and 241

Motorway landscape: this junction is on the M2 near Rochester in Kent

more slow lorries blocking the inadequate highways for mile after mile. But, of course, little could be done about it until after 1945.

In fact, it was not until 1959 that Britain's first motorway was opened. This was the M1, between London and Birmingham, offering about eighty miles of three-lane carriageways, free from obstructions. Despite its lateness in comparison with other countries, there was justifiable pride in this fine road. By 1970 there were over seven hundred miles of motorway in use, and by the mid-1970s it is hoped that most of the major cities in Britain will be linked by motorway. When the M6 is finally complete, it will probably be possible to drive from London to Glasgow in about six hours. Other major roads, like the A1, have been greatly improved, with dual carriageways, and by-passes around the worst bottlenecks. By the late 1960s the government was spending over £500 million every year on roads. All these improvements have naturally caused problems. Valuable agricultural land has been taken over, and a good deal of property destroyed to make way for them. In towns, car parks have caused more trouble. They have to be provided, yet there is no solution which will satisfy everyone. Street parking causes congestion, and

Below: A modern articulated lorry. Such lorries make the most of Britain's expanding motorway system. *Right:* Britain's principal motorways in the early 1970s

242

has been discouraged by various means, notably by parking meters. Yet off-street car parks, whether on the surface or as multi-storey buildings, are unsightly and use up valuable land.

Usually, everything has been done to keep to a minimum the harmful effects of road improvements. Indeed, many would argue that the motorways, at least, have been so well designed that they actually improve the landscape. Certainly, such magnificent structures as the Forth and Severn Bridges could be said to add to the beauty of the surrounding countryside. It is none the less true that much wanton destruction has taken place due to bad planning, and that is really the price which has been paid for tackling the problem of the roads too late.

Society's Debt to Motor Transport

Economically, the country has gained very much from motor transport. The movement of goods has become much easier, especially over short distances. The ability to carry freight from door to door, without the transhipment necessary with rail transport, has been the telling factor. (Very large loads and bulk goods such as coal in quantity usually go by rail, though sometimes even these go by road.) This was the basic cause of the difficulties of the railways from the 1920s, but the economy has not suffered from the decline of rail services, because the overall volume of internal freight transport has risen enormously with effects similar to those of the railways in the nineteenth century.

As one example of how good road transport can affect a particular area, let us take Severnside. Before the building of the M4, M5 and Severn Bridge this was not one area but two — either side of the river, with no direct road links.

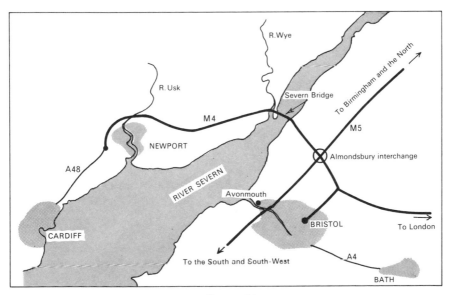

Severnside

243

The Severn Bridge. This magnificent bridge carries traffic on the M4 between London and South Wales

They were important regions but were not showing the growth which their potential promised. The new roads have produced a completely different scene. Now Severnside is a single, fast-growing region, with rapid economic expansion. New life has been given to South Wales industries, and Bristol is the centre of what could be one of the most prosperous areas in Britain.

Socially, the motor age has had an equally important effect. We hardly need to describe in detail here the benefits which have come to ordinary people. Nearly all of us, every day, enjoy these benefits – perhaps they can be summed up as freedom of movement. Other forms of transport have enabled people to move about the country with ease, but always according to a timetable, and dependent upon the decisions and operations of others. The motor car has removed this dependence. We can now travel quickly and comfortably whenever and wherever we choose, from door to door, resting when we feel like it. Families, tourists, businessmen – all have gained tremendously from this ease and convenience. Even those who do not own a car still gain in a multitude of ways – from more regular and efficient services and distribution of goods, especially in remote areas. Motor vehicles, like railways before them, have welded the nation more closely together.

The Evils of Motor Transport

Unfortunately, there is another side to the coin. First of all, the environment has suffered. The general deterioration of the world about us is looked at in more detail later on (see Chapter 17), but we must note here that the motor vehicle has played a large part in it. It is not just that new roads have carved their way through beautiful cities and countryside: the exhaust fumes of millions of cars and lorries have polluted the air we breathe; the noise, day and night, of traffic thundering by, is a tremendous strain on those who live near busy roads; all of us have had experience of the nervous tension caused by dense traffic, whether as drivers, passengers or pedestrians; the whole pace

244

of life has accelerated, almost beyond endurance. Some people suffer more than others, of course, but perhaps all of us suffer more than we realise. It would be a fair generalisation to say that slowly, but surely, the whole nation, and the people in it, are being poisoned, physically and mentally, by the motor car. This is an alarming thought, and it is not too well appreciated. The change has been gradual, and memories of more peaceful days have receded. The problem is not yet completely beyond solution, but time is running out. Already fifteen million vehicles represent one to every twenty-five yards of road. As the population increases and becomes more affluent, and as the economy demands more and more freight capacity, the number of vehicles on the road is likely to grow beyond all recognition, and then it will be too late.

Next, there is the question of safety. The motor car has killed many hundreds of thousands of people in Britain. Even with improved roads, and better vehicle design, the car is still a lethal weapon in the hands of an unskilled, tired or drunken driver. In 1969 no fewer than 7,383 people were killed and 345,811 injured on the roads. Every day about twenty people were killed and nearly a thousand injured. This is a staggering total. In order to cut it down, or at least to keep it in check, many steps have been taken: tests for learner drivers, a general speed limit of 70 m.p.h., stringent laws about drinking and driving (the 'breathalyser') – all these have certainly helped to prevent accidents and to save lives. During the 1960s accident figures rose only a little. But death and injury are still never far away on the roads.

Perhaps there is one way in which, unintentionally, these problems may be reduced. The cost of motoring is getting very high indeed. The purchase price, tax, cost of petrol and repairs are all vast compared with the years before 1939. It has been estimated that the average cost of running a car is now about eight pounds per week, and this is bound to go on rising. However affluent people become, they may find it impossible to meet these higher costs.

PUBLIC TRANSPORT IN CITIES

So far, we have dealt mainly with transport on a national scale, but to a great many people the means of transport within cities or towns matter far more. When towns were small, this was not so important, as it was easy to walk from one place to another. But as towns grew in size this became more difficult. Even so, it was a long time before adequate urban services for ordinary people were introduced. The rich, of course, could always travel in their own carriages, or hire cabs. But the poor could not, and it was not at all unusual for working people to walk many miles to and from work, or to visit friends and relatives.

The earliest form of public transport was the horse-drawn bus. In London the first service was opened in 1829 between Paddington and the Bank of 245

England. This example was soon followed throughout London, and in other large towns. Later on, horses were replaced by steam buses, and then finally by motor buses. The first motor buses ran in London in 1898, and by 1913 there were 3,500. The most famous was the 'B' type, which carried thirty-four seated passengers. It was introduced in 1910, and ran for many years before being superseded by more modern buses.

Tram services were also started in the mid-nineteenth century. The first in London was opened in 1861, and soon a network of rails was laid throughout the capital and elsewhere. At first, trams were pulled by horses, or even winched up steep hills by cables (as at Highgate Hill in London). Later electricity took over as motive power, and this ushered in a very successful era for trams. As time went on, however, they proved to be a nuisance to the increasing volume of motor traffic, and services were gradually withdrawn. The last tram in London ran in 1952, though others survived elsewhere for a time. Today, in London, one can still see the old Kingsway tram tunnel. It is now a road underpass, but it was once a busy tram route. It even had a tram station underground.

Another form of city transport given up only recently was the trolleybus. This was a bus which drew electricity from overhead wires. Like the tram, it ran smoothly and was cheap to operate. After being pioneered in northern towns from about 1911, it was put into service elsewhere, but today the trolleybus too has disappeared from most parts of Britain.

Lastly, we must mention the Underground. Main-line and suburban railway lines, of course, ran into city centres, but it soon became clear that there was room for special urban rail services, which could only be underground (although Liverpool did build an overhead railway system in the 1890s). The first underground service in London ran from Paddington to Farringdon Street, and was opened in 1863. It was operated by steam at first, and this must have been extremely dirty! Later it was converted to electric power. The

Left: early days of public transport in London: a horse-drawn omnibus photographed in the late nineteenth century. *Below:* an early London tram

246

route is now part of the Metropolitan Line, and if one travels along it one can see that it is just a shallow cut, hardly a proper underground railway at all. The first 'tube' (so-called because the trains ran in tubes in tunnels bored deep underground) ran between the City and the Elephant and Castle in 1890, and other lines followed. By the time that all London's transport was taken over by the London Passenger Transport Board in 1933, there were over 200 underground route miles. There were also smaller systems in Glasgow and Liverpool. In 1969 the new Victoria Line was opened, and there are plans for yet another – the Fleet Line – to be built in London, and for the Piccadilly Line to be extended to Heathrow Airport.

Today, Britain is far better provided than many other countries with urban public transport. Services are on the whole efficient, though far from cheap. In a sense this may not seem as important as it did when there were few private cars. In another sense, however, good public transport can be seen as the key to movement in the cities of the future. Already the streets are almost incapable of coping with the congestion, and planners are showing growing interest in the possibility of expanding existing networks of public transport, possibly using new developments such as the electrically-powered minibus for use in city centres. On a smaller scale, movement around shopping precincts can be assisted by moving pavements and escalators, as has already happened at Chester and Birmingham. The time may soon come when private cars have to be banned altogether from heavily used areas in favour of public transport: this was actually tried as an experiment on a limited scale in Birmingham at Christmas 1970, with considerable success. In other countries with problems of urban congestion, such as Switzerland, Holland, Japan and the U.S.A., better public transport is increasingly regarded as the answer. In particular some exciting hints of the possibilities that may lie in the future were to be seen at the Tokyo World Fair of 1970, where monorails, minibuses and travelators were used in combination.

Modern public transport: a Victoria Line Underground train arrives at Seven Sisters Station. Though these trains carry operators, the services are in fact fully automatic

Suggestions for further work and discussion

1. Consult railway timetables of former years and see how the times of journeys differed from those of today. David and Charles Ltd have published reprints of Bradshaw's Railway Guides, which would help you in this.

2. Make a list of railway lines in your locality which have been closed down. Find out when they were built, and when and why they were closed. In some cases you can walk along such lines and see interesting railway relics.

3. Make a list of the principal cars produced in Britain:
   (a) before 1914, (b) from 1914 to 1939, (c) since 1945.

4. Make a fuller study of the working of:
   (a) the internal combustion engine, (b) the diesel engine, (c) the Wankel rotary engine.

5. Write an account of the life and achievements of either Lord Nuffield or Lord Austin.

6. Visit one of the many motor museums in Britain. The most well known is probably the Montagu Motor Museum at Beaulieu, in Hampshire.

7. Subjects for an essay or discussion:
   What are the problems which British railways have faced in the twentieth century?
   How have they been tackled?
   In what ways has the environment (the world in which we live) been affected by the motor-car?
   What do you expect to be the chief means of public and private transport in the year 2000?

Books for further reading:

E. L. Ahrons and O. S. Nock, *The British Steam Locomotive* (2 volumes), Ian Allan, 1963.

G. N. Georgano, *The Complete Encyclopaedia of Motor Cars 1885–1968*, Ebury Press, 1968.

D. Kaye, *Buses and Trolleybuses Since 1945*, Blandford, 1968.

E. T. MacDermot and O. S. Nock, *History of the Great Western Railway* (3 volumes), Ian Allan, 1963.

T. R. Nicholson, *Passenger Cars 1863–1904*. Blandford, 1970.

Ed. D. StJ. Thomas, *A Regional History of the Railways of Great Britain* (5 volumes published so far), David & Charles, Vol. 1 published in 1966.

11 : Farming – the Circle of Change

PROSPEROUS PEACE AND WAR-TIME BOOM: 1750–1815

With the coming of the Agricultural Revolution the history of agriculture has to be told in a new way. Formerly it had been chiefly a matter of describing the way people grew their food, or if they were landowners, managed their estates. The principal variable factor had been the weather. Now, however, agriculture was becoming geared to a market economy, and demand was coming to be as important – and almost as variable – as supply had been before. Thus attention begins to focus more and more on rising or falling prices, and on farmers' attempts to adjust their techniques to produce what they think the market will buy.

The growth of population in the second half of the eighteenth century was a great stimulus to agriculture, as we have already seen. More and more food was produced, but still there was not enough to satisfy the demands being made. The level of these demands was further raised by the fact that, as the country grew richer, the standard of living went up, and the average requirement of food increased. At the same time, many of the trades and industries which were flourishing at this time used as their raw materials the products of agriculture – wool for cloth and hides for leather goods are obvious examples. In this way agriculture and industry fed on each other – another example of the way in which all aspects of economic history are interwoven and dependent on each other.

Since, while the prices of their goods were rising, the farmers were often successful in cutting their production costs, this period was one of solidly based prosperity for the agricultural community, taken as a whole. The farmers were not completely successful, however, in keeping up with the demand, and an increasing proportion of Britain's food had to be imported from the continent of Europe. In 1767, a year of grain shortage in England, 500,000 quarters of wheat had to be brought in, and there were large imports also in 1774–75 and 1783. On the other hand, there were still some years, such as 1776 and 1779–80, when sizeable quantities of wheat were actually exported. The general picture was becoming clearer despite these fluctuations – Britain could no longer rely with certainty on her ability to feed herself from her own resources. This was recognised to some extent when the laws governing the import and export of corn were modified slightly in 1773 and again in 1791. In fact, the load of wheat imports averaged about 174,000 quarters a year during the 1780s.

From about 1750 onwards, therefore, the demand for the products of agriculture grew rather faster than the farmers could satisfy it, and so the average level of prices rose slowly but steadily, in the case of meat, and with more violent variations in the case of wheat. (This variation is a common pattern with wheat prices, since the product is so very dependent on climatic factors which, in Britain at least, are unreliable.)

WHEAT AND MEAT PRICES, 1750–93

	Wheat (shillings per quarter)	Meat (shillings per stone)
1750	26	1
1756	48	1
1761	23	1
1766	50	1s. 7d.
1769	30	1s. 7d.
1774	52	1s. 9d.
1778	33	1s. 9d.
1783	51	1s. 6d.
1786	40	1s. 9d.
1790	50	1s. 9d.
1793	44	1s. 9d.

So long as Britain was at peace the balance adjusted itself with relatively little trouble. But from 1793 to 1815, with only one short break at the Peace of Amiens (1802–03), Britain was at war with France. This exceptionally long war was fought at a very high intensity, with few of the lulls which had tended to characterise earlier eighteenth-century wars, and as time went by more and more use was made of economic weapons. The idea of economic warfare was not at all new – medieval kings had tried to destroy each other's trade, and the whole mercantilist system of the eighteenth century had been based on ideas about trade war. But the plan for economic warfare laid down by Napoleon in his Berlin and Milan Decrees (1806 and 1807) was a great deal more far-reaching than anything previously attempted. He tried to close the whole of Europe to British goods, and at the same time to starve Britain by cutting off all supplies. Britain retaliated with the Orders in Council of 1807, designed to put an end to seaborne trade which might help Napoleon's schemes. Both schemes were over-ambitious; but the strength of the contestants was sufficiently great, and sufficiently equal, to cause great destruction, loss and hardship, before economic warfare was virtually abandoned by both sides in 1812.

In Britain the effects of the struggle were varied. Everybody, however, was equally affected by one general shortage, which at some times was desperately severe – a shortage of food. The delicate, self-adjusting balance of peacetime was destroyed by the war, and though British sea-power ensured that trade in food was not stopped, it was to some extent disrupted. The chief Continental sources of grain were less accessible, and were sometimes cut off altogether; and the newer sources, in particular America, were not very certain – from 1812 to 1814 Britain and the U.S.A. were at war.

The import difficulty only really became serious, however, in connection with the fact that several of the war-time years saw exceptionally poor harvest yields of grain, which would have made for difficulties even in normal circumstances. The winter of 1794–95 was one of the three worst winters of the whole eighteenth century (the others had been 1708–09 and 1739–40). It was followed by a summer so exceptionally cold that in late June severe frosts killed thousands of new-born sheep in the fields. Consequently the harvest was as much as a fifth or a quarter smaller than usual. It so happened that this catastrophe came on top of a sufficiently bad harvest in the preceding year. So it is not surprising that prices of grain reached an all-time record.

This record, however, was to be beaten almost immediately. Every following year until 1800 was remarkable for some sort of weather freak, and harvests were so consistently bad that by 1800–01 grain prices had reached crisis levels again, as the accompanying table clearly shows.

WHEAT PRICES, 1793–1815

	Shillings per quarter
1790–94	49s. 7d.
1795–99	65s. 8½d.
1800–04	84s. 10½d.
1805–09	84s. 7d.
1810–14	102s. 6d.

(Figures are given in approximate annual averages per five-year period.)

Part of the reason for these high prices was to be found not in simple shortage, but in monetary inflation. This had the effect of pushing up prices even when supply was adequate. None the less, the levels shown above (representing averages often surpassed) brought acute hardship for poor people – whose wages might well not be going up as fast as the prices of food which they had to buy. In 1811 and 1812, particularly bad harvests, perhaps as little as half the normal size, occurring at the same time as outbreaks of disease among sheep, produced something close to famine conditions. The government did what it could to encourage imports of grain by paying bounties, and to discourage wasteful uses of it for such purposes as milling it into hair-powder. These may have had some success; other policies of 251 economy, such as attempts to persuade poor people to eat rice or potatoes instead of bread, or at any rate bread made of something cheaper than wheat-flour, seem to have been almost entirely unsuccessful.

Amid all this distress the farmers flourished. Their profits soared, and in many cases so did their ambitions. Land was in great demand, and vast loans were raised to buy farms in the expectation of quick profits. One observer, writing after the event, in 1838, remarked that 'Every purchase of land previous to 1811, whether made with or without judgement, turned out favourable according to the then market rates and it was supposed, in consequence, that money could in no way be so profitably employed as in buying land.' In order to ensure maximum returns, farmers embarked on great improvement schemes – enclosures went ahead at a great pace (see diagram on p. 31) and lands previously considered worthless were brought under the plough to return yields which, although marginal in terms of quantity, were still valuable in terms of the prices they fetched. Heavy clay lands fit for nothing but pasture (until they were drained by nineteenth-century methods), thin chalky soils on downlands, and acid, sterile moorland, all were ploughed and sown with grain. The marks of these Napoleonic fields can still be seen in some deserted places, for they were abandoned soon after the war, and arable cultivation has never advanced so far into the waste again.

The worst result of this reckless policy was that many of the improvement schemes had required the outlay of great quantities of capital, and farmers had raised loans of enormous size, for this purpose, often at steep rates of interest. In addition to this, the days of prosperity had also been days of greater expenditure. The running costs of farming 100 acres of arable land nearly doubled between 1790 and 1813, according to an enquiry made by the Board of Agriculture at the time.

The costly purchase and improvement of land, and the increasing expense of farming at all – these were the unavoidable results of farming in a boom time. The outlay was great, but so, for the time being at least, was the profit. A good many farmers, however, spent their profits in a way that caused a great many wiseacres to shake their heads disapprovingly – particularly after 1815, when the bubble burst. Not that they were generally reckless, at least as a class; but as their wealth increased they, and perhaps particularly their wives, felt naturally tempted to indulge themselves a little in what had previously been considered items of luxury, quite unsuitable for an honest plain farming family. Carpets on the parlour floor, fine china instead of pewter on the table, mahogany furniture instead of deal or oak, perhaps even a piano in the front room! This sort of expenditure may not have made the difference between solvency and bankruptcy when the pinch came; but it probably helped to make the contrast between prosperity and hardship more painful than it might otherwise have been.

DEPRESSION AND THE CORN LAWS: 1815–1846

After 1815 profitable war-time abnormalities gradually came to an end. The home demand for farm produce did not slacken, except in so far as depression in other parts of the economy reduced purchasing power. But the restraints which had operated against imports were now removed, and farmers feared they would have to stand unprotected against the blast of foreign competition. With this in mind they put such pressure on the government that in 1815 a new Corn Law was passed. This was the famous law which gave its name to the great controversy about agricultural protection which occupied much political and economic attention in the nineteenth century. But the idea of Corn Laws as such was nothing new – the import of grain had frequently been regulated before. The Act of 1815 was designed to protect British farmers against overseas competition by keeping foreign corn off English markets until prices had reached what in pre-war times had been considered famine levels – 80s. per quarter for wheat, 40s. for barley and 27s. for oats. This, it was hoped, would keep the price of home-grown corn both steady and 'reasonably' high. In fact the Corn Law in its simple form was a failure, and even after it had been modified, as it was several times before its final repeal in 1846, it could do little to achieve

The rich rejecting cheap imported corn and letting the poor starve in order to maintain a high price for home-grown produce: a savage cartoon by George Cruikshank

its declared objectives. When corn was plentiful prices could not be kept up; when it was scarce, they could not be kept down. So both farmers and consumers suffered, though their reactions were different, in that the former demanded more protection as the solution, while the latter clamoured for less.

Seen from a safe historical distance, the Corn Laws were a failure. In so far as they were designed to protect the corn-growing farmers, they might also seem to have been narrowly selfish. Certainly they were fiercely attacked at the time, and have come in for a lot of abuse since. To be fair, though, we must remember that agriculture was of vital importance to the nation as a whole. It contributed over a third of the national income; it gave employment to the same proportion of the total employed population; it provided all but a tiny proportion of the nation's food; and of course the agriculturalists were consumers too, whose buying power assisted the prosperity of British industries. These and similar arguments were powerfully advanced by some of the foremost economists of the period, and had a great deal of influence, in Parliament particularly.

It is important that we should get the Corn Laws into the right perspective, because of the great controversy that came to rage about them in the first half of the nineteenth century. The argument was centred on Parliament, where the Laws were debated, altered several times (notably in 1828 and 1842) and finally repealed in 1846. But what happened in Parliament was merely a reflection of the great discussion that agitated the whole country, with increasing force. After the settling of the Reform issue in 1832 (when the electoral system was altered) the Corn Laws came to be the most important of all domestic issues.

They attracted so much attention because they came to stand as a symbol of agricultural supremacy at a time when new pressure groups were rising up and attempting to assert themselves. In short, the attack on the Corn Laws was really the spearpoint of an attack on the social and economic system that had produced them. This is sometimes represented as a struggle of the middle classes against the aristocracy. But that is much too narrow a view of the affair. Two completely different ideas about society were at issue. Richard Cobden, one of the leaders of the Manchester-based Anti-Corn Law League, which played a leading part in the controversy, summed the matter up well during a speech to the House of Commons in 1845, when he appealed to the landowners to sanction repeal, in their own interests.

This is a new age: the age of social advancement . . . ; you belong to a mercantile age; you cannot have the advantage of commercial rents and retain your feudal privileges, too. If you identify yourselves with the spirit of the age, you may yet do well; . . . but your power was never got, and you will not keep it by obstructing that progressive spirit of the age in which you live.

Richard Cobden

John Bright

Meanwhile on the farm, life got gradually more competitive. Despite all the tinkering and tampering with the Corn Laws, grain prices slipped steadily downwards between 1815 and 1820, and though they improved thereafter, there was nothing to match the halcyon days of war-time. Meat prices also fell, though less steeply, and with shallower troughs.

WHEAT AND MEAT PRICES, 1815–46

	Wheat (shillings per quarter)	Meat (shillings per quarter)
1815	75	4s. 6d.
1817	97	4s.
1821	48	3s. 1d.
1828	66	3s. 9d.
1835	40	3s. 1d.
1838	68	3s. 9d.
1846	53	3s. 9d.

During this post-war depression period, bad harvests reduced the British farmer's share of the home market on a number of occasions, while a series of outbreaks of disease devastated flocks and herds. Other factors, of a more financial nature, also had their effect. The heavy debts contracted in war-time prosperity still had to be paid off as the instalments fell due; and after the resumption of cash payments in 1819 they had to be paid in gold – which would often be higher in value than the notes in which the loan had been made in the first case. Meanwhile taxes bore heavily on the landed classes – both national taxes designed to pay off the vast war debts, and local taxes, or rates, particularly those connected with poor relief under the so-called Speenhamland system.

The load of national taxation was lightened gradually in the 1820s and 1830s, and the Poor Law was changed in 1834, but conditions as a whole did not improve greatly. The evidence was clear to see – marginal lands abandoned, tenancies terminated, smallholders forced to sell up, much discussion in the Press of the virtues of emigration, with a sharp rise in the numbers of those actually leaving, especially for North America, and finally an alarmingly large number of actual bankruptcies. In 1821 William Cobbett wrote in his *Rural Rides*:

> ... nothing can be clearer than that the present race of farmers, generally speaking, must be swept away by bankruptcy, if they do not, in time, make their bow, and retire.

William Cobbett

Cobbett was one of the most famous propagandists of his day, and a figure well worth noticing for his own sake. He was born in 1773, the son of a farmer in Farnham, Surrey. After a wandering early life – with the army in Canada, living by his wits in revolutionary France and the U.S.A. – he began to carve out a career as a freelance journalist. His most famous ventures were the *Weekly Register* (from 1802), the *Parliamentary Debates* (from 1804) and *Rural Rides* (from 1821). Unlike Arthur Young and William Marshall, the propagandists noted in an earlier chapter, he was not concerned principally with the techniques of farming; his interest was rather in the politics of agriculture, and still more in questions of social reform. His attitude in these matters has been described as radical conservatism. He was in many respects an ardent fighter for reform – he campaigned for liberty of the Press, for humanitarian causes (in 1810 he was fined £1,000 and imprisoned for two years because he had attacked flogging in the army), and for economic and social justice and freedom.

William Cobbett

Look at these hovels, made of mud and straw; bits of glass, or of old cast-off windows, without frames or hinges frequently, but merely stuck in the mud wall. Enter them, and look at the bits of chairs or stools; the wretched boards tacked together to serve for a table; the floor of pebble, broken brick, or of the bare ground; look at the thing called a bed; and survey the rags on the backs of the wretched inhabitants; and then wonder if you can that the gaols and dungeons and treadmills increase, and that a standing army and barracks become the favourite establishments of England!

On the other hand Cobbett's ideas for the improvement of English society were essentially backward-looking. He regretted the disappearance of the small, independent, yeoman farmer, who was being squeezed out by the big commercial estates. He reserved some of his bitterest language for the new sort of landowner who made a fortune from trade or industry and then bought an estate to make himself respectable, or even as a speculation. He wrote and spoke violently in favour of reform; but he wanted reform in order that revolution might be avoided. Near Lincoln in 1830 he saw

three poor fellows digging stone for the roads, who told me that they never had anything but bread to eat, and water to wash it down. One of them was a widower with three children; and his pay was eighteenpence a day; that is to say, about three pounds of bread a day each, for six days in the week: nothing for Sunday, and nothing for lodging, washing, clothing, candlelight, or fuel! Just such was the state of things in France at the eve of the Revolution! Precisely such; and precisely were the causes.

By 1835, when Cobbett died, Parliament at least had been reformed; but there had been little improvement in conditions on the land.

The Progress of Improvement

Of all the many people who wrote about the distress of the farming community, Cobbett did so most powerfully and most feelingly. But like practically everybody else, he failed to see what the trouble was really about. A close examination of the figures shows that imported food, although it increased considerably in terms of quantities (wheat imports averaged 816,000 quarters a year in the 1820s, and 1,468,000 quarters a year in the 1830s) was actually a diminishing proportion of the total food consumption. Similarly, although prices fell below the war-time peaks, they still represented a consistently higher level than the pre-war average.

The fact was that the improvements of the Agricultural Revolution, aided by the abnormal conditions of the wartime boom, had enabled farmers to raise the level of their production to the point where it had very nearly caught up with the demand, greatly though this latter had expanded. When this equalising process was nearly complete, prices were bound to fall. Then the 257 farmers who had invested too heavily for the final profit-level to sustain their repayments, or those who had the misfortune to farm land (such as the heavy Midland clays) requiring high running costs, were bound to feel the pinch.

Lord Brougham summed up the reality of the situation in a Parliamentary debate in 1816:

> Not only have wastes disappeared for miles and miles, giving place to houses, fences and crops; not only have even the most inconsiderable commons, the very village greens, and the little strips of sward along the wayside, been in many places subject to division and exclusive ownership, cut up into cornfields in the rage for farming; not only have stubborn soils been forced to bear crops by mere weight of metal, by sinking money in the earth, as it has been called – but . . . the work of both men and cattle has been economised, new skill has been applied, and a more dexterous combination of different kinds of husbandry been practised, until . . . I am sure that five [blades of grass] grow where four used to be.

These new conditions placed a premium upon efficiency, which many farmers accustomed to the easy profits of earlier years found uncomfortable or even impossible to pay. Despite failures, the general trend was towards more improvement – drainage schemes, new buildings, improved rotations and increasing use of machinery. Labour costs were pruned to a minimum – the average wage of 12s. to 15s. a week in 1814 fell to 9s. or 10s. in 1822, and barely rose above that until the 1840s, at least in real terms. Even new social habits could be turned to economic advantage, according to Cobbett: 'Why do not farmers now *feed* and *lodge* their work-people, as they did formerly? Because they cannot keep them *upon so little* as they give them in wages.'

Looking at the situation as a whole, therefore, it was a tough, competitive farming community that faced the repeal of the Corn Laws in 1846.

THE GOLDEN AGE: THE 1850s AND 1860s

> The farmer's business is to grow the heaviest crops of the most remunerative kind his soil can be made to carry, and, within certain limits of climate which experience has now defined, the better he farms the more capable his land becomes of growing the higher qualities of grain, of supporting the most valuable breeds of stock, and of being readily adapted to the growth of any kind of agricultural produce, which railway facilities or increasing population may render most remunerative. In this country the agricultural improver cannot stand still. If he tries to do so, he will soon fall into the list of obsolete men, being passed by eager competitors, willing to seize the current of events and turn them to their advantage.

So wrote Sir James Caird in 1852, and his words could serve as a summary of the new style of farming that emerged from the difficulties of the post-war depression, and came to be known as 'high farming' in the prosperous period that followed. Caird was the Arthur Young of his time. In his principal book, *English Agriculture in 1850–51*, he described a tour of the English countryside undertaken in the same spirit as that which had inspired Young. Caird was well aware of the resemblance; indeed, he did not hesitate to draw the comparison himself.

His work was extremely valuable in its time. His approach was more methodical and businesslike, and his technical knowledge was probably greater, than that of Young. On the other hand, the more detailed his recommendations were, the more chance they stood of being wrong – as some of them later turned out to be; and if Young dealt in rather more general terms, he also had a rather bigger object in view – the whole notion of agricultural 'improvement', compared with which Caird's 'high farming' is a much more limited notion. These facts probably explain why Caird's name is now less famous than that of his predecessor.

He first became prominent in 1848, when, in the aftermath of the Corn Law Repeal, he published a pamphlet with a long title which can be abbreviated to *High Farming, the Best Substitute for Protection*. From then onwards he constantly pressed for large farms, on which a high level of capital investment would be possible, so that full advantage could be taken of new scientific knowledge of soils and how to treat them, by draining, the use of chemical fertilisers and the growing of special crops. New buildings, new roads, new machines were high on the list of priorities. Every use was to be made of the latest aids, including the railway to take goods to market. 'Unnecessary obstructions to economical tillage' – hedges, for instance – were to be eliminated. And, since competition from abroad was making it increasingly unwise to concentrate on corn-growing, the wise farmer would swing his activities more towards pasture and dairy farming. This need not mean the elimination of arable altogether – Caird in fact advocated a more sophisticated version of the old 'mixed farming' in which crops and cattle supplemented each other. The centre of high farming, the area from which all others took their lessons, was to be found in Scotland – in the Scottish Lothians, the Carse of Gowrie and southern Perthshire. Norfolk, the old pioneering area, fell into something like conservatism as the farmers there persisted with the ideas which had brought such success to earlier generations.

Science and technology were at the base of the new improvements. They had, of course, begun to affect agriculture a long time before. A threshing machine had been invented in 1784, and had gradually come into common use during the period of depression, thus changing the whole pattern of winter work on the farm. In 1800 a horse-tedder had been invented for tossing hay. As iron became cheaper it had been more and more used for implements

Agricultural innovation in the 'Golden Age': a trial of steam ploughing machinery in 1862. Notice the crowd of interested spectators

(such as ploughs and harrows), and for fences and gates, especially in the North of England, where it was most readily available. But the tide had not really begun to run until the 1840s.

A symbolic step was taken with the formation of the Royal Agricultural Society in 1838, to advance the cause of efficient farming through its *Journal*, shows and other activities. In 1840 a scholar named Liebig published a book with the imposing title *Organic Chemistry in its Applications to Agriculture and Physiology* – a book which was to be of great importance in showing how science could aid the farmer. In 1843 an agricultural research station was set up at Rothamsted, and in 1845 an Agricultural College was founded at Cirencester. During the 1840s a host of new ploughs, harrows, tedders, drills, cultivators, reapers and machines of all sorts came on to the market, and in the 1850s the range was further extended by the application of a new source of power – steam – though this was too clumsy to make a great deal of difference in field operations. By 1867 only 200,000 acres were steam-drilled. Steam threshing, on the other hand, was nationally common; it was often carried on by firms of machinery contractors. Their machines were usually driven by belts running from great traction engines, huge and heavy, though often beautifully engineered.

Chemical fertilisers were rapidly developed, and became increasingly popular during this period. Superphosphate and basic slag were the by-products of Britain's own Industrial Revolution. Guano, on the other hand, was a natural product – accumulated bird-manure – and had to be brought from Peru. Nitrate came from Chile, and from the 1860s potash was imported from Germany. The speed with which these were taken up is illustrated by the figures for guano imports – less than 2,000 tons in 1841, but 300,000 tons in 1847.

Perhaps the most important improvements of all were those connected with drainage. Undrained land is bad for crops and animals alike. Unfortunately

Steam threshing. Heavy steam-driven machinery was more economical in the
farmyard than in the fields

large parts of England are covered with heavy, 'strong' soil, which holds the
heavy English rainfall and prevents it from filtering away. These areas, consequently, had always been difficult to farm, especially as arable land. After the
war, it was these areas that suffered most in the cost-and-efficiency struggle.
But such land, though difficult to work, is often very rich if it can be drained.
Consequently, efforts had been made to overcome the problem.

The digging of trenches across the field had obvious disadvantages; but this
was practised instead of any better way, until superseded in the 1830s by the
idea of using a network of shallower trenches filled with stone and covered
over with furze. Early in the 1840s an essential advance was made when the
principle of the underground tile-drain was discovered, and it was not long
before machines were invented both for making and for laying such tiles. This
extract from the Royal Agricultural Society's *Journal* describes the results as
displayed at the Great Exhibition of 1851.

Twelve years ago draining-tiles were made by hand, cumbrous arches with flat
soles, costing respectively 50s. and 25s. per 1,000. Pipes have been substituted for
these, made by machinery, which squeezes out clay from a box through circular
holes, exactly as macaroni is made at Naples, and the cost of these pipes averages
from 20s. down to 12s. per 1,000. . . . [It is wonderful] to see two horses at work
by the side of a field, on a capstan which, by an invisible wire-rope, draws towards
itself a low framework, leaving but the trace of a narrow slit on the surface. If you
pass, however, to the other side of the field, which the framework has quitted, you
perceive that it has been dragging after it a string of pipes, which, still following the
plough's snout, that burrows all the while four feet below ground, twists itself like a
gigantic red worm into the earth, so that in a few minutes, when the framework has
reached the capstan, the string is withdrawn from the necklace, and you are
assured that a drain has been invisibly formed under your feet. [The machine
referred to in the second part of this excerpt is Fowler's mole-drainage plough.]   261

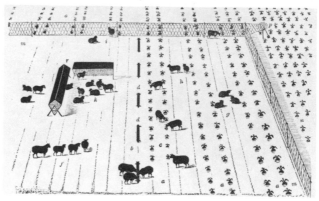
Feeding sheep on turnips, from a late nineteenth-century farming manual. Notice the light, portable fencing

All this innovation none the less cost a great deal of money; it was an essential part of Caird's scheme that the farmer invested heavily in the hope of equally heavy profits. However, it became a point of honour with the leaders of the agricultural community to take up every possible improvement, regardless of whether it actually increased profits at all – though in doing so they were betraying the principles of Caird. The Duke of Northumberland, for instance, invested nearly £1,000,000 on his estate for a trifling $2\frac{1}{2}$% return – he could have got more from government stocks with far less effort. A farmer on the Duke of Bedford's estate, one Jonathan Bodger, seems to have had an inkling of the real situation. The Duke inspected his farm after a great reorganisation, and observed gravely, 'Great improvements, Jonathan,' to which Jonathan replied 'Great *alterations*, your Grace.' Much of the money invested in this way could never be recalled; and the decline of the great landed aristocracy in the fifty years that followed 1870 was due in part to their injudicious behaviour in the so-called Golden Age.

We must now turn to justify the term 'Golden Age' itself. How was it that the ending of agricultural protection in 1846 became the signal for a period of exceptional prosperity? The answer is that while demand expanded rapidly, foreign competition remained still comparatively insignificant; improvements in technique enabled the farmer to supply the needs of the market more accurately, and the development of railways cut his transport costs and therefore enlarged his margin of profit; finally, prices for most agricultural products rose steadily by from 20 to over 50% after 1850. In other words, the fuss over the Corn Laws had, in an economic sense, been misplaced, and once their disturbing influence had been removed agriculture was able to join the rest of the British economy in the great mid-Victorian boom, when almost everybody earned more and spent more in the most prolonged bout of solidly based prosperity that the country has ever known.

(Indices: average of 1865 and 1885 equals 100)

	Prices, total agricultural products	Overall national prices
1840–44	125	114
1845–49	114	105
1850–54	105	104
1855–59	122	120
1860–64	116	119
1865–69	119	116
1870–74	122	120

Prices: meat prices doubled between 1840 and 1870. Wheat prices remained roughly constant.

Income: average national income (net, per head) went up by 50% between 1855 and 1875; farmers' profits approximately doubled.

A famous prize heifer, the product of intensive breeding. (This print was made and sold to raise funds for the breeder, who had gone bankrupt – a fate that befell many over-ambitious farmers in the later nineteenth century.)

Having tried to explain why the Golden Age was given its name, it is necessary to add that the description as given is capable of misleading. There were bad years from 1849 to 1853, and again in 1859 and 1860. In 1864 there was drought, and again in 1868. Cattle-plague and a form of animal pneumonia ravaged the country so severely in 1865–66 that the government had to step in, slaughtering herds and restricting movement in a manner that foreshadowed twentieth-century policies. At all these troubled times, many farmers must have come close to the brink of ruin, and some would have fallen over it.

Then there were those who had less to lose, because they subsisted on so little in the first case. In 1851, of all those who occupied more than 5 acres of land — that is, of those who were farmers in any real sense of the word at all — no less than 62% occupied less than 100 acres each. By the 1880s the figure was still over 60%. Since Caird's notion of high farming required a farm of at any rate 300 acres to begin with, his doctrines clearly had only a limited relevance. It is doubtful whether he had much impact on the farmers whom he himself saw on the Sussex Downs near Brighton, laboriously tilling the ground with wooden ploughs drawn by teams of six oxen, just as their medieval ancestors had done.

Finally, there were the agricultural labourers — the most consistently depressed class of the nineteenth century. Caird described the life of one who lived on Salisbury Plain in 1850:

> We were curious to know how the money was economised, and heard from a labourer the following account of a day's diet. After doing up his horses he takes breakfast, which is made of flour with a little butter, and water 'from the tea-kettle' poured over it. He takes with him to the field a piece of bread and (if he has not a young family and can afford it) cheese to eat at mid-day. He returns home in the afternoon to a few potatoes, and possibly a little bacon, though only those who are better off can afford this. The supper very commonly consists of bread and water. The appearance of the labourers showed, as might be expected from such meagre diet, a want of that vigour and activity which mark the well-fed ploughman of the midland and northern counties. Beer is given by the master in hay-time and harvest. Some farmers allow ground for planting potatoes to their labourers, and carry home their fuel — which on the downs, where there is no wood, is a very expensive article in a labourer's family.

The *Daily News* summarised the weekly expenditure of a typical Warwickshire labourer's family in 1872 rather more succinctly: 'Wages, father 12s.; son 3s.; 15s. per week. The week's bread and flour, 9s. 4d.; one cwt. of coal, 1s. 1d.; schooling for children, 2d.; rent of allotment (1 chain), 1d.; total, 10s. 8d. Leaves for butcher's meat, tea, sugar, soap, lights, pepper and salt, clothes for seven persons, beer, medicine and pocket money, per week 4s. 4d.'

Evidently things in some parts had not changed very much, despite the Golden Age.

Averages are difficult to strike when talking about wages. Caird, for instance, noticed that in 1850 the labourers in the north were getting wages a third higher than those in the south (11s. 6d. as against 8s. 5d.). There were many differences from district to district, and of course men had many skills, some more valuable than others. Roughly speaking, however, the main regional differentials tended to close during this period, and average wages rose from about 9s. 6d. a week in 1850 to 11s. in 1860 and 12s. in 1870. The

Life on the land: a magnificent early photograph of nineteenth-century farm labourers

movement of real wages was also irregularly upward. But certainly this was no particularly Golden Age for those who worked on the land, as opposed to those who owned or farmed it.

The number of those so involved fell between 1851 and 1871 by over 250,000, or 22%. The 1873 figure was 989,000. The figure actually disguises the tremendously high rate of migration from the land – over 75,000 people a year throughout the second half of the nineteenth century. What happened was that the rural population reproduced itself at a tremendous rate, and at the same time streamed off at an even faster rate into the towns – or even abroad. The net effect was thus a gentle fall. This 'flight from the land', as it was sometimes called, was symptomatic of the changing position of agriculture – no longer the greatest force in the national economy, soon to be no longer even the country's major industry.

THE END OF AN ERA: 1870–1914

British agriculture from the 1870s onwards was affected like every other part of the British economy by the development of a world economic system unfavourable to the continuation of British economic supremacy. The early stages of the change were obscured for farmers at the time by a sequence of outstandingly bad weather years in the 1870s. Production was disrupted by rain and cold, and the harvest of 1879 was actually the worst of the century. In these circumstances it was only to be expected that large quantities of imports would be brought in, and farmers tided over their losses as best they could, and waited impatiently for a return to the 'normal' conditions of, for instance, 1868, when Caird had calculated that 80% of the food consumed in Britain was also produced there.

But things had changed for good. In the Baltic lands and southern Russia, and still more in Canada and the U.S.A., a great surge of agricultural colonisation was bringing into cultivation vast new tracts of rich earth. In North America, particularly, this process was quite largely the work of British emigrants, and aided by British capital and technical skill. The produce of these new farms could now be hurried over great distances by railway, and sent on by fast steamship, at comparatively low cost, to flood the British market. And this is what it continued to do, even when the British producers had the goods to compete with it. In a sense, the fears of those who had opposed agricultural free trade in the 1840s were justified at last.

The rise in grain imports, and particularly wheat, was the most impressive of all. The methods of high farming had of course tended to diminish the quantity of wheat grown at home, so that foreign producers already had rather more than a foot in the door. In fact, by the early 1870s they were supplying nearly half the wheat consumed in Britain. During this period, however, they rapidly improved their position still further. Gross average annual imports of wheat increased from 58,314,000 cwt. in 1875–77 to 99,257,000 cwt. in 1893–95. This latter figure represented 77% of the nation's consumption. Imports of barley also rose dramatically; those of oats rather less sharply.

At the same time that the grain market was falling into foreign hands, the meat market – something a good deal more important to the high farmer – was also under attack. Here the new lands were Australia and New Zealand, and once again transport improvements played an essential role in bringing the goods to Britain at competitive prices. In this case, railways and steam-

Competition for English graziers: frozen meat being shipped from Australia in the S.S. *Victoria*

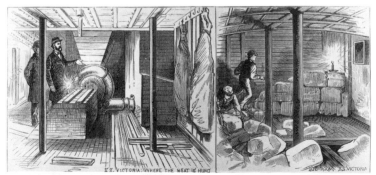

ships had to be supplemented by a new invention – refrigeration. A British patent for a refrigerator had been taken out by an American called Jacob Perkins as long ago as 1834, but most of the development work was done by a Scot, James Harrison, who emigrated to Australia and was struck by the possibilities of applying the principle to ships, which could then carry meat to arrive virtually fresh in England. There was a good deal of controversy about the safety of this revolutionary process, but trade in refrigerated meat was legalised in Britain in 1877, and in 1880 a small sailing ship, the *Strathleven*, arrived in London with a cargo of meat that proved to be completely sound. After this the practice spread rapidly. In 1895 28% of the beef and veal, 31% of the mutton and lamb and 49% of the pigmeat consumed in Britain was imported – though not all of this came in as dead, carcass meat. This represented roughly a 30% rise in total meat imports over the previous thirty years.

In the face of this new abundance of supplies, prices fell, as the following figures make clear.

AGRICULTURAL PRICES, 1870–1900

Wheat (shillings per quarter)

1870–74	55s.
1875–79	47s. 8d.
1880–84	42s. 5d.
1885–89	31s. 7d.
1890–94	29s. 8d.
1895–99	27s. 10d.
1900–04	27s. 4d.

(Figures are given in approximate annual averages for each five-year period.)

Meat prices fell by approximately 25% between 1883 and 1887, having held up well until then. Beef and mutton prices moved separately in the period 1887–96; average prices of beef were 13% below those of 1871, and of mutton, 3% below.

These figures on their own would seem to indicate a total disaster for British farming. In fact, things were not so bad as all that. Although food prices fell, production costs, apart from labour wages, fell too, so that it was possible throughout the period to find farmers who were quite content with the way things were going. Population rose during the depression by the fantastic number of ten million; so the market was continually expanding, particularly for farmers who could see what was wanted. The answer lay in a change in the pattern of farming.

Change was further assisted by new developments in eating habits – diet.

As wages rose for the great masses of townspeople, they began to demand more varied and interesting food. The growing volume and range of imports assisted this movement, and spurred the British farmers to respond in their turn. At the same time, doctors and scientists were urging changes on grounds of health, while advances in techniques of preserving and keeping food (bottling, canning and refrigeration) further extended the scope of even a working man's diet. The old reliance on bread and potatoes gradually died away, and there was an increase in the consumption of meat and dairy products, green vegetables and fresh fruit. Potato-eating seems to have reached its peak, in fact, in 1871, and then to have declined by as much as one-third by the end of the century.

Those farmers who could responded to this by changing their style of operations. The classic mixed arable system, in which crops and animals supported each other, was abandoned in favour of concentration on one of the big selling lines – livestock, dairying, vegetables or fruit. Cattle-feed was bought, not grown. A small, but significant, number of farmers close to the big towns took this process to its logical conclusion and converted themselves into market gardeners, cultivating small areas of ground intensively for special crops.

Unfortunately, this sort of option was not available to all farmers everywhere. Some were prevented from taking it up by simple physical factors – they were too far from a railway, or from a densely-settled urban area, for the operation to pay. Others had the wrong sort of soil – once again, heavy soil often proved a drawback. For these reasons chiefly, land values fell particularly badly in Essex and parts of Suffolk, Wiltshire, Berkshire, Hampshire and Gloucestershire.

Probably still more farmers were troubled by sheer lack of the capital on the scale that was necessary to finance any conversion operation. The great investments of the Golden Age had been carried out by the landowners, who had been able to afford them because rents, reflecting agricultural prices, stood at a high level. Thus the landlords had had income to spare. Now that prices were low, rents fell too, and so the landlords were short of income, at any rate for such purposes as further investment in farms which, as we saw in the last section, could already be reasonably regarded as very highly capitalised. The tenant farmers could not move on their own accounts. They would not usually have the resources, and even when they did they would very commonly hold their land on a short lease or even as tenants-at-will (that is on six month's notice) – terms which effectively made it impossible for them to embark on improvement programmes themselves.

In these difficult circumstances, the most that a good many farmers could think of doing was to go in for 'low farming', as opposed to 'high farming'.

RENT OF AGRICULTURAL LAND IN ENGLAND AND WALES,
1870–1914
(*Index: 28 shillings per acre equals 100*)

1870–74	101
1875–79	104
1880–84	94
1885–89	83
1890–94	79
1895–99	74
1900–04	72
1905–09	74
1910–14	75

That is to say, they pared their costs to a minimum (often by working long hours themselves, and dispensing with some of their hired labour), took as little out of the farm in the way of profits as they could possibly manage on, and hoped to weather the storm. The long years of boom had made them basically optimistic, and many of them stuck it out in the hope of better times until they were too hopelessly in the red ever to pull themselves out again. Even for the luckier ones, this penny-pinching was a miserable business.

For the labourer wages rose slightly, especially during the period of Joseph Arch's Agricultural Labourers' Union in the 1870s, but still remained on average below 15s. At some times and in some places they dipped well below this figure. Government-inspired attempts to improve conditions of housing and education in the countryside were of little avail and the flight from the land went on apace. An ambitious scheme, the smallholdings movement, aimed at stopping it by restoring an independent, property-owning peasantry. Two Acts of Parliament were passed, in 1892 and 1907, to assist in the formation of miniature farms of a few acres each, capable of being tilled by one man and his family, who would derive their livelihood entirely from them. By 1914 there were 14,000 such smallholdings, with an average size of 14 acres. But these were still relatively insignificant. A labourer could only get two-thirds (allowing for payments in kind) of an industrial worker's wage. A tenant farmer or smallholder could not be sure of covering his costs. Even a landlord was beginning to look upon an estate as something of a liability — especially after a Conservative Chancellor of the Exchequer, Goschen, had introduced the idea of Death Duties in 1889, an idea which was taken up and vastly expanded by the Liberal Harcourt in 1892.

The numbers of people making their living from the land therefore continued to dwindle. In 1871 there were said to be 249,735 farmers and graziers in England and Wales. In 1881 the figure was 223,943; in 1891,

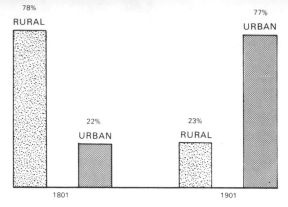

Changes in distribution of population

223,610; in 1901, 224,299; in 1911, 208,761. The figures for agricultural labourers fell from 988,824 in 1871, to 798,912 in 1891, and to 665,258 in 1911. This last represented only 7·6% of the total working population. Agriculture was no longer the country's major industry.

Finally, the great estates began to break up; this was, admittedly, not so much a result of agricultural depression, as a response to government taxation policies, and a consequence of a change in the whole social and political position of the landed aristocracy. But if the reasons were complex, the process itself was clear; in 1913 alone no less than 800,000 acres changed hands.

The consequences of this break-up, together with the decline in the general position of agriculture, were enormous; the whole fabric of English rural life as it had been for 200 years was torn up and thrown aside. We are still only just beginning to grapple with the new situation.

THE RETURN OF PROTECTION: 1914–39

The gradual evolution of British agriculture was sharply disrupted by the First World War. The effects of the war were variable; in certain respects, it accelerated existing trends – as for instance in reducing further the influence of the old landowning aristocracy; in other respects, it had a reactionary effect – particularly in producing a temporary swing back to grain production; most important of all, it pointed the way to future developments, especially those concerned with government policies.

When war broke out in 1914 Britain was more dependent than ever before on foreign foodstuffs. When one considers the extent of this dependence, it is amazing that nothing significant was done to regulate the situation until 1916, and that over the war as a whole the average number of calories available per adult male hardly fell below the pre-war figure.

270

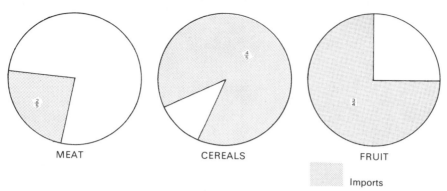

MEAT   CEREALS   FRUIT

Imports

Food production and consumption in Britain, 1914

	Calories per day
1909–13	3,442
1917 (the worst year of the war)	3,320
Safe minimum	3,300

Awareness of the need for controls was forced on the government chiefly by U-boat sinkings in 1916, and when Lloyd George became Prime Minister in December of that year he appointed a Food Controller, who proceeded from 1917 to fix prices, regulate the supplies and organise rationing. There was something of a panic during the winter of 1917–18, but the government's measures proved adequate. Regulations extended more and more widely, partly at least because of a natural spreading tendency which led them on from one thing to another, but chiefly because it is not possible to regulate supply without regulating production as well. Farmers were directly affected. From the end of 1917 the government was active in ordering the slaughter of livestock and controlling the sale of carcasses; from the spring of the same year it was busy urging farmers to grow more wheat – supplying labour (316,000 women, some of them organised in a Land Army, and 22,000 men, many of them prisoners of war), fertilisers, and newcomers to the farming scene, tractors – several thousand of them. Finally, increasing use was made of subsidies to encourage farmers to produce foodstuffs of the type required, and at the same time to keep the price low for the consumer; £50 million a year was paid out for wheat alone between 1917 and 1920, and 4 million acres of grassland were ploughed up in 1917 and 1918 alone.

Clearly this was intervention on a scale undreamed of in the *laissez-faire* years of the nineteenth century. It was begun reluctantly, in response to a danger of national calamity far more urgent than anything that had happened in the French wars a hundred years previously. People accepted it, because it

271

was so obviously necessary; but they did not like it. The farmers were hurt in their pride when they had to work and produce to rule. A. G. Street, who was farming as a young man under his father during the war, wrote in his book *Farmer's Glory*:

Although my father was making money out of his farming at that time, neither he nor the men had any joy in it. There was no definite system. If the labour shortage made it impossible to do a certain job at a certain season, the fact of its being left undone was resented strongly. For instance, to have a good plant of rape and turnips, and to be unable to get them hand-hoed and singled out, rankled. Thinning them out by repeated harrowing was reckoned a poor job. To see banks untrimmed, ditches uncleaned, field corners not dug, and one's farm generally untidy, hurt one's proper pride. But there it was. There was only barely enough labour for essentials, and the frills had to be cut out. From 1916 the farms in the countryside were allowed to deteriorate or to 'go back', a local term which describes the situation admirably.

When the war was over, there was a general desire to get back to the good old days, so far as society at large was concerned. The case of agriculture was more complicated. For one thing, it was simply not possible to drop all controls immediately, since shortages of food were if anything rather more severe immediately after the fighting than they had been while it was still going on. Milk control did not *begin* until the winter of 1918–19. Secondly, the farmers had seen something of the advantages that protection, in the shape of controls, could bring to their flagging concerns, and they were not at all sure that they wanted to be thrown back on their own resources.

A war-time Act of Parliament, the Corn Production Act of 1917, had offered guaranteed prices and wages to farmers and farmworkers as encouragement to produce large quantities of corn, and this policy of government guarantees was continued and extended by the Agriculture Act of 1920. Unfortunately, no sooner was this passed than grain prices came crashing down from their war-time peaks.

WHEAT PRICES, 1914–39

	Shillings per quarter
1910–14	32s. 11d.
1915–19	66s. 7d.
1920–24	44s. 3½d.
1925–29	11s. 2d.
1930–34	5s. 11d.
1935–38	7s. 1½d.

(Figures are given in approximate annual averages for each five-year period)

This meant that the government was faced with the horrifying prospect of having to pay out enormous sums in subsidies to the farmers – possibly as much as £20 million. Rather than do that, they promptly repealed the Acts (1921). The farmers – and their labourers – were thrown on the cold world.

With some difficulty, therefore, they went back to the pattern which they had been following before the war had turned everything upside down – less arable, more pasture; more meat, dairy products, vegetables and fruit. Demand for all these goods continued to rise, not so much now because of an increasing population, but rather because the standard of living was going up and people were eating more and better and more varied food. However, if British farmers had an eye for the urban market, so had their foreign competitors. Foreign costs were falling fast, techniques of packing and preserving were improving and transport was speeding up still further with the arrival of motor vehicles. So the share of the home market enjoyed by British farmers continued to dwindle, and depression became ever darker.

As demands for government aid grew more and more insistent, some limited help was given. The Smallholdings Acts of the pre-war period were revived and extended in 1919, 1926 and 1931. The position of tenant farmers was improved by the Agricultural Holdings Act of 1923. Loan facilities were made available by the Agricultural Credit Act of 1928. And lastly, the government intervened directly to set up two new branches of agricultural activity, which in course of time proved to be valuable aids both to farmers and to the nation. The first of these was the Forestry Commission (1919); originally designed to repair the ravages of war-time on Britain's timber reserves, it has since become an important part of the national system of land economy. By 1939 it had acquired and planted one million acres. The other new venture was a brand new sugar-beet industry (1925). Heavily subsidised, the crop was a success. By the mid-1930s it was grown on 350,000 acres, and provided employment for 32,000 men in the fields, as well as many more in factories. In 1936 a fresh Act reorganised production, and created the British Sugar Corporation (B.S.C.) Ltd, a largely government-controlled body, to supervise the industry. This was a significant step – a move towards the modern system of state management.

This aid, however, was much too limited to satisfy the farmers, and events in the late 1920s strengthened their hand in demanding more protection. North America, Australia and Argentina flooded the world with wheat, so that prices fell by nearly 50% between 1929 and 1931. The world slump sent governments everywhere scurrying into the shelter of tariffs to protect their industries, and Britain followed suit in 1931. Why should British agriculture be left to face the blast alone?

Agricultural protection in fact returned in the years 1931 to 1933, in a series of Acts of Parliament, following a conference of Dominion representa-

The tractor comes to English farms: harvesting in Wiltshire, 1934

tives meeting at Ottawa. Imports were limited by a system of protective duties. Production and supply were regulated by a number of government Marketing Boards – for milk, potatoes, hops, bacon and pigs. Prices, and thus profits, were stabilised, manipulated and, if necessary, subsidised. As a result, depression in the 1930s was far from absolute. Output rose above pre-war levels, and techniques continued to improve, particularly with respect to fertilisers, pest and weed control, and machinery. Combine harvesters, milking machines and, above all, tractors – 55,000 of them by 1939 – helped to raise individual productivity by some 20% per person between 1921 and 1941; and crop yields also went up in many cases.

The manpower picture, however, was gloomy. Whereas in 1911 agriculture had accounted for 7·6% of the total working population, by 1920 it was down to 6·3%, and by 1938 to 3·9%. This in itself might have meant just economy of manpower; but of the 10,000 men who left the industry each year the greater part were young. It was the old men who stayed, and their wages – 28s. per week in 1924, 32s. 4d. in 1936 – were only a third of the wages paid to a skilled bricklayer.

An overalled mechanic drives a 1970 combine harvester. How long before the hedges go?

Milking machine

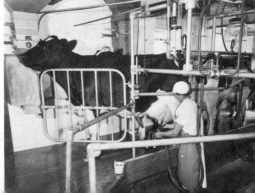

In good times the surest sign of agricultural prosperity is a rise in the number of owner-occupied holdings. The break-up of the great estates had begun a trend this way shortly before the war, when farmers had seemed to be getting the measure of the depression; and the brief post-war boom had enabled it to continue.

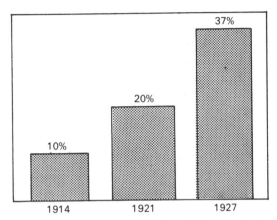

Proportion of farmers occupying their own land,
1914–1927

After 1925, however, buying virtually ceased.

The state of agriculture in the late 1930s was summed up by a government document, the Scott Report, published in 1942.

> Less arable land was to be seen in the landscape; the number of derelict fields, rank with coarse matted grass, thistle, weeds, and brambles, multiplied; ditches became choked and no longer served as effective drains; hedges became overgrown and straggled over the edges of other fields; gates and fences fell into disrepair; farm roads were left unmade. Signs of decay were to be seen also in many of the buildings ... the landscape of 1938 had, in many districts, assumed a neglected and unkept appearance.

THE NEWEST NEW FARMING: 1939 TO THE PRESENT DAY

The pattern of the First World War was to some extent repeated in the Second, so far as the history of British agriculture was concerned. A shortage of imported food, made acute by U-boat sinkings, once again led to massive government intervention and radical reorganisation of the industry in the interests of higher output. Many of the techniques employed were the same – administration through a system of centrally directed County War Agricultural Committees, a Women's Land Army and so on. Some of the mistakes were copied too.

275

Given these basic similarities, however, there are also great differences to be noted. Britain started the war even more dependent on imported food than she had been in 1914; the leap in productivity caused by war-time re-organisation was startlingly greater the second time round; and both the measures taken during the war and the way in which they were pursued afterwards had a genuinely revolutionary effect on the position of British agriculture.

The best way to measure Britain's dependence on imported food is in terms of calories. By the late 1930s about 70% of the country's calorie consumption came from abroad. The effect of government policies, which were applied from 1939 onwards, was to raise home calorie production by 70%, distributed in such a way that about half the import total of food was saved. Put another way, home production of food accounted for 42% of consumption in 1938, and 52% in 1946.

Once again, a major part of the effort was directed at raising the arable acreage. From June 1939 subsidies (initially of £2 per acre) were paid for the ploughing up of old grass. As a result, by the end of the war, the arable acreage had been raised from nearly 12 million to nearly 18 million acres. Animal farming naturally diminished, except in the case of cattle, which went up in numbers from 8 million head to 8,700,000, chiefly for their value as milk suppliers.

Almost more striking than the increase in the sheer quantity of arable was the great improvement in yields, that is, in the quantity of crop successfully harvested from every acre. The yield of wheat per acre, for instance, rose from 17·7 cwt. in 1938 to 19·7 in 1942. This was not achieved by a heavier application of labour to the land, although of course it was part of the war-time policy to raise the number of labourers, as it had been in 1914–18. The key factors were the use of machines and fertilisers, as will be seen from the following table.

AGRICULTURAL CHANGES DURING THE SECOND WORLD WAR

	1939	1946
Quantity of fertiliser used (tons):		
Nitrogen	60,000	165,000
Phosphate	170,000	359,000
Potash	75,000	101,000
Lime	1,300,000	2,000,000
Numbers of machines used:		
Tractors	56,000	203,000
Combine harvesters	29,500	48,300 (1942)
Total mechanical horse-power	2,000,000	5,000,000

This feature of the war effort – increased productivity achieved by means of technology – is of central importance to the history of farming in Britain in the last thirty years. It is in fact the newest form of new farming, and its limits have apparently not yet been reached.

Government subsidies, often on a high level, are obviously essential to this type of policy now that the old type of 'improving landlord' has disappeared from the scene. During the Second World War a pattern emerged of subsidies, loans and grants running sometimes as high as 75% of the cost of a project.

Backing on such a scale clearly indicates that an entirely new importance was attached to agriculture after 1939. But the critical period in the recent history of agriculture came in the years following the end of the war. As after 1918, the immediate post-war period saw food shortages and difficulties if anything greater than those which had been experienced during the war itself, so that there could be no immediate question of dismantling controls or relaxing the drive for higher productivity and output. In fact, bread itself, popularly regarded as the most basic of all foods, actually had to be rationed temporarily in 1946 – something that had never happened before. But once the most urgent need for regulation had passed away, there was still no move to abandon the position established during the emergency. A socialist government was in office, untroubled by doubts about the desirability of state management, and for their part the farmers, though not on the whole socialist in their political views, were too firmly convinced of the benefits of this sort of protection to want to go back to pre-war miseries.

An important Act of Parliament, the Agriculture Act of 1947, sent British farmers marching down the road denied to their predecessors in 1921. Annual price reviews and guaranteed markets were to banish the spectres of failure and bankruptcy which had hung over the land during the long years of depression, and taken the heart out of so many men. Government encouragement was given to mechanisation and improvement programmes, particularly where these were undertaken in the context of a scheme of mixed farming. This helped to maintain a relatively high arable acreage. Finally, the industry was given planned objectives to work for – a 20% increase in output over a period of five years, with the emphasis especially on import-saving crops. In fact, this target figure represented no less than 150% of the pre-war output; incredibly, it was almost achieved – the final tally for 1950–51 was 146% of pre-war output. The rewards of success were golden – average farm incomes in the same period climbed to six times their pre-war peak.

From this point on, one success led to another. The Conservative government which took office in 1951 changed the mode of protection given to farmers, but the basic idea remained the same. Agriculture was still encouraged to expand, and the government was still prepared to intervene in 277 support of profits and to give aid to improvement schemes. But the idea of rigidly planned growth targets and close, prescriptive controls over crops and techniques was relaxed. Instead, farmers and consumers were to have greater freedom of choice, and the market was to find its own level.

Meanwhile, the stress on increased productivity remained unaltered. Output rose sharply in the early 1950s, and again in the middle 1960s, as the table shows.

AGRICULTURAL OUTPUT AFTER THE
SECOND WORLD WAR
Index: 1958 equals 100

	Agriculture, forestry, fishing	Gross domestic product
1946	78	75·6
1948	80	79·8
1950	88	85·7
1952	92	87·0
1954	96	94·3
1956	100	98·4
1958	100	100·0
1960	111	110·1
1962	115	113·5
1964	125	124·3
1966	129	129·2

This was achieved against a background of sharply falling employment from the war-time levels (though, with a predicted total manpower figure of 805,000 for 1970, agriculture was not far below its 1911 level of employment). Instead, the increase in productivity was achieved mainly by means of an ever higher concentration on technical and mechanical aids. The 1966 figure of 446,000 tractors meant that there was an average of 1·5 tractors to every holding of any size. This revolutionised methods and was accompanied by a tremendous increase in the number and type of tractor-hauled or power-operated machines, for every possible farming operation – tilling the land, harvesting, hedging and ditching, dairy work, package and transport, sheep and cattle handling, and so on. Mechanical skill came to be one of the principal requirements for a good farm labourer. The use of new materials has produced further significant changes; light and even prefabricated portable metal structures replacing permanent wooden or masonry buildings, for storage, and animal and poultry management. These, together with changes in harvesting and cattle feeding techniques, have made redundant the old type of farmyard, with its bars, byres, pig-sties and stacks of corn and fodder. The buildings are often pulled down or converted for grain-drying or other mechanical operations, and the empty stack-yard, concreted over, becomes a parking and loading bay.

This change in the traditional face of farming is only one of many. A more generally striking change is being brought about by the final abandonment of 'organic' farming, and the wholesale adoption of regulated chemical methods. This process really began in the Golden Age itself, with the advanced practices of high farming, but it is only now being taken to its logical conclusion. The fertility of the soil, its freedom from vegetable and animal 'pests' and the health of the crops are more and more regulated by the application of chemical compounds, often spread from the air by helicopters or light aeroplanes. The idea of cultivation as a self-sustaining balancing operation is giving way to a view which sees the soil as basic material, to be adjusted to suit the desired crop. As a necessary consequence of these mechanical—chemical methods, the shape of the landscape is changing, like the shape of the farmyards. Inconveniently small fields are being merged by the grubbing up of hedges and the levelling of ditches; timber is being cut down, and the 'unnecessary obstructions to economical tillage' spoken of by Caird a century ago are being removed at a faster rate than ever before.

This means, in fact, that the pattern of the countryside slowly built up during the 200 years that followed the enclosure of the open fields is now being a great deal more rapidly changed back to the medieval pattern – except that there is no forest, no fen and no waste.

The changes in animal and poultry farming brought about by developments in scientific, and particularly in bio-chemical, knowledge have made less impact on the eye, but have perhaps gone furthest of all in changing farming practice. Apart from the light sheds mentioned above, the chief outward sign of change is the appearance on many farms of tall silo towers, in which cattle feed is processed. Most people, however, have heard of the battery system for

Broiler-houses on a poultry-farm (Hampshire)

Inside the broiler

managing calves and poultry, using intensive care to minimise the space required for each bird or animal, while ensuring maximum return in the shortest possible time. Chemically treated feeds, mechanically administered and often supplemented by injections or other 'adjusting devices', are joined to regulated conditions of heat, light and air to 'process' the subject creature at high speed through the required part of its life cycle.

This side of the new style of intensive farming has attracted a good deal of hostile comment from people who object to animals being treated in such a ruthless way. More recently, however, the 'exploiting approach' has come in for even sharper criticism, actually based on scientific grounds. It is being alleged that the precarious balance of biology is being too radically and rapidly altered, and that 'control' measures may in fact produce a situation which is out of control. As examples of this danger, biologists point to the threat of dust-bowls which can develop (and possibly have already begun to develop in East Anglia) where large tracts of bare soil, not bonded together by roots or sheltered by windbreaks, are exposed to rain, frost and wind; to the possibility that certain pests may acquire immunity to all known methods of control and flourish unchecked by natural agents – as has already happened with rats in certain parts of Wales and the Midlands; and to the incalculable results of breaking a natural chain of biological dependence – as happens for instance when the chemical poisoning of a certain type of insect produces the accidental sterilisation and eventual extermination of a certain type of bird which preys on the insect.

At the same time as criticisms of this sort are mounting, the whole position of agriculture is being questioned by those who feel that, if we are to achieve a high quality of life on this increasingly crowded island, we must plan, not merely individual industries and activities, but everything in co-ordination. For the past thirty years agricultural expansion and efficiency have been pursued as ends in themselves. It is now being suggested that it may be necessary to grade our priorities, and, in some areas at least, to place a higher value on the use of the countryside as a complement to the town for purposes of amenity and recreation, rather than for food production. Food supplies can be drawn from the empty lands of the world, so long at any rate as we can exchange them for the industrial goods which are now the chief British products. Green spaces, trees and every type of natural habitat cannot be imported, and these, it is argued, are essential components of a complete and civilised life.

Thus we end on a note of paradox; the innovations of the Agricultural Revolution have worked themselves out in a circular way, to the destruction of the farms of the Agricultural Revolution itself. More important still, the pursuit of commercial efficiency, so long regarded as beneficial, has itself come to be regarded with suspicion.

East Anglian dust-bowl: field dykes on a Suffolk farm after a high wind. Where are the hedges?

Suggestions for further work and discussion

1. Examine the farm-buildings in a selected area. When were they built, and for what original purpose?

2. Study a great estate, and see what effect its history has had on that of agriculture in the district.

3. From the figures given in the chapter, construct a graph showing fluctuations in agricultural prices over the last 200 years.

4. Farming is often described as a way of life; does it still deserve this compliment? Talk to people who have worked on the land for a long time, and find out how they view the changes of the last 50 years.

5. Subjects for essays or discussion: describe the major changes in government policy to agriculture over the last 200 years, and estimate their significance.

What is the likely effect on British agriculture of Britain's merging with the Common Market?

What does the mug tell you about the life of a farmer in the mid-nineteenth century?

How many farming implements can you identify? What were they used for?

Books for further reading:

William Cobbett, *Rural Rides*, 1885.

The novels of Thomas Hardy.

A. G. Street, *Farmer's Glory*, Faber & Faber, 1956.

A. G. Street, *The Gentleman of the Party*, F. A. Thorpe, 1965.

R. Blythe, *Akenfield*, Allen Lane, The Penguin Press, 1969.

12 : The Twentieth-century Economy – War and Slump

The First World War broke out after a period in which it seemed as if the British economy had completely recovered from the problems which troubled it in the last quarter of the nineteenth century. From about the 1840s to the 1870s the economy boomed. Industry and commerce mushroomed, helped by railways, free trade and British investment in foreign countries. Britain became both the workshop and the market-place of the world, the centre of world industry, trade and finance.

Yet in the last part of the century signs appeared that all was not well. Exports actually stagnated, and partly because of this, industrial growth slowed down. This period is sometimes called 'The Great Depression', but the phrase is misleading. Except in agriculture, where special conditions existed, there were no very obvious difficulties. There was certainly no widespread unemployment or closing of factories, as was to happen in the 1930s. In fact, because of lower food prices, the standard of living of most working-class families actually improved.

On the other hand, there were undoubtedly serious problems below the surface, even though they were not fully recognised at the time. These problems and their causes were complicated. The basic fault, however, was that British industry was becoming less efficient by international standards. Too few industrialists were adopting the new techniques which were helping the industrialisation of new trading rivals. Two examples among many will show this: the Gilchrist Thomas steel-making process, described in Chapter 7, was adopted only slowly in Britain (even though invented in London!) and electric power was in use far sooner in American and German factories. Other countries began to produce goods more efficiently, and therefore more cheaply.

As a result of such competition exporters found it more difficult to sell abroad, especially in those countries, like the United States, which imposed heavy tariffs against foreign products. British industry depended very much on exports, and so a slump in trade was bound to hit industrial output. Fortunately, the opening up of new colonies and other territories in the late nineteenth century gave fresh opportunities for trade and investment. Exports and industry recovered, and the years before 1914 were prosperous ones for business. The problem appeared to have been solved. Unfortunately this was not really so, for the basic weakness of industrial inefficiency remained. Little

283

A view of late nineteenth-century German industry, which offered a growing challenge to Britain

was done to bring industry more up to date in its methods, for there seemed nothing to worry about. This is why the economic position in 1914, though it seemed secure enough, was in fact dangerously exposed. Britain depended so much on trade (and on foreign investment) that any major upset to the existing world trading and financial system was certain to have disastrous effects.

This is exactly what happened. In this chapter we tell the story of how Britain coped with the strains of war, only to find that this effort, and the after-effects of the war, brought the old problems out into the open. The economy, so strong and dominating in the nineteenth century, suffered the greatest collapse since the start of industrialisation. But we also show, in Chapter 13, how the challenge was met. A process of reconstruction began which, despite the effects of another major war, led eventually to the prosperous conditions of today.

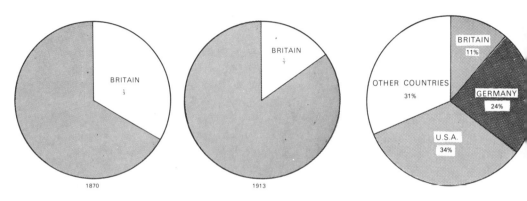

Britain's share of world trade 1870 and 1913

World output of chemicals 191

The Problems

The outbreak of war in 1914 came as a shock to many people in Britain. There was little anxiety, however, and it was generally thought that the war would be a short one, perhaps over in time for Christmas. The government, led by H. H. Asquith, seemed to share this view. It was very slow to make adequate arrangements. One member of the Cabinet, Winston Churchill, spoke publicly of the need for 'business as usual', implying that there was no need for any changes in the economy or national way of life.

This was an understandable point of view, for few wars in which Britain had been involved had really affected the people at home. Fighting usually took place far away and, on the whole, life in Britain carried on as normal. But the First World War turned out to be quite different from expectations. The scale of fighting was greater than anything previously seen. Far from being over quickly, it dragged on for years. The casualties on all sides proved frighteningly high, and the cost in men and money was enormous; at least ten million men were killed altogether.

The government came to realise gradually that if the war was to be won several things had to be done: a huge sum of money had to be found to pay for it; industry had to be properly geared to the needs of war; the civilian population had to be moved into a war effort no less important than the fighting at the fronts. In fact, the idea of 'total war', involving the entire population, emerged for the first time. None of this could be done by private enterprise and voluntary effort alone. The government had to abandon the idea that it could stand aloof. It had to step in and take control where required. This involved very great changes in economic and social life. Changes did not come easily or quickly. There was no set plan. Few men had an overall understanding of what had to be done. But as the war went on, and the needs became clear, more and more was done. By the end of the war, in 1918, the situation had been completely transformed. The government was in control of much of the economy, and practically everyone was in some way bound up with the war effort.

Paying for the War

One thing that was clear from the start was that the war would be expensive, however long it lasted, and extra money would have to be found to pay for it. The amount turned out to be far greater than anyone forecast; the government's expenditure between 1914 and 1919 was about £9,500 million. In addition, it made loans to allies totalling £1,825 million, including £556 million to Russia.

The first way to raise this money was to increase taxes. Income tax went up

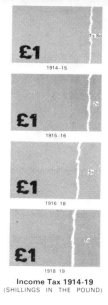

Income Tax 1914-19
(SHILLINGS IN THE POUND)

1914-15

1915-16

1916 18

1918 19

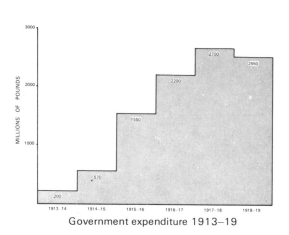

Government expenditure 1913–19

several times until it reached six shillings in the pound in 1918. Indirect taxes on goods like tobacco and spirits were also raised. A new tax was introduced in 1915, called the 'Excess Profits Tax'. Any business making a profit above a certain amount had to pay at a tax on the extra, at a rate which eventually rose to 80%. The aim of this was not only to bring in more revenue, but also to discourage some firms from taking advantage of the war to put up prices and make huge profits ('profiteering').

Despite these increases, taxation only covered about 30% of government expenditure. The government soon had to turn to the traditional war-time method of borrowing from the people. Government securities, called 'War Loans', were sold, and an active National Savings Movement gave poorer people the chance to contribute. Borrowing in these and other ways pushed up the National Debt from £650 million to £8,000 million.

Even so, this was still not enough, and two other sources of money had to be tapped. British investors had built up a large reserve of shares and other property abroad in the nineteenth century. Some of this was now sold, voluntarily at first, but compulsorily after 1917. It is not clear just how much was sold, and some new investment overseas took place until stopped in 1916. It seems probable, however, that between £300 and £500 million, about 10% of Britain's total holdings, was raised on balance in this way. None the less, Britain still had to borrow from overseas, mainly from the United States. Loans usually took the form of credit for the materials and equipment supplied to Britain, and total borrowing from this source was about £1,300 million.

The government was anxious to save money wherever possible, and it
286 particularly wanted to keep up its reserves of gold. Other financial measures

were therefore taken, and in particular the gold standard was abandoned in practice in 1914, the first time for nearly a century. This meant that banks no longer had to pay gold instead of banknotes to any customer who asked for it. 'Treasury Notes' of £1 and ten shillings were put into circulation and these rapidly replaced gold sovereigns and half sovereigns, which were never brought back. In 1915 the Chancellor of the Exchequer, Reginald McKenna, put customs duties on various goods, such as motor vehicles, films, watches and musical instruments. This was to prevent unnecessary imports from using currency reserves and wasting shipping space. These were the first new customs duties since the coming of free trade in the nineteenth century. From 1915 no new shares could be issued on the Stock Exchange without special permission. Most other aspects of trade and finance were brought under government regulation at some stage in the war. By these means the war was financed. It is worth noting that a large proportion of the cost (two-thirds) was met out of borrowed money. This placed a heavy burden on the future generations who had to pay it back.

Production for the War

The problem was to make sure that enough goods were produced for the armed forces without reducing too much the amount available for civilians. The Defence of the Realm Act (DORA), 1914, gave the government widespread powers, including the right to take over any industry or service. This had happened at the start of the war in the case of railways, though for purely military reasons. The jute industry was also taken over very quickly, to ensure that enough cheap sandbags were available for use in the trenches. Otherwise the government was reluctant to use its powers and, to begin with, it continued to buy war materials – guns, shells, uniforms, food and other essentials – from private manufacturers.

This proved to be a mistake. As the government bought on a huge scale, prices rose. This always happens if there is heavy buying in a free market. Moreover, private firms were sometimes unable to keep up with orders and some of the goods produced were of a poor standard. This was especially true of shells. Soldiers on the Western Front were often bitter about the low quality of their ammunition, which cost lives unnecessarily. The climax came when many of the shells used in the Gallipoli campaign of 1915 failed to explode. This 'shell scandal' helped to bring about a change of organisation.

In 1915 munitions factories were taken over by the government, and a Ministry of Munitions set up to supervise them. David Lloyd George was appointed Minister of Munitions. He was a man who understood the need for vigorous action at home if the war was to be won. He began with a tiny staff and no proper offices. By 1918 the Ministry had a staff of fifteen thousand, directing three million workers in two hundred and eighteen factories, **287**

David Lloyd George

including specially built 'National Shell Factories'. The quality of shells improved markedly, as did that of all the other weapons of war which the Ministry produced.

The success of Lloyd George and the Ministry of Munitions was important. He became Prime Minister in 1916, and immediately set about reorganising the war effort, and establishing new controls over industries and services. By the end of the war, control had been extended to shipping services, coal-mines, cotton- and flour-mills, and also distilleries. Licences were needed for any new building work. Control must not be confused with nationalisation, which means state ownership. These industries were not owned by the state, but controlled by it for the duration of the war. In most cases the owners continued to manage the companies.

Food supply was a special problem. British farmers increased their output considerably, but imports of food were still essential, as were raw materials for industry. The Germans knew this and tried to starve Britain into submission by submarine warfare. In the whole war German U-Boats sank nearly eight million tons of British, allied and neutral shipping. By early 1917 Britain was running very short of some supplies, especially wheat. If an answer had not been found to this menace, it is possible that Britain might have been forced into negotiation or surrender, as the hardship already caused was considerable. The danger was only averted when the convoy system was introduced in 1917. Merchant ships were required to sail in convoys, sometimes containing more than a hundred ships, protected by naval destroyers. This cut down losses considerably and eventually overcame the threat.

Labour supply was another problem. With so many men, many of them craftsmen, joining the forces, it was essential to find workers to man the factories and to keep vital services running. By June 1915 nearly 20% of male engineering workers had volunteered to fight, and by the end of the war

A German U-boat of the First World War

a total of six million men had joined up. This left large gaps to be filled at home. The government's policy was not altogether successful, but it managed to cope. Early in 1915 an agreement was reached with all the Trade Unions, except the Miners' Union. They agreed to settle all disputes by arbitration, and not to strike. They also agreed to allow unskilled workers, including women, to do what were regarded as skilled jobs. This was called 'dilution' of labour, and it was widely practised. On the whole the Unions kept to their word, though there was difficulty late in the war, as some men became bitter at the hardship of life. The presence in the Cabinet of some Labour Party leaders, like Arthur Henderson, helped to smooth matters over, but the government still had to take legal powers to prevent key workers from joining the forces, to direct them to certain jobs and to prevent them from changing their job without permission.

One other attempt to improve production was the tightening up of the laws relating to public houses, in the hope of keeping some workers more sober. The restriction on 'opening hours', laid down then, still operates. In Carlisle and Gretna, where there were large munitions factories, the government actually nationalised the public houses, and runs them to this day (though it was proposed in 1971 to sell them to private enterprise).

New ministries were founded to deal with the extended work of the government. By 1918 there were Ministries of Labour, Food, Shipping, National Service and Transport. The Civil Service was enormously expanded from the days of 1914 when, for example, there had been only twenty clerks in the Army Contracts Department!

There were some gaps, of course. Food rationing was begun only in 1918, and was far from complete even then. None the less, compared with the situation in 1914, the economic picture was very different. The government employed the majority of British workers, either directly or through other controls. It made sure that essential supplies reached the troops, and also reached those fighting on the home front. Whatever mistakes were made, this was a great achievement.

The People and the War

The aspect of war-time life which affected ordinary people most closely was the fighting itself. For the first time the great majority of the nation's young men were required to fight. At the start of the war the regular army had far too few men to fight a war on the Continent. It had to be expanded by reserves and, initially, by volunteers. During the first eighteen months of the war, 2,476,000 volunteers responded to the appeal of Lord Kitchener, the Secretary for War, helped by his famous recruiting poster with its commanding finger pointing at the reader, above the words 'Your Country Needs YOU'. But as the casualties mounted in actions from the Marne to the Somme these volunteers proved to be insufficient. Compulsory national service, or conscription, was started in 1916, for bachelors only at first, and later for married men as well. It did not apply to Ireland, where it would have been bitterly opposed in the South. None the less, tens of thousands of Irishmen, from both North and South, did serve as volunteers in the British forces.

All this meant that practically every family in Britain had at least one member, and often several, away at the war. With the casualties so high (much higher in proportion than in the Second World War), each family lived in dread of a telegram announcing the death of a relative. Asquith, Prime Minister until 1916, himself lost a son, killed in action in France. The war memorials which stand in nearly every town and village in Britain, and throughout the Commonwealth, remind us today of how many men and women died for their country.

Another effect of the war was to help to alter the status of women in society. In the years before the First World War many women, led by the 'Suffragettes', had been campaigning for the vote and other 'women's rights'. The war brought them the chance to show that they were worthy of equal rights with men, and they took it. Apart from those who served in some way with the forces, perhaps as nurses or as ambulance drivers, great numbers of women went to work for the first time to help with war production. By the end of the war 800,000 women were working in engineering, 750,000 in offices and 250,000 on the land. They did men's jobs which were often skilled, sometimes in unpleasant and dangerous conditions, as in the munitions factories, and always with long tiring hours. Their economic contribution was very important, and this was one of the things which was taken into account when the vote was first given to women over thirty in 1918.

Other economic changes also affected the people. It made little difference to the majority of those who remained at home whether they worked for the government or for a private employer, but the state of prices and wages did concern them. The government realised the importance of keeping prices down to prevent undue hardship. It had some control over coal prices and rents, but it was not successful in restraining most prices in the shops. Food prices in particular rose rapidly, and the result was that the cost of living doubled during the war. This caused hardship early on, but after 1917 wages rose rapidly. This was because of the scarcity of labour, and because the government gave way to wage demands to avoid trouble. Conditions were therefore rather better in 1917 and 1918.

Morale in Britain was good, on the whole, despite the high casualties and social changes. The government helped with good and effective propaganda, to keep spirits up. One interesting example of this, only recently falling into some disuse, was the custom of playing the National Anthem at performances in cinemas and other places of entertainment.

Of course some despaired, which was understandable. A very few men, called 'conscientious objectors', who believed that war was wrong, actively opposed it, and refused to fight. Some, like Bertrand Russell, the mathematician and philosopher, were imprisoned because of this. There were others who saw the war as a golden opportunity to make some money, for profiteering in some branch of business, and they longed for it to continue. The majority of people, however, were anxious for the war to be won, whatever the cost. This determination grew the longer the war went on. It was just as well that few, except the troops, understood the real horrors of the fighting.

Conclusion

The war was finally won in 1918. Britain would not have been on the winning side but for the enormous changes which had taken place in British

Bertrand Russell (*left*) leaving court in 1918. The famous mathematician and philosopher was one of many conscientious objectors sent to prison during the First World War

life, in support of the fighting forces. Somehow the money was found; production was reorganised; the civilian population was brought wholly into the war effort; the government machine was extended to deal with unprecedented tasks. Lloyd George was rightly praised for his role in all this. He was a great war leader, who provided drive, inspiration and organisation when it was most needed – when the war was at a stalemate and no end was in sight.

His war policy has been called 'war socialism'. This is because the situation in 1918 resembled a modern socialist state, with close government control and supervision of a wide part of economic and social life. But this was a system which appeared by trial and error, and not according to any set plan. It involved practically no actual nationalisation, only control for the duration of the war. None the less it created a state which was almost a dictatorship, and this was completely against the British tradition of individual freedom and enterprise. Thus it was very unpopular, and was tolerated only because it became clear that the war could not be won without it. Just as soon as the war was over, there were strong demands for a return to the pre-war situation. The system had served its purpose, and it was soon dismantled.

THE ECONOMIC EFFECTS OF THE WAR

Any major war creates grave economic and social problems which have to be solved once it is over. These problems were particularly difficult after the First World War, partly because Britain had no recent experience of dealing with such matters. In fact, some of the results of the war were good. The improvement in the social position of women, for example, was a goal which had long been fought for. Trade Unions emerged from the war with more members and with a political party – the Labour Party – much strengthened by the participation of its leaders in the Cabinet. In the long run the customs duties imposed by McKenna made it easier to do away with free trade when this became urgent in the 1930s. Industrialists learned much from taking part in the large scale business organisation made necessary by the war. Above all, political leaders learned lessons for the future. When the Second World War came in 1939 the government had experience to draw on, and moved at once into the necessary controls of national life.

Apart from these general points, however, the results of the war were damaging to the economy.

Harmful Effects of the War

1 Loss of Manpower. Britain lost 750,000 killed in the war and $1\frac{3}{4}$ millions injured, many of them permanently. The dead represented 9% of all men between twenty and forty-five years old. This was a huge total, but it is not clear just how much it harmed the economy. In terms of actual numbers, the loss was probably not so severe as was once supposed. This is because the years before the war saw high growth in the population, and the loss was soon made up. In terms of quality, however, it was a much more serious matter; many of the dead were skilled men, and most of the officers killed might have been expected to go on to positions of responsibility in business or the professions. This certainly harmed Britain. A subsidiary problem which the government had to face in consequence was the payment of £100 million a year in war pensions.

2 Damage to Industry. Industry also faced serious problems of readjustment. Some industries, like cotton, had been deliberately run at a low level, lest resources be wasted on production which was not essential. The diagram on p. 294 shows how this affected the output of the cotton industry. Industries like this had to be brought back up to their former level, and this proved much harder than expected. Other industries had been run flat out all the time, and there had been little opportunity to replace machinery and equipment. This was so in the case of the railways, iron and steel works, coalmines and the land, which were near exhaustion and needed a thorough overhaul. They had been producing for war-time needs for over four years, and it was difficult to switch over to peace-time production again.

Britain suffered very little damage to property from enemy action, except to her shipping, in which losses were made good very soon. Britain's large merchant fleet and shipbuilding industry was therefore maintained, but unfortunately it found a post-war world in which demand for shipping services and new vessels was to be low for many years. Otherwise, apart from Zeppelin raids and a few bombardments of coastal towns, like Felixstowe and Sunderland, there was no physical damage to Britain's factories and plant. This was something of a mixed blessing. France and Belgium, who suffered so much devastation, were forced to build again in many cases from the beginning. They did so using the latest techniques. There was no such need or opportunity in Britain.

3 Damage to Trade and Finance. Before the war Britain's balance of payments was in a healthy position, but it depended on the survival of the delicately balanced pre-war international situation. This balance was completely upset by the war. British exports were naturally cut right down, while imports remained steady. It was hoped that the old situation would soon be restored, but Britain found that the world in 1919 was very different from what it had been in 1914, and that the old position could not easily be re-established. The chief countries of Europe, which had been such good markets and producers, were unable to trade on a large scale until they had recovered from the war. Other, more distant markets, in America and the Far East, for example, had been cut off from most British exports during the war. Some, like India, began to make their own goods instead. Most turned to rising industrial powers, like the United States and Japan, for at least some of

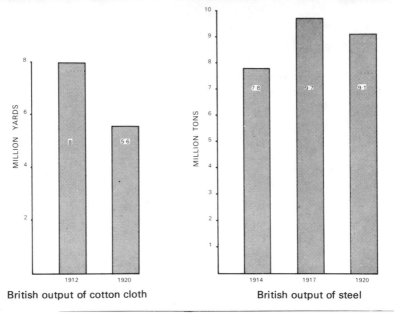

British output of cotton cloth

British output of steel

their supplies. American industrial production went up by 20% during the war, and the Japanese by 75%, taking advantage of these opportunities. British industry, therefore, found it much more difficult to export.

BRITISH BALANCE OF PAYMENTS
(CURRENT ACCOUNT)

	£ million
1913	+237
1919	−128

Britain also lost some financial business, such as insurance and banking, during the war, to centres like New York and Zürich. Much of this returned to London in due course, but not all, and profits from this source were not so reliable as they had been. All these changes made Britain's balance of payments much weaker than before 1914.

4 Debt. Perhaps the most important change was that Britain was now a nation in debt. She still had large overseas assets, of course, but we have seen how about 10% of the pre-war total had been sold on balance to help pay for the war. More was lost after the Russian Revolution in 1917, when the new Communist government refused to pay back any of the money borrowed during the war, and also seized foreign property without payment. This made it even more difficult for Britain to pay back the £800 million still owed to the United States in March 1919. Since that time Britain has never been out of debt to foreign countries.

These were some of the problems which faced Britain after 1918. They lay **294** at the heart of the economic crises of the 1920s and 1930s.

Problems of the Post-war World

The men who returned from the fighting looked forward to a land 'fit for heroes to live in'. For a while it seemed as if they would not be disappointed. Demobilised soldiers were absorbed into industry without much difficulty, and during much of 1919 and 1920 there were boom conditions. Very soon, however, these gave way to a slump, which lasted throughout the next two decades. Trade declined, sections of industry collapsed, unemployment reached record levels and great social hardship resulted. It was not a completely black picture: some years were less bad than others, and some industries, together with the areas in which they were located, enjoyed relative prosperity. This was a most important side of the story, and we shall deal with it later. But it cannot be allowed to obscure the great hardships which so many people had to endure for so long.

We have seen how the war effort had serious consequences for British industry, though some of the difficulties went back much earlier, and were merely brought to the surface by the war. International trading and financial systems were transformed, and economic historians can see now that Britain was certain to face an extremely difficult task in regaining the prosperous position which she had enjoyed in 1914. In 1919, however, few people had any doubt that Britain would quickly recover. This confidence was based on a complete failure to realise that the conditions of 1914, which had favoured Britain so much, had gone for ever. A new world had come into existence. Failure to realise this, and to make necessary changes quickly enough, accounted for much of the difficulty which arose. It is worth while to look in more detail at four particular features of this new situation, in order to stress the point:

1 The Slow Recovery of World Trade. It was not until 1929 that world trade again reached its 1913 level. It then dropped rapidly, and had barely recovered its position by 1939. The main cause was the devastation which the war caused in Europe. The German economy in particular had been ruined, even though the country had not been invaded. Matters were made worse by some of the terms of the Treaty of Versailles (1919). The allies insisted that Germany should pay huge reparations (damages) as compensation for losses suffered by the victor powers. The bill eventually presented amounted to £6,600 million. This 'squeezing' was economically absurd, because Germany simply could not afford to pay, and attempts to force her to do so (such as the seizure of the industrial Ruhr area in 1923) made it quite impossible for Germany to build up her economy quickly, and so resume her leading position in world trade. Instead, the German economy was struck by a terrible inflation, which caused complete chaos.

295

This stagnation of world trade was a very serious matter for Britain, as she depended far more on trade than any other country. Healthy exports and imports, together with the revenue from shipping services, were vital. British trade fell in real terms (that is, taking account of the effects of price changes) for much of the inter-war period and, at the worst time in 1933, the level was 55% below that of 1913. Revenue from shipping services was no higher in 1938 than it had been in 1914, and Britain's merchant fleet was one million tons smaller.

2 The Harm to the Staple Industries. Stagnation of world trade was, of course, something which affected all countries, but it hit Britain especially hard, not only because she depended more on trade but also because the greatest trading difficulties were experienced in those goods which had always made up the bulk of British exports. These were the products of the staple industries – shipbuilding, iron and steel, coal and cotton. These industries had either been under great strain during the war or, in the case of cotton, had been run down deliberately. They had not been particularly efficient by international standards before 1914, and the war lost them vital markets. Now, demand was falling off. Sluggish trade meant little demand for new ships. New fuels and sources of power, such as oil and hydro-electricity, were being developed to replace coal. Artificial textiles, like rayon, began to compete with cotton. Heavy industry found itself badly placed in the cut-throat competition for the limited trade available.

These are the reasons why the depression in Britain was mainly connected with the staple industries, and why the worst effects were felt in the areas in which they were to be found. The diagrams show the extent of the collapse which took place in the exports and output of some staple products. Such industries could not prosper without a high level of exports, for the domestic market was too small. New industries were slow to fill the gap, and so inevitably men were thrown out of work in growing numbers.

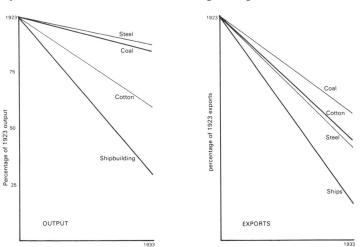

The decline in output and exports of staple products 1923–33

3 Government Actions. In the early years the depression was probably made worse by certain actions which the government took. Two of these were especially damaging. The first was the handing back to private ownership of those industries and services which had been controlled by the state during the war. This policy was understandable, as at that time no government considered nationalisation to be an acceptable policy. Moreover, the general public seemed anxious to 'get back to 1914'. But so far as coal and heavy industries were concerned (as well as the railways), a strong case for national-isation could be made out. The reasons were that private owners were incapable of raising the capital needed for urgently needed investment and reorganisation. The Miners' Union, in fact, did urge this course on the government, without success, and all controls were lifted by 1921. Another harmful move by the government was to restore the gold standard in 1925 at an unrealistically high rate of exchange. This was a technical matter, but the effect was to increase British export prices by about 10%. For the coal industry, fighting to keep up exports in a highly competitive world market, this move was disastrous, and, as we saw in Chapter 8, it brought the General Strike very much nearer.

4 Dependence on the United States. One other very important and quite new feature of the post-war world was the extent to which nations depended on the United States for economic well-being. The war finally revealed the United States as a major world power, and her economic supremacy was greatly strengthened. She was the only leading industrial nation to emerge from the war in a stronger economic position, and so her role in world trade and finance became crucial. Of particular importance was the fact that the allied powers were greatly in debt to the United States, as a result of loans made during the war.

Unfortunately, it is clear now that the United States exploited this position largely for her own good. This is not surprising, of course, especially in view of the disgust felt in the United States towards the terms of the Versailles Treaty. High tariffs prevented many foreign goods from competing in American markets, and insistence on the payment of war-debts hindered European economic recovery. On the other hand, American financiers made large loans overseas and international trade, however slowly it grew, owed a good deal to this investment.

This is why, though economic conditions were bad enough in Britain in the 1920s, there was always some hope of improvement so long as the United States continued to play an active role in world affairs. Unfortunately, in 1929, after a decade in which it seemed as if the American economy had reached a state of permanent growth and prosperity, a complete collapse began. In the week following 24 October 1929 the American stock market plummeted downwards, and this heralded a devastating depression throughout the economy. Because so many other countries relied on American prosperity, the events of 1929 had world-wide repercussions. As American trade and investment fell off, the one remaining prop was knocked away. European economies deteriorated much more seriously, without any obvious prospect of recovery.

Unemployment and Its Evils

In Britain the unemployment rate rose in proportion to the fluctuations and difficulties of trade and industry. Today, unemployment can be serious, but the national rate seldom exceeds $2\frac{1}{2}$%, and even then those who are unemployed are well provided for by the state. In the inter-war years unemployment was a very different matter. Its scale and effects were unprecedented, and it came to form a kind of canker, eating away at the very heart of the nation.

The first thing to bear in mind is the staggering size of the problem. There were never fewer than one million men out of work between 1921 and 1938, which meant an average rate of at least 10%. Some years were very much worse than this, and in 1932 two million eight hundred thousand had no employment – a rate of 23%. In other words, almost one man in four was unable to earn his own living. This was a scale of unemployment which far exceeded even the worst periods of the nineteenth century, when the rate is thought to have reached even 10% only rarely.

Because unemployment was highly localised, the problem was worse than even these figures suggest. The staple industries, which bore the brunt of

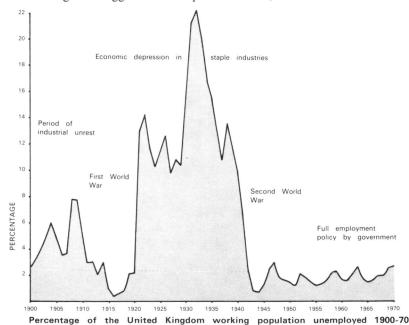

Percentage of the United Kingdom working population unemployed 1900-70

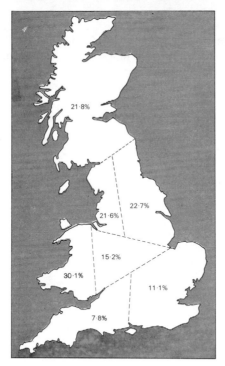

Average unemployment rates in Britain 1929–36

redundancy were centred in areas which were economically favourable to
them. These areas were broadly the North of England, South Wales and parts
of Scotland and Northern Ireland. Entire regions depended on the staple
industries – the workmen employed in them, and those who provided the
shops and other services in the towns where they lived. In some cases practically everyone in a town depended in some way on a single large firm.
Palmers shipyard at Jarrow (Durham) employed ten thousand men, for example, and so did the Vickers shipbuilding and engineering works at Barrow
(Lancashire). When such firms began to lay off workers it meant that whole
townships suffered. In 1933, when Palmers yard closed down, the unemployment rate in Jarrow reached 80% for a time. Only two men in every ten could
find work of any kind. In 1934 70% of the work force in Merthyr Tydfil was
unemployed, and in the whole county of Glamorgan only two men in three
had jobs. Other examples on this scale can easily be found. Moreover, unemployment tended to be cumulative – that is, the worse it got, the worse it
was certain to become. Everyone who could afford to do so, such as shopkeepers, moved away from destitute areas. As amenities and services
dwindled others were driven away. There was virtually no chance of new
industry being attracted to such unpromising regions to break into this
vicious circle of stagnation and decay. Those dark days saw the beginning of   **299**

the so-called 'regional problem' — the problem of large areas with declining industry, high unemployment and a much lower standard of living than in the rest of the country. It is a problem which seemed almost insoluble in the 1930s, and one which has still not been completely mastered.

UNEMPLOYMENT PERCENTAGES IN THE STAPLE AND
NEW INDUSTRIES

	1932	*1937*
The Staple Industries:		
Coal-mining	33·9	14·7
Cotton	28·5	11·6
Shipbuilding	62·2	23·8
Pig-iron	43·5	9·8
The New Industries:		
Motor vehicles	20·0	4·8
Electrical engineering	16·3	3·1
Food industries	16·6	12·4
Distributive trades	12·2	8·8

Statistics can never adequately describe the real story of unemployment in human terms. The prospect of prolonged unemployment seems so remote to most of us today that we may be in danger of underestimating the full horror of chronic unemployment. Imagine the lives of men and their families who for month after month, year after year, tramped the streets looking for work, or sat at home in poverty, knowing that it was almost impossible that they would find jobs. For many older men there was the near-certainty that they would never work again, and the bitter frustration of knowing that their skills would never more be used. As George Orwell wrote, 'It is a deadly thing to see a skilled man running to seed, year after year, in utter, hopeless, idleness.' Dignity and self-respect, especially of men with families to support, were undermined by long periods of unemployment. A man's natural desire is to work, to earn his own living and support his dependents, without having to fall back on the state for a meagre subsistence.

It is hard to make these conditions seem real to those who have not experienced them. Perhaps it is best to read some of the books of the 1930s which convey so movingly an understanding of the period and its problems. Of special interest are *Love on the Dole*, a play by Walter Greenwood mentioned earlier in Chapter 1, and *The Road to Wigan Pier*, by George Orwell. The first contains a deep and emotional insight into the human problems caused by unemployment, and when the play was first performed it had a wide influence. Orwell's book, from which the quotation above was taken, is probably the best factual account of the effects of unemploy-

ment. He lived and travelled in the North during the worst years of the de-

George Orwell

pression, and set down his impressions of what he saw. These make harrowing reading, and more passages are quoted from the book later in this section. It is hardly possible, after reading such works, not to be deeply moved by the tragedy which affected the lives of so many honest and decent people.

Of course, there was the 'dole' to fall back on, but government aid to the unemployed had two drawbacks. The first was the 'means test', which required men to go through humiliating procedures before they could draw any money at all. Moreover, because of the way in which the scheme operated, families were sometimes forced to split up. Not surprisingly, the means test was most unpopular, especially as many men were ashamed of having to apply for assistance anyway. When the money was finally handed out, it was completely inadequate to provide more than the barest standard of living. A family of five received about 35s. each week. A single man got 17s. In Wigan, in 1936, about one person in three lived on the dole, and it was impossible to maintain a household in any comfort on it. It was enough for survival, but no more. As a result, the conditions in which people had to live were very bad. We must not exaggerate, because conditions in industrial towns had always been bad. But it was now almost impossible for people to maintain their basic dignity and self-respect.

Orwell described conditions on a Wigan caravan site in these terms:

Along the banks of Wigan's miry canal are patches of waste ground on which the caravans have been dumped like rubbish shot out of a bucket. Some of them are actually gypsy caravans, but very old ones and in bad repair. The majority are old single-decker buses (the rather smaller buses of ten years ago) which have been taken off their wheels and propped up with struts of wood. Some are simply wagons with semi-circular slats on top, over which canvas is stretched, so that the people inside have nothing but canvas between them and the outer air. Inside, these places are usually about five feet wide by six high (I could not stand quite upright in any of them) and anything from six to fifteen feet long. Some, I suppose, are   **301** inhabited by only one person, but I did not see any that held less than two persons, and some of them contained large families. One, for instance, measuring fourteen feet long, had seven people in it – seven people in about 450 cubic feet of space; which is to say that each person had for his entire dwelling a space a *good deal* smaller than one compartment of a public lavatory. The dirt and congestion of these places is such that you cannot well imagine it unless you have tested it with your own eyes and more particularly your nose. Each contains a tiny cottage kitchener and such furniture as can be crammed in – sometimes two beds, more usually one, into which the whole family have to huddle as best they can. It is almost impossible to sleep on the floor, because the damp soaks up from below. I was shown mattresses which were still wringing wet at eleven in the morning. In winter it is so cold that the kitcheners have to be kept burning day and night, and the windows, needless to say, are never opened. Water is got from a hydrant common to the whole colony, some of the caravan-dwellers having to walk 150 or 200 yards for every bucket of water. There are no sanitary arrangements at all. Most of the people construct a little hut to serve as a lavatory on the tiny patch of ground surrounding their caravan, and once a week dig a deep hole in which to bury the refuse. All the people I saw in these places, especially the children, were unspeakably dirty, and I do not doubt that they were lousy as well. They could not possibly be otherwise. . . . Some of the people have been in their caravans for many years. Theoretically the Corporation are doing away with the caravan-colonies and getting the inhabitants out into houses; but as the houses don't get built, the caravans remain standing. Most of the people I talked to had given up the idea of ever getting a decent habitation again. They were all out of work, and a job and a

Despair: this well-known photograph sums up all the evils of unemployment. It was published in *Picture Post* in 1939, when over a million men were still out of work

302

house seemed to them about equally remote and impossible. Some hardly seemed to care; others realized quite clearly in what misery they were living. One woman's face stays by me, a worn skull-like face on which was a look of intolerable misery and degradation. I gathered that in that dreadful pigsty, struggling to keep her large brood of children clean, she felt as I should feel if I were coated all over with dung.

In such conditions, why, one may ask, did working people not react violently? This is not an easy question to answer. In some other countries in Europe unemployment did produce violence and political change, but in Britain there was hardly any disturbance. One reason was that the Trade Unions were weak, and the whole idea of militancy had suffered a blow with the humiliating collapse of the General Strike. More important, however, was the peculiar nature of the evil of unemployment itself, which had a numbing and bewildering effect. It was still thought of as the result, not of any fault in the economy, but in some way of the workers themselves. Unemployment was somehow shaming, in a way which would be unthinkable today. The vast scale and totally inexplicable nature of the problem left workers adrift from their normal bearings. Long periods of idleness and boredom drove any fight from them. George Orwell saw very clearly the despair of 'decent young miners and cotton-workers gazing at their destiny with the same sort of dumb amazement as an animal in a trap.'

They simply could not understand what was happening to them. They had been brought up to work, and behold! it seemed as if they were never going to have the chance of working again. In their circumstances it was inevitable, at first, that they should be haunted by a feeling of personal degradation. That was the attitude towards unemployment in those days: it was a disaster which happened to *you* as an individual and for which *you* were to blame.

When a quarter of a million miners are unemployed, it is part of the order of things that Alf Smith, a miner living in the back streets of Newcastle, should be out of work. Alf Smith is merely one of the quarter million, a statistical unit. But no human being finds it easy to regard himself as a statistical unit. So long as Bert Jones across the street is still at work, Alf Smith is bound to feel himself dishonoured and a failure. Hence that frightful feeling of impotence and despair which is almost the worst evil of unemployment – far worse than any hardship, worse than the demoralization of enforced idleness. . . . Everyone who saw Greenwood's play *Love on the Dole* must remember that dreadful moment when the poor, good, stupid working man beats on the table and cries out, 'O God, send me some work!' This was not dramatic exaggeration, it was a touch from life. That cry must have been uttered, in almost those words, in tens of thousands, perhaps hundreds of thousands of English homes, during the past fifteen years.

So the unemployed did not react violently, many sank into the sullen despair which Orwell describes, while others tried to bear up with scarcely   **303**

Jarrow marchers passing through a village near Bedford on their way to London in 1936

felt cheerfulness. There were some demonstrations, but these were usually peaceful and orderly. The most famous was the 'Jarrow Crusade', a hunger march which took place in 1936. Volunteers from that stricken town marched to London, covering about twenty-five to thirty miles each day, and holding political meetings at the end of every stage. Their intention was to draw attention to their plight, and in this they were most successful. Their dignity attracted national sympathy, though little practical good came of it at the time. For the most part, the unemployed waited and waited for better times to come. Eventually the tide turned, but the bad days were never forgotten. It is not surprising that many men were permanently scarred, and that attitudes hardened, as a result of the bitter experiences of those years.

The Response of the Government

Strong government action was needed to overcome industrial recession on such a scale. Unfortunately, as we saw earlier, the government had already shown its inability to appreciate the danger signals in the 1920s, and it was equally slow to see what had to be done when the situation deteriorated after 1929.

It was not that the authorities were unaware of what was happening, though sometimes it seemed as if officials in London were misled by the relative prosperity of the South-East and Midlands. The trouble was that most people in authority really did think that unemployment was beyond their control. Many regarded it as 'an act of God', something inevitable which time alone could cure. The government was prepared to provide some relief, though rather reluctantly, since some Ministers still believed that unemployed men

The police dealt firmly with these disturbances in London in 1932

should be treated as harshly as possible to discourage slacking. But so far as getting the economy going again was concerned, the government felt itself to be powerless. All it could offer was constant encouragement to people to be thrifty, and to 'tighten their belts'.

This may seem an unbelievable attitude today, but we must not be too harsh in our judgement of those concerned. The study of economics was still in its infancy, and some leading economists supported the official viewpoint. But a few younger economists thought differently. One was John Maynard Keynes (1883–1946), later to become Lord Keynes. In time he was acknowledged as perhaps the greatest modern economist, and his work influenced economic thinking deeply. But in the early 1930s he was known only as a brilliant teacher at Cambridge University. He had attracted attention with far-seeing attacks on the Treaty of Versailles, and on Winston Churchill, who was Chancellor of the Exchequer when the gold standard was restored in 1925. Keynes was convinced that unemployment could be solved, but only if the government acted in a positive way. He advised it to make massive investment in such projects as roads, hospitals and other public works. Also required were cuts in taxes, an increase in the dole and rises in salary for everyone employed by the state. The effect of all this would be to stimulate the economy into activity, and after a time this would become self-generating. The government, as Keynes put it, 'should prime the pump'.

We know today that Keynes was basically right. In the United States President Roosevelt applied similar ideas in the 'New Deal', which did much

Lord Keynes, photographed just before his death in 1946. He was the most influential economist of modern times

to help American industry to recover from a far worse situation. But Keynes' advice, given in the report of the Macmillan Committee (1931), was ignored in Britain. Instead the government preferred to adopt the traditional policies recommended by the May Committee (1931). It proceeded to follow the opposite course from that suggested by Keynes. In particular, government spending was slashed and this involved reductions in unemployment benefit (by 10%) and in the salaries and wages of all state employees, from Cabinet Ministers to the armed forces. The amounts ranged from 5% to 15%, and naturally the cuts were very unpopular among the lower income groups and the unemployed, especially as the government in power when they were proposed was the Labour administration of Ramsay MacDonald. Disgruntled sailors, stirred up by communist agitators, even staged a short-lived mutiny in the fleet stationed at Invergordon, in Scotland.

Such a policy could not only do no good; it was certain to make matters worse. MacDonald's government fell at the end of 1931, after splitting over the issue. Its fall also followed a serious financial crisis, as a result of which MacDonald had to form a National government. This was a coalition between the different parties and one of its first measures was to abandon the gold standard (1931). It put the May Committee recommendations into effect, but after a time the harsh policy was gradually abandoned. The policy of the National government, under both MacDonald and his successors, Stanley Baldwin and Neville Chamberlain, then began to improve.

By 1939 it had done much more, in several different ways. Unemployment benefits were extended. The Special Areas Act (1934) and subsequent legislation of the same kind gave help to the worst-hit areas. Staple industries were encouraged to reorganise into more efficient units: in 1936, for example, a Coal Cartel was established for greater security, and in the same year a Spindles Board began a programme of cuts designed to remove surplus capacity in the cotton industry. In 1939 the British Iron and Steel Federation was set up to promote greater efficiency, and similar moves took place in shipbuilding at the initiative of the government – which also gave subsidies for the completion of the *Queen Elizabeth* and *Queen Mary*, saving many jobs on Clydeside. Subsidies were also given to farmers, as agriculture was in a bad state. Industry was given protection by tariffs imposed according to the Import Duties Act of 1931, a measure which brought to an end the long era of free trade. Finally, the government also encouraged the growth of newer industries, which are described in the next chapter, and must be given some credit for the recovery which followed.

Suggestions for further work and discussion

1. Talk to people who remember the First World War, particularly those who fought in it. Ask them to relate their experiences.

2. Make a fuller study of the life and achievements of Lloyd George. If you are in North Wales, visit the Lloyd George Museum near Criccieth in Caernarvonshire.

3. Visit the Imperial War Museum in Lambeth Road, London S.E.1. This has many fascinating exhibits of both World Wars.

4. Subjects for an essay or discussion:

What were the problems which faced Britain during the First World War? How were they overcome?

Why was there so much unemployment between the wars? What did governments do about it? How successful were they?

5. Try to obtain first-hand accounts (from your father or grandfather, for example) of what life was like during the 1930s. What did it actually feel like to be unemployed? How did unemployed men manage to keep their families? How did they spend their days?

6. Building was one industry which did flourish during the 1930s. What evidence is there of this in your area? How many houses around you date from that time, especially council houses?

Books for further reading:

W. Greenwood, *Love on the Dole*, Cape, 1966, Penguin, 1969.
Ed. T. Hopkinson, *Picture Post 1938–50, Penguin, 1970.* [There is a moving account in the issue of 1939 of the life of an unemployed man.]

G. Orwell, Down and Out in Paris and London, Secker & Warburg, 1949, Penguin, 1969.

G. Orwell, *The Road to Wigan Pier*, Secker & Warburg, 1959. Also in Penguin.

A. J. P. Taylor, *The First World War*, Penguin, 1970.

Ed. A. J. P. Taylor, *History of the Twentieth Century, vols. 1–3*, Purnell (Part Work).

13 : The Twentieth-century Economy – War and Reconstruction

It is remarkable how quickly Britain recovered from the slump described in the previous chapter. It is often thought that this recovery began only with the new demand created by the Second World War, and with the changes which took place after 1945. This is not so. The origins of recovery are to be found long before, in the beginnings of a process of reconstruction of the economy, resulting from the growth and prosperity of the so-called 'new industries'. These began to flourish in the dark days of the depression itself. The war, and later changes, were certainly vital for stimulating this process but it was essentially continuous, right through to the present day, and that is why we look first at the whole story of the new industries.

THE NEW INDUSTRIES

The new industries were those which became prominent during the inter-war years. Most had actually begun before 1914, but did not play an important role until after the war. The future clearly lay in the new industries because of the high demand for their products – such as motor vehicles, aircraft, machine tools and chemicals. World production and trade began to adjust accordingly, at the expense of the traditional industries. In Britain, however, the economy was still dominated in the early 1920s by the staples, and new industries were of little relative importance for some time. The fact that they did not expand quickly enough to fill the vacuum left by the staples is one reason why the depression hit Britain especially hard.

The new industries did take root, however, and soon began to grow, encouraged by more positive government policy in the 1930s. Apart from their products, the new industries had common features which distinguished them from the old. These were a greater emphasis on technology and scientific research; more efficient organisation, especially in the use of mass-production and automation; location in relatively non-industrialised regions; and a much smaller dependence on exports. As we look in more detail at the new industries, we shall concentrate on these features, presenting the main facts and figures in diagrammatic form.

Engineering

In the nineteenth century the quality of British engineering products was high. Ships, locomotives, agricultural and textile machinery were sold

309

throughout the world. As demand for these traditional products eased, however, the accumulated experience had to be adapted to new forms of engineering. Change was rather slow at first, but after a time the old reputation was re-established in new fields:

1 Motor Vehicles. In the early days of road transport many cars and lorries had to be imported, as home production was very small. Manufacturers were encouraged by war-time demand, however, and some useful protection was given by a $33\frac{1}{3}$% tariff imposed in 1915. Henry Ford's mass-production techniques were taken up by Morris and Austin in the 1920s, and the industry was firmly established (see p. 238). Despite the depression, most middle-class incomes held their own, and so demand for cars and motor-cycles was strong. Production rose accordingly. The industry was centred in the Midlands, though factories were later built in other areas. A few large companies came to monopolise output, and in 1939 the two biggest − Morris and Austin − controlled 60% of the total production of motor vehicles. Only an eighth of this output was exported, partly because the smaller cars favoured in Britain were unsuitable for use in other countries.

During the Second World War the efforts of the industry were switched to producing military vehicles, but it was not difficult to readjust afterwards. As demand for private cars and commercial vehicles grew, the industry enjoyed boom conditions, providing work for eight hundred thousand people. Exports expanded and brought in badly needed foreign currency. In recent years, however, the industry has suffered from bad labour relations and much overseas business has been lost as a result of strikes and allegedly bad after-sales service. Home buyers have again begun to turn to foreign cars. Only one large firm − British Leyland − is still free of American control, and altogether the outlook for the industry is bleaker than it was ten years ago.

A number of other industries have also prospered as a result of the demands of road transport. The oil industry, though not very important in Britain before 1945, has grown rapidly since. Its strength has been the demand for petrol and commercial fuels, but it has also branched out into other fields, such as domestic central heating. Rubber manufacturers, like Dunlops whose production went back to the early days of the bicycle, were given new life by the demand for car tyres and tubes. Production of light metals and electrical instruments also responded to new requirements.

2 Aircraft. The British aircraft industry was slow to get under way, but it soon drew on the experience of skilled engineering workers. From the start it relied heavily on orders for military aircraft, and these were increased when the period of rearmament began in the later 1930s. Thirty thousand men were employed in the industry at that time, and this workforce was greatly expanded as soon as war broke out. Enormous numbers of aircraft were needed, and production increased tenfold between 1938 and 1944, in which year twenty-six thousand planes were built. This was a fine achievement, and it had an important effect on the course of the war. Further details of this period and of the industry since 1945 are given in Chapter 9.

3 Electrical Goods. Little use was made of electricity in British industry in the late nineteenth century. Output was insignificant compared with that in Germany and the United States, but the gap was quickly narrowed after 1918. Electricity supply was at first controlled by private enterprise or by municipal corporations, but this arrangement was not always very efficient, owing to the use of several different voltages. Finally, in 1926, a National Grid was established, giving employment to 100,000 men. It gave Britain a first-rate supply system, and provided power both for public services, such as street-lighting and trams, and for industrial and private consumers. There were only 730,000 consumers in 1920, yet by 1938 nine million people had direct access to mains electricity. Most of the rest of the population had it connected after 1945.

Not only did industry in general benefit from the use of electricity but new industries producing electrical goods were also able to exploit it. This field had been opened up so much that even in 1937 it employed 367,000 workers. The home market was protected by tariffs, and demand was particularly strong in the 1930s among the higher income groups. When electricity became available to everyone, record sales of electrical equipment were an indication of the general rise in the standard of living. Sales of cookers, fires, radios, televisions, refrigerators, washing machines, vacuum cleaners, irons and dish washers all shot up.

In recent years technological developments have begun to transform the industry. New fields in electronics such as radar, computers, transistors and telecommunications, have been opened up. Britain is among the most

Deptford Power Station. It was here that electricity was first produced on a large scale in Britain

Modern electronics: an I.C.L. 1901A
computer installation

advanced nations in electronics, and has much to offer the world. Exports of electrical goods have always been good, and even in 1937 Britain's share of world trade was 28%. More recently, world-famous firms such as E.M.I. and G.E.C.–A.E.I. have earned millions of pounds abroad with exports.

Chemicals

By international standards the chemical industry was backward in the years before 1914. It was badly organised and relied on out-of-date techniques. It was so inadequate that some dyes for army uniforms had to be imported from Germany! Only in the production of margarine and soap were techniques at all advanced.

This state of affairs changed after the war. Two great companies emerged in control. One was Imperial Chemical Industries (I.C.I.), founded in 1926. The other was Unilever, created by a merger in 1929 between Lever Brothers (which monopolised soap production in Britain) and a Dutch concern. These two companies have dominated the chemical industry ever since.

Explosives, dyestuffs, gases, fertilisers, cosmetics, drugs and plastics are among the wide variety of goods produced. Before 1939 production was geared mainly to the home market, but after 1945 the collapse of the German chemical industry and the rising international demand, for drugs and plastics in particular, opened up valuable export opportunities.

Primitive methods in the chemical industry:
a nitric acid plant around 1890

The modern chemical industry: the same I.C.I.
nitric acid plant today

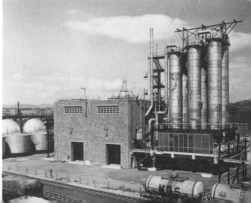

First steps in artificial textile manufacture: spinning rayon yarn at Courtaulds' Coventry factory in 1905

A modern spinning machine producing high-tenacity rayon yarn. The machine spins, chemically treats, washes and dries the yarn, finally winding it on to bobbins

Artificial Textiles

At present, I.C.I. and another firm, Courtaulds, control the production of artificial textiles, which is really a by-product of the chemical industry. Though early research in this field was done in France, much of the pioneering work was carried out in Britain before 1914. Rayon, which is derived from cellulose, was the first semi-artificial fibre to be developed, and Courtaulds were responsible for its commercial exploitation. At this stage Britain led the world, but research and production slipped back during the war. In Britain rayon was not as popular as the natural fibres, and in any case it had to be strengthened by cotton in the early stages. For these reasons British rayon was overtaken in world markets by Japanese and Italian products.

Since 1945, however, many new and cheaper artificial textiles have been developed, among them nylon and terylene. Such materials have become very popular for a wide variety of purposes, but particularly for clothes. As a result, textiles made from natural fibres, such as cotton, wool, silk and linen, have been facing severe competition. It is ironic that cotton and woollen textiles, once the basis of Britain's prosperity, are now looked upon as something of a luxury.

Other Industries and Services

Progress in all branches of industry had increasingly to be supported by high-quality instruments and machine tools. There was little difficulty in making the changes in the 1920s, thanks to Britain's strong tradition in these fields. Since then machine tools in particular have earned valuable revenue from exports.

A number of other new industries have appeared in the twentieth century, **313** and most older ones have been completely transformed. They include for example food-canning, furniture and glass manufacturing, and the generation of nuclear power. In the 1930s building also assumed a more important role in the economy. The cinema, radio and television have created completely new entertainment industries, and a wide variety of new service industries, from travel agencies to betting shops, have come into existence.

Summary

All these new industries were important in their early stages because they offered employment and created demand for raw materials. They helped to make prosperous the regions in which they were situated. Although some plants, especially in the chemical industry, were located in the older industrial areas, most new industries were centred in the South and Midlands. There were several reasons for this: there was already some industry there, but the depression had a far less serious effect than in the districts where the staple industries predominated – unemployment certainly rose, but this merely made skilled labour available to the new industries; a higher proportion of the upper income groups lived in the South and Midlands, offering the kind of market for which the new products were best suited; finally, the use of electricity, and the new kind of raw materials required, meant that there was no need for the new industries to be situated near to the coal and iron supplies of the older industrial regions.

As a result, some towns like Bristol, Oxford, Swindon, Slough and Reading recovered very quickly, shaking off the signs of slump. Rapid economic growth and much improved social conditions soon produced a totally different kind of environment from that described earlier. It may seem strange, therefore, that in the 1930s the unemployed from the destitute areas of Britain did not flock to the South to get work. Some did, of course, but a great many were loth to uproot or to leave their families and settle in quite unfamiliar surroundings, even when given financial assistance by the government. In one case a number of Cumberland miners who had been given work in Kent felt so unsettled after a time that they gave up and walked all the way home.

But despite the sluggishness of labour at that time, the prosperity generated by the new industries slowly filtered through the economy and helped to start the process of recovery. Government policy, rearmament and war carried on the task. Although we should never forget the great distress in Britain between the wars, it is also possible to see in this period a great deal of good. Diversification of the economy, which began then, was essential to enable Britain to adjust to new conditions. By building on the foundations laid in the 1930s this adjustment was safely carried out, and this is the secret of the totally different economic and social picture of the years after the Second

World War.

THE SECOND WORLD WAR (1939–45)

The outbreak of war in 1939 had mixed results for the economy. On the one hand, it solved very quickly the problem of unemployment. On the other, war naturally brought very great economic and social difficulties, of the kind which had faced the country after 1914. This time, however, the government was ready to deal with them. The basic problems were the same – how to pay for the war, how to produce enough goods, and how to bring the population into the war effort, without reducing the standard of living to a point where morale would suffer. Many mistakes had been made after 1914, and the lessons were not forgotten. Long before war broke out, preparations were made, and the government was able to move swiftly. It soon established controls over most sectors of the economy. These controls were similar to those which had eventually been set up between 1914 and 1918, but they were more extensive and better organised as part of a general plan. As well as firmer controls over industry and finance, taxes were increased and large loans raised both at home and abroad, particularly in the United States, which also supplied vast quantities of war materials on favourable terms. All this was vital to meet the total cost of the war to Britain of £28,000 million.

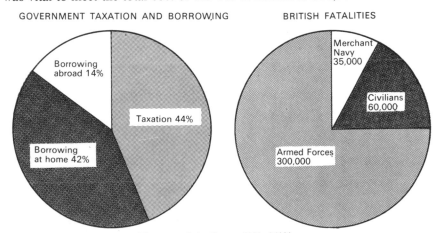

GOVERNMENT TAXATION AND BORROWING

Borrowing abroad 14%
Taxation 44%
Borrowing at home 42%

BRITISH FATALITIES

Merchant Navy 35,000
Civilians 60,000
Armed Forces 300,000

The cost of the Second World War

For the individual, personal freedom was rather less than it had been in the First World War: conscription was introduced straight away, and restrictions were placed on movement and other civil liberties. These were generally accepted as necessary so long as the emergency lasted. Naturally, the war brought social hardships of many kinds. The hours of work were very long, and conditions hard, both for men and for the millions of women who were again brought into manufacturing industry and into the public services. Many goods were in short supply, and despite a much better system of rationing, the standard of living inevitably fell. The fighting brought fewer casualties than in the First World War, but even so 388,000 were killed, and few families escaped a personal tragedy.

Moreover, bombing, which was a quite new factor, brought the civilian population right into the front line. Throughout the war German bombers and (in the later stages) rockets attacked the major cities. The devastating effects of bombing had been anticipated, and preparations were made. Millions of children were evacuated to the country in a well-organised operation which undoubtedly saved many lives. Anti-aircraft defences were set up, and these were helped by the invention of radar just before the war by Sir Robert Watson-Watt. Radar gave the defences valuable extra time in which to intercept enemy aircraft, but even so, the majority were able to get through.

The result was that large areas of the main industrial centres were laid waste. London, Glasgow, Liverpool, Manchester and Coventry suffered especially badly, and so terrible were some of the raids that 'fire-storms' swept through hundreds of properties before they were brought under control. In all, 6% of the buildings in Britain were destroyed during the course of the war. Naturally, many people lost their lives or their homes as a result of bombing. Even those who were lucky enough to escape direct hits still had to spend night after night, often for weeks on end, in bomb-shelters or underground stations while raids were on.

Bomb damage in Coventry in 1940. Fire caused much of the destruction during bombing raids. Coventry suffered particularly badly, and its great cathedral was burned down

Winston Churchill, photographed in 1939. He was soon to become Prime Minister and the inspiring leader of Britain's war effort

The British people endured the 'blitz' with great courage, and victory over Germany and Japan was finally achieved in 1945. Great sacrifices had been made, and war had brought the nation much closer together. Bombs did not distinguish between the social classes, and the common experience of total war was a great social leveller – much more even than in the First World War. The old divisions could no longer be tolerated. A much more united people now faced up to the problems of adjusting to peace, determined to build up a prosperous society. To fail would mean that victory had been thrown away.

PROSPERITY AND ITS PROBLEMS

The end of the war certainly brought many problems. Although the new industries had been stimulated, all sectors of manufacturing had been run to capacity for years and were badly in need of fresh capital. Demobilised troops had to be absorbed. Raw materials, food and consumer goods remained in short supply for some time. In fact, rationing of some foodstuffs continued until as late as 1954. World trade had to be built up again.

These were not easy problems to deal with and things did not go very well at first. The winter of 1947 brought particular hardship. The weather was unusually severe, and supplies of coal and electricity ran short. Factories had to close down, unemployment rose and there was much social distress. Even when the winter passed, the government still had to appeal for patience, hard work and economies. As late as 1949 a financial crisis forced it to devalue the pound.

317

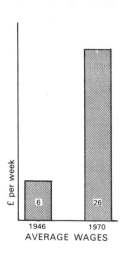 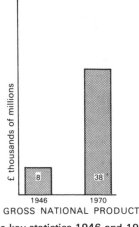 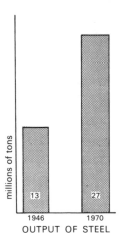

| 1946 | 1970 | 1946 | 1970 | 1946 | 1970 |
| AVERAGE WAGES | | GROSS NATIONAL PRODUCT | | OUTPUT OF STEEL | |

Some key statistics 1946 and 1970

But these difficult early years gave way to better times. The Festival of Britain, an exhibition held in London in 1951, on the South Bank of the Thames, commemorated the Great Exhibition of 1851. It also seemed to symbolise Britain's recovery from the war, and to be the signal for the start of a long era of prosperity, which has produced the so-called 'affluent society'. In it, affluence (prosperity) is the general rule, and poverty the exception. All the evidence shows that a great rise in the standard of living has taken place. Figures for production and wages (see diagram), together with hours of work, reflect the enormous improvement in economic conditions. With prosperity have come dramatic changes in social habits. Longer and more expensive holidays, more leisure, greater consumption of what were once luxury goods, like cars, electrical equipment, televisions and so on – these are some of the outward signs of the affluent society. Of course, not everyone has shared equally in this rising prosperity. But even allowing for the exceptions, and also for the increase in prices, there can be no doubt that the standard of living has risen out of all recognition.

When we remember the depression which took place after the First World War, the contrast is remarkable. How can we explain it? There are many explanations, but the most important is that the mistakes of the 1920s were not repeated. Lessons had been learned, not only about how to conduct total war but also about how to deal with the peace-time problems which it created. This was true of all governments, and helps to explain the very different picture after 1945.

THE REVIVAL OF WORLD TRADE

World trade revived very quickly after 1945, and this was a vital factor in Britain's economic recovery. The mistakes of the peacemakers of Versailles were not repeated (indeed there was not even a Peace Conference as such). No reparations were demanded, and the United States, realising the importance of preventing another world depression, made loans to many countries to help them repair their economies. When these loans proved to be insufficient, the American government decided to give money to any country in serious need of help. 'Marshall Aid', which was named after the American Secretary of State, General George Marshall, eventually amounted to over fifteen billion dollars. This money was distributed among sixteen European nations, including Britain. Such generosity was a most important factor in the revival of world industry and trade, and within a remarkably short time the effects of the war had been shaken off. Moreover, a new system of international finance came into existence, supervised by the International Monetary Fund, and this helped to give greater security.

These developments were naturally helpful to Britain. Building on the foundations laid down before the war, modern industries with high export potential continued to grow and to replace the old staples in the forefront of the economy. This continuing change, which allowed Britain to take full advantage of world demand, was at the heart of the affluent society. There were other important causes, however, and these were related to government policy, which became much more enlightened, in several different ways:

GOVERNMENT POLICY

1 Nationalisation. In the last chapter we saw how weak government policy in the 1920s helped to make the depression worse. In contrast, the war-time coalition, led by Winston Churchill, was determined to plan for the future, and it accepted the need for its active policy to continue once the war was over. To the surprise of most political experts, however, the election of 1945 produced a massive Labour majority. This seemed to indicate that the electors wanted a new government which promised even more decisive policies, including considerable social reform. Accordingly, Clement Attlee became Prime Minister, and it was his Labour administration (1945–51) which had to deal with the immediate problems of post-war reconstruction.

In those difficult years its policy was controversial. But in two respects at least it seems now to have been wise. Economic controls were continued as long as they were necessary (these included food-rationing and building restrictions); and certain industries and services were nationalised. The motives behind the nationalisation programme were partly political, for it had always been the ambition of socialists to bring important industries under state ownership. But in the case of coal and the railways the financial situation was such that nationalisation was the only way to prevent complete collapse, and so to avoid the great hardships which would result from such a disaster. The industries which were nationalised between 1946 and 1951 were coal,   **319** iron and steel, gas, electricity, railways, road haulage, canals, British European Airways, cable and wireless companies and the Bank of England. (Iron and steel, with road haulage, were largely returned to private ownership in 1951, but steel was renationalised in 1967.)

Not all of these industries were unprofitable. The Bank of England was certainly not, but it was taken over for reasons concerned with the national interest. But some were in serious trouble, and only state funds could help them to survive or to be profitable in the future. The coal industry has been skilfully run down to meet changing demand conditions, and this task has been achieved without creating mass unemployment. The manpower on the railways has also been cut, but as with the other industries the railways have been modernised and their losses reduced. There have certainly been many critics of nationalisation, and the Conservative government elected in 1970 expects to 'hive-off' to private ownership some of the activities of the state enterprises. None the less, it is arguable that nationalisation has been partly responsible for the strong position of the economy, at least until the early 1960s.

Revolution in coal-mining: all Britain's coal is now cut by machines of this kind

2 Full Employment. Another new departure in government policy after 1945 was the acceptance of responsibility for ensuring full employment. Lord Keynes acted as economic adviser to the Treasury during the war, and his ideas have been influential in official circles ever since. Broadly speaking, the government tries to keep up full employment by influencing the economy in different ways: by monetary policy, which means controlling credit (such things as hire-purchase and bank loans); by fiscal policy, which means altering taxes and the government's own expenditure; and by a variety of more direct measures, which are designed to give special help to certain regions, industries or firms.

320

Partly because of such policies, unemployment has always been kept below 3% since the war, and the rate has usually been very much lower. This is a very low figure when compared with the high levels of the depression years. Some governments have placed more emphasis on such policies than others. Conservative governments have preferred not to get too closely involved in industry, believing that it should have as much freedom of action as possible. For this reason, in the 1950s, when there was little danger of unemployment, intervention was kept to a minimum. This was certainly the correct policy at that time.

3 The Welfare State. The welfare state, which is described in more detail in Chapter 17, was also created by the post-war Labour government. It was not entirely new then, and it has been expanded since, to become a most important feature of the affluent society. Despite its defects, it has given security of living to the great majority of the population.

PROBLEMS OF THE 1960s

Harold Macmillan (Prime Minister 1957–63) once made the remark 'You've never had it so good'. In the election of 1959 the electorate seemed to agree, for it returned the Conservative government to power with an increased majority. Britain never had been so prosperous. But though they were not clear in 1959, new problems emerged. Three of them in particular became increasingly obvious in the early 1960s:

1 Price Inflation. The prices of goods and services went up by 40% during the 1960s. In times of economic expansion prices do tend to rise, but such a rate of inflation was exceptionally high, and it continues to mount. It is harmful for two reasons. The first is that it lowers the purchasing power of the pound, which means that a pound buys less and less as the years go by. The real value of wages is greatly reduced. Many workers, in strong Trade Unions, can keep ahead of inflation by obtaining frequent wage increases, but others cannot do this. Old-age pensioners, for example, and those who live

Labour unrest: Ford workers outside the Dagenham plant during the ten-week strike early in 1971. At one time, 50,000 Ford men were on strike, and the Company was losing £2 million a day

321

on relatively fixed incomes, suffer considerable hardship as they see the real value of their pensions or savings steadily eaten away. The second reason is that inflation does serious damage to exports by putting up the costs of production.

The causes of inflation are complex, and ministers have had great difficulty in trying to bring it within reasonable bounds. Many different measures have been tried, including a Prices and Incomes Board (1965) and legal checks on price increases, but none of these seems to have been very successful. By the end of 1970 inflation was running at an annual rate of about 7%, without any sign of it being controlled.

2 The Balance of Payments. The balance of payments began to get into serious difficulties in the late 1950s, though this fact was not appreciated at once. There were two main causes of the difficulties. The first was that the gap between imports and exports of goods ('visible trade') became much wider. Because of the need to import large quantities of raw materials and food there had nearly always been a deficit in visible trade. But now imports began to increase rapidly, as prosperity created new demands, especially for foreign manufactured goods. At the same time, inflation was pushing up the costs of producing exports and making it more difficult to sell them abroad. Strikes made matters worse. In earlier years this situation would not have been alarming, because Britain had always been able to cover losses on visible trade by earnings from 'invisible' trade. This includes the profits from shipping and financial services, tourism and investment overseas, which had normally been large. Now, however, foreign competition began to be felt in these fields too, and profits on invisible trade began to fall.

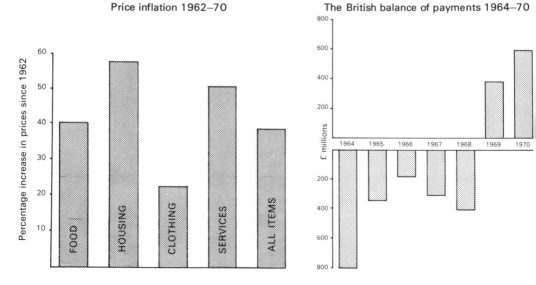

Price inflation 1962–70

The British balance of payments 1964–70

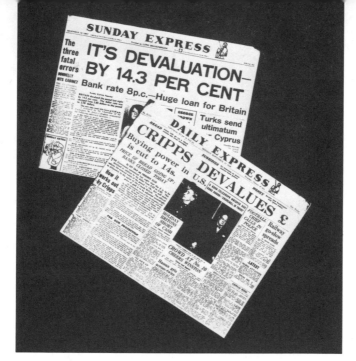

Devaluation headlines: the news announced in 1949 and 1967.

In 1964 the overall deficit on the balance of payments reached £800 million. This was a huge loss, which could only be met by loans from other countries. The new Labour government, elected in 1964, tried many ways of improving the situation. It became much more deeply involved in economic affairs than any previous peace-time government. But in the end it was forced to resort to the ultimate weapon of devaluation. After a grave financial crisis in 1967 the pound was devalued by about 14%. The effect of devaluation was to lower export prices and raise import prices, which helped to redress the balance. It gave a breathing space in which the problems of the economy could be put right. Subsequent economic policies seem to have been success-ful, as the balance of payments has returned to surplus. In 1970 this surplus was about £600 million, and Britain was able to repay much of the money which had been borrowed during the years of crisis. The rapid rate of inflation and continued sluggishness of industrial output, however, make the future uncertain.

3 The 'Regional Problem'. The regional problem arises from the fact that some areas of Britain have not shared fully in the general rise in the standard of living. These regions are mainly those in which depression hit hardest in the inter-war years, and even now they have still not recovered completely. Unemployment in these regions is higher and wages are lower than the national average, and there is a good deal of migration away from them.

Apart from the social hardship involved, any unemployment means a waste of national resources, and so it is important to try to solve this problem. During the 1960s many forms of aid were given to the regions, which were named 'Development Areas'. By 1970 the total cost of regional policy was about £300 million, and much of this went into schemes designed to attract new industry to the Development Areas, in order to provide employment and to stimulate growth. The most important weapon of this policy was the Regional Employment Premium introduced in 1967, for a period of seven years. The Premium is a grant to manufacturers in development areas of £1·50 a week for each full-time male employee, with smaller amounts for women and young people. Other measures have included tax incentives, the provision of government-owned factories at cheap rents, and the establishment of Regional Planning Boards to work out long-term development plans for their respective areas.

It is arguable whether these measures have done anything to solve the problem, but at least it has not got any worse. The Conservative government of 1970 intends to wind up much of the regional policy which it inherited, in the expectation that the regions will share in the general economic advance which is anticipated.

BRITAIN AND THE EUROPEAN ECONOMIC COMMUNITY

In 1957 six European countries (France, West Germany, Italy, Holland, Belgium and Luxemburg) joined together in the Treaty of Rome to form a new economic community. This is usually known in Britain as 'The Common Market'. Britain was given a chance to join then, but she declined because at that time there did not seem to be any advantage to be gained from membership. The E.E.C. has had many difficulties, but these have been slowly overcome. Industry and trade within the community have prospered, and the standard of living in all six countries has risen quickly, exceeding that in Britain in most cases.

While the E.E.C. was getting stronger, Britain's economic difficulties led to second thoughts about membership. As a temporary device, Britain took the initiative in 1960 in forming, with six other countries, the European Free Trade Association (EFTA), which was a much looser form of organisation. Bitter debates about the merits of joining the E.E.C. continued throughout the 1960s, for there are many arguments both for and against membership. Eventually the leaders of both main political parties have come to the conclusion that Britain has more to gain from entry than from staying out. The feeling is that membership would give British industry unlimited access to a huge market, and that this would be the best way of stimulating the economy into more rapid growth, and solving all the basic problems.

Such arguments outweigh all the potential disadvantages, such as the harm to Commonwealth trade and to British farmers. Three separate applications for membership have therefore been made. The first two were rejected, in 1963 and 1967, mainly as a result of political objections raised by President de Gaulle of France. The third application, however, has led to more productive negotiations in 1970 and 1971, and these look like being successful. If all goes according to plan, Britain should join the E.E.C. some time after 1971, and other countries may follow. There will be many difficulties of adjustment, of course, but if the hopes of the 'Marketeers' are fulfilled, the long-term result should be a period of unprecedented growth and prosperity. This would bring to a fitting end the story of the fundamental reconstruction of the British economy in the twentieth century.

Suggestions for further work and discussion

1. If you live in an area (in the Midlands or South of England) where the 'new industries' were established in the inter-war period, locate evidence of this. For example, find out when the factories were set up, and what difference they made to the life of the area.

2. Reconstruct the events of the Battle of Britain in 1940. Are there any war-time airfields in your locality? If so, try to find out what part they played in the war.

3. There are many people who can tell you about life during the Second World War. Ask them to tell you about bombing, the evacuation, the fighting and other aspects of the war.

4. In 1970–71 a T.V. series called 'A Family at War' showed the experiences of a Liverpool family during the war. What were the experiences of *your* family?

5. Select any nationalised industry and describe its progress since nationalisation.

6. Subjects for an essay or discussion:

What were the achievements of Winston Churchill? Why is he generally considered to have been such a great war leader?

Why has Britain been an 'affluent society' in the last twenty years? What have been the signs of affluence?

What are the economic problems of the area in which you live?

State the arguments for and against British membership of the E.E.C.

Books for further reading:

N. Balchin, *The Small Back Room*, 1963.

W. S. Churchill, *The Second World War*, Cassell, 1948–54.

Ed. T. Hopkinson, *Picture Post 1938–50*, Penguin, 1970.

N. Longmate, *How We Lived Then*, Hutchinson, 1971.

Ed. A. J. P. Taylor, *History of the Twentieth Century*, vols. 4–6.

E. Waugh, *Men At Arms*, Chapman & Hall, 1952, Penguin, 1970.

E. Waugh, *Officers and Gentlemen*, Chapman & Hall, 1955, Penguin, 1970.

E. Waugh, *Unconditional Surrender*, Chapman & Hall, 1961, Penguin, 1970.

14 : Social Patterns

The majority of people at the beginning of the eighteenth century lived in a fairly narrow circle of friends and neighbours and had little opportunity of learning what went on in the wider world beyond. One of the most striking social developments of the past two and a half centuries is the development of means of communication that have put an end to the former isolation and made men all over the country, and indeed all over the world, neighbours if not friends.

The earliest means of spreading news other than by word of mouth, the hand-written letter, was still important at the beginning of our period. Professional letter-writers in London used to make a living by composing accounts of current affairs which were circulated in the provinces for a small charge. Already, however, this method was effectively obsolete: it had really been out of date since the invention of printing 200 years before. The seventeenth century had seen the first pioneering efforts at printed news-sheets and pamphlets, and in 1695 the first successful regular newspaper was founded in England. It was a local paper – the *Lincoln, Rutland and Stamford Mercury* – and it still flourishes today. The first daily paper was the *Daily Courant*, established in 1702, and these were followed by so many imitators that we can fairly say that the age of newspapers began with the eighteenth century. By 1724 there were sixteen papers in London alone, not counting numerous journals and periodicals such as *The Tatler* (founded 1709) and *The Spectator* (founded 1711). Many of these early papers, especially those based in the capital, had a strong political bias, and some of them – such as *The Craftsman*, which flourished for a while in the 1720s – were so damaging to the government that it was felt they ought to be controlled. Partly for this reason, and partly for the sake of revenue, a government tax, known as Stamp Duty, was introduced in 1712. This continued to be levied at varying rates until 1855, and since any paper which paid it was likely to be fairly respectable, and any paper which did not was liable to be prosecuted, it acted as a form of censorship. It was far from being completely effective, though: in 1763 John Wilkes' *North Briton* attacked Lord Bute's government so fiercely that Bute fell that year.

On the whole, therefore, eighteenth-century papers expressed themselves very freely – much more freely than their descendants today. This was

327

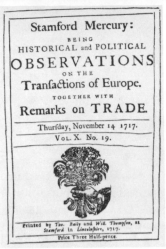

The earliest surviving frontispiece of the *Stamford Mercury* – 11 November 1717

particularly the case with the provincial papers, which, since there was no system of national distribution, were the only ones read in their locality. They carried no illustrations, but a large variety of advertisements – chiefly of the type that would nowadays go in the personal columns – and a weirdly assorted collection of articles and reports.

The great national newspapers as we know them today began to appear at the end of the eighteenth century, when the Transport Revolution made it possible for them to be carried to all parts of the country within a reasonable time of their being printed. *The Times* was founded in 1785, though it did not take that name until 1788. At the same time the old type of journal and periodical was adapted for mass distribution, and there was established a group of powerful intellectual reviews such as the *Edinburgh Review* (1802) – showing the importance of Scotland at this time – and the *Quarterly Review* (1809). These reviews were a great influence on thought and ideas in the early nineteenth century.

The influence of the Industrial Revolution affected the newspapers directly with the introduction of steam printing in 1814, which led to a further expansion. By 1815 there were no fewer than 252 newspapers in the United Kingdom, exercising tremendous weight in the formation of public opinion. Most of their content was still political (Lord Palmerston actually ran his own party paper), and the majority of their readers were naturally members of the middle and upper classes. But as technical changes continued prices fell and the scope of readership was widened, with a consequent tendency to widen the content as well. The price of *The Times*, for instance, fell from 7d. in 1815 to 3d. in 1861, and its circulation at the latter date was 70,000. The *Telegraph*, an evening paper, sold 150,000 copies, however, and *Reynolds' Weekly*, a still more popular affair, sold 350,000. Many papers of various sorts were founded deliberately to cater for a taste in light literature; one of the most famous was *Punch*, which began in 1840. The general style even of the most popular papers at this time, however, was dignified and restrained; periodicals such as the *Illustrated London News* were adorned with elaborate etchings which were often considerable works of art, but otherwise illustration was impossible, and the content was similarly serious and sober. This applied even to the radical journals which appealed directly to the discontented working classes in the 1820s, '30s and '40s; the *Black Dwarf* and the Chartist *Northern Star* were examples of this type.

In 1880, however, a new era was opened by the founding of *Tit-Bits*, a collection of gossipy items with some scandal interest and no political or intellectual content. Further technical advances made possible a livelier and more attractive style of presentation, which was rapidly developed by Alfred Harmsworth, who launched the *Daily Mail* in 1896, and Arthur Pearson, who founded the *Daily Express* in 1900. In catering for a mass market these papers were in tune with the other trends of late Victorian England, such as the growth of a popular franchise and the development of powerful Trade Unions. The established newspapers had to follow their lead to some extent, and in 1914 even *The Times* reduced its price to 1d.

The newspapers reached their peak of popularity and influence in the period between the wars. Aided by the development of photography and drawing vast incomes from the surging advertising industry, they achieved tremendous circulations and became more powerful as framers of opinion than ever before. The most striking success was scored by one of the newest comers to Fleet Street, the *Daily Mirror*. Founded by Harmsworth in 1904, this paper rapidly became popular with the working classes and achieved the biggest circulation of any newspaper in the world.

Modern newspaper printing presses

Even at this time of high prosperity, however, the writing was on the wall for the newspaper industry. Radio was developed principally by an Italian, Guglielmo Marconi (1874–1919). It made great technical strides in the early years of the century, and in 1922 a company was set up to make nationwide broadcasts over the air. This developed in 1926 into the British Broadcasting Corporation, a government-backed organisation with a monopoly over public transmissions. Under a forceful Scot with a high sense of public responsibility – John Reith. later Lord Reith – it rapidly became a great influence. News came through to the listener with a speed and immediacy which the newspapers could never hope to match and, as listening is so much easier than reading, the voice of the BBC achieved more impact in twenty years than the newspapers had managed in two hundred. Not only was British society bound together as never before – regional accents, for instance, began a rapid decline before the onslaught of 'BBC English' – but British people were brought into direct contact with the world outside their own borders. This was a major factor, for example, in bringing about British interest in the Spanish Civil War.

Under this impact the Press began to change. Local papers, already hard hit by the competition of the nationals, weakened still further – and the strength of local life probably weakened with them. The national papers came to concentrate more on comment, and on the one field in which radio could not compete, picture reportage. This last stronghold, however, was threatened by the cinema newsreels which were popular from the 1930s onwards, and then destroyed by the growth of television. T.V. was invented by a Scotsman, John Logie Baird (1888–1946) in the 1920s. It first came into prominence in the late 1940s, but owing to post-war economic difficulties did not become really widespread until the late 1950s. (Commercial T.V. began in 1955.) Since then there have been numerous technical improvements, including the introduction of colour T.V. in 1968.

The young Marconi photographed shortly after his first arrival in England in 1896, with his apparatus for 'telegraphing without wires'

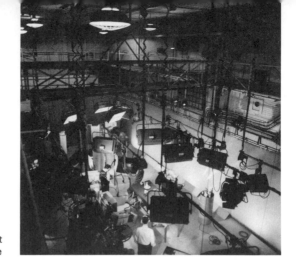

The first T.V. studios, at
Alexandra Palace

The role of T.V. in modern society is still a subject for endless discussion. It is by no means clear what precise effects it has; but there is no doubt that it is the biggest single influence in most people's lives in modern Britain. Some 96% of all households possess a T.V. set, and almost all other forms of entertainment and social activity have been to some extent abandoned in favour of nightly watching. Small children are growing up literally around the T.V. set. It has combined the roles of the Press, the pulpit and the pub, as well as the theatre, the schoolroom and the sports stadium, to achieve a cultural dominance that is almost frightening in its completeness.

Whether we approve of this or not, it has brought about many changes in our awareness of other people and has done so in a way that is in line with all the other developments in British society. The telegraph (invented 1837), the cheap postal system (begun 1840) and the telephone (invented 1876) were diminishing the isolation of the individual long before television was ever thought of, and the whole history of transport in the last 200 years has moved us in the same direction. The world is a smaller place and the importance of the individual is diminished in consequence.

A crystal set, forerunner of the radio,
complete with operating instruc-
tions

An early Bell telephone

331

Although Shakespeare has claims to be the world's greatest dramatist, the British theatre has not a particularly distinguished history, on the whole. During the first half of the eighteenth century it was quite remarkably dull, with few great actors and fewer authors. This was partly because, from the time of Sir Robert Walpole, governments limited the number of theatres in London and controlled the plays that could be put on, as part of a policy of political censorship that extended also to cover the Press. Whereas the Press flourished despite restrictions, the theatre languished, both in the capital and in the provinces. One of the few notable actors of this period, David Garrick, was responsible for continuing the tradition of Shakespearian performance; but, since he was in the habit of amending Shakespeare's texts to suit what he considered 'good taste', even this was a mixed blessing.

In the second half of the century there was still only one important dramatist, Richard Sheridan (1751–1816); his sparklingly witty plays, such as *The Rivals*, *The Critic* and *The School for Scandal* give a brilliant picture of the elegant and sophisticated society of the time. But even they fall short of great art.

So far as public entertainment was concerned, the eighteenth century had a better record in musical matters. The opera was a favourite social meeting place, and some people even listened to the music. All significant social events would be adorned by the presence of a small orchestra, and there was a slow but steady growth in the number of regular concerts. The German-born George Frederick Handel (1685–1759) was particularly popular, especially since he had the enthusiastic support of the royal family; and the great English tradition of choral singing, which has flourished on such works as *The Messiah*, really dates from this period.

For less sophisticated entertainment there were pleasure gardens in London and most of the social centres such as spas and watering-places. At Vauxhall, Ranelagh and similar resorts, anybody who was tolerably well-dressed and could pay the entrance fee could find a mixture of the pleasures of a night-club, a music-hall, a gambling club, a restaurant and a fun-fair. Most of them were probably pretty tawdry affairs; but the best must at times have been places of glittering magic.

The Evangelical revival of the early nineteenth century, described elsewhere, had a depressing effect on most sorts of public entertainment. The pleasure gardens were closed down altogether, the theatres became still duller, and even the concerts became less distinguished, with a tendency to consist largely of 'sacred music'. This may seem to indicate a total decay in entertainment standards; but in fact throughout the eighteenth and nineteenth centuries such activity was virtually confined to the upper classes and the inhabitants of

Vauxhall Gardens in about 1800. By Thomas Rowlandson

London; thus trends in the theatre, for instance, never really affected most British people, who were accustomed to find their amusement elsewhere – in sports, particularly.

Such popular public entertainment as survived was often of a debased and even depraved type. This extract describes the state of the London music-halls (as we would call them) in the 1850s and 1860s:

In many of the thoroughfares of London there are shops which have been turned into a kind of temporary theatre (admission one penny) where dancing and singing take place every night. Rude pictures of the performers are arranged outside, to give the front a gaudy and attractive look, and at night time coloured lamps and transparencies are displayed to draw an audience. These places are called by the costers 'Penny Gaffs'; and on a Monday night as many as six performances will take place, each one having its two hundred visitors.

It is impossible to contemplate the ignorance and immorality of so numerous a class as that of the costermongers, without wishing to discover the cause of their degradation. Let any one curious on this point visit one of these penny shows, and he will wonder that *any* trace of virtue and honesty should remain among the people.

(From Henry Mayhew's *London Labour and the London Poor*)

An Edwardian music-hall; crowded, but no longer disreputable

The music-hall was not rescued from the depths described by Mayhew until the last quarter of the nineteenth century, when the general slackening of the Evangelical strait-jacket led to a revival of all sorts of entertainment. The trend towards a mass culture, noted elsewhere as beginning about this time, produced a great flowering of popular entertainment and music-hall stars such as Harry Lauder became national figures, admired by all classes.

In the serious theatre, the low standards of the mid-Victorian period were raised by a group of playwrights who were largely influenced by the widespread reaction against conventional values that was common at the time. Their plays of social comment – particularly those by the Irishman George Bernard Shaw (1856–1950) – achieved a period of genuine quality in English theatrical history. This revival did not outlast the First World War, though. The standard of drama in the 1920s and '30s can be gauged from the fact that Noel Coward was its most successful and distinguished figure. Only after the Second World War did English playwrights recover the fire and conviction that makes for powerful drama; when they did so, it was once again under the influence of strong left-wing political and social views, which ensured that the theatre remained a minority taste.

In terms of society as a whole, public entertainment in the twentieth century has been dominated by an entirely new form – the cinema. The first films appeared before 1914, and in the inter-war years they swept the country. Sound was added to pictures in 1927, thus widening the scope of the medium, and rapid technical improvements made possible ever more ambi-

Charlie Chaplin in one of his most famous roles – 'The Tramp'

Mary Pickford, heart-throb of the 'twenties

tious and impressive projects. In the often drab world of the Slump the cinema offered to many people an escape into a dream world of fantasy, glamour and excitement. Cinema-going became a habit, a necessity; it was calculated that 40% of the population of Liverpool went to the cinema once a week, and 25% went twice – most of them relatively poor people. The music-halls, by contrast, were deserted.

This boom lasted until the 1950s, when it was destroyed almost overnight by the rapid rise of television, made available to the masses of ordinary people by the spread of hire-purchase credit schemes. Despite some remarkable technical refinements, particularly in the field of colour, the film industry found itself operating all too often at a loss, and many cinemas were closed down or converted into bingo halls.

After a short period of genuine mass entertainment, therefore, the popular culture of the twentieth century has turned away from the idea of the public show. Private and domestic amusement is the rule, and public occasions are enjoyed mostly by a cultural *élite*. Thus the pattern of the eighteenth century is to some extent re-emerging.

The Roundhouse: a relic of the Industrial Revolution at Chalk Farm, London, turned into a citadel of *avant garde* culture

Early Sports

No picture of British society would be complete without sport, for this has always been a most important part of British life. By the start of our period most of the martial sports like archery and jousting, which had been so popular in medieval times, had died out. This was partly because they were no longer essential as a training for war. But many old sports survived and new ones were adopted. For the rich, hunting of all kinds – for foxes, otters, stags, hares, even wolves (the last wolf was killed in Scotland as late as 1743) – shooting and fishing were almost universally enjoyed when in the country. The poor too could often join in, as spectators, or illegally poaching game from local squires. In general, one could fairly state that sport was the only part of life in which all classes could mingle together on more or less equal terms.

Many spectator sports, which seem very cruel to us today, enjoyed a wide following among all classes of people. Cock-fighting, bear-baiting, bull-baiting, dog-fighting, 'ratting' (in which specially bred dogs tried to kill as many rats as possible in an enclosed pit) – all these drew large excited crowds. Very few people saw anything wrong or cruel in these sports and in fact Queen Elizabeth I herself had given them encouragement and prestige. Of course, betting was an important part of the interest, and hundreds of pounds were won and lost on single fights. The 'Bear Garden' in Southwark, London, was a very popular attraction and many public houses incorporated rat-pits or cock-pits. Despite efforts to stamp them out these sports survived well into the nineteenth century. It needed a large body of police and troops in 1840 to put an end to one notorious annual event, held at Stamford in Lincolnshire. This was a 'bull-running'. Amid riotous scenes, an unfortunate bull was driven through the streets, running a gauntlet of people armed with all kinds of weapons, until it was either killed, or forced into the River Welland and drowned.

Humanitarian feelings eventually put an end to all these cruel sports, and others were saved by changes in organisation. Football was popular from early times, though it was rather different from today's game. Teams of any number, often hundreds on each side, played from one end of a village to the other. Sometimes entire villages, including women and children, made up the teams. The object was 'to get the ball into the opponent's goal by any means short of murder', as one rule-book put it! The 'pitch' might be several miles long and include rivers, ditches, main roads and any other natural obstacles. No quarter was given or asked and not surprisingly there was a great deal of bloodshed; even deaths sometimes resulted. For this reason football was officially discouraged in the eighteenth century. It was revived in more

The Stamford Bull-Running

modern form chiefly by the public schools. It was at one of these, Rugby, that in 1823 William Webb Ellis (in the words of a plaque set up later at the school) 'with a fine disregard for the rules of football as played in his time, first took the ball in his arms and ran with it'. So was born the game of rugby football.

Cricket is a game of ancient origin, for it was certainly played in the sixteenth century and probably before. It was played mostly in the South of England and, though the top hats and curved bats seem strange to us today, the rules were basically the same. In the eighteenth century the principal club was at Broadhalfpenny Down, Hambledon, in Hampshire, and nearly every village in the South had a team, in which anyone – squire, parson or labourer – could play. As early as 1728 a county match was held between Kent and Sussex, and in 1787 the Marylebone Cricket Club (M.C.C.) was formed. This club gradually took over administration of the game, and moved to Lord's (named after the owner of the land, Thomas Lord) in 1814.

Racing was also very popular. Foot-racing attracted large crowds and some remarkable races were held. On one occasion it is said that a fish-seller ran seven miles in forty-five minutes with 56 lb. of fish on his head (a feat which seems almost impossible!). Horse-racing was popular from Stuart times, and Charles II was such a frequent visitor to Newmarket that he had a house built there. The Jockey Club was founded in about 1760, and most of today's 'classic' races were inaugurated in the later eighteenth century. The Derby, for example, was first run in 1780.

Boxing was another favoured sport. With fencing, it was one of the arts or skills learned by many, even of the finest gentlemen, and men of all ranks flocked to the great fights between the leading pugilists of the day, like Mendoza and Broughton. Fights were hard, with bare fists, and often went to

337

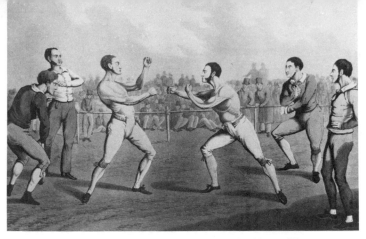

A prize fight. By the great sporting artist, Henry Alken

eighty or ninety rounds. Not until 1866 did the Queensberry Rules give a modern, safer organisation to the sport. Until then most fights were in fact illegal, but few magistrates dared to try to break up such popular events when they were held in their localities. In fact, boxing (or 'the fancy' as the sport and its followers were often called) fell into the hands of rogues and criminals in the early nineteenth century and lost repute.

Other sports of the time included bowls, real (or royal) tennis, coursing, handball, wrestling, golf, stoolball, bat and trap and hurling – to mention just a few. In winter, skating and curling could be enjoyed. There were few people who did not take part in, or enjoy watching, sport. For the gentleman, sport was a proper part of his upbringing and way of life. To be a 'sporting man' was a mark of social class. For the poor man, sport, with its exercise and associated festivities, provided an outlet, a kind of safety valve, from the hard life and working conditions of the time.

Up to the mid-nineteenth century sport was normally just a matter of local interest. But as time went on and communications improved, many changes took place. Sport began to be organised on a national, and even an international, basis. Controlling bodies were set up and uniform rules laid down. Leagues and other competitions were organised. A distinction arose between amateurs – those who took part in sport purely for pleasure – and professionals, who made their living from sport. None of these things was entirely new, of course, but they were given a great impetus a century or so ago, in line with the general changes in society, particularly the rapid replacement of local by national feeling. Many sports became big businesses and their leading exponents became, if not (until recently) rich men, then at least national heroes. Let us follow these developments in more detail, as they have affected

a few of Britain's major sports.

Association Football

Modern soccer really dates from the foundation of the Football Association in 1863. The F.A. was followed by similar associations in the other home countries, and these bodies gave direction and organisation to the game, which soon became Britain's undisputed national winter sport. Some of the early milestones in the history of modern soccer were: the start of the F.A. Cup (1871); the first international match (in 1872, a goalless draw between England and Scotland); the formation of the Football League (1882) with twelve professional clubs; the formation of F.I.F.A., the international controlling body (1904).

The English take their pleasures sadly: 92,000 people came Up for the Cup in 1928 — Huddersfield Town *v.* Blackburn Rovers

Soccer was carried to all corners of the world by British emigrants and workers, and today it is one of the few truly international games. In 1970 F.I.F.A. had 135 member countries. For many years the standard of British soccer was considered to be rather superior; few international matches were ever lost on foreign soil, and never at home. Thus it was a sensation and a humiliation when Hungary beat England 6–3 at Wembley in 1953 and when British teams went on to suffer more defeats in the next few years. Since the early 1960s, however, British soccer has regained something of its old reputation, particularly with the triumphs of England in the 1966 World Cup, and of Celtic and Manchester United, winners of the European Cup in 1967 and 1968 respectively.

For years soccer attracted enormous crowds, and it still does on occasions. As early as 1901, 110,000 people watched Tottenham Hotspur, then a non-league club, win the F.A. Cup at Crystal Palace. Vast crowds became commonplace, especially in Scotland. But, as with many other sports, soccer suffered from declining attendances after the 1950s, partly because of the effects of television, which tended to keep people at home. This decline continued until 1966, since when the influence of England's World Cup success (though not repeated in Mexico in 1970) and a high standard of play has brought back some of the missing millions.

The great players of the past are familiar names to the modern soccer fan — Alex James and Charlie Buchan (Arsenal), Billy Wright (Wolves), Dixie Dean (Everton), Tom Finney (Preston), Stanley Matthews (Blackpool) and George Young (Rangers). These are just a few of the stars who entertained millions. Yet they were very poorly paid for the pleasure which they gave. This was a result of the imposition of a maximum wage, which was still only twenty pounds per week when it was lifted in 1961. Since that time wages and transfer fees have shot up and modern soccer 'super-stars', like George Best and Bobby Charlton (Manchester United), Jimmy Johnstone (Celtic), and Bobby Moore (West Ham), earn over a hundred pounds per week. They travel in luxury, stay in the best hotels and many have agents to handle their business and financial affairs. Such a world would have been unthinkable twenty, or even ten, years ago.

However, such players, and the great teams of soccer history — Huddersfield in the 1920s, Arsenal in the 1930s, then Wolves, Tottenham, Manchester United and Leeds, with Celtic and Rangers in Scotland — represent only the tip of the iceberg. The real heart of soccer still lies, as it always has done, in the thousands of smaller clubs all over the country. It lies in the Sunday morning game on the sloping pitch hired from the local council and in the scratch games got up in school playgrounds, or in the streets. The popularity of the game is really just as strong at the grass roots as it ever has been.

Cricket

As we saw earlier, cricket already had some organisation by the early nineteenth century. Most counties had a team which played friendly matches and the M.C.C. exercised an overall control. But, like soccer, cricket expanded on a wider scale after the middle of the century. The principal landmarks were: the formation of the County Championship (first won by Surrey in 1864, but reorganised in 1873); the first Test Match, won by an English touring side in Australia in 1876; and the presentation of the 'Ashes' to the M.C.C in 1883. These 'Ashes', kept in an urn at Lords, became the symbol of supremacy in the series of matches which have been held between England and Australia every two or three years since.

Cricket was another sport which British emigrants took with them to other countries, but it only took firm root in the Empire. As a result, Test Matches have also been played against the West Indies, South Africa, India, Pakistan

'W.G.' by Spy, 1877

Compton, the cavalier of cricket

and New Zealand. Until the 1950s, only Australia put up any serious opposition, but since that time the West Indies and South Africa have both had excellent teams, and have beaten England.

Once, cricket had a great following. Enormous crowds flocked to see great English players like W. G. Grace, G. L. Jessop, Jack Hobbs, Frank Woolley, Wally Hammond, Wilfred Rhodes, Denis Compton, Len Hutton and many others, quite apart from visiting stars like Don Bradman and Gary Sobers. Unfortunately a very big drop in attendances in the last twenty years has brought professional cricket to a point of crisis. Test Matches still draw the crowds, but County Championship games normally attract very few. Most county clubs are in financial difficulties. In an effort to save the situation several innovations have been tried, including the Gillette Cup competition (begun in 1963), and the Sunday League (1969). The M.C.C. has given up some of its powers to other bodies, and overseas players have been allowed to play for English county clubs. These measures have proved popular and successful, according to general opinion, but much remains to be done to win back those spectators who have forsaken the traditional form of the game.

Away from the county grounds, however, cricket remains a popular game for many thousands of amateurs. Club and village cricket continues to flourish, still the backbone of the game. It is a familiar sight throughout the countryside at weekends in summer. It is still true that nothing seems more typical of England than the cricket match on the village green on a hot afternoon in summer. Nor must we forget that many women play cricket, and there have been several Test Matches between representative sides from England and Australia, as well as much domestic competition.

341

Rugby Football

After William Webb Ellis made his epic transgression of the laws of football at Rugby School, the new handling game soon caught on and clubs like Guy's Hospital (1843) and Blackheath (1858) were formed.

In 1871 the Rugby Football Union was founded, and other countries at home and abroad followed this example in time. In this year, too, Scotland beat England at Edinburgh in the first international match. In 1889 a County Championship was started. These early years were not entirely happy, because of various disputes. It was not until 1890 that the R.F.U. finally settled an argument with the other home countries over the laws of the game. Almost immediately another crisis arose over the question of professionalism. Rugby union football has always been an amateur game and attempts to introduce some payment for players, in the 1890s, were firmly resisted. This led, in 1895, to the secession of twenty-two northern clubs from the R.F.U. and the formation of a professional Rugby League. The professional game has different laws and has a strong following in the North of England. Recent television coverage of matches has brought the game to a wider audience, and it is also played in some other countries. Some of the trouble arose because rugby union, partly because of its strength in the public schools and at Oxford and Cambridge, tended to exclude working men. This was not true in Wales, where the social pattern was different, but in the other home countries there was a definite social standing attached to the game. For many the match itself was not so important as the social activities which followed in the clubhouse. It has taken a long time for this image to fade even slightly.

Although it has remained an amateur game, rugby union has kept its majority support and many international matches have been played. It continues to spread abroad and the centenary matches and events held in England in 1970–1 attracted even more interest.

Horse-racing

British racing has a most impressive history. Since the days of Charles II royal patronage has given the Turf respectability and prestige. Indeed, racing is sometimes called the 'Sport of Kings'. Yet although favoured, and controlled, by the aristocracy, the sport has always had room for the ordinary people. Without them, in fact, racing would have been on a much smaller scale, for it depends chiefly on betting. Many enjoy the Turf for its own sake, of course, but there can be no doubt that betting has always been the chief interest in it. British punters are lucky, for they have a choice of betting facilities second to none. The efforts of the Jockey Club over the years have stamped out all but isolated cases of dishonesty, and British racing is now perhaps the fairest in the world. Classic races, like the Derby, St.

'Derby Day', by W. P. Frith. Not so much a race-meeting, more a way of life

Leger and Oaks, which as we saw were founded in the eighteenth century, have kept attention focused on the sport. So have great steeplechase races, like the Grand National and Cheltenham Gold Cup. Good breeding has produced famous horses like St. Simon, Hyperion, Golden Miller, Arkle and Royal Palace (as well as building up a prosperous British blood-stock industry).

Yet, despite all this, racing has been in financial difficulties for some years as a result mainly of falling attendances. In the nineteenth century race-meetings attracted vast crowds, not just for the racing but for all the fun of the fair, shops and entertainments, which formed part of the meeting. These lost their appeal as other forms of entertainment became popular. Now many punters prefer to stay at home and watch the races on television, placing their bets in local betting shops. The sport has lost a good deal of money in this way. In order to help it, a Horse-race Betting Levy Board was set up in the 1960s to plough back money into racing. The proceeds of a betting tax have been used for ground improvements and for increases in prize money. In this way it is hoped that racing will be able to withstand the challenge from abroad and from other sports.

Britain and the Olympic Games

In 1896, following a suggestion by Baron de Coubertin, a French nobleman, the ancient Olympic Games were revived in a new form. They had last been held 1,600 years before, and their revival was an attempt to foster international peace and understanding. The first of the modern series was held in Athens in 1896 and the Games have been held every four years since, **343** except in war-time. From the start, Britain has played a major role in the Olympic movement.

London has twice been host to the Olympic Games – in 1908 and 1948. The first occasion was memorable for the Marathon Race, in which the Italian, Dorando, was helped exhausted across the line by anxious officials, only to be disqualified. The 1948 Games gave Britain a chance to show how she had recovered from the ravages of war, and they were most successful.

British sportsmen and women have had their share of success, especially in the early years. For example, the Marquess of Exeter, now the President of the International Amateur Athletics Federation, won the 400 metres Hurdles at Amsterdam in 1928. But in more recent times it has become more difficult to match the strength of other countries and British Gold Medal winners have been rarer. In Mexico in 1968 only five were won, perhaps the most notable being that won by David Hemery, again in the 400 metres Hurdles, in which he set a new world record.

Other Sports

Finally, we must at least mention a few of the many other sports which have enjoyed periods of national popularity. Greyhound racing and speedway were once very popular, but they no longer command national followings. Boxing revived in respectability at the end of the nineteenth century, and several British world champions emerged. As the risks to health became known, however, its following declined.

Motor-racing, a natural consequence of the development of the motor car, has always owed much to British designers, technicians and owners. Before the Second World War Brooklands (now part of the British Aircraft Corporation works at Weybridge) was almost the cradle of the sport, while many British drivers, like Graham Hill and Jim Clark, in recent years, have carried off the World Championship. In lawn tennis, Britain enjoyed great success in the 1930s, with Fred Perry winning at Wimbledon and leading his country to several Davis Cup victories, which helped to give the game immense social popularity at that time. Since 1945, however, golf has spread from Scotland to become the principal 'social' sport. International success by British golfers was rare until Tony Jacklin's outstanding victories in the British and United States Open Championships (1969 and 1970).

Recent Attitudes to Sport

There are three generalisations which may be made about sport in Britain in the last twenty years or so. These are, that spectator sports have become less popular; that individual pursuits, mainly for recreation, as opposed to competitive team games, have become more popular; and that 'affluent' sports, needing money and equipment, have been taken up by a much wider circle of people.

The reasons for these changes are all linked. On the one hand, television and other forms of 'instant' entertainment have kept people away from spectator sports. On the other, the increased tensions of life and work have made the need for escape and exercise even greater than in the past. A shorter working week gives more time to take part in sport. But the standard has risen so much that no one can hope to succeed in competitive sport without many sacrifices. In any case, among younger people, the discipline required for team games makes them less acceptable in an age when authority and discipline are less welcome.

This helps to explain why, aided by better facilities and by much greater general prosperity, many have turned to sports which were once available only to the rich minority. Fifty years ago this need for individual recreation and exercise could only be met by inexpensive activities like cycling, angling and rambling, and these had a wide following, as they still do. But now it is golf, sailing, judo, climbing, water-skiing and winter sports which are attracting followers and this change is bound to continue as society develops. For we can see that sport is, in a way, the mirror of our affluent society, reflecting all the changes which take place.

COSTUME AND FASHION

Fashions in clothes changed just as often at the start of our period as they do now. Practically every year in between saw something new in the way in which men and women dressed. Of course, until recently, only the rich could afford to keep right up to date with new fashions. But in time new styles worked their way down and affected the clothes of ordinary people as well. Because of this constant change, it is impossible to describe in detail how modern dress has evolved. Let us, instead, take several different years within our period, and see how fashionable people dressed then. In this way we can obtain an overall picture, which will show how much fashion is a mirror of social attitudes and change.

1750

In the eighteenth century fashion in Britain was very much influenced by French design. Every innovation in Paris was quickly followed in London. The main features of ladies' dresses were the rich materials used – silks, velvets and satins – brightly coloured and embroidered with exquisite designs. Gowns were worn over hoops made of metal or whalebone. The hoops were attached to corsets, which kept waists in, and they were so large and cumbersome that a collapsible model was introduced, to allow ladies to pass more easily through narrow entrances! Ruffles and bows were popular, and much use was made of powder in arranging the hair.

Male attire was very elegant and colourful, reflecting the gay spirit of the 345 times. The well-dressed gentleman might wear, for example, a green flared velvet coat, with a satin waistcoat embroidered in gold, green woollen breeches and silk stockings. A white cravat, black leather shoes with buckles, cane and black tricorne hat surmounting a powdered wig or pigtail completed his ensemble. Such dress became even more exotic in the following years, until it reached a climax in the heyday of the 'dandy' during the early nineteenth-century Regency period.

Fashionable society satirised: Hogarth's 'Taste in High Life', engraved in 1742

1850

In the reign of Queen Victoria, in keeping with different social ideas, a reaction set in against such gay clothes in favour of quieter, more sober dress. For example, when Benjamin Disraeli attended the House of Commons for the first time in 1837, wearing a bottle-green coat, a white waistcoat covered in gold chains and a large black cravat, he was ridiculed by other members. Instead, the fashion for men became staid and sombre: tail-coats, trousers, cloaks, top hats and boots became uniform, and wing collars came in soon afterwards. Colours were dark and individual touches could only be displayed in the moustaches and side-whiskers which were universally worn.

In ladies' dress, too, the tendency was towards a more sombre uniformity. Skirts were very full, with several layers of petticoats or under-skirts beneath. Six or seven was quite a usual number! The crinoline – a petticoat stiffened with horizontal whalebone bands – became popular, and of course corsets were compulsory to achieve the target of a seventeen-inch to nineteen-inch waist. Bonnets were worn and were made very popular by Queen Victoria,

Frith's 'Paddington Station'. The painter believed that every picture should tell a story; this tells several

whose wardrobe was simple and homely. A few dresses even revealed the ankles, but these were rather daring and rare.

1925

After the First World War there was a general reaction against the Victorian period and this was certainly felt in fashion. The trend in men's clothing was towards greater comfort. The lounge suit came into its own, though trousers were much wider than today. Sports jackets and flannels made their appearance and shoes replaced boots. Fewer men wore hats, and those who did favoured the bowler or trilby. There was a brief fashion at this time for 'plus-fours' (still worn sometimes by golfers) and for 'Oxford bags', which were enormously wide trousers, popular at the university.

Ladies' fashion was dominated by the greater personal freedom which women were enjoying. Strangely, this made them want to disguise all signs of femininity in order to play down the differences between the sexes! Dresses

Left: The 'flapper' and the 'silly ass': fashion in the 1920s.
Right: From *Vogue*, May 1929

347

did come up to the knee – a feature regarded by older people as disgusting and sinful – but they were straight, tubular or sack-like in style, without waists, the intention being to hide the figure rather than to enhance it. Silk stockings, cloche hats and straight hair were also typical of the times.

Today

Modern fashion has undergone a revolution, like so many other aspects of society. The desire for personal freedom has been reflected in quite new departures in design and a return to the more exciting styles of the past, and these have been given new dimensions by the use of artificial textiles. Because of more general prosperity and because manufacturers have been careful to produce good-quality, fashionable clothes at reasonable prices, these changes have affected everyone, of all ages and incomes. Britain has set the pace in a world-wide transformation and Carnaby Street has become a place of pilgrimage.

In men's wear the emphasis is not so much on new fashions, as on a return to the elegance of the eighteenth century. The cut, material and colours of modern clothing draw heavily on Georgian and Regency fashions. Even nineteenth-century military uniforms have had a brief revival! Such fashions have influenced formal and informal dress alike.

For women, a completely new fashion came with the mini-skirt. Throughout the 1960s skirts crept higher and higher, until they could rise no more and tights had to be worn for the sake of decency as well as for convenience. The 'mini', though still enormously popular, now seems to be under severe competition as the styles of the past – the 'maxis' and 'midis' – come back into favour.

Over the years then, fashion has clearly reflected changes in social attitudes and values. In the eighteenth century, styles were geared to the whims of the aristocracy. In the nineteenth, they were determined much more by middle-class conventions. Today, fashion is for everyone, and perhaps the future lies in the modern trend towards 'unisex' – identical clothes for both men and women, perhaps the ultimate in equality between the sexes.

TENSIONS IN SOCIETY

The Classes

In the eighteenth and nineteenth centuries the class structure of British society was much more clearly marked than it is today. Everyone was expected to know his place in the system of layers, to be satisfied with it and to behave according to the standards generally thought to be appropriate to his 'station'. The structure was like a pyramid. At the top were the members
348   of the upper class. Their distinction lay not in wealth alone, though most were

Carriages in Rotten Row, Hyde Park, about 1900

rich and some had enormous fortunes. Equally important, if not more so, were birth, upbringing and occupation. The old aristocracy was joined by newcomers over the years, but several generations might pass before 'new' families could gain proper acceptance. To be of 'good birth' was the surest key to social standing and success, though of course some degree of wealth, obtained preferably from land, was necessary to pay for the luxurious style of living which was expected of the upper class.

But though it was perfectly possible for newcomers to buy estates and even titles, no one could buy social acceptance or the qualities needed to be a 'gentleman'. These qualities were indefinable, and came to refer to standards of behaviour as much as status. It was said that the only real test of gentility was to be accepted as a gentleman by others.

The middle class was a much broader section of society. Birth and breeding were still important, especially for the humbler country gentry and professional men; but any man of wealth, whatever he made his money by and however undistinguished his origins, was regarded as being of the middle class.

Beneath came the mass of society. The working class was not uniform – indeed, Victorians usually referred to the 'working classes'. They ranged from skilled craftsmen ('artisans'), many of them quite comfortably off, to unskilled factory operatives, domestic workers, navvies and labourers in the fields. These men and their families made up the great majority of the population, yet they were regarded as inferior, because of their background and the nature of their work.

These lines were not drawn as firmly as in some other countries. Indeed, it was always possible for working-men to better themselves and rise up in the social scale. Self-improvement was, within limits, an accepted virtue in the nineteenth century. With industrialisation, the middle class expanded rapidly and some leading industrialists, such as Josiah Wedgwood and Sir Robert Peel the Elder, moved freely in even the highest circles (as merchants had done in earlier times).

But we must not exaggerate the degree of flexibility which the Industrial Revolution brought to British society. In fact, many historians believe that the end of the eighteenth century actually saw a rise in social tensions caused by class differences. In so far as these tensions got worse, they did so because the Industrial Revolution altered the environment in ways that made social divisions seem actually less tolerable than they had been before. There is evidence that the highly stratified social system was not greatly resented before industrialisation occurred. It was tolerated and even defended as the natural and God-given order of things. True, some ambitious men might fret at restraints, but most were brought up not to question the position. Moreover, the middle and upper classes had responsibilities as well as privileges. It was an accepted duty of the fortunate minority to help the poor – a duty usually discharged by means of charity. So long as these responsibilities were met and economic difficulties did not become too great, the social pattern of pre-Industrial Britain was rarely challenged. In time, however, the economic changes brought about by the coming of industry began to weigh heavily on the old order. The vast increase in population centred mainly in towns; the dependence of people on factory employment; the hardships of factory life and of periods of unemployment – all combined to make the existing system of social inter-dependence increasingly out of date. The upper and middle classes could not cope with their social responsibilities in the towns and many gave up trying. The state was slow to fill the vacuum thus created. Not surprisingly, therefore, restlessness grew and the bitterness of the workers was directed especially against the middle class. It was generally felt that the hardships of life were the fault of the latter, and especially of the industrial capitalists, who were thought to be exploiting labour in order to line their own pockets. This was the kind of idea which Karl Marx (1818–83) and other socialists put around. They urged workers to rise up together in revolution and break their 'chains'.

These ideas certainly had a wide influence in Britain, as well as in other countries, but revolution did not take place. This would have been a disappointment to Marx, who did most of his writing in Britain and felt that revolution was certain to happen in a country where the classes were so sharply divided. However, the upper classes were shrewd enough to yield to political pressure peacefully in 1832, 1846 and 1867, and the middle classes joined them in reforms which kept the social temperature down. The coming of democracy; changing attitudes with regard to social legislation; improvements in the economy – these changes drew the sting of violence. None the less there were many uneasy moments and the years before the First World War were particularly dangerous times. By then the old supremacy of the landowners was in rapid decline. Many estates had been ruined by agricultural depression and the social structure in the countryside began to change

Sunday morning in Paradise Gardens, 1856

for good, as new men took the opportunity to buy land at low prices. Land was never again to have the same degree of dominance. It was at this time, too, that radicals like David Lloyd George began to attack the aristocracy directly. On one occasion he referred to the landed classes as 'parasites, who toil not, neither do they spin', a remark which drew a reproof from King Edward VII.

Thus by the outbreak of the First World War the traditional class divisions were under attack and patterns were changing. Since that time further evolution has taken place, for which war and economic changes have been responsible. In both World Wars, especially the Second, all classes united together in the interests of the nation and this brought an easing of the social tensions which had preceded each conflict. The tremendous leap forward in the economy, described in Chapter 13, together with the Welfare State, has brought a much higher standard of living and removed the worst economic distress. The progressive development of a democratic form of government has given everyone a share in the responsibility for social and economic progress and has thus helped towards a more democratic society. Though modern political parties still do, in a way, represent classes, this is by no means as clear as it was even twenty years ago, and there were signs that this was changing further in the late 1960s.

Today, some deference is still paid to the old ruling classes, particularly to the aristocracy, but most of the old distinctions based on birth have gone. That is not to say that modern Britain is a 'classless society'; instead, it is wealth, education and ability that matter. It is not easy to say whether people are any happier under this new system than under the old one; but at least it is generally felt to be more reasonable and democratic, and therefore less likely to produce tensions in society.

The Youth Culture

No doubt young people have always chafed at restrictions imposed upon them by their parents or society. But, until very recently in the history of British society, such feelings were rarely expressed forcibly. Family ties and parental authority were strong and few children dared to question them openly. They could not afford to do so, since most of them depended financially on their parents until well into their adult lives. A combination of fear, respect, tradition and, above all, economic necessity limited the scale and effectiveness of most young people's self-assertion. It is true that there were times, like the 1920s, when they scandalised their elders by their behaviour, but these were phases which hardly seemed to pose fundamental questions.

The last twenty years or so, however, have told a very different story. The younger generation has emerged as a quite distinct and powerful force in society. A wide and potentially harmful division is developing, often called the 'generation gap', because it is basically a division between two different generations. Several things have brought this conflict out into the open, of which the most important is economic change. A more affluent society provides jobs for all, and the welfare state supports those who cannot or will not work. Millions of teenagers have therefore grown up without experiencing anything but prosperity. Many have never been short of food or clothing and only a few have had to struggle for survival, as their grandparents often had to do. At the age of fifteen, a boy or girl can, at will, take up a well-paid job and earn enough to lead an independent life. In consequence the economic ties which helped to bind families together have snapped. Even the law, by reducing the age of majority to eighteen (in 1970), has assisted in this process.

Economic independence has brought with it new expressions of the desire for personal freedom of action. These have taken many outward forms, but they all have in common the desire to get away from uniformity and tradition. Completely new styles in dress have influenced all age-groups (see p. 348), and the rejection of a conventional style of life is also considered a sign of freedom. In the arts, a new 'pop culture' has emerged, in which old forms and modes have been done away with. In music and dancing the uninhibited rock-and-roll of the 1950s was followed by the beat style of the 1960s, pioneered by the phenomenally successful Beatles. The new sounds were matched by a distinctively 'pop' style of visual art and decoration, and with great rapidity – partly assisted by purely commercial forces – the pop-culture extended to cover all aspects of teenage life.

These trends are not socially harmful in themselves. New tastes and fashions have aroused controversy before now. What may be harmful is the way in which personal freedom has been abused by a small minority. Some

young people, who do not remember any other kind of society, have come to

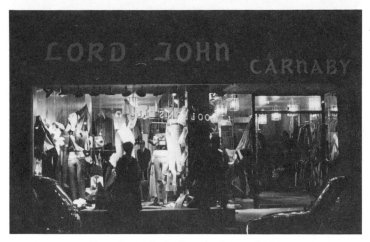

Saturday night in Carnaby Street, 1970

feel that they owe nothing to it, and consequently feel no responsibility. Moral standards, codes of behaviour, respect for authority and the law – these are seen as myths, invented as means of keeping order and suppressing the individual. Some therefore reject society totally; others merely demand the right to opt out and to deviate from accepted standards of behaviour.

Naturally, older people are bewildered by such changes, and particularly by attacks on ideas and institutions which they see as the cement holding civilised life together. It is true that in strictly political matters some of the protests of young people have attracted support from a wide cross-section of society; but more often than not protest movements have taken on the characteristics of campaigns in a cultural war – and some incidents, such as the mêlée outside the American Embassy in Grosvenor Square in 1966, have been very like real battles.

Certain groups of young people have caused particular disquiet. 'Teddy boys', 'mods', 'rockers', 'greasers', 'Hell's Angels' and 'skinheads' have all briefly hit the headlines, and there has been much alarm in connection with drug-taking and sexual indulgence. Not surprisingly, there has been a reaction against such manifestations, leading to much misunderstanding. The whole of the younger generation has fallen into the danger of being tarred with the same brush as the extreme and harmful minority, whereas a great majority are really only affected by such exterior trappings as long hair or 'way-out' clothes. On the other side there is much impatience, not least among the large numbers of genuine idealists. Where the generation gap divides the defenders of society from those who would be happy to see it destroyed, it is regrettable enough; but where it divides them also from those who wish to strengthen and improve the structure, it is far more dangerous. This is at present one of the more serious of the many tensions produced by Britain's venture into urban industrialism.

353

'The permissive society' is a phrase coined to describe the effects of the relaxation of moral standards which has taken place in recent years. A society is generally described as permissive when it accepts (or permits) personal opinions, unrestricted by general standards and conventions, as the sole guides in moral matters. As commonly used, the phrase often carries an additional suggestion that this system of personal choice produces less desirable behaviour than the previous system of social rules. Finally, it is most frequently applied to sexual matters. It is, in fact, a subject surrounded by muddled thinking and uncertainty and it is probably not surprising that a lot of people, when talking about it, confuse attitudes with behaviour.

In the case of sex, for instance, careful study of the behavioural patterns of men, at least, shows that there has been relatively little significant change in the last 250 years. Women, it is true, appear to have changed their pattern to some extent since the Second World War; but the extent even of this important change should not be over-rated. In attitudes, on the other hand, there have been great changes. During the eighteenth century, very free behaviour was accepted in many parts of society, but lip service was generally paid to the orthodox rules. In the nineteenth century this easy-going compromise was rejected in favour of a demand for more outward observance of the rules; but while 'middle-class Victorian morality' was undoubtedly seriously practised by a great many people, much evidence has come to light recently that eighteenth-century habits went underground, rather than dying out. In the present century this attitude in turn has come to be regarded as hypocritical or repressive, or both, and a massive change in opinion has taken place. Sex is now a subject which is openly discussed. Divorce, formerly difficult and shameful, has become relatively easy and (to a rather lesser extent) acceptable. Changing ideas about sin, together with effective contraceptives (especially 'the pill') and legalised abortions, have made for a quite different attitude towards sexual behaviour. Prostitutes and homosexuals were given more freedom by changes in the law in the 1950s and '60s. All these developments have doubtless encouraged a great many people to stop paying even lip service to the conventions and numbers have done what they would not previously have dared to do. The exact extent and significance of the 'sexual revolution', however, has probably been over-estimated.

Rather more serious, perhaps, are the implications of the permissive society for thought and culture. The most striking feature here has been the attack on censorship in literature, drama, films and other forms of art and entertainment. The idea that people should be allowed to decide for themselves what they should and should not read, watch or listen to has been taken far and fast. A famous test case was the prosecution for obscenity, in 1960, of the publishers of *Lady Chatterley's Lover*, by D. H. Lawrence. The prosecution failed, and this opened the way for the publication of other 'outspoken' books.

The theatre censorship powers of the Lord Chamberlain were abolished in 1968, and since then every kind of sexual behaviour, together with scenes of extreme violence, has been represented on stage. The same is true of the cinema and, to a lesser extent, of television. Sex has also been very freely used as an aid in advertising – even, in one case, to publicise a road-safety campaign!

Many people regard these trends as a serious social problem, in the sense that society may suffer from unscrupulous exploitation if no holds are to be barred. This problem is seen in a particularly advanced form in connection with the habit of drug-taking. There is no doubt that the use of drugs, especially among young people, grew suddenly and became widespread in the 1960s (in this respect it differs from sex – something which was far from new). In fact, drugs have become very much part of the youth culture described above, despite legal penalties and despite the clear medical evidence that they are all more or less harmful, and frequently very dangerous indeed. For some people their danger is part of their attraction. Many, on the other hand, merely go along with the crowd. But some at least deliberately turn to drugs as a way of dropping out from the strains and stresses of modern life. Thus drugs are in a peculiar sense a social problem.

All these matters are so controversial that statements of fact tend to get mixed up with judgements whenever they are discussed. Many people see Britain as a pioneer in social liberalism; others condemn the changes as undermining traditional European values, particularly those of Christianity, and leading to national decadence. It is clear that this division of opinion reflects a division in society and that both sides consider that basic values are at stake. This makes for grave tensions in British society.

It is also clear that these tensions arise at root from the relative failure of twentieth-century Britain to adapt to the new life of an industrial urban society, surrounded by vast affluence, but unsure of its values. Whether such adjustment is possible remains to be seen.

Suggestions for further work and discussion

1. If you live near a provincial theatre, find out how it is financed. What sort of plays are most popular? How many people attend it out of the local population?

2. Investigate the history of your local paper; in what main ways has it changed since its foundation?

3. Give a fuller account of one of the sports mentioned in this chapter. Alternatively, choose another sport in which you are interested and describe its development in Britain.

4. Apart from the styles of dress mentioned, there have been a great many others in the last two hundred years. Find out about some of these and, if possible, make drawings of them. How have *your* clothes been influenced by former styles?

5. Subjects for an essay or discussion:

What can sport tell us about the society in which we live?

Is modern fashion part of a wider feeling against authority?

Why has the revolution which Marx forecast not come about in Britain?

6. What sort of social distinctions matter most in modern British society?

7. Which do you think matter more in forming social attitudes — ideas (including religion) or economic and environmental facts?

Books for further reading:

C. Hole, *English Sports and Pastimes*, Batsford, 1949.

J. Laver, *A Concise History of Costume*, Thames and Hudson, 1969.

K. Chesney, *The Victorian Underworld*, David and Charles, 1970.

R. Hoggart, *The Uses of Literacy*, Chatto & Windus, 1957, Penguin, 1969.

15 : Learning and Belief

We have frequently noticed in previous chapters that, although Great Britain is really quite small in area, its different parts – England, Scotland, Wales, Ireland – have often had quite distinct histories. This is particularly so with education; Wales can be taken, roughly speaking, with England, but Ireland and Scotland both go their own ways.

Educational history in Ireland can be briefly summed up by saying that most parts of the country suffered in this as in other respects from being unfairly governed – or rather, neglected – by England. Education was almost entirely a religious matter in the eighteenth and nineteenth centuries, and since the Roman Catholic majority in Ireland were very poor, it was notorious that the Irish peasantry was virtually uneducated. Later on the schools of southern Ireland became focus-points for nationalist propaganda; but this takes us beyond the point where Eire became independent of England, early in the twentieth century.

Though Scotland also has a distinct educational history, the reason for this is quite the opposite. Scottish education was for a long time vastly superior to English. Throughout the eighteenth and nineteenth centuries Scotsmen, at any rate in the Lowlands, enjoyed a fine system of efficiently run schools and universities, where they received an education notable for its thoroughness and rigour, as well as its relative modernity – there was much emphasis on mathematics and practical subjects. All this was provided cheaply, by means of carefully run charities rather than through state action. The influence of Calvinistic religion, with its stress on hard work and self-improvement in education as in other matters, was particularly important. Throughout these two centuries, the proportion of Scots receiving secondary and university education was usually much higher than in England. It seems very likely that is gave the Scots an advantage and it is probably no accident that we find so many Scotsmen among the pioneers of the Industrial Revolution and foremost in medicine, law, politics, engineering, science, business and imperial or military matters.

In this chapter, however, we propose to concentrate on English education, partly at least because its complicated history has much to tell us about the problems facing an evolving industrial society.

Education is a topic which is rather hard to get into perspective. The truth of this has been demonstrated very clearly in recent years, when it has caused as much argument as any issue in British domestic politics. It is not difficult to see why this should be so. Education nowadays affects everybody, in a very intimate and personal way; it has an important impact on family relationships, which arouse very deep emotions; it often touches very sensitive subjects, such as religion; and since it is concerned with the shaping of citizens, it is of crucial importance to the society in which we live. It is not surprising that many people have very strong and radical views about it. But these ideas may involve something very close to experimenting with children and that in itself will often rouse further passions.

THE EIGHTEENTH CENTURY

In view of the high priority which we give to education today, it may come as a surprise to find that it mattered a great deal less to most people in the eighteenth century. That is not to say that English society then was an uncultivated society. On the contrary, many people look back to this period as a time when civilisation reached new peaks, and there are even some who believe it has been in decline ever since. But this very highly polished culture was an essentially aristocratic affair, confined to a relatively small proportion of the population. Even for these fortunate people, formal education was relatively unimportant. Many of the richest noblemen never troubled with schools or universities for their sons – they hired private tutors and sent the boys on Grand Tours of Europe. This was because 'civilisation' was conceived at that time much more as a way of life, an approach to living, a matter of cool poise and elegant taste, rather than of actual knowledge. A civilised man was distinguished by his social qualities, not by certificates to say that he had passed a certain number of examinations.

That is not to say that there were no schools, or that they were entirely unimportant. But it may help to explain why the educational picture was so peaceful in the eighteenth century, and it will be important to compare the attitudes described above to those shown by reformers in both the nineteenth and the twentieth centuries.

The state had nothing to do with education in the eighteenth century, nor was there any suggestion that it should have. All the schools that existed were either privately run for profit, or else were charitable foundations – and a good many of the latter were corruptly managed so that the headmaster or some other person was able to make private profit illegally. It was not compulsory for anyone to go to school and the vast majority of the population got very little schooling indeed. One consequence of this was that many people could neither read nor write. (This can be seen immediately from a look at any church register of the period; in the place where they were supposed to sign their name, thousands could only put a large X. This was known as 'making one's mark'.)

Very small children might be sent to a 'dame school'. This was a sort of nursery school, run by an old lady, who might (or might not) be able to teach little children their alphabet and numbers. If a child was fortunate, he or she might then be able to go on to an elementary school, usually run by a religious body – a Church of England educational society or its nonconformist counterpart. Not every village had such a school, and not even every town possessed one. From 1780 onwards, therefore, a voluntary movement grew up to provide at any rate some schooling for poor children, by means of Sunday Schools staffed by volunteer adults, usually of the middle classes. Robert Raikes of Gloucester (1735–1811) was a principal figure in organising and extending the Sunday School movement.

Virtually no children of the lower classes were educated beyond the age of ten or twelve. It was generally felt that, since their business in life was to labour with their hands, it was unnecessary to overload their minds with useless book learning. Besides, it might unsettle them and give them ideas above their station. There were people who were convinced that too much education could cause revolution; in a sense you may think they were right.

Secondary education was therefore confined to the middle and upper classes. It was provided, patchily, by grammar schools, often of Tudor or even medieval foundation. These were charitable in origin and intended for local dayboys, but in some of them the masters had been able to add to their salaries by taking in boarders as private pupils. This practice, already common in the better endowed or better run schools, was the origin of some of the public schools which developed during the next century.

An eighteenth-century grammar school: Hipperholme, in Yorkshire

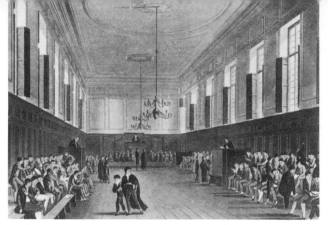
Eton in the eighteenth century

The quality of the education offered at all these schools would seem to our eyes very limited. Reading, writing and arithmetic were taught in elementary schools by mechanical methods which involved a great deal of copying out and learning by heart. In the grammar schools this approach was taken even further, in the study of Latin, and sometimes mathematics, to which they were almost entirely devoted. Languages, history, English literature and, of course, science were all entirely ignored as school subjects. Severe punishment was used freely and universally, for bad work as well as any kind of misbehaviour. (There was no particular concern about the wisdom of this. Apart from anything else, children were just not very important – they were widely treated as 'incomplete humans'. The high birth rate probably encouraged the idea that they were expendable, or at least less significant than productive adults.)

Historians are accustomed to describe the two ancient universities of Oxford and Cambridge as 'sunk in torpor' or 'stagnant' during this period. This is not entirely true, in that there were men of tremendous learning to be found there at all times and a certain proportion of undergraduates worked hard and were well taught. Generally speaking, however, most dons did little work and lived very comfortably, while most undergraduates followed their example. Officially and in law, the universities were supposed to have a religious character and purpose; but this was widely ignored, apart from the rules which prevented anyone except members of the Church of England from entering. In consequence, there were many examples of careful parents (for such people did exist, then as at any other time) deliberately preferring to send their son on a carefully planned European Tour of two or three years rather than to university.

These Grand Tours were, as has already been suggested, of great importance in the education of a young aristocrat. In company with a tutor, he

would visit courts and capitals, meet great men and useful acquaintances, learn the manners of international society and (if he was at all serious) acquire a taste for and some knowledge of the classical civilisation on which most of contemporary European culture was based. The Grand Tour gave the British aristocratic culture of the eighteenth century an international, cosmopolitan flavour that was notably lacking in the nineteenth century.

Sometimes its influence could have great effects. A short tour of twelve months in 1714 and 1715, for instance, made by the young Earl of Burlington, may have had first-rate importance in developing the Earl's taste· for classical architecture which he later displayed so brilliantly as the chief founder of the so-called Palladian style in England. (He designed Chiswick Villa and many other beautiful houses and palaces.) Though this was a rather shorter journey than most, it took in the main towns of Belgium, Holland and the Rhineland, Geneva in Switzerland, the Alps, Turin, Genoa and a long stay in Rome, followed by a rather shorter one in Venice (which was a sort of eighteenth-century Las Vegas); then the Earl came home through France, with a stay in Paris and a visit to Versailles. Other travellers on the Grand Tour often went to Dresden, Berlin and Vienna, and some to Madrid, or St. Petersburg in Russia, but Lord Burlington was interested chiefly in classical architecture and that meant above all Italy.

1800–1870

The changes at the end of the eighteenth century did much to disturb the pattern of educational activity that had become so comfortably established in England. In simple terms, the needs and the outlook of society both changed. There were more people to be educated than ever before and they could not be catered for under existing arrangements. The Industrial Revolution created new demands (e.g. for scientific knowledge) in education as it did in other fields. The French Revolution brought a new wave of ideas and aspirations in

Chiswick Villa, one of the early masterpieces of English Palladianism

361

mental as well as political matters. For these and other reasons the aristocratic culture which had found it possible to dispense with an elaborate system of formal education declined and dwindled slowly away.

The new society which began to emerge in England during the early nineteenth century was dimly aware of these factors, and aware that the educational picture was changing in consequence. People were still reluctant to do very much, though. Many of the pioneer figures of the new middle class were self-made men, inclined to despise book-learning. In addition, very strong feelings were aroused by two questions – what should happen to religious instruction in an expanded educational system, and how far should the state intervene in educational affairs? Violent controversy on these points effectively slowed up the rate of educational change during the first three-quarters of the nineteenth century and limited the business of education to charitable efforts, usually of a religious nature. Because England during this period was immensely wealthy by the standards of the time, and because many middle-class citizens felt that they had a positive duty to give money for work of this kind, the achievements were surprisingly great. But by comparison with France or Germany, England fell notably behind in the national 'education league'.

The sheer problem of numbers began to attract attention at an early stage and methods of teaching were adapted to meet it. Two men were prominent in this, Joseph Lancaster (1778–1838) and Andrew Bell (1753–1832). (In view of the superiority of Scottish education, it is noteworthy that Bell was himself a Scot.) The system which both men claimed to have been the first to invent was an interesting product of the Age of Industrial Revolution; Lancaster described it as a 'new mechanical system', and it has a lot in common with the techniques pioneered by Arkwright in the cotton industry. The idea was very simple: a teacher would give an item of knowledge, or a whole lesson, to a class of, say, twenty; they would learn it off by heart, and then go and repeat it to other classes. In this way one master could 'teach' several hundred children in one hall. The pupil-teachers were called 'monitors', and so the system as a whole became known as the 'monitorial' system – though it was often also called the Lancasterian system. The claims made for it were very high, but often exaggerated.

It is significant that Lancaster and Bell were religious as well as educational rivals, and the societies founded, in competition, to advocate their ideas, were also committed to particular slants in religious education. The Royal Lancasterian Association (founded 1810) was a Nonconformist body which developed in 1814 into the British and Foreign School Society. Its rival, the Anglican National Society (For Promoting the Education of the Poor in the Principles of the Established Church) was founded in 1810. Each deserves credit for the founding of hundreds of schools; and yet the chief effort of each

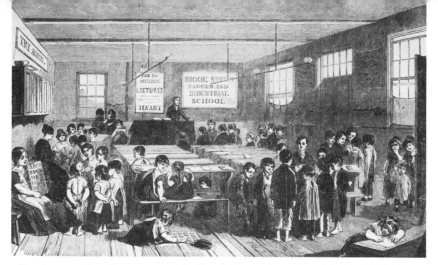

The Lancasterian System at work: Brook Street Ragged and Industrial School, 1846. Note the text on the left

was directed towards beating the other one down and struggling for advantage in whatever plans the state might have for assisting educational expansion.

In fact, the whole history of education in Britain (and especially in England) in the nineteenth century revolved around religious disagreement. There were two main reasons for this. First, great importance was attached at that time to the forms of religion, which consequently loomed large in all school arrangements. Second, education was in any case traditionally part of the business of the Churches, and particularly of the Established Church of England. This second argument perhaps grew in significance as the century went by, for, with the state or other non-religious bodies taking over more and more of the other 'social' functions of the Church (poor relief, in particular, and the care of the sick and the aged), churchmen hung on especially grimly to this last sphere of influence. The Church of England made a tremendous effort. Of the 8,798 schools which received state aid in 1870, no fewer than 6,724 were Anglican and there were hundreds more which received no assistance at all. Between 1811 and 1870 the Church of England raised £15 million for education, and from 1870 to 1883 another £12¼ million. This indicates the importance attached to the business of education. It is not surprising, therefore, to find that Anglicans would not tolerate any religious instruction which was not strictly Anglican in tone being given in a school which they supported. In addition, they expected that, as the state Church, their brand of religion ought to prevail in all schools supported by the state. But Nonconformists were violently angry about this demand, saying that they could see no reason why they should pay taxes to support the teaching of a form of religion with which they disagreed. So the argument went on indefinitely and seriously limited the amount which the state was able to give in aid. **363**

The idea that the state might itself run schools with no particular religious bias had very few supporters in the first half of the nineteenth century. But the reasonableness of at least some state financial aid was admitted from 1833 onwards. In that year Parliament voted £20,000 'for the purposes of education', and the money was shared between the National Society and the British and Foreign School Society. This grant was increased slowly over the years that followed and in consequence the government gradually developed methods of administering the money and making sure it was properly spent. Eventually, therefore, they found themselves considering questions of efficiency.

A government department of education was formally set up in 1856, and in 1858 a parliamentary commission of inquiry, under the Duke of Newcastle as chairman, was asked to investigate elementary education. The commission concluded that the great majority of children were now getting some form of elementary schooling; but it was often of poor standard and needed to be tightened up. Dame schools, for instance, are described to them as follows:

> The usual scene of these schools is a cottage kitchen, in which the mistress divides her time between her pupils and her domestic duties. The children sit round the room, often so thickly stowed as to occupy every available corner, and spend the greater part of their time in knitting and sewing. At intervals the mistress calls them up, one or two at a time, and teaches the alphabet and easy words . . .
>
> The dames most commonly have only one room for every purpose and their scholars may often be seen sitting round the sides of a four-post bed . . .
>
> I have seen the children as closely packed as birds in a nest, and tumbling over each other like puppies in a kennel.

The dame schools and other private schools, however, were less important than the schools run by the great national societies, often with financial aid provided by the state. The commissioners estimated that only $4\frac{1}{2}$% of children of school age were not actually receiving elementary education of some sort. Their estimate was too high, and even so it disguised serious weaknesses, such as the fact that attendance was often very erratic. Most children left school for good at eleven.

The chief weakness, however, was the *quality* of the education offered. The fault was principally with the teachers.

> Sometimes teachers are appointed because they are pious people; sometimes because they can do nothing else . . . sometimes because it is very erroneously supposed that a person in too weak health for ordinary employments is strong enough to keep a school. . . . In one large parish the master just appointed was said to be a man of notoriously bad character . . .

Schoolmasters who played the petty tyrant were all too common in
364 Victorian schools and their surroundings frequently matched them well.

A long room, with three long rows of desks, and six of forms, and bristling all round with pegs for hats and slates. Scraps of old copybooks and exercises litter the dirty floor.... There is a strange, unwholesome smell upon the room, like mildewed corduroys, sweet apples wanting air, and rotten books. There could not well be more ink splashed about it, if it had been roofless from its first construction, and the skies had rained, snowed, hailed, and blown ink through the varying seasons of the year.

(from *David Copperfield*, by Charles Dickens)

Perhaps we may be rather less surprised than the Newcastle Commissioners apparently were to find that, despite all the time and money spent on them, the majority of children ended their elementary education still not really masters of reading, writing and arithmetic. To deal with this, the commission proposed a typically Victorian solution:

... to institute a searching examination by competent authority of every child in every school to which grants are to be paid, with the view of ascertaining whether these indispensable elements of knowledge are thoroughly acquired, and to make the prospects and position of the teacher dependent, to a considerable extent, on the results of these examinations.

This system was actually put into practice in 1862, and lasted more or less unchanged until 1897, while examinations of course are still with us. The importance of the change was tremendous. In particular, it gave solid form to the idea that education was a matter of meeting 'requirements' and acquiring 'qualifications' – an idea which in turn led by easy stages to the view that schooling ought to fit the pupil for a particular job or function in life, in other words an increasingly technical ideal.

The Newcastle Commission was followed in 1861 and 1864 by two other similar commissions, enquiring into secondary schools of different sorts – the old public schools and the grammar schools. The public schools – that is, the most famous of the ancient grammar schools – were found to be in a very mixed state. Some were still stuck in the corrupt eighteenth century, but others had followed the lead set by Dr Arnold, the famous headmaster of Rugby (from 1828 to 1842), and had improved their teaching, their discipline and the quality of their boarding life, often on the foundation of a religious revival. The famous boys' book, *Tom Brown's Schooldays*, written by an enthusiastic ex-pupil of Dr Arnold called Thomas Hughes, was immensely popular and influential among the middle classes in spreading the new ideas about education at this level.

This reform of the public schools continued throughout the nineteenth century and led to many new foundations, such as Wellington and Haileybury. It was a most important development. First, it meant that secondary education as a whole was improved; public schools, such as Rugby, 365

Uppingham and Loretto, were in fact among the chief educational pioneers of the century. Second, it satisfied a critical need at a vital moment – a need for men. The business of government began to grow very rapidly at this time and the later expansion of the Empire accelerated this trend still further. As a result there was a demand for honest and public-spirited men to do the work. Because the demand was met, we have come to take the existence of such people for granted; but if we look closely at the period before the middle of the nineteenth century we do not see many of them around. They were a type which the new public schools specialised in producing, taking as raw material the new middle classes, who thus found a role and a place in society apart from the making of money. Of the two new schools mentioned above, for instance, Wellington supplied chiefly officers for the army, and Haileybury civil servants for India. This is a fact of considerable interest to the social historian, since it marked the beginning of a new social pattern which was to last until the Second World War.

The grammar schools, like the public schools, were found by their commission of inquiry to vary widely, but the average picture was rather worse. Some were immensely wealthy: Christ's Hospital had an income of £42,000 a year from land. Others were very poor: some had as little as £5 a year from endowments. Some were a scandal: Thame Grammar School, run by New College, Oxford, had £300 a year income, two masters and one boy. Others, such as Manchester Grammar School, were of first-rate quality. One hundred towns of 5,000 or more inhabitants had no adequate secondary school at all, but the state could do nothing to help until it had put the elementary system into better order. Instead, there was a growth in secondary schools owned privately by individuals or corporations. Many of the first sort were found 'lamentably unsatisfactory' in 1861, and indeed these were the schools which Dickens attacked in such novels as *Nicholas Nickleby* ('Dotheboys Hall'). But some of the corporation-run schools were outstandingly good, especially those founded by the Rev. Nathaniel Woodard, which were designed to provide a complete range of education, suitable for all social classes – a typical Victorian idea.

Secondary schools for girls were only just beginning to appear on the scene. The pioneers here were Dorothea Beale (1831–1906) and Frances Mary Buss (1827–94), who were responsible for the success of Cheltenham Ladies' College and the North London Collegiate School for Girls, respectively. They showed that girls could benefit from education, and that a school for girls could be run with no more difficulties than a boys' school need encounter. Thus they overcame the prejudice which up till this time had hampered projects for girls' education, apart from the 'finishing school' type of institution.

The universities were also affected by the new movements in education

Arnold of Rugby   Miss Buss   Miss Beale

around the middle of the century. Oxford and Cambridge were investigated by commissions in the 1850s and, though there was much conservative resistance to change, the old religious barriers were gradually taken down and new subjects, particularly science, made their appearance. The famous Cavendish laboratory, where Rutherford later split the atom, was given to Cambridge University by the Duke of Devonshire in 1871. Meanwhile, the movement to found new universities had also begun, starting with London in 1828 and Durham in 1832.

Apart from these developments in schools and universities, the middle of the nineteenth century saw another educational movement which is of the greatest interest to social historians. This was the tremendous growth in self-education, or as the Victorians called it 'improvement', by adult members of the working class, especially skilled craftsmen. This was a direct equivalent of the public school movement among the middle classes. In each case you find a new class, virtually created by the Industrial Revolution, attempting to improve its economic and social position and in the process discovering and developing new ideas and new standards. The difference was that the adult workers had to pull themselves up by their own bootlaces. The state did nothing at all to help at first (it was only in 1850 that Parliament passed an Act allowing public libraries to be set up), and employers were usually totally unsympathetic. All the same, the efforts of philanthropists met with a tremendous response. The Society for the Diffusion of Useful Knowledge (founded 1827) published a *Penny Magazine*, filled with articles of an informative nature, covering a wide range of subjects in what was at the time considered a 'popular' style. Hundreds of Mechanics Institutes, where working-men could meet for educational and social purposes, were set up after 1823, when the first one was begun in Glasgow. In 1854 a group of Anglican churchmen who believed in a Christian form of socialism established a Working Men's College in London. (They included Charles Kingsley, the author of *Westward Ho!*, and Thomas Hughes, who wrote *Tom Brown's Schooldays* – an interesting direct link with the public school movement.) Inspired by the stories of success which they read in such books as Samuel Smiles' *Self Help* (almost a textbook of Victorian social attitudes; it sold 150,000 copies between 1859 and 1889), the artisans devoured eagerly as much as they could get. This passionate desire to better oneself, linked to a conviction (which made very good sense in those times of economic boom) that such virtues as thrift and hard work really could bring golden success, is a hallmark of the age. Its influence can be seen in the careers of such men as Thomas Cooper (1805–92), the Chartist leader and public lecturer, who devoted his life to preaching the value of education, and turned himself into a mine of information on a great variety of subjects.

Unfortunately, too much of the material so eagerly snatched by the artisans was practically useless to them in their search for career success. The *Penny Magazine* is full of articles on picturesque Kentish castles, opium smuggling in China and the habits of the musk-rat; but it could not have been much help to an ambitious plumber.

THE PENNY MAGAZINE
of the
Society for the Diffusion of Useful Knowledge.

515.] PUBLISHED EVERY SATURDAY. [April 11, 1840.

NEWCASTLE IMPROVEMENTS.—No. II.

[Royal Arcade.]

Part of the front page of a *Penny Magazine* of 1840

This was a great flaw in the whole educational pattern of the period. What was it all for? The old system had originally been designed to produce scholars, lawyers and clerics. It had been found possible to adapt it to produce gentlemen as well – particularly when, as in the eighteenth century, schooling had not seemed to matter much anyway. Now it was being required to do all sorts of new jobs for which it was not at all fitted. In short, people had not yet realised that education must be practical and that the needs of the time had changed. As a case in point, Leeds, with a population of 250,000 in 1867, re-

lied for its livelihood almost entirely on the industrial uses of science; yet in that year the only technical instruction in the whole city was to be found in a single cellar, where one teacher held a class in chemistry for an annual grant of £11. One consequence of this was that when the manufacturers of Leeds went to the Paris Industrial Exhibition of 1867, they were alarmed to find that their products were in many cases hopelessly outclassed by those of their Continental rivals, simply on the score of technical efficiency. Dr Lyon Playfair, reporting to the chairman of the Schools Inquiry Commission, wrote:

> I have just returned from Paris, where I acted as a juror in one of the classes of the Exhibition ... I am sorry to say that, with very few exceptions, a singular accordance of opinion prevailed that our country has shown little inventiveness and made but little progress in the peaceful arts of industry since 1862 ... out of 90 classes there are scarcely a dozen in which pre-eminence is unhesitatingly awarded to us ... the one cause upon which there was most unanimity of conviction is that France, Prussia, Austria, Belgium, and Switzerland possess good systems of industrial education for the masters and managers of factories and workshops, and that England possesses none.

By the late 1860s therefore it had become clear that England urgently needed a purposeful system of education, organised on a national scale and covering a much wider age-range.

1870–1944

A tremendous step was taken towards this goal with the Education Act of 1870, which was largely the work of one man, W. E. Forster (1818–86: responsible for government education policy 1868–74). This effectively provided, almost free, elementary schools for every child who wanted them – compulsion did not come in until 1880, when it was introduced for children under twelve. The really significant part of this Act was the principle that the state should provide schools of its own where voluntary effort had not set up any so far. Existing schools were not touched, but on the contrary continued to receive aid. But the state had at last grasped the nettle of direct action, and with it the thistle of religious bias – the state schools were to be non-denominational. That is to say, they were not to be controlled by any one religious body. (A strong Christian influence of a general sort was assumed as a matter of course.)

The Education Act was prompted quite largely by the Parliamentary Reform Act of 1867, which had brought large numbers of working men within the franchise for the first time. It was widely felt that it would be dangerous if these new voters were allowed to remain uneducated. 'Now we must educate our masters,' one politician had said, with a touch of sardonic bitterness. The success of the Act in this respect at least can be seen from the fact that at the General Election of 1886, out of 2,416,272 votes cast, only 38,547 were those of illiterates.

Chelsea Oratory Infants' School in the late nineteenth century

The 1870 Act was, however, only a start. After a period of digestion in the 1870s (very necessary after the controversy which had been caused by its passage), there was a spate of commissions and enquiries in the 1880s and '90s, rather like that of the 1850s and '60s. In 1889 the Technical Instruction Act set up the beginnings of a proper system of state technical education. And ten years later, in 1899, the government machinery for administering education was overhauled and a new Board of Education was set up. In addition to these, a number of local authorities were beginning to provide their own, limited, schemes of secondary education, to supplement the inadequate number of grammar schools; and government grants were being paid to the universities, which were themselves increasing steadily in number.

The trend towards secondary education was reinforced by an important Education Act of 1902 (Balfour's Act), which reorganised the method of administration (Local Education Authorities – L.E.A.s – appeared for the first time), and created a proper machinery for state secondary schools. It was considered a great achievement that by 1911 no less than 8% of 14–15-year-old children were still undergoing full-time education, though most of them were fee-payers of one sort or another.

Another important feature of the 1902 Act was the increased control which it gave to the state over the 'voluntary' elementary schools. This was to prove the beginning of another long process, the gradual development of a state monopoly of the educational system. A number of the grammar schools also came under L.E.A. control after 1902.

Almost at the same time, in a striking outburst of educational activity, six new universities were established (including Birmingham, Manchester and Bristol), together with a number of university-type colleges and institutes of technology. All these were increasingly linked to the secondary level by scholarship schemes. (Similar scholarship schemes operated between the elementary level and the secondary level.)

Adult students also got help from 1904, when the Workers' Educational Association was founded. By 1914 it had 179 branches and 11,430 members.

Apart from organisational changes and a strengthening of the trend towards secondary education (by 1938 21% of all 14–15-year-olds were still receiving full-time education), there was relatively little change in the system between the wars. This was not because people were satisfied with it – on the contrary, there was a great deal of debate about it, and one very important committee report, the Hadow Report of 1926. The trouble was simply that the country was going through a very difficult time economically, and could not afford to embark on educational expansion which might have been thought ideal. There was some irony in this situation, because when Britain had had the money, in the mid-nineteenth century, she had dragged her feet over education; now, when she wanted to do more, she could not. The irony may go even deeper, in that part at least of her economic difficulty in the twentieth century arose from her inadequate investment in education earlier on.

Apart from the great shortage of secondary education, the chief weakness of the English education system up to the Second World War, in many eyes at least, was the way in which it matched and actually strengthened class distinctions. This seemed particularly vicious where the class distinctions were a matter of advantages or disadvantages – as they usually were. In general, the working classes received an elementary education and left school at 14 (the age established by Act of Parliament in 1918). The middle classes went on to grammar schools, often helped by scholarships, and they might then go on to one of the newer universities. The upper middle and upper classes enjoyed a completely separated system of private education, starting with expensive private preparatory schools, going on to the public schools, which had rapidly become much more expensive – and exclusive – than they had been in Dr Arnold's day, and finishing at Oxford or Cambridge.

This pattern had developed in the first case largely by accident, at least in the sense that educational changes had not been designed to give any one class a positive advantage over another. But once an advantage had emerged, the people who benefited from it were quick to press it as far as they could – and the people who got no advantage could do nothing about it. Thus education actually widened social gaps, even when it was thought of as a social improvement. This was in a sense the penalty of treating it purely in economic terms, as a matter of vocational training and national assets. Was this to be the answer of the Victorian question, What is education for?

1944 TO THE PRESENT DAY

The 1944 Education Act, often known as Butler's Education Act after the Minister who was chiefly responsible for it, seemed at first sight to extend rather than change the pattern described above. It made no attempt to fit the 'private sector' (prep and public schools, etc.) in with the state side. Also, by continuing and reinforcing the method of selective awards of scholarships, it did nothing to satisfy the complaints of people who felt unfairly handicapped in the process of selection.

The term 'elementary' was dropped and replaced by 'primary' education. This covered the years up to eleven. At that age all pupils at state-run or state-aided schools would take an examination (the '11-plus') which would decide their future in secondary education. Those who were considered most able to benefit from academic work would go to grammar schools, while those whose abilities seemed more suited to 'practical' education would go to 'secondary modern' schools. In theory, this was supposed to give pupils the education most likely to be useful to them in afterlife and was thus in the direct line of descent from the examination system which we have traced from the report of the Newcastle Commission. But rising criticism was voiced against this approach, principally on the ground that the system of selection tended to emphasise and continue social divisions, which more and more people were beginning to attack as wrong and irrelevant. In this sense the 1944 Act was a 'conservative' piece of law-making.

On the other hand, it did finally achieve the goal defined by the Hadow Report of 1926, but kept out of reach by the economic hardships of the inter-war period. Free secondary education was made available to all and provision was made to raise the school leaving age to 16, which was done in two stages; it went up to 15 in 1947 and, though the original timetable failed, later measures put it up to 16 with effect from 1972–73. In addition, under the Act schools became centres of welfare services, where children received free milk and low-priced meals, medical inspection and free medical and dental treatment. In its actual operation, therefore, it was the forward-looking aspects of the Education Act that dominated over the old-style parts. Its most important impact, though, was a very simple one. It gave so many more children a secondary education that the rigid old divisions were just blown apart. The weakening of social barriers that followed seemed very much in tune with the spirit of the years after the war, which had levelled out so many differences.

In the new social climate further educational change followed rapidly. The universities flooded with students and eight new ones had to be founded in the 1960s in England alone. The system of selective scholarships broke down, not administratively but socially, and a merging of the different types of secondary school, to include semi-independent grammar schools, produced the comprehensive school movement. The purely private sector, sharing in the general boom, flourished largely in isolation, despite threatened attacks by state action; but it no longer monopolises the most advantageous part of the

educational system and is becoming increasingly a provider simply of special types of schooling – still sometimes a sign of social divisions, but much less a cause of the divisions.

Along with this revolutionary expansion, and forcing it along from within, there has been a great change in the whole manner of education. Someone from the 1850s visiting a schoolroom of the 1930s would certainly have found a good many differences, but could have settled in without too much difficulty. Since the last war, technical improvements have transformed many aspects of teaching and learning quite beyond recognition; but attitudes have changed even more profoundly.

To take the technicalities first, books are more plentiful, and they are supplemented by aids of many types – television, slides, films, tape-recordings, maps and charts. Whole lessons can be given on television or in language laboratories. Buildings and facilities are – in the case of new schools at least – both efficient and luxurious to a degree that makes the old ones seem prison-like.

The new buildings are not only more comfortable; they can be used for new and different purposes. The rigidities of the Victorian classroom have vanished and instead 'teaching spaces' change shape as partitions are put up or taken down, classes split into groups for projects or join to act a play, and teachers acting as a team move about supervising a wide range of activities, often of a practical and even noisy sort that would have been dismissed as mere play a hundred years ago. These changes have gone furthest in the lowest age-ranges of education, but they are spreading upwards – not without provoking a good deal of argument. The very newest school buildings in fact embody completely new ideas about the function and purpose of a school. At Countesthorpe, near Leicester, for instance, the school buildings will be used for all the educational needs of the community, from small children through to adults; in addition, the school will act as a completely equipped community

An aerial view of Countesthorpe College, near Leicester

centre, with facilities for sports, drama, meetings and every type of social activity. This calls for a method of planning and construction which is highly flexible and technically very advanced; but the building is no less advanced than the ideas which inspire it.

Changed attitudes, in fact, are the key to the new education. Some changes can be simply defined; the widespread abandonment of corporal punishment would be a good example of these. But the changes go very deep. Some teachers, for instance, prefer to do without all 'traditional' forms of discipline, and aim at collaboration with their pupils instead. This probably reflects the fact that, since the 1930s, the majority of those concerned with education have moved into the position of social pioneers. Believing, in many cases, that a child's 'environment' is more important than his 'heredity' in shaping his life, they have been swept by a quite remarkable wave of idealistic enthusiasm. Their teaching has been designed more and more to develop their pupils, rather than fit them into society's mould, and they have on the whole tended to place increasing stress on learning by exploration, feeling and experience. Many have reacted against examinations and even against certain subjects of study which appear particularly 'irrelevant'.

The more extreme 'progressives' have provoked a good deal of opposition from people who condemn their approach as anti-intellectual, destructive of quality and liable to cause social confusion. Much of the argument has gone on at high levels, but most people in England have been affected by it in one important respect, which is concerned with educational organisation. The Labour government of 1964–70 pressed vigorously on Local Education Authorities to convert their schools to the comprehensive system. Under this, all the children of a district are supposed to attend the same school, regardless of distinctions of social class or ability. There was fierce opposition from supporters of the grammar school system, who believed that separation and special treatment of the brightest children was best for all concerned. In addition, many L.E.A.s felt that 'comprehensivisation' was being forced upon them as a means of compulsory social change, rather than as a genuine measure of educational improvement. However, most areas had begun to toe the line when the Labour government fell in 1970.

All these changes have altered education almost beyond belief in living memory. In a sense, despite the controversy, the movement has been back, as well as forward – back to an older ideal. To the Georgian gentleman, formal schooling was only part of the training for life and social training mattered at least as much. The Victorians, faced with new problems, placed increasing stress on the formalities of education – and ran themselves into a dead end where examinations and technical qualifications loomed larger and larger. In the first half of the twentieth century it became the object of administrators to

extend the benefits of formal education to as many people as possible. But

Voluntary work in school: a boy at Sevenoaks teaches a blind boy to read

society changed faster than the examinations and critics began to ask, 'What's it all for?' The answers, and the recipes for improvement, vary greatly; but at least there are signs that we are getting out of the dead end of merely formal education and realising once more that social training and formal learning can be blended in one.

RELIGIOUS BELIEF

A great deal has been said in this chapter about the importance of religious controversy in deciding the course of educational development in the nineteenth century. Religion was in fact a force of major social importance throughout this period and, though it is not possible to give here a full history of every aspect of the religious scene, we cannot leave the subject without outlining some of the main ways in which Christianity affected the way men thought and behaved.

For much of the eighteenth century the officially established Church of England was in a sleepy state. Its senior clergy were generally members of the landed classes; its organisation was slack and sometimes corrupt; and its business usually seemed to be the defence of the existing order both in politics and in society. Many ordinary clergymen, it is true, lived decent if uninspiring lives, and church-going and Christian attitudes were part of the regular framework that made life meaningful to common people, particularly perhaps in the countryside. But there was little vitality or evidence of social conscience.

The Roman Catholics were a tiny and mostly unimportant minority throughout the century, though occasionally they became the unhappy objects of frightful outbreaks of crude prejudice, such as the terrible Gordon Riots that devastated central London in 1779. The English Nonconformist sects — Baptists, Congregationalists, Quakers and others — were a good deal more active and influential. They were strong in the towns and in certain parts of the countryside such as East Anglia, and were particularly well supported 375

The results of religious intolerance: troops fire on the Gordon Rioters, 1780

by the artisan classes, who may have found such relative vigour more suited to their arduous life than the comfortable ease of the Church of England. Some historians find a connection between this fact and the strenuous efforts of the Industrial Revolution pioneers. (It is generally agreed that the strict Presbyterianism which dominated Scotland was a major factor in encouraging Scottish enterprise.)

It is certainly true that Nonconformists were prominent in both educational and scientific fields in the eighteenth century. 'Dissenting academies' were famous for the quality of their schooling, and men such as Joseph Priestley (1733–1804: famous for his isolation of oxygen and his theory of electric attraction) were among the foremost minds of their times. In a different field, Quaker families such as the Gurneys of Norwich were well known for their prominence in banking.

Even the Nonconformists, however, seemed by and large to be content with society as they found it, and men of conscience who looked around them at the state of the poor, particularly as the Industrial Revolution made its effects felt, were often unhappy at the lack of Christian social action. One whose dissatisfaction drove him to action was John Wesley (1703–91). Although an Anglican priest, his activities in unauthorised preaching and missionary activity led him into conflict with the Church authorities, so that by 1784 he had – reluctantly – set up what amounted to an independent sect, the Methodists. His objective was to bring Christianity to the neglected working classes, particularly such downtrodden groups as the Cornish tin-miners; he was not principally concerned with charity or other good works. His colleague, George Whitefield (1714–70), took a similar line, except that he concentrated on the conversion of the upper classes. (He made a considerable impression on George II's son, Frederick, Prince of Wales.)

John Wesley   William Wilberforce

In due course, however, the direct and indirect success of such efforts at reviving Christian ideals in society was so great that social as well as individual morality underwent a change. The beginning of the nineteenth century saw a widespread interest in simple, vigorous and outward-looking religion. This attitude, known as Evangelicalism, affected all Protestant religious groups more or less and was at the root of many of the most important movements for social reform in the first half of the new century. Among its particular triumphs may be noted the suppression of slavery, largely the work of William Wilberforce (1759–1833); the Factory Act of 1833; the educational reforms described above; and the work of Lord Shaftesbury (1801–85), who achieved tremendous reforms in mental hospitals, factory hours and conditions, the treatment of orphans, charity education, the safeguarding of chimney sweeps' climbing boys and many other fields. It would be no exaggeration to say that Evangelicalism became the conscience of early Victorian England. Nor was the effect confined to charity from above; it provided the motive force for much of the early labour movement, as seen in episodes such as the Tolpuddle Martyrs, and in the careers of Labour pioneers like Keir Hardie and George Lansbury.

As time went on, however, there is no denying that Evangelicalism became smug and stuffy; it became more concerned with manners than morals and often degenerated into the hypocritical narrowness which is what the phrase 'Victorian religion', perhaps unjustly, means to many people nowadays. Its influence as a motive force remained powerful throughout the century, however, and there is no doubt that it was at least part of the inspiration which drove later generations of Victorians to explore, evangelise – and colonialise – Africa and other unknown regions of the world. In its different sectarian forms, it did much to give meaning to the lives of the new industrial classes. And if its influence was generally exercised to preserve social stability, whether by encouraging reforms or, later on, by discouraging change, it

'The Present Revival of Christian Architecture': a vision of the Gothic Revival by the romantic Roman Catholic architect A. W. Pugin

probably played a valuable role in regulating the potentially explosive process of rapid social evolution.

Increasingly, however, as the century went on, criticism of orthodox religion mounted. Some of the critics were satisfied by fresh religious revivals – the Oxford Movement of the 1830s stressed the ancient links of the Church of England with the colourful Middle Ages; and the Roman Catholic Church began to grow in strength from about the same time. But to some people these movements were merely further evidence that Christianity, divided and preoccupied with the past, had little to say for modern man.

These doubts were intensified by the scientific discoveries which followed each other so rapidly in the nineteenth century. The early inventions of machinery were generally regarded as striking examples of man's God-given ingenuity; but the work of geologists such as Sir Charles Lyell (1797–1875: published *The Principles of Geology* in 1830–33) and biologists such as Charles Darwin (1809–82: published *The Origin of Species* in 1859) seemed to undermine the Biblical account of world history and caused much heart-searching. The drift away from religion was accelerated by the comparative failure of the Churches to come to grips with the problems of organisation raised by the growth of the new towns, and by about 1900 it was clear to many people that religion in Britain was no longer the dominant force that it had been around the middle of the century.

The First World War, when it came, had the effect of accelerating this trend away from religion. Many people found they could not believe in a God who could let such things happen – or, more simply, they were just shocked out of their conventional habits of mind and realised that they had never believed in anything at all. Even more powerful, though, in the years that followed, was the effect of rising standards of living and material comforts in encouraging a habit of materialism that made religion seem irrelevant. The Church seemed unable to cope with this apathy; its traditional roles in education, the care of the poor and the social services had been taken away from it by the state and it found difficulty in adjusting to the position of a private, voluntary body. Britain by the 1960s was only nominally a Christian country, with fewer than 10% of the population at all actively committed to religion. (This compares with a figure of $7\frac{1}{4}$ million, out of a total population of some 17 million, attending church on 30 March 1851 – a total which was thought shockingly low at the time.)

Much of the enthusiasm that had once gone into religious causes was reserved instead for science and its achievements. Brilliant advances in all fields – most strikingly perhaps those connected with medicine, surgery, electronics, nuclear power and the conquest of space – made the real or potential power of man seem almost unbounded. Since many, if not all, of the scientific triumphs of the twentieth century seemed to improve human life, they became sufficient aims in themselves. Consequently the prevalent mood of Britain in the late 1960s was indicated by a leading academic, delivering a radio lecture: 'Men,' he said, 'have become gods.' On the other hand, the stir caused by this outspoken assertion can be more than matched by the

Below: Belief at the grass roots. Freedom of meeting and freedom of discussion are basic rights; so is freedom to laugh. A Socialist in 1910 has trouble with his hair. *Right:* Speakers' Corner, 1970; still the same problem

Socialist. "I'M THE FRIEND OF THE WORKING-MAN!"
Morose Hairdresser (at back of crowd), "WOT! WITH NINE-PENN'ORTH OF 'AIR-CUTS OVERDUE!"

reactions to Christian attempts at 'revisionism', often referred to collectively as the 'New Morality'. An example would be the furore over Bishop John Robinson's book, *Honest to God* (published in 1963), in which he demanded a 'new image for God'. Religious feeling, if confused, is far from dead; indeed it may be thought in part responsible for the dissatisfaction, evident in many quarters, with the spiritual sterility of much of modern urban existence.

Suggestions for further work and discussion

1. Ask your parents and other relatives how the school which they attended was different from the one you go to now.

2. Trace the history of your own school; pay particular attention to the importance at various times of (*a*) personal and private enterprise and initiative, (*b*) local and municipal enterprise and initiative, (*c*) state enterprise and initiative.

3. Experiment with the Lancasterian system of teaching. What are its drawbacks?

4. Search in country houses for evidence that past owners went on the Grand Tour.

5. Ask your local vicar or rector if he will show you how to trace, in his parish registers, the pattern of church attendances over the last 150 years.

6. Subject for essay or discussion: why have girls been given an educational treatment so different from that of boys?

7. Find out more about the Gordon Riots (*see* illustration on p. 376: there is a gripping fictional account in Charles Dickens' *Barnaby Rudge*). What do these Riots tell the historian about eighteenth-century London society?

Books for further reading:

Charles Dickens, *Nicholas Nickleby*, 1838 (the horrors of Yorkshire schools for unwanted children).
Thomas Hughes, *Tom Brown's Schooldays*, 1856 (the beginnings of modern public schools).

16 : Aristocracy into Democracy

The word 'franchise' means, basically, freedom; but it is generally used to refer to a freedom of a particular sort, namely the right to vote at elections. In Britain today everybody over the age of 18 who is not disqualified for some special reason has this right. The classes who are excluded are peers of the realm, since they sit in the House of Lords in any case and do not need double representation; lunatics; criminals serving sentences of more than twelve months; and people who have been convicted of misusing the right to vote, by behaving corruptly at previous elections. Apart from these, there will always be some people who, though full British citizens, have failed to get their name on to the register of electors for any area, as a result of some oversight or a change of address, and so may not be able to vote until the the register has been revised in the following year. Otherwise Britain enjoys the widest possible franchise, namely 'universal adult suffrage' – 'suffrage' being another, and more precise, word for the right to vote.

The fact that historians often refer to suffrage as *the* franchise indicates the importance which this right carries in the British scheme of things today. It is regarded as the foundation of a democratic system, since it enables the people to choose a government that will do their will, and to make this choice quite freely. This approach to politics is almost universally accepted as the most desirable for modern Britain, since it is generally considered to be a good thing that individual people should have some say in the running of their state, particularly when the state affects so much of their daily lives. In fact, it is often claimed that democracy is actually the highest and best form of politics.

Setting such enthusiasm aside, however, it is possible to see the modern democratic system as a reflection of modern British society. Greater economic equality than in the past and the disappearance of old social distinctions have produced a situation in which people can claim that all are roughly speaking on the same level. In this case, political equality is a natural consequence of social and economic equality.

These conditions have not always applied in the past and so it should be no surprise to find that democracy is a fairly recent growth in Britain, and that the franchise has only been universally enjoyed for quite a short time. In the eighteenth century, at the beginning of our period, society was quite differently organised, and politics likewise. At that time, indeed, the word   **381** 'democracy' was very generally detested – and not only by those whom we might expect to lose by its introduction! It was thought that common people were not fit to govern themselves, let alone to rule the nation by weight of numbers; and anybody looking at the poorer classes then would have been almost bound to agree with this argument (even though he might then have gone on to wonder *why* they were so outstandingly stupid and violent). The complicated and serious business of politics was reserved for those people whose position in society marked them out as leaders and men of influence and whose background and upbringing qualified them to undertake its tasks. Thus local government was in the hands of squires and rich merchants (industrialists, too, as these gradually rose to wealth and power), while national politics were in the hands of the aristocracy and their landed and propertied supporters.

This is not the place for a detailed explanation of the British constitution, nor for a full history of its development. But a brief account of the way in which Parliament evolved, and particularly of the changes in the franchise, is a valuable way of illustrating the social and economic history of the eighteenth and nineteenth centuries. So we will begin by looking at the composition of the House of Commons (the House of Lords, though it plays an important political role, does not claim to be a representative body in any wide sense and so responds far less to the changes of the period). There were in the late eighteenth century about 560 Members of Parliament (M.P.s), as compared with about 630 nowadays. They were drawn from a relatively narrow section of society: in 1796 one observer calculated that 222 M.P.s were connected to titled families, 151 were professional men and 172 were country gentlemen. This was not thought to be an odd or improper state of affairs. Robert Jenkinson, later Earl of Liverpool and Prime Minister from 1812 to 1827, spoke for the vast majority of British people at that time when he stated in the House of Commons in 1793:

We must be all agreed that the House of Commons is meant to be a legislative body, representing all descriptions of men in this country . . . He supposed every person would agree that the Landed interest ought to have the preponderant weight. The Landed interest was, in fact, the stamina of the country. In the second place, in a commercial country like this, the manufacturing and commercial interest ought to have a considerable weight, secondary to the Landed interest, but secondary to the Landed interest only . . . There were other descriptions of people, which, to distinguish from those already mentioned, he should style *professional people*, and whom he considered as absolutely necessary to the composition of a House of Commons. By professional people, he did not mean to use that expression in the narrow and confined sense in which it was generally used; he meant those Members of the House of Commons who wished to raise themselves to the great offices of the State; those that were in the army; those that were in the navy;

those that were in the law; and he maintained that these several descriptions of persons ought to be able to find some means of entering the House . . .

Notice the capital L for Landed!

To produce a House of Commons made up in this way the system of elections was quite different from that which applies in Britain today. For a start, there was no attempt to split the country up into roughly equal voting areas, or constituencies. Instead, each county was allowed to send two M.P.s to Parliament and a number of 'boroughs' also had the right to elect two M.P.s. These boroughs were not necessarily all towns – some of them, though once large, had dwindled into tiny villages, and one or two, such as Old Sarum near Salisbury, had ceased to exist altogether, so that the local land-owner controlled the 'election' entirely. On the other hand, some growing towns, such as Manchester, Leeds, Birmingham and Sheffield, had no M.P.s at all, because they had been unimportant when the first arrangements for Parliament were being made – that is, in the later Middle Ages and the sixteenth century. This pattern of representation seems not merely unfair, but ridiculous, to people who are convinced of the superiority of democracy; however, it was tolerated in the eighteenth century, because it worked in favour of the classes described by Robert Jenkinson in the passage quoted above. Some boroughs were so completely in the control of an influential man that they were referred to as 'pocket boroughs'.

The power of the propertied classes was increased by the fact that very few people at that time had the right to vote. No women possessed the franchise, for a start, nor did anyone dream that they should. Apart from that, the rules governing the franchise varied widely from place to place. In the counties there was a fairly simple and relatively low property qualification, the owner-ship of a small plot of freehold land (the 40s. freehold). In the boroughs there was every kind of oddity. At Preston, in Lancashire, anybody could vote at an election who spent the night before in the town; in others, only freemen of the borough could vote, or members of the (self-appointed) town corporation, or those who paid certain local taxes, or occupied certain specified properties – the variety was almost endless. The origin of this confusion was the great variety in the ancient royal charters which permitted a borough to send M.P.s to Parliament. But few people thought it worth altering, since it seemed to work well enough by their non-democratic standards. The total number of people thus qualified to vote was about 400,000 in England and Wales together. The Scots had a different system since the government, through the aristocracy, virtually nominated M.P.s.

The way in which elections were managed was also totally different from modern practice. Instead of voting secretly by marking a piece of paper in a voting-booth, as happens nowadays, the eighteenth-century voter declared out

A vivid view of the corruption, intimidation and fraud that characterised elections in the eighteenth century: Hogarth's 'The Polling'

loud his preference at a meeting arranged in the market place or town hall. Partly because of this, there was a great deal of intimidation and even open violence. At Southwark, in London, for instance, where there were several breweries, the draymen – a notoriously rough lot – were regularly hired by candidates to beat up the opposition. At Gloucester in 1761 two men were killed when they were caught by 'the other side', drenched in brandy and then stuffed (presumably with others) into a stiflingly airless carriage. Such extremes could hardly be defended; but more moderate rowdyism was frequently treated as a good joke – particularly if it gave the mob a chance to bring the aristocracy down to earth! A French visitor in 1818 was impressed by the way in which English noblemen had to put up with the attentions of a rough crowd:

> I saw Lord Nugent with one side all black. Lord Molyneux's face resembled a pug's. Lord John Russell attempted with difficulty to wipe off the stinking patches of dirt which continually bespattered his cheeks.

Equally intolerable to modern eyes, and equally tolerated by the eighteenth century, was widespread bribery. Even when a candidate had no opponent, the electors expected to be handsomely treated to food, drink and souvenir-type presents. When there was an actual contest, expenses soared. In 1807 William Wilberforce (the great anti-slavery agitator) stood for a Yorkshire county seat. He and his supporters spent some £35,000, and won; but his unsuccessful opponents were said to have spent £100,000 each. As this example shows, it was not always the side that spent the most that won the election and this was sometimes offered as a defence of the system. Others maintained that, just as it did the aristocracy good to be rolled in the mud

384

'A prime facer' from Lord Castlereagh for Sam Whitbread, the Radical brewer. A cartoonist's comment on the rough-and-tumble of aristocratic politics in 1815

occasionally, it was a good thing that they should be forced to spend heavily at election times and thus put money into the pockets of the poor.

We have devoted a good deal of attention to the eighteenth-century system, for several reasons. First, it operated for a large part of our whole period — in fact, it was not greatly altered until 1867. Second, it is so very different from the modern democratic system that it is rather hard to understand unless painted in some depth. Finally, it represents in a very important way the structure and values of British society before the Industrial Revolution.

This last point is in fact the clue to the changes which took place in the nineteenth century. The Industrial Revolution altered the whole shape of English society, so that the political system which, in a ramshackle and shambling way, had served the eighteenth century to most people's satisfaction, became just too obviously unsuitable for the new needs.

Even before the end of the eighteenth century demands for change had been heard from such men as John Wilkes, who whipped up much popular support in the 1760s and 1770s. On the whole, though, these early efforts were directed more at reducing the bribery and corruption of M.P.s by the government, which was thought to be increasing the power of the Crown, than at making the franchise any different or changing the system of election. They were provoked more by government inefficiency (in the 1780s Britain lost the American colonies) than by democratic ideas. And indeed when real democracy appeared on the scene in the shape of the French Revolution, most Englishmen were so horrified by it that they dropped any ideas they might have had about further Parliamentary reform. In 1802 things were certainly quiet enough in Appleby:

The Fact is that yesterday morning, between 11 & 12 I was unanimously elected by one Elector, to represent this Ancient Borough in Parliament, and I believe I am the very first Member returned in the whole Kingdom. There was no other candidate, no Opposition, no Poll demanded. So I had nothing to do but thank the said Elector for the Unanimous Voice by which I was chosen ... On Friday Morning I shall quit this Triumphant Scene with flying Colours, and a noble Determination not to see it again in less than seven years.

In the 1820s, however, after prolonged agitation by a few 'Radicals', such as Sir Francis Burdett, Major Cartwright, Francis Place, Henry Hunt and William Cobbett, interest in reform began to revive. This time, too, there was a distinct smack of democracy to the demands and, though universal suffrage was still hardly even considered, a widening of the franchise became a more and more popular idea. Still it may be doubted whether the reformers would have got very far if it had not been for the support of many members of the middle classes. These people, often made wealthy by trade or industry, were becoming increasingly impatient with a political system that was run exclusively for the benefit of the 'Landed interest' (in Jenkinson's phrase), and those associated with it. The new men wanted a share. They were not supporters of democracy as such. But they were willing to use the enthusiasm of democratic reformers to serve their purpose.

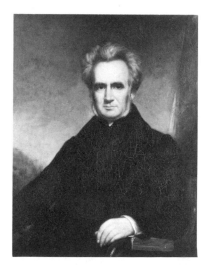

Francis Place

An important preliminary step was taken in 1829, when the last penalties imposed on people who refused to belong to the Church of England were removed by the Duke of Wellington's government. If religious equality was to be permitted it would be hard to defend political inequality, at least in its extreme form. None the less, the struggle for Parliamentary Reform was long and bitter, and marked by extremism on both sides. The Duke of Wellington himself said in the House of Lords that

> I never read or heard of any measure up to the present moment which in any degree satisfies my mind that the state of the representation can be improved.

He later added darkly that

> A democracy has never been established in any part of the world, that ... has not immediately declared war against property.

The gentry, perhaps a little more realistically, were afraid that:

> In a Reformed Parliament, when the day of battle came, the country Squires would not be able to stand up against the active, pushing, intelligent people who would be sent from the manufacturing districts.

The other side resorted to violence:

> The whole of Bristol was on the verge of destruction; the mansion-house, custom-house, excise-office, and bishop's palace, were plundered and set on fire; the toll-gates pulled down; the prisons burst open with sledge hammers, and their inmates, criminals and debtors, set at liberty amidst the exulting cries of the populace. During the whole of Sunday the mob were the unresisted masters of the city. Forty-two offices, dwelling houses, and warehouses were completely destroyed, exclusive of public buildings. The loss of property was estimated at half a million. The number of rioters killed, wounded or injured, was about 110.

(From a contemporary account.)

The burning of Nottingham Castle during Reform riots, 1831

Eventually, the Great Reform Bill was passed in June 1832. The old jumble of voting qualifications was replaced by a simpler and uniform set, still dependent on property. As a result, the size of the electorate in England and Wales was increased from about 435,000 to about 652,000. This meant that about one adult male in five had the right to vote. (The proportion in Scotland after 1832 was one in eight.) At the same time 143 seats were redistributed – that is, they were taken away from the worst of the pocket boroughs and given to the new industrial towns. The result was by no means a triumph for the reformers – the rural and aristocratic South of England still returned 371 M.P.s, as compared with 120 from the industrial North. Nor did election behaviour change very much, as the following extract shows:

> On the morning after my arrival at the Star Inn ... several hundred electors assembled in military array, under my windows, and on my appearance greeted me with three cheers. One of the leaders of this worthy band of brothers – who, to do them justice, were no hypocrites, but came immediately to business – then spoke out thus:
>
> 'Now, Gronow, my old boy, we like what we have heard about you, your principles, and all that sort of thing; we will therefore all vote for you if —' Here every man in the crowd struck his breeches-pocket several times with his open hand. After this expressive pantomime, the speaker continued, 'You know what we mean, old fellow? If not – you understand – you won't do for Stafford.'
>
> (From an account of the first 'reformed' election.)

In fact, little was changed in 1832 – except, perhaps, the idea that the constitution could never be changed. The leaders of the middle class, once they had entered the charmed circle of political power, rapidly became relatively conservative and dropped the working-class allies who had helped them to their success. The great majority of M.P.s were still drawn from the 'Landed interest'.

Not all of the disappointed lower classes were prepared to accept this tame result and some of the more fiery spirits tried to renew the agitation in the years 1839 to 1848. They made their position clear enough, when they presented their first petition to Parliament in 1839:

> It was the fond expectation of the friends of the people, that a remedy for the greater part, if not for the whole of their grievances, would be found in the Reform Act of 1832 ... They have been bitterly and basely deceived. The fruit which looked so fair to the eye, has turned to dust and ashes when gathered. The Reform Act has effected a transfer of power from one domineering faction to another, and left the people as helpless as before.

They therefore demanded a 'People's Charter' (for which reason they were called Chartists), based on six points. The six points were: universal manhood
suffrage, the secret ballot, the ending of a property qualification for Members

The Chartist meeting on Kennington Common, 1848. Notice the police officer (far right)

of Parliament, the payment of M.P.s, the formation of equal constituencies and the calling of regular annual Parliaments. These measures, they hoped, would put effective power in the hands of the people. Three times, in 1839, 1842 and 1848, they presented their petition to Parliament, but each time they were ignored. Their leaders, especially an Irishman named Feargus O'Connor, were uncertain what to do and a few rather desperate attempts at violence produced no good results. Their last effort, a massive demonstration at Kennington Common, in London, on 6 April 1848, collapsed ridiculously when the Chartists were actually outnumbered by the thousands of special constables enrolled for the occasion, and dispersed miserably in pouring rain. The 5,706,000 signatures claimed for their third and last petition, which O'Connor presented to Parliament after the demonstration, turned out to be under 2,000,000, with many forgeries (including 'Queen Victoria' and 'Mr. Punch'!) even in that number. The movement died with little more ado.

The reason that underlay the failure of the Chartists, however, was really an economic one. The movement had been born from the misery of poor men, suffering from the frequent slumps that convulsed the British economy in the second quarter of the century. They hoped that if they could win control of the political machine, they could manage the economy in such a way that their troubles would be ended. The hope was probably vain, but in any case the economy entered a new phase – the mid-Victorian boom – in the late 1840s and their agitation was swallowed up in prosperity. On the other hand, the fact that their demands were in a real sense in tune with the political trends of the century as a whole, is proved when we look at the British constitution today: the first five of the six Chartist points have all been granted, and the sixth has been rejected for practical, rather than political, reasons.

389

By contrast with the great struggles of 1832, and even the Chartist movement, the later stages in the history of franchise reform seem peaceful and almost tame. Both the Liberals and the Tories took up the reform cry hoping for political advantage, and the next step – the Second Reform Act, 1867 – was marked by scenes of extraordinary bargaining in the House of Commons, as Gladstone and Disraeli tried to outbid each other for popular support. This Act further reduced and simplified the qualifications for suffrage, so that in the towns at least virtually everybody down to and including the artisans (upper working class) got the vote – excluding the women, of course. The countryside came off less well, but the electorate as a whole went up from 1,056,000 to 1,994,000. At the same time there was another redistribution of seats, which at last brought North and South on to something like equal terms in the House of Commons.

In a sense, this Act came about so easily because it was the result of 35 years' evolution. The first Reform Act had shown the way and made it possible to consider altering the sacred shape of the constitution a second time. Still more, it had established the principle that classes newly rising to positions of respectability in society should be rewarded by a share in political power. It will have been noticed that between 1832 and 1867 the electorate expanded by 400,000 without any change in the qualifications; this represented the result of mid-Victorian prosperity which enabled many more people to satisfy the 1832 requirements. At the same time, more people still were rising from even further below and claiming the prize for their more modest but still striking success. The strength of their case was recognised by Disraeli in 1859, when he referred to the 'mechanic' whose 'virtue, prudence, intelligence, and frugality entitle him to enter the privileged pale of the constituent body of the country'. Gladstone committed himself similarly in 1864, when he said that every man 'who is not presumably incapacitated by some consideration of personal unfitness or political danger, is morally entitled to come within the pale of the constitution'. Such language would have shocked the Duke of Wellington; but now the day of the 'Landed interest' was, if not yet over, beginning to draw to an end.

The new political system encouraged the formation of parties of a recognisably modern type, designed to organise electors in support of one group of leaders or another. And in 1872 a further step towards modern democracy was taken with the passing of the Ballot Act, which introduced the voting system that is still in use today. This removed most of the traces of earlier violence, while corruption (already growing practically impossible by reason of the increased size of the electorate) was also attacked by laws (the Corrupt and Illegal Practices Prevention Act, 1883).

The electorate continued to grow by natural means and with the spread of
democratic principles there was little real fuss about the passage of the Third

Reform Act in 1884. This gave suffrage on equal terms ('household suffrage') to town and country dwellers alike and pushed up the numbers from about 3,000,000 (note the increase over the 1867 figure) to about 5,000,000. At the same time, the old distinction between town and country constituencies was finally abolished and the modern system of equal divisions was introduced.

The final step towards adult male suffrage, without any significant qualifications being required, was taken after the appalling sacrifices of the First World War had produced a feeling that if a man was to be called upon to risk his life for his country (conscription was introduced in 1916), he must at least have some say in running it. The franchise was therefore extended in 1918 to all men over 21, apart from those small categories mentioned at the beginning of this chapter (Fourth Reform Act). Taken together with the reduction in the powers of the House of Lords which had been accomplished by the Parliament Act of 1911 (following a long and critical constitutional struggle), this marks the achievement of effective political power by the masses of ordinary people in Britain. The story of democracy cannot be considered complete, however, until we have examined the status of women.

Below: 'Franchise Bill' issues his challenge to the House of Lords, 1884. A cartoon from *Punch.* *Right:* Population and the franchise

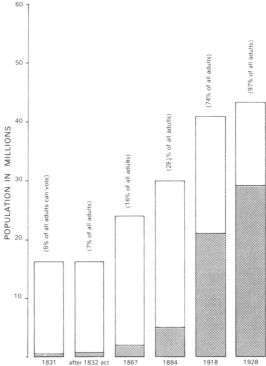

The Industrial Revolution and related changes made a certain amount of difference to the economic position of women in Britain; but their social status hardly altered at all and their legal status remained unchanged almost until the end of the nineteenth century.

The growth of female employment in cotton-mills and other factories, from the late eighteenth century onwards, obviously meant that there would be a good many women who were in theory able to earn their own living. But in practice women were still regarded as inferior to men and were expected to be dependent on a man either as husband or father. So they were treated as an easily bullied source of cheap labour and were paid lower wages than a male doing the same job. It is significant that most of the nineteenth-century Factory Acts and Mines Acts classed women together with children as the classes of labourers both most seriously oppressed and least capable of looking after themselves. As standards of living rose in the middle of the nineteenth century, the labour market for women tended to contract, and they became increasingly confined to a limited area of industry, particularly in the textile and clothing trades, together with the great category of domestic service. In 1851 the chief female occupation groups were as follows:

FEMALE OCCUPATION GROUPS IN 1851

Total female population:	10,736,000
Agriculture	227,000
Domestic service	905,000
Cotton manufacture	272,000
Milliners, dress-makers, seamstresses	340,000
Wool manufacture	113,000
Washerwomen	145,000
Silk manufacture	80,000
Linen manufacture	56,000
Lace manufacture	54,000
Charwomen	55,000

At the other end of the scale there were 54 railway employees, 28 shipyard workers, 23 sawyers and 19 commercial clerks.

Whatever a woman's work or wages, her position in law remained unaltered for most of the nineteenth century. If she was under 21 and single, she was subordinate to her father. If she married, she became subordinate to her husband – to such an extent that all her property and income became his (unless they were protected by very complicated legal devices). Even if she remained single and earned her own living, she still suffered various disadvantages which made her in effect a second-class citizen. She could not vote, nor take any part in politics. Nor could she enter the majority of attractive jobs and professions, since these were barred to her by convention or, in some cases, by law. This subordination was reinforced by an educational system which, in so far as it took any account of girls at all, was designed to make them into nothing more than housekeepers for husbands; they were taught nothing that would help them to get a job.

In view of the depressed position of most working women, it is not surprising that pressure for change came chiefly from women of the middle class. Some of them found it intolerable that they could not retain and dispose of their own property after marriage; and some were sickened by the common Victorian attitude to women, summed up in the words of a popular song of the late nineteenth century – 'I'm only a bird in a gilded cage'. A real effort to provide education for girls was followed by changes in the law. In 1882 and 1893 Married Women's Property Acts were passed by Parliament to give wives a fair degree of equality with their husbands in this respect. At the same time women made considerable progress in breaking into two of the professions, namely medicine and teaching.

There were still a good many formal obstacles to be overcome, however, and more important than any formality there was the entrenched social convention of male superiority. A famous play first performed in London in 1889, Ibsen's *Doll's House*, made a tremendous impression by its revolutionary assertion of the spiritual freedom and equality of women and the conclusion which it drew, that marriage ought to be an equal partnership. Shortly after this, in 1891, a notorious lawsuit seemed to confirm this point of view when the Court of Appeal declared that a husband had no lawful right to detain his wife in his house against her will. These happenings certainly did a

The effect of Ibsen's *Doll's House*; but who needs emancipating?

IBSEN IN BRIXTON.
Mrs. Harris, "YES, WILLIAM, I'VE THOUGHT A DEAL ABOUT IT, AND I FIND I'M NOTHIN' BUT YOUR DOLL AND DICKEY-BIRD, AND SO I'M GOING!"

393

lot to bring the problem of female emancipation before people's minds; but they could hardly change the centuries-old traditional outlook overnight.

In the first years of the twentieth century the issue of whether or not women should get the vote became the focal point in the whole emancipation controversy. People took sides, not so much on political or constitutional grounds, but because they wanted to assert or deny male superiority. A body called the Women's Social and Political Union was formed in Manchester in 1903 to fight for the vote. Its head was Mrs Emmeline Pankhurst, who with her daughters Christabel and Sylvia played a leading part in the struggle for emancipation. Because they demanded the suffrage, or right to vote, they became known as the suffragettes.

At first they employed the tactics of normal political propaganda and agitation. But in 1905 they began to disrupt election meetings and moved towards what we would now call 'civil disobedience'. They harassed the Liberal government with persistent and forceful demands for franchise Bills, using tactics that became steadily more militant. From interrupting meetings and sittings of Parliament, they moved on to disregard of the law and resisting arrest, and on again to protest demonstrations (such as chaining themselves to railings in public places, while shouting slogans until they were silenced) and minor attacks on property, such as the breaking of Cabinet Ministers' windows. 'The argument of the broken pane is the most valuable argument in modern politics,' declared Mrs Pankhurst.

If they had gone no further than this, they would have done nothing that was exceptional by the traditional standards of radical political movements in Britain. But the early 1900s were dangerous and feverish years in many ways, when the whole constitution and fabric of society seemed to be threatened by violence in Ireland, over the House of Lords, in labour relations and in many other ways. Although the suffragettes started off as a serious and high-minded

Mrs Pankhurst arrested yet again. She has just attacked Buckingham Palace. (1914)

body, they were affected by the current unrest and irresponsibility. Indeed, they began to attack the very foundations of the democratic system which they were claiming the right to join. This involved them in a vicious circle; their extremism stiffened the opposition, so that a moderate proposal which would normally have stood a good chance of acceptance was defeated after long negotiations in 1912. The suffragettes in turn felt that they could only respond with still more violence. After 1912 Christabel Pankhurst led a campaign of outright terrorism, though it was directed against property rather than people. Empty houses, schools, a railway station and a church were among many buildings and installations attacked with fire, and bombs were also used. When arrested, the suffragettes went on hunger strike and some of them positively tried to make martyrs of themselves. One at least succeeded, when she committed a dramatic suicide on Derby Day, 1913, throwing herself under the hooves of the King's horse at Tattenham Corner as the field thundered towards the winning post.

It is difficult to say where this rapidly escalating campaign would have led to; but it was abruptly ended by the First World War. During the war women of all classes made immense contributions to the war effort – working in munitions factories, nursing the wounded and filling the jobs of men who were called to the front. When the question of the suffrage was raised again at the end of the war, in connection with the Fourth Reform Act, it did not seem at all surprising that the former Prime Minister, Asquith, should say in the House of Commons: 'Some years ago I ventured to use the expression, "Let the women work out their own salvation." Well, Sir, they have worked it out during this war.' Consequently, in 1918, women were given the vote, provided they were over 30 and could satisfy a residential qualification. The conditions attached to the grant represented the last lingering remains of anti-

Horror at Tattenham Corner. Emily Davison's suicide, 1913

She earned emancipa-
tion. Munitions worker
at Vickers, July 1915

female prejudice, and in 1928 the Fifth Reform Act dropped them, so that women enjoyed the franchise on exactly the same terms as men.

The suffragettes had focused the emancipation controversy on the vote and had then distorted the issue by allowing their enthusiasm to run away with them. Subsequent events have shown that there is much more to female equality than the law of civil rights. When the First World War brought women the vote, it demonstrated that it is women's *function* in society that matters most. Economic and social developments have in fact changed many things for women since 1918; but curiously enough the factors have balanced out to a large degree, so that although women in Britain today lead lives very different from those of their grandparents, they are in many ways hardly more powerful or independent. This contrasts with the situation in certain other countries, such as Soviet Russia, where they enjoy much greater freedom (75% of Russian doctors, for example, are women).

On the side of emancipation, it is easy to trace the rise of well-paid office employment for women, following the invention of the typewriter; the development of automation in light industry, offering acceptable employment in this field; the multiplication of labour-saving devices in the home, freeing women from domestic drudgery; the trend towards smaller families and birth control; welfare legislation such as widows' pensions and family allowances, designed specifically to help women; and the relaxing of the law on divorce. At the same time women's opportunities have been vastly improved by equal education, and one after another exclusive male preserves have been opened – Parliament, academic life, the law and big business. Women still tend to get paid less than men for doing the same job; but there has been a strong movement recently towards ending this discrimination.

On the other hand, the organisation of the more private aspects of society has changed too, and here the results have been much less helpful to women. Families have become smaller not only in terms of the number of children born to an average couple, but also in terms of the number of relatives living in the same house or in the near neighbourhood. Most families nowadays consist of father, mother and children – the minimum nucleus. (Hence they are called 'nuclear', as opposed to 'extended' families.) In such families the burden of looking after the house and the children falls squarely on the mother. If they are under a certain age, she is not allowed by law to go out leaving the children alone. At the same time the pattern of town life has changed too, so that, while the upper and middle classes have lost their servants, the old idea of a 'community' (a street, an area or a parish) has also virtually disappeared. This means in practice that a family has to rely on its own resources to a much greater extent than was true in the past. In consequence, house and family are, if anything, more demanding than they were a hundred years ago. It is true that an increasing number of women marry at an early age, and so are able to return to their jobs after raising a family. But for the majority a career still seems too often to be an alternative to a married life, and most women are just as reluctant as men to give up the comforts of marriage. And yet the 'nuclear' family – which is the invention of the last 50 years in this country – is proving a rather unsatisfactory form of social organisation, especially for women. No amount of gadgetry can make up for human help and comradeship in the daily business of life; women are as far from emancipation in the real sense as ever they were.

Suggestions for further work and discussion

1. Trace the history of the constituency in which you live. Has it ever been notably corrupt?

2. Read Dickens' account of the Eatanswill election in *Pickwick Papers*; how is a modern election different?

3. Subject for an essay or discussion: describe the origins of modern British political parties.

4. Find out how many people have the vote today. How many actually use it at election times (both local and national)?

5. The aristocracy used to dominate political affairs; is it possible to identify a class which exercises particular influence today?

6. The illustration on p. 384 shows the scene on polling day at an eighteenth-century election; describe what is going on.

7. Ask your mother — when she is not too busy — what she thinks of Women's Lib; on another occasion, ask her if she feels tied to the house, and if she says she does, what should be done about it? If you are a girl, what do *you* think?

Book for further reading:

John Galsworthy's, *The Forsyte Saga*, (Heinemann 1950, Penguin 1967), a picture of middle-class life around the turn of the century, shows particularly well the progress of women towards emancipation.

17 : A Modern State

The 'welfare state' is a term used to describe a system of social responsibility. The whole community, through the government, takes on the responsibility of ensuring that all citizens enjoy a minimum standard of living, or welfare. It also tries to ensure that this standard rises whenever possible. An important stage in the development of the ideal was marked by the publication of the government-commissioned Beveridge Report in 1942. Sir William Beveridge (later Lord Beveridge) wrote of the need for society to be free from 'want', 'disease', 'ignorance', 'squalor' and 'idleness'. These, he said, were 'giants' obstructing the path towards social progress, and they could only be overcome by state action and a policy of social security 'from the cradle to the grave'.

Origins

The Beveridge Report had much influence, and it helped to persuade statesmen to build up the modern welfare state. But Beveridge was not the first to put forward such ideas, and the origins of the welfare state went back much earlier. In the nineteenth century social security as we understand it was not regarded as part of the responsibility of government at all. It came to be recognised only gradually that many people in need of help were in difficulties through no fault of their own and that only state action could help them, despite all the charity which was so freely given at that time. This idea only took root slowly, because people often felt that state action would increase what they took to be idleness and lack of personal responsibility on the part of the poor.

Yet, despite these views, change began to come about, particularly in the ministries of Gladstone and Disraeli. A system of state education, available to all, was built up after 1870. The same period also saw the start of slum clearance and other measures to improve public health and living conditions. (The chief social reforms of the nineteenth century are listed in the Appendix on page 423.)

All these measures were piecemeal, however, and did not deal, in a way acceptable to the working people of the time, with the most important problems of all, namely the welfare of the sick, elderly and unemployed. It is true that the state accepted that no one should be allowed to die from want. There

Oliver Twist asks for more. The famous drawing by Cruikshank

was almost always some kind of help available as a last resort, provided either by charity or by parish authorities. But much of it was given in a way deliberately designed to be as humiliating and unpleasant as possible, to deter what was called 'malingering'. Thus, when the new Poor Law came into effect after 1834, all able-bodied people requiring aid had to go into a 'workhouse', where families were split up and conditions were harsh and miserable. Charles Dickens, in his novel *Oliver Twist*, gave a very good idea of life in a workhouse, and it is not surprising that many people preferred to die in their own homes than to live in such surroundings.

This was the situation which a new Liberal government set about changing in 1905. Among the factors which influenced it were two very disturbing and widely read Reports about the social conditions in London and York (by Charles Booth of the Salvation Army and Seebohm Rowntree respectively). These revealed that over one-third of the population of these cities was living below the 'poverty line'. Agitation by the 'New Unions' and the emerging Labour Party at this time showed the growing anger which working people felt about their conditions, and the success in Germany of a limited scheme of

The latest in poor relief, 1867. Note the texts

The first pension payment:
1 January 1909

state assistance (started in the 1880s) was carefully noted. Most important, the Liberal government included two dynamic men – David Lloyd George and Winston Churchill – who felt strongly that more urgent state action was needed to solve the social problems of the country.

As a result, several important measures were passed. One was the Old Age Pensions Act of 1908, under which the state paid 5s. a week to people over 70 years old. In 1909 Labour Exchanges were set up, making it much easier for the unemployed to find work. The National Insurance Act of 1911 established a scheme whereby small unemployment benefits and some medical treatment could be obtained in return for insurance contributions paid each week, in part by employees, in part by employers, and the remainder made up by the state out of general taxation. (At first the total was 9d., made up in the proportion of 4d. : 3d. : 2d.)

These measures were very limited in scale and helped at first only a minority. But it is from these small seeds, sown before 1914, that the modern welfare state has grown.

The Inter-war Years

The inter-war depression put a severe strain on the National Insurance scheme. In 1920 the principle of insurance had in practice to be abandoned. The government was more or less forced to give unemployment benefit (the 'dole') to many workers who were not strictly entitled to it under the existing arrangements. Though the payment of contributions continued, and was later extended to all workers, the 'stamp' became really just another tax, and the idea that social services should be enjoyed only by those who paid for them was dropped.

401

Beveridge explains his plan

However, unemployment pay and other forms of public assistance were only given after a rigorous 'means test', or investigation into all the financial means of a family; this was felt to be humiliating and was widely resented. But at least these changes meant the end of the old Poor Law in 1930, when many new responsibilities were handed over to local authorities.

After Beveridge

With the war came a rethinking of the role of government in modern society. The Beveridge Report, mentioned above, showed how inadequate social policy had been and how much could and should be done in the future. The devastation of war gave an opportunity for social reconstruction, and the war-time government gave notice in 1944 of its determination to act. Apart from the important Education Act of that year, it set out in a White Paper its acceptance of most of Beveridge's proposals.

Since that time, successive governments have tried to put these ideas into effect, both by legislation and by a new approach in economic policy. As Keynes had advocated in the 1930s, governments have used their vast economic influence to maintain full employment – an essential element in social security. But it was new legislation which provided the framework for the welfare state and much of it was passed in the post-war Labour administration. The Family Allowances Act (1945), derived directly from Beveridge's proposals, gave allowances for each child after the first, paid for out of general taxation. The National Insurance Act, passed in 1946, extended the existing scheme to cover all workers and included a wide variety of additional benefits, such as maternity grants. Only part of the cost was to be met by contributions.

The keystone of the modern welfare state, however, was the National Health Service Act of 1946, the responsibility of the Minister of Health, Aneurin Bevan. It set out to organise a state system of medical and dental services, available to all, either free of charge or at nominal cost.

This was generally agreed to be a great step forward, for it meant that millions of people could now have medical care for the first time, including the expensive hospital treatment which previous measures had been unable to provide. The National Health Service came into operation in 1948 and, though the law allowed private practice to continue, about 95% of all doctors and dentists eventually joined, at least in part. Some doctors, and others, attacked the scheme strongly, saying that it was bound to encourage hypochondria and 'sponging' off the state. These fears seemed to be justified at the start, as surgeries were swamped by patients. But this was mainly a result, not of a desire to get something for nothing, but of years of medical neglect.

The National Health Service has certainly had its difficulties, particularly with regard to staffing. It has had to recruit staff from many parts of the world and yet it is still short of qualified personnel. Many old buildings and poor facilities can still be found, and treatment which is not urgent may involve a long wait. But at least no one now has to go without attention because he cannot afford it (though some people have undoubtedly suffered from the charges which have been imposed over the past few years, even though these are far below the full cost of treatment). Taken in association with advances in medical science – particularly in the use of drugs – and in surgical techniques, the National Health Service has gone a long way towards conquering the physical misery which was so universal before the present century. Today, preventive medicine has greatly reduced the likelihood of a major epidemic of any serious disease; the death rate is at practically its lowest point ever; organ transplantation is already bringing new hope to many who seemed to have no chance of living; in time research may even bring a cure for cancer.

Housing is another field in which the government has become more active. In the nineteenth century only a few local authorities, in Birmingham and Leeds, for example, built houses for the poor at low rent. Little effort was made in this direction until the 1920s. Housing is now the responsibility of local authorities, aided by subsidies from the central government (though this system was due to be changed, according to proposals published in 1970). During the Second World War about one-third of Britain's houses were destroyed or damaged by enemy action, and so rehousing was of great importance. In a remarkably short time war damage was made good, and the opportunity was taken to clear many slum areas. Housing is a constant problem, as many slums remain to be cleared and the population continues to grow. Despite petty disagreement over policy, successive governments have done their best to meet demand, by encouraging local authorities to build more council houses and flats, and by giving some help to private builders. Rents were brought under closer control by the Rent Act of 1957, but despite all these measures much remains to be done before the shortage is brought within reasonable limits. Even so, 378,000 new houses were built in 1969 (about half of which were council houses) and, though this is not the highest total for a single year, it certainly represents a creditable achievement.

Certain changes have been made in the social services since the post-war overhaul. In particular, a much more effective 'Ministry of Social Security' was set up in 1966 to give better direction. In 1970 the new Conservative government announced changes which, in effect, acknowledged the principle of a minimum income for all. Its proposals may go some way towards curing the poverty that remains. For despite everything that has been done, an estimated seven million people still live in poverty, according to the standards of the early 1970s (the 'poverty line' rises, of course, as the national standard of living goes up). The size of this figure indicates how far we are from the ideal of a state in which everybody shares and from which everybody benefits.

The welfare state has caused bitter political controversy and continues to do so. Many people feel that the system is abused and that it should be cut down, especially in a time of more general prosperity. Others object to the forcible redistribution of wealth. Some people are too proud to ask for help on such a basis. There are many critics of the complicated administration. On the other hand, as the supporters of the social services point out, millions are still in difficulties and it does not really matter if a few people abuse a system which does enormous good for the majority. The welfare state cost £2,600 million in 1969/70 – a sum which does not include local government expenditure on education. It is a large amount, but it could fairly be argued that it is cheap, when one considers the security of living which it brings.

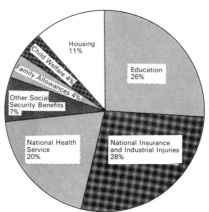

Public expenditure on social services
and housing 1969/70

The great social improvements described in the previous section were brought about by the action of the state, not only in passing laws but in administering the many services which a complicated modern society needs. Although much of this action has been influenced by socialist ideas, as we have seen, Conservative and Liberal governments have both contributed to the process in their time. In fact, all parties in the state have joined together to support and run this elaborate system.

This general agreement has led to the development of an organisation which differs considerably from those both of countries which are entirely state-controlled, such as Soviet Russia, and of countries where opposition to state interference has limited the growth of welfare services, such as the United States. In Britain the principle of a welfare state is generally accepted, but there is room within the system for a good deal of variety in the ways by which it is administered. The Conservative government elected in 1970, for instance, seems anxious to reduce the role of the state to that of a watchful guardian and adjuster of the public interest, rather than that of a general workhorse, doing everything itself.

However, no matter which way opinion swings, one thing goes on growing steadily, and that is the sheer amount of administration. Whether the state does the job itself, or whether it confines itself to seeing that someone else does it properly instead, there is a continuously expanding army of people looking after us. In 1966 the number of people qualifying for the description 'civil servant' was some 800,000; this included employees of the Post Office, which at that time was a department of government, but did not include those who worked in the nationalised industries such as the railways and coal-mining. Even reforms designed to increase the efficiency of government by cutting out wasteful effort tend to increase the total manpower. The efforts of Mr Wilson (Prime Minister 1964–70) to streamline economic planning actually multiplied the number of officials concerned in the business, and the plans of Mr Heath (Prime Minister 1970–   ) for the speeding-up of Civil Service decisions have started with the establishment of a number of new offices and organisations.

This seemingly unending expansion is partly, no doubt, the result of the tendency, which many organisations have shown in the past, for the business of administration to become a self-supporting industry, with more and more people spending more and more time organising each other. This was humorously defined as a 'Law' – Parkinson's Law – by Prof. C. Northcote Parkinson: 'Work expands to fill the capacity available for it.'

However, there is a better reason for the process than this self-generated momentum. As our standard of living rises we demand more and more in the   405

Faceless bureaucracy? New government offices

way of services, and with services comes regulation. To take just one example, of a simple sort, but one that affects the great majority of people directly or indirectly: the enormous growth since the last war in the number and use of private cars has led to a steep and shocking rise in the level of accidents. Concern about this has caused the introduction of a system of government-supervised tests for cars over a certain age, together with a rapid growth in official efforts to control and regulate drivers' behaviour on the roads, by means of speed limits, publicity campaigns and so on. In these ways the rise in our national prosperity, and perhaps also the development of our feelings of concern for victims of road accidents, have produced an increase in state intervention, under one form or another.

This pattern of state regulation and control is often referred to as 'bureaucracy'; this ugly, made-up word describes a state of affairs in which people cannot make for themselves the decisions which affect their comfort and their livelihood, but have to accept the rules laid down by officials in 'bureaux', or offices. It is of course easy to exaggerate the extent to which this has come about in Britain. Even where the amount of central regulation is considerable, as in the field of health, it is generally accepted that the intentions behind the system are admirable – people sometimes grumble that we are living in a 'nanny state', but no one seriously believes that there is anything sinister or deliberately wicked about this nanny. (Compare the picture of a perverted bureaucracy in George Orwell's novel *Nineteen Eighty-Four*.) All the same, there are a number of sound reasons for keeping a watchful eye on developments.

One of these reasons is undoubtedly the relative weakness of the political
system which itself brought the bureaucracy into existence. The Civil Service

operates under laws passed in Parliament, but Parliament knows next to nothing about what goes on in the offices which its own Acts set up. This is chiefly a matter of the volume of government business and the time available for checking it – nobody could hope to keep a close control over such an enormous range of activities. But this does mean that the elected representatives of the people cannot always be sure that the country is being run as the people may want. Various devices are being tried, such as the appointment of a Parliamentary Commissioner, or 'Ombudsman', to examine grievances, and M.P.s themselves form committees to investigate specially important areas of administration. Fortunately, it is generally agreed that the British Civil Service has quite unusually high standards of honesty and integrity and even when left on its own continues to function well, so far as these characteristics are concerned.

Another reason for sensible concern has to do with planning. A complicated and changing modern society requires planning, but the taking of planning decisions leads on to further planning, sometimes involving consequences which cannot be foreseen. This affects ordinary people particularly in such matters as house-building and road-making, where it covers everything from the erection of garden sheds on private property (for which permission is often required) to the construction of multi-million-pound motorways. But both big and small issues are meshed together in a growing web of management. Thus the decision to build another airport to serve London turns out to mean that the road and rail systems of a whole region, together with its industrial development, land use, housing, educational and social welfare policies are all drastically affected, as well as many other matters. All this leads to more administration, more bureaucracy.

A third reason for feeling that bureaucracy must be carefully watched is of a quite different type. It is connected with the actual techniques of administration. The first great expansion of administrative activity was greatly helped by the development of the typewriter. One of the first really effective machines was patented by an American, Christopher Latham Sholes, in 1878. But the invention did not really become popular until the early 1900s. In the Civil Service, its triumph was completed by the First World War, when the male clerks who had conducted laborious correspondence using quill pens were called up to the army in France and replaced by young women using the new machines. The typewriter revolution was associated with the rise of 'forms' – quick and relatively easy ways of carrying on business and acquiring information in a regular and uniform style, which became increasingly necessary under the heavy administrative pressures of war-time. In fact the two great wars in which Britain has been involved in the present century have done almost as much as the growth of the welfare state to bring about the rise of bureaucracy. Now, however, the typewriter and the form are being surpassed   **407** as the tools of bureaucratic power by electronic aids, and particularly by computers. These have speeded up routine administration, and by extending the range of calculation they have made possible planning of a far wider-reaching nature than could ever be contemplated before. But the most important consequence of the electronic revolution in government is probably the capacity to store, for almost instantaneous reference, enormous quantities of information. This information can be of the most personal sort and affect individuals at every level. Some people therefore fear that the existence of such 'data banks' could make possible invasions of privacy of a type never previously dreamt of. This threat is not posed by the state alone; indeed, the state data banks are probably the least important part of the problem, which is much more serious in the field of private business, particularly where finance is concerned. But once again the danger of bureaucratic rule cannot be ignored.

THE CONSUMER SOCIETY

The bureaucratic state described in the last section is a direct result of the rapid growth of our crowded, complex, industrial society. In the same way, practical economic pressures are at work on the way ordinary people live. In the case of government administration, we noted a tendency for the work to begin feeding on itself; and a similar type of process can be seen operating on more purely economic affairs, such as the jobs people do and the way they spend their money.

Some indication of what is happening can be drawn from the following figures:

EMPLOYMENT STATISTICS

1920:

Total working population	20,617,000
Industrial production, agriculture, forestry, fishing	11,003,000
Transport and communication, distributive trades and other services	8,009,000

1968:

Total working population	25,825,000
Industrial production, agriculture, forestry, fishing	11,258,000
Transport and communication, distributive trades and other services	12,869,000

It is obvious that the rise in the numbers of those engaged in what is often called 'productive' labour has been a good deal slower than the rise in 'service' industries of one sort and another. Nor do these figures tell the whole story, since there has been a rise also in the numbers of those receiving

408

education who would previously have been working, from 340,000 (over the age of 15) in 1920 to approximately 1 million in 1966.

At the same time the pattern of industrial production itself has been radically changed; we have seen how the old 'heavy' industries have declined in relative importance, while new 'light' industries have risen beside them. These light industries are concerned largely with the production of small articles in metal or plastic, or with such specialities as electrical goods, and very often their end products will be intended for use as domestic consumer goods, frequently designed to save labour (kitchen gadgets) or give pleasure (gramophone records).

A last point that should be noticed is the reduction of actual hours spent working and the higher standard of living made possible by improved wages. These together add up to a vastly expanded place for leisure in the lives of ordinary people; it is not surprising that a whole 'leisure industry' is growing up to absorb the spare time and spare money which are now more plentiful than ever before.

These three fundamental and important changes in themselves point to a big reorganisation of British society. From being the 'workshop of the world' Britain has become a 'consumer society', that is to say, a society in which the production of basic goods is less important than the arrangements made for spending the rising tide of national wealth. This is, so far as we can see, the usual pattern of growth for what are called fully developed economies. It can only happen, of course, where the country concerned has a certain particularly favoured position in the world economic system. It is usually associated

Left: Small beginnings: one of the first Sainsbury's shops, 1888. *Right:* Consumers in the machine

with the growth of retailing systems specially suited to a high level of consumption, such as supermarkets and mail-order firms.

However, the expression 'consumer society' has another shade of meaning which we must not ignore. This meaning is connected with the need of producers (any producers, including those who deal in luxuries) to maintain, and if possible expand, their sales. If the market becomes saturated, producers go out of business. And so businessmen, principally in America to begin with, developed the idea of 'built-in obsolescence'. This means manufacturing an article in such a way that within a limited period of time the consumer will come back for another. This may be done by using materials that will simply wear out, rather than those which will last (as in the case of electric light bulbs); or it may be achieved by manipulation of fashion. In either case, consumption, disposal and fresh purchase become a sort of merry-go-round on which industrial prosperity is based. The process has been considerably assisted by the development of lightweight, short-life materials, particularly plastics and the various types of wood-pulp product (including paper); so disposable plastic bottles and paper panties may almost stand as symbols of the consumer society, using the phrase in this special sense.

By the rules of this game, if an article has not actually worn out in quite a short time, the customer must be persuaded to think that it is none the less high time that it was changed for another, newer, 'better' model. The fashion system is most obviously seen at work in such areas as clothing and personal accessories. But it is very powerful also in many other fields — many people feel ashamed if they have not got the latest year's model car, the newest kitchen gadget, or just anything that Mrs Jones has got next door. 'Keeping up with the Jones's' is a particularly powerful slogan in the entertainment industry — the whole of the commercial pop scene, especially, depends on it. This constant stress on the desirability of change has been so successful that for many people the value which, in all societies until the present day, has been given to an object by its age and associations, has been neatly turned upside down, so that now there is something positively disreputable about the possession of old goods. The word 'old', too, has changed its meaning and can signify anything that is not brand new.

These changes have happened almost unnoticed; and the use of all sorts of appeals to stir us into action without our being fully aware of the reasons is a regular and important part of the great advertising business. Advertising is in fact such an important aspect of the consumer society that it almost deserves a section of its own. For one thing, it is very big business. As long ago as 1907 it was estimated that advertising in the press (at that time far the most important way of advertising) was running at the rate of £22 million a year; by 1930 it was £60 million, and in 1968 the press advertising bill was calculated at £154,073,000. Needless to say, the advertisers would not have paid such high fees if they had not expected to make a profit overall. But by the 1930s other forms of advertising were growing rapidly in importance, ranging from new versions of older methods such as posters and handouts, through 'stunts' of every type (including novelties such as air races and give-away campaigns or competitions with glamorous, up-to-date prizes such as motor cars), to the latest technical breakthrough – films. An Advertising Association was formed in 1926 (though it was not the only such body) and advertising agents formed themselves into a professional-type group, with their own rules and standards. By 1938 it was estimated that £106 million a year was being spent on advertising; this included press advertising, but novel techniques were very popular. Some of these techniques lasted only a short time – the use of aeroplanes, for instance, to write messages in the sky; others have dwindled in importance – cigarette cards are still issued occasionally, but are insignificant nowadays, whereas between 1900 and 1939 they were enthusiastically collected, and indeed good specimens of the oldest cards are highly prized nowadays by connoisseurs.

There have been many changes in advertising during the post-war period. More use has been made of postal services (often in connection with mail-order retailing), but more important still was the appearance of television advertising which brought with it revolutionary new styles. This developed at tremendous speed after the setting up of independent television companies which were permitted, unlike the BBC, to carry advertising in order to cover their costs. (ITA was established in 1955.) By 1968 the amount spent on this type of advertising alone had risen to a staggering £143,520,000, and the total advertising expenditure of the whole country was estimated to be £297,593,000.

Not everyone was happy about this mushroom growth. Many people were inclined to regret the standardisation of taste which seemed to follow nation-wide saturation with a uniform type of advertising. There were doubts about the threat to small firms and businesses which could not hope to compete with their bigger rivals in such expensive campaigns – would advertising cause monopolies? Fears were expressed about the exploitation of certain specially vulnerable groups, in particular the teenage market which was created by the spread of relative affluence down the age scale. Certain advertising methods were condemned on grounds of taste, particularly those which made special use of sex, and others were attacked as unethical – for instance, 'subliminal' advertising on television (the flashing of a message on to the screen so fast that the eye does not consciously register it, but transmits it none the less to the subconscious memory).

Despite a steady flow of such doubts and controversies, advertising has continued to grow, and with the exception of a ban on subliminal advertisement very few holds are now barred. It is possible, however, that in the near future some of the more aggressive methods of 'inertia selling', by which goods are delivered unasked for and the recipient is virtually blackmailed into paying for them, will be effectively outlawed.

The continuing prosperity of the advertising industry, in fact, reflects its vital role in the machinery of the consumer society – it is the oil which helps the wheels of supply and demand to go round at an ever-increasing speed. One other factor in this machinery must be considered, however, before we leave the consumer society, and that is the power itself – the purchasing power which makes it possible for the consumers to acquire the goods which they so quickly discard.

The rise in wages is obviously important in this connection, particularly when we are considering the smaller items of purchase involved in leisure and entertainment. But the significant majority of consumer goods have usually been just a little too expensive to buy straight out of the weekly wages. An extensive credit system is therefore the financial basis of a consumer society, enabling people to buy what they cannot immediately pay for, in terms of ready cash.

The traditional source of credit is of course the banks. Equally traditionally, though, the banks until well into the present century drew their clients from the middle and upper classes of society, the people with assured salaries or substantial private incomes, who could invest money in relatively large quantities. Since the last war the banks have made big efforts to get rid of this image and have tried to persuade anybody with any money at all to use their services, including manual workers and students. Their efforts have been only partially successful, though, and great numbers of people still remain without a bank account. The commercial banks have made very large sums of money available by way of special loans and overdrafts to their customers; but most of these people would have enjoyed private arrangements with traders to a greater or lesser degree in any case, so that although the banks have undoubtedly assisted the consumer boom, they have not created it.

The great credit-maker of twentieth-century Britain has been the hire-purchase arrangement. This is familiar to most people nowadays. A customer puts down a deposit (usually a fixed proportion of the total purchase price) on the goods he wishes to buy and enters into an agreement with the trader. Under the terms of this agreement, the buyer pays so much per week (or month) over a fixed period of time, until he has paid the whole of the original purchase price, plus a certain amount of interest. While he is paying the money the article remains the property of the seller, who is technically only hiring it out and can reclaim it in case the buyer defaults on his payments. For the same reason the buyer cannot usually dispose of the article until he has finished paying for it. When the payments are completed the article becomes finally the property of the buyer. This system enables people who have a regular income but little or no spare cash to equip themselves with goods which they might otherwise never be able to afford, since small savings are slow to accumulate and depressingly easy to spend.

The idea of hire-purchase first spread in Britain during the 1890s, when it was pioneered by the promoters of a major sales campaign for sewing machines. At first it met with a good deal of resistance. This was due largely to inherited ideas about the dangers of getting into debt; indeed, there were plenty of people who claimed that 'H.P.' was actually sinful. Such ideas gradually disappeared in the period between the wars, when instalment-paying became fairly common. The scale of individual purchases made in this way was still usually fairly small – bicycles, carpet sweepers and the best sitting-room furniture were typical subjects. Finance was usually arranged directly by the seller. In fact, there was a lasting prejudice against the suggestion that a third party – a Hire Purchase Finance Company, specialising in lending money for H.P. purposes – should be brought in. This prejudice was not finally broken down until the great consumer boom of the 1950s increased the demand for H.P. finance far beyond the point where it could be supplied by the sellers themselves.

H.P. has now spread from the working classes to the middle classes – partly because the middle classes have lost ground in the incomes scale, and need the facilities of H.P. as much as anyone. The debt accumulated in this way has grown very fast in the last 15 years; in 1957 it stood at £369 million, in 1964 at £900 million and in 1969 at £1,295 million. This rise reflects not only the growing number of H.P. transactions but also the increasing size of the individual arrangements, which now cover cars, colour television sets and yachts among other expensive items.

The enormous credit facilities unleashed by this method of finance have proved something of a headache to Chancellors of the Exchequer, among other people. H.P. loans now have to be counted in as part of the national financial system, and the government controls the rate of interest which can be charged on them, together with such matters as the proportion of the purchase price which must be paid over in the deposit and the length of time over which payments can be spread. By altering the regulations covering these details, it is possible for the Chancellor to affect the rate of spending of millions of ordinary people and thus to change the balance of the whole national economy.

The achievements of H.P. were seen most strikingly in the late 1950s and early 1960s, when after a long period of hardship and relative stagnation the standard of living leapt dramatically, until 91% of British households had electric irons, 82% television sets, 72% vacuum cleaners, 45% washing machines and 30% refrigerators, most of them bought for the first time between 1958 and 1963. Since then the number of people enjoying these

413

advantages has continued to rise and the range of commodities has widened, but the rate of increase has been less dramatic.

The threat of Pollution

We have seen how the idea of 'disposability' is a central feature of the consumer society. Nothing has been said, however, about *where* or *how* the worn-out or redundant consumer goods are disposed of. Some of them, of course, are given back to traders in part exchange; but many types of goods cannot have much return value, and some – including a wide range of plastic goods – are deliberately designed with none at all. This creates straightaway a problem of which we are only just beginning to realise the size. It may seem odd at first sight that the problem strikes one most strongly in the country-side, the area least directly affected by the consumer revolution. But this is because towns generally have disposal arrangements which keep rubbish out of sight, if not entirely under control; the countryside is less well off in this respect, and in fact the towns tend to exploit the countryside as a dumping ground – regrettably, official bodies do this as well as private individuals. So we see all sorts of metal, plastic and paper rubbish littering the hedgerows and choking the streams, immune to the natural processes of decay, at least in the short run. In fact, although the fouling of the countryside has an obvious visual impact, it is only the tip of an iceberg, of which the greater part is to be found in and around the towns. So far Britain has managed to avoid serious trouble by a mixture of good luck and good management. But the shape of the future may possibly be seen in places like New York, where the rubbish disposal problem has reached nightmare proportions in certain areas. Nor is rubbish the worst thing to be faced. Waste chemical products and gases are rapidly polluting and destroying whole regions of our environment and pose a threat to human life itself.

Such pollution, ironically, is something that only a wealthy, or 'affluent', society can afford. It is the result of high-speed mass-production of highly artificial goods and materials, which are lavishly used and freely disposed of, but cannot easily be broken down by the action of nature. Some are likely to produce dangerous concentrations of substances such as mercury, plutonium or carbon monoxide, capable of destroying both animal and plant life. Pollution has of course been a product of industrial societies since the beginning of the Industrial Revolution, but it is only recently that it has threatened to grow to catastrophic proportions. The urgency of the problem has become so obvious just recently that a number of countries have taken government action to deal with it. In Britain, for instance, a Department of the Environment was set up in 1970 to handle all such matters, together with the planning which is essential if they are to be controlled and avoided.

It's a dirty bird that fouls its own nest – and man is the dirtiest bird of all

The growth of pollution is the result of a number of factors, but they are all related to the population explosion with which this book began. Britain is one of the most densely populated countries in the world; since it is also one of the richest, its pollution problem is unusually severe. It seems unlikely that any really effective solution can be found which does not involve a limitation and probably a reduction of the population. Obviously a policy of this sort would be very controversial, whatever form it took.

Some people, however, advocate going even further than the management of population; they believe that a modern, affluent society can, and possibly must, take steps to control its whole environment, adjusting it to its needs and in accordance with certain principles of civilisation, for example the desirability of protecting wildlife, preserving old buildings and limiting the dominance of machines.

In a sense, this would only be a logical conclusion of the policy which man has been pursuing for many generations. But whereas our ancestors thought of themselves as struggling with hostile and powerful forces of nature, it is possible that our children may come to think of themselves as managers of a pliant and subdued environment. This can only be done, however, at enormous cost – it is the ultimate stage of affluence; and yet affluence, as we have seen, is itself the source of the pollution that is poisoning the globe. Some economists demand an end to economic growth, or at least its dethronement from the position of unquestioned shibboleth, so that the death-ride can be stopped. But it is not easy to see how this can be done, given the present momentum of change.

415

The new urban environment at its best: a corner of Cumbernauld New Town, Scotland

The Future for an Industrialised Society

Whether the answer is sought in more growth or less, one thing is almost inevitable – the remorseless advance in the power of the state. We have traced the beginnings of the modern state from the time when the first stresses and strains of the Industrial Revolution called into being a power greater than that of the little local communities who had hitherto regulated their own affairs, free from all but the lightest load of government interference. The rapidly evolving problems of an urbanised, industrial society allowed no respite in the onward march of state power, no matter how reluctant the politicians of the time might be. It is an ironic commentary on the nature of the process that many of the most important steps have in fact been taken by parties most deeply committed to the welfare of the individual – the Liberals in the nineteenth century, the Labour Party in the twentieth. In pre-industrial times such encroachments would have been passionately resisted in the name of liberty. Industrial man came to feel that life was more important than liberty. On present trends it may not be too long before the state receives the ultimate licence to power, in the shape of a recently coined slogan: 'Human life is more important than human lives.'

Suggestions for further work and discussion

1. Find out what benefits your family is receiving or has recently received from state welfare schemes.

2. Subject for an essay or discussion: should we pay more for the Welfare State?

3. Find out how many civil servants there are today. Compare this figure with the total of the working population.

4. Metric measurements are coming into more general use very rapidly. Who is responsible for this? Why?

5. Are you conscious of being influenced by advertisements? How many (including T.V. jingles, etc.) can you remember?

6. Find out what is meant by 'growth economics'. Can such growth go on indefinitely?

7. What do you think are the chief practical pollution threats today?

Book for further reading:

Michael Harrington, *The Accidental Century*, Penguin, 1967.

Appendices

Because it is not possible to cover all subjects in detail in a book of this length, some important facts and complicated topics have been mentioned only briefly and in passing. We feel, however, that readers will want to know more about these subjects, and so we include here some brief notes on them, in five appendices.

Appendix A Ministries from 1721

1721–42	Sir Robert Walpole
1742–43	(change of ministry)
1743–54	Henry Pelham
1754–56	Duke of Newcastle
1756–57	Duke of Devonshire/William Pitt the Elder
1757–61	Duke of Newcastle/William Pitt the Elder
1761–62	Duke of Newcastle/Earl of Bute
1762–63	Earl of Bute
1763–65	George Grenville
1765–66	Marquess of Rockingham
1766–68	Duke of Grafton/William Pitt the Elder (created Earl of Chatham 1766)
1768–70	Duke of Grafton
1770–82	Lord North
1782	Marquess of Rockingham
1782–83	Earl of Shelburne
1783	Duke of Portland/Lord North/Charles James Fox
1783–1801	William Pitt the Younger
1801–4	Henry Addington
1804–6	William Pitt the Younger
1806–7	Lord Grenville/Charles James Fox ('Ministry of all the Talents')
1807–9	Duke of Portland
1809–12	Spencer Perceval
1812–27	Earl of Liverpool
1827	George Canning
1827–28	Viscount Goderich

1828–30	Duke of Wellington
1830–34	Earl Grey
1834	Viscount Melbourne
1834–35	Sir Robert Peel
1835–41	Viscount Melbourne
1841–46	Sir Robert Peel
1846–52	Lord John Russell
1852	Earl of Derby
1852–55	Earl of Aberdeen
1855–58	Viscount Palmerston
1858–59	Earl of Derby
1859–65	Viscount Palmerston
1865–66	Earl Russell (created Earl 1861)
1866–68	Earl of Derby
1868	Benjamin Disraeli
1868–74	W. E. Gladstone
1874–80	Benjamin Disraeli (created Earl of Beaconsfield 1876)
1880–85	W. E. Gladstone
1885–86	Marquess of Salisbury
1886	W. E. Gladstone
1886–92	Marquess of Salisbury
1892–94	W. E. Gladstone
1894–95	Earl of Rosebery
1895–1902	Marquess of Salisbury
1902–5	A. J. Balfour
1905–8	Sir Henry Campbell-Bannerman
1908–15	H. H. Asquith
1915–16	Asquith Coalition
1916–19	D. Lloyd George
1919–22	Lloyd George Coalition
1922–23	A. Bonar Law
1923–24	Stanley Baldwin
1924	J. Ramsay MacDonald
1924–29	Stanley Baldwin
1929–31	J. Ramsay MacDonald
1931–35	MacDonald's National Government
1935–37	Baldwin's National Government
1937–39	Neville Chamberlain's National Government
1939–40	Chamberlain's War Government
1940–45	Winston Churchill's War Government (followed by a brief Conservative ministry)
1945–51	C. R. Attlee

1951–55	Winston Churchill (knighted 1953)
1955–57	Sir Anthony Eden
1957–63	Harold Macmillan
1963–64	Earl of Home (Sir Alec Douglas-Home)
1964–70	Harold Wilson
1970–	Edward Heath

Appendix B Reform Movements of the Early Nineteenth Century

POPULAR AGITATION

Popular agitation in the early nineteenth century was chiefly aimed at bringing about parliamentary reform. This demand went back into the previous century, but it had been driven underground during the wars against France (1793–1815). After 1815, however, economic distress produced further agitation for political reforms which were expected to improve the conditions among the working people. Middle-class radicals, such as Henry ('Orator') Hunt and William Cobbett provided the leadership. The chief instances of this agitation were:

1816 The Spa Fields Riot
1 This began as a meeting in Spa Fields, London, addressed by Hunt.
2 Part of the crowd got out of hand and seized guns from a shop.
3 The mob was dispersed by force.
4 As a result, the government suspended the Habeas Corpus Act (this meant that suspects could now be held without trial).

1817 The March of the Blanketeers
1 A group of distressed workers, carrying blankets for shelter, set out from Manchester to walk to London, in order to petition Parliament for reform.
2 The leaders were quickly arrested, and most of the marchers dispersed at Stockport.
3 The rest gave up at Macclesfield.

1819 'Peterloo'
1 About 50–60,000 people met in St Peter's Field in Manchester, to hear Hunt.
2 The crowd was very orderly, but the local magistrates lost their heads and called in cavalry to arrest Hunt.
3 In the panic which followed, eleven people were killed and four hundred injured. Some accounts give even higher casualty figures.
4 With memories of the Battle of Waterloo (1815) fresh in people's minds, the 'massacre' became known as the 'Battle of Peterloo'.

5 It created intense indignation in the country, but the government reacted by passing the 'Six Acts' of 1819.
6 These Acts were popularly called the 'Gag Acts' because they placed many restrictions on individual freedom, and helped to prevent further agitation.

1830–32 Reform Riots
1 Agitation revived during the Reform Act crises (see Chapter 16), and there were riots in places such as Bristol and Nottingham.
2 These riots helped to persuade Lord Grey's government to pass the Act.

1838–48 Chartism
Disappointment with the results of the 1832 Reform Act was a major cause of the renewed agitation associated with the Chartist movement, which is described more fully in Chapter 16.

There was one other movement in which popular pressures played an important part in the early nineteenth century. This was:

1834–45 The Anti-Poor Law Movement
1 A great many people objected to the terms of the new Poor Law (described in Appendix C) and resisted it, especially in the north of England, where townspeople were particularly affected.
2 By the later 1840s, however, improving economic conditions drew the sting from this opposition.

THE ANTI-CORN LAW LEAGUE

The League was a good example of several movements which were particularly strong among the middle classes, and which sought to improve conditions for the people.
1 The League was opposed to the Corn Laws, which were thought to be responsible for high bread prices (see Chapter 11).
2 Its leaders were Richard Cobden (1804–65), John Bright (1811–89) and George Wilson (1808–70). They were prominent businessmen in Manchester.
3 Between 1838 and 1846 the League organised monster demonstrations, attracting wide popular support.
4 These activities were partially responsible for persuading Peel to repeal the Corn Laws in 1846.

THE FACTORY REFORM MOVEMENT

A strong movement, centred in Lancashire and Yorkshire, developed to improve working conditions in factories. Its leaders included several well-known factory-owners, such as Robert Owen, Sir Robert Peel the Elder and

John Fielden. Supporters of the movement wished to introduce safety regulations, and to stop the exploitation of women and children by limiting the number of hours which they could work. Some reformers also wished to restrict the hours which men could work, but it was very hard to get Parliament to agree to this. However, since most factories could not operate without women and children, it was hoped that protecting them would also help men. The goal of these reformers was a 'Ten Hour Day' for women and young persons, and thus indirectly for men as well.

Other leading figures apart from the factory-owners were Michael Sadler, Sir John Hobhouse, Richard Oastler and, most important, Lord Shaftesbury (1801–85). Although he was Lord Ashley until 1851, he is usually known by his later title. Shaftesbury was an Evangelical and a philanthropist who devoted his whole life to the cause of social reform. Apart from factory legislation, he was associated with practically every other reform movement, especially those concerned with public health, education, lunacy and emigration. There is a recent book about Lord Shaftesbury by G. Best, which gives fuller details of his selfless career.

THE MOVEMENT FOR PENAL REFORM

The law was very harsh in the early nineteenth century. Men and women were executed for what we consider to be minor offences today. The theft of five shillings, for example, was a capital offence. As a result of such harshness, many juries refused to convict men on trial, and the law came into some disrepute. Moreover, conditions in British prisons, and in the colonies to which many thousands of prisoners were transported, were often very bad and cruel. There was no properly organised police force.

Several outstanding humanitarians worked to improve this situation. They included John Howard, Sir Samuel Romilly and Mrs Elizabeth Fry. Sir Robert Peel (the Younger), who was Home Secretary during the 1820s, also worked hard for change.

Lord Shaftesbury

Many people were concerned at the bad state of sanitation in towns. Public health was undermined, disease spread easily and the death rate was high. Although many laws had been passed about the matter, the responsibility for carrying them out was either not clear or ignored by the self-appointed town corporations which controlled local government until 1835.

Lord Shaftesbury, Dr Southwood-Smith and Sir Edwin Chadwick were among those most concerned with public health. Chadwick (1800–90) was not a politician. He was an administrator, who wished to see government in all fields become more efficient. His main work was with the Poor Law Commission and the General Board of Health, and though his tactless manner made him many enemies, his strong will and devotion to duty brought invaluable changes. Chadwick was knighted in 1889, just before his death.

Edwin Chadwick

Appendix C The Chief Measures of Social Legislation in the Nineteenth Century

This Appendix includes only legislation passed in the nineteenth century. Later changes, in attitudes and in the law, are described fully in the book. Legislation relating to Trade Unionism and to Education is dealt with in Chapters 8 and 15. The names of the persons chiefly responsible for the most important measures are included in brackets.

FACTORY AND MINES LEGISLATION

1819 Factory Act (Sir Robert Peel the Elder)
1 Employment of children under 9 forbidden.
2 Hours of work of children aged 9 to 16 limited to 12 a day (excluding meal times).
3 No provision for enforcement.

1833 Factory Act (Michael Sadler and Lord Shaftesbury)
1 Employment of children under 9 forbidden.
2 Hours of work of children aged 9 to 13 limited to 9.
3 Hours of work of young persons aged 13 to 18 limited to 12.
4 These hours had to be worked between 5.30 a.m. and 8.30 p.m.
5 The Act applied only to textile factories.
6 It was enforced by Factory Inspectors.

1842 Mines Act (Lord Shaftesbury)
1 This followed a sensational Report by a Committee of Inquiry.
2 Employment of women and girls underground forbidden.
3 Boys under 10 forbidden to work underground.
4 The Act was enforced by Inspectors.

1844 Factory Act (Lord Shaftesbury)
1 Hours of work of children under 13 cut to $6\frac{1}{2}$.
2 Hours of work of women limited to 12.
3 Safety regulations for factories introduced.
4 The Act still applied only to textile factories.

1847 Factory Act (John Fielden)
1 Hours of work of women and young persons aged 13 to 18 cut to 10.
2 Employers used a relay system, however, to keep factories going.
3 This move thwarted the intention of the Act, which was to limit the hours of men as well.

1850 Factory Act (Lord Shaftesbury)
1 The relay system was banned.
2 But the hours of work were extended to $10\frac{1}{2}$.

1850 Coal Mines Inspection Act
Laid down and enforced safety regulations in mines.

1860–67 Factory Acts
Extended regulations to cover most trades and industries.

1872 Coal Mines Act
1 Made safety regulations more stringent.
2 Required managers of mines to possess a certificate of competence.

1874 Factory Act
Finally established the 10-hour day.

1875 'Climbing boys' Act (Lord Shaftesbury)
The most important of several measures controlling the employment of children as chimney-sweeps.

Before 1834 poor relief was given by parish authorities to those in poverty. Paupers were given 'outdoor relief', which meant that they could remain in their own homes.

1834 The Poor Law Amendment Act (Edwin Chadwick)
1 Outdoor relief was to be given only to the sick and aged.
2 Everyone else (including the sick and aged where outdoor relief was not possible) could receive help only in workhouses.
3 Conditions in workhouses were to be hard, in order to discourage unnecessary applications for relief.
4 Poor Law administration was reorganised:
  a Parishes were grouped into Unions, under locally elected Boards of Guardians.
  b Guardians were responsible to a central Poor Law Commission.

1847 The Poor Law Board took over these powers.

1871 The Local Government Board assumed control of the Poor Law.

LOCAL GOVERNMENT AND PUBLIC HEALTH

1831–33 Cholera Epidemic
This killed many thousands of people and led to temporary local Boards of Health.

1835 Municipal Corporations Act (Joseph Parks)
1 Reorganised local government on a more democratic basis.
2 Gave voluntary powers over public health matters to the new councils.

1845 Lunacy Commission established (Lord Shaftesbury)
The most important measure to improve conditions for people with mental disorders.

1848 Public Health Act (Lord Shaftesbury and Edwin Chadwick)
1 Passed after renewed cholera (1847) and after several Reports had shown the bad state of sanitation in towns.
2 A central Board of Health was established, with powers to set up local Boards, in order to improve conditions.

1851 Lodging Houses Act (Lord Shaftesbury)
Checked abuses in the provision of accommodation for lodgers, especially in 'doss-houses'.

1854 The Board of Health lost some of its powers. It was disbanded in 1858.   **425**

1871 The Local Government Board was established (James Stansfeld)
1 This followed another cholera epidemic 1865–66, and a Royal Commission of Inquiry.
2 The Board took responsibility for both the Poor Law and for public health.

1875 Public Health Act (Sclater Booth)
1 This brought together, into one Act, over a hundred previous measures.
2 It was much more effective, and paved the way for a complete overhaul of responsibility for public health and sanitation.

1875 Artisans' Dwellings Act (Richard Cross)
1 Local authorities empowered to clear slums.
2 Though voluntary, it was taken up in some areas, such as Birmingham.

1875 Sale of Food and Drugs Act (Sclater Booth)
Designed to prevent the sale of goods containing harmful substances.

1888 Local Government Act
Established County Councils and County Borough Councils.

1894 Local Government Act
Established Parish Councils.

PUBLIC ORDER

These dates are not all exact, for some measures took a long time to come into full effect.

1820s Reform of the Penal Code and improvement of conditions in prisons (Elizabeth Fry and Sir Robert Peel the Younger)

1829 Establishment of the Metropolitan Police (Sir Robert Peel)

1839 Extension of the Police Force to the rest of Britain.

1853 Abolition of the Transportation of Convicts

1853 Reform of the Civil Service (Sir Stafford Northcote and Sir Charles Trevelyan)

1872 Licensing Act (Henry Bruce)
1 Enforced licensing of public houses.
2 Controlled the quality of drink sold, and checked some obnoxious practices.

1868–74 Army Reforms (Edward Cardwell)
Cardwell was Secretary of War in Gladstone's Ministry. He undertook
many important reforms in the army. Among these were:

One of the first 'Peelers' or 'Bobbies'

1 The abolition of flogging in peace-time.
2 The abolition of the purchase of commissions.
3 The reorganisation of the War Office, and of many regiments.
4 Improvements in the terms of enlistment and service in the army.
5 The introduction of more efficient weapons, such as the breech-loading rifle.

The result was that the British Army became much more efficient, and morale improved greatly.

Appendix D Banking

Before 1800

1 There were four main kinds of financial institution:

a The London Private Banks.
 i These catered mainly for merchants and members of the aristocracy.
 ii They were relatively strong, but had little connection with industry.
b The Bank of England.
 i Founded in 1694, it was very strong and had many privileges. It was the only joint-stock bank permitted.
 ii It operated purely for profit, however, and though it sometimes made loans to banks in difficulties, it took no responsibility for doing so.
c The Country Banks.
 i These were situated outside London.
 ii They varied greatly in security and usefulness.
 iii Because of legal weaknesses and inexperience, many collapsed.

427

d The Bill-brokers.
  i These dealt mainly with Bills of Exchange, which were credit notes generally used in business.
  ii Thus they were very useful for the smooth running of industry and trade.
2 There was no national banking system as such, however, and the whole structure was weak.
3 As a result, many banking crises took place, for example in 1772, 1783 and 1793. These were harmful to industrialisation.

1800–1900

1 The main changes in the nineteenth century were:

a The development of the Bank of England as a 'Central Bank', with responsibility to the whole banking system.
b The strengthening of other banks.
c The emergence of the City of London as the main banking and financial centre of the world.

2 The changes took place in several stages:

1826 a Joint-stock banks, which were more secure, were permitted, provided that they were at least 65 miles from London.
  b This restriction was to protect the privilege of the Bank of England, which was, however, required to open up branches in provincial cities, in order that other banks could be helped more easily.

1833 The 65-mile limit was removed, and joint-stock banks grew rapidly in number.

1844 The Bank Charter Act
  a The Bank of England was given full control over the issue of almost all bank-notes.
  b The quantity of notes which could be issued was severely restricted in an attempt to stop price inflation.

1857 135 banks collapsed.

1866 Overend, Gurney and Company, one of the largest and most famous banks, collapsed, together with many others.
  As a result of these two great crises, the Bank of England decided to abandon much of its private business and to concentrate on strengthening the banking system.

1890 The Barings crisis showed the new role of the Bank of England, which organised help for Barings, a famous bank in financial difficulties.

The Bank of England at the beginning of the nineteenth century

1900–1970 Three main changes have taken place:
a Amalgamations among banks, which have produced four very large and strong firms. (Lloyds, Barclays, Midland, National Westminster.)
b The extension of services offered by banks, which now carry out every conceivable kind of financial business.
c Nationalisation of the Bank of England, in 1946.

Appendix E British Investment Overseas in the Nineteenth Century

One of the most striking consequences of Britain's economic expansion in the nineteenth century was the huge investment of capital overseas.

1 *The Scale of Investment*
Between 1800 and 1914 British citizens and companies invested about £4,000 million overseas.

2 *The Reasons for Investment*
  a As the wealth of Britain increased, from industry and trade, more and more money was available for investment.
  b After the first great industrial boom of the early nineteenth century, and the 'railway mania' of the 1840s, there were fewer opportunities for investment at home.
  c Overseas investment, though often risky, was usually very profitable.

429

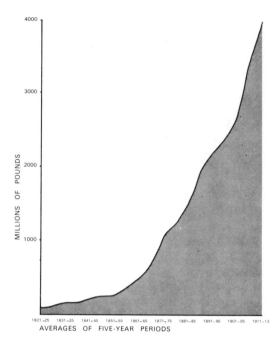

4000

3000

MILLIONS OF POUNDS

2000

1000

1821–25 1831–35 1841–45 1851–55 1861–65 1871–75 1881–85 1891–95 1901–05 1911–13
AVERAGES OF FIVE-YEAR PERIODS

The growth of British
investment overseas 1821–1913

d Many businessmen wished to help other countries to develop as good markets for British goods and as sources of raw materials for British industry.

3 *The Pattern of Investment*

a Investment took place in a great variety of projects, notably railways, but also in docks and harbours, mines and factories, water and gas works, banks, farming, electricity and telegraph services.

b At first, investment was mainly in Europe, but it soon spread to North America, and then to all parts of the world, especially Australia, South America and Asia.

4 *The Gains*

a The expansion of world trade.

b The growth of British trade and industry, which supplied goods to expanding markets.

c The development of the City of London as the centre of world finance, shipping and other services.

d Favourable effects for Britain's balance of payments. The annual income from overseas investment was about £190 million by 1914.

e A reduction in the price of imported food at the end of the nineteenth century, resulting from improved communications systems. This produced a rise in the standard of living for poorer people.

f The build-up of a reserve of funds which proved invaluable to Britain in the First World War.

5 *The Losses*

    a Investment helped other countries, especially the United States, to industrialise and so to challenge Britain's industrial supremacy in the long run. But this was inevitable.

    b British farming was seriously harmed by imports of cheap food.

    c Much overseas investment was in unsuccessful or even fraudulent projects. Such capital might have been more usefully invested at home.

    d Britain came to depend too much on her overseas income which covered up real difficulties in the economy at the end of the century.

Index